Symbolism
and American Literature

Symbolism
and American Literature

By Charles Feidelson, Jr.

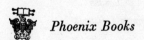

Phoenix Books

THE UNIVERSITY OF CHICAGO PRESS

CHICAGO AND LONDON

The University of Chicago Press, Chicago & London
The University of Toronto Press, Toronto 5, Canada

Copyright 1953 by The University of Chicago. Published 1953
First Phoenix Edition 1959. Sixth Impression 1966
Printed in the United States of America

To my mother and father

Acknowledgments

I am very grateful to the colleagues and friends who have given me counsel and encouragement in the writing of this book: in particular, to Stanley T. Williams, under whose guidance the work was first undertaken; William K. Wimsatt, Jr., John C. Pope, and Maynard Mack, who have made a number of valuable suggestions; and Norman H. Pearson, who has shown unfailing interest in the project for a long time. I owe special thanks to Richard Ellmann for many promptings; to Lionel Trilling for his helpfulness; and to my wife for her abundant good will.

For permission to quote from copyright material I am very much obliged to the following: Alfred A. Knopf, Inc. (*The Counter-*

Acknowledgments

feiters, with *Journal of "The Counterfeiters,"* by André Gide, trans.
Dorothy Bussy and Justin O'Brien; *Democracy in America,* by
Alexis de Tocqueville, trans. Henry Reeve *et al.;* and *Ideas of
Order,* by Wallace Stevens) ; American Book Company (*Herman
Melville: Representative Selections,* ed. Willard Thorp) ; Charles
Scribner's Sons (*The Art of the Novel,* by Henry James) ; Harper
and Brothers (*Language and Myth,* by Ernst Cassirer, trans. S. K.
Langer) ; Houghton Mifflin Company (*The Journals of Ralph
Waldo Emerson; Young Emerson Speaks;* and *The Writings of
Henry David Thoreau*) ; Librairie Gallimard (*Les Faux-mon-
nayeurs* and *Journal des faux-monnayeurs,* by André Gide) ; and
Perry Miller (*The New England Mind: The Seventeenth Century*).

YALE UNIVERSITY
NEW HAVEN, CONNECTICUT

Contents

Contents

Introduction

*As a vast, solid phalanx the generation comes on,
they have the same features, and their pattern is new
in the world. All wear the same expression,
but it is that which they do not detect in each other.*

EMERSON, *Journals*

The unified phase of American literature which began with the tales of Hawthorne and Poe and ended with Melville and Whitman was not recognized as such by the men who made it. Certainly none would have described it as a symbolist movement; indeed, none would have called himself a symbolist. Yet today the family likeness can be discerned, and the pattern is that of symbolism. The Representative Man of the era was Emerson himself:

All our works which we do not understand are symbolical. If I appear to myself to carry rails into the shed under my barn, if I appear to myself to dig parsnips with a dung-fork, there is reason, no doubt, in these special appearances as much as in the study of metaphysics or mythology, in which I do not see meaning. We are greatly more poetic than we know; poets in our drudgery, poets in our eyes, and ears, and skin.

The mania of Ahab and the dreams of Pierre were the projection of Melville's own habits of thought, which made or found value in the world only by taking the world as symbol. For Melville, as for Ahab, the doubloon contained a reality that was pointedly not measurable in terms of money and arithmetic:

> One morning, turning to pass the doubloon, he seemed to be newly attracted by the strange figures and inscriptions stamped on it, as though now for the first time beginning to interpret for himself in some monomaniac way whatever significance might lurk in them. And some certain significance lurks in all things, else all things are little worth, and the round world itself but an empty cipher, except to sell by the cartload, as they do hills about Boston, to fill up some morass in the Milky Way.

It was symbolism that lured Hawthorne into those byways of the spirit from which he was always rescuing himself by platitude. Something in him responded to a "rag of scarlet cloth":

> My eyes fastened themselves upon the old scarlet letter, and would not be turned aside. Certainly, there was some deep meaning in it, most worthy of interpretation, and which, as it were, streamed forth from the mystic symbol, subtly communicating itself to my sensibilities, but evading the analysis of my mind.

The neurotic Poe frankly devoted himself to "l'exception dans l'ordre moral"—the extreme opposite of the world that is given to intellectual analysis and measured by the cartload. Like the friend of Roderick Usher, he gazed in fascinated reverie upon objects that seemed to swim in "an atmosphere peculiar to themselves":

> What was it—I paused to think—what was it that so unnerved me in the contemplation of the House of Usher? It was a mystery all insoluble; nor could I grapple with the shadowy fancies that crowded

upon me as I pondered. I was forced to fall back upon the unsatisfactory conclusion, that while, beyond doubt, there *are* combinations of very simple natural objects which have the power of thus affecting us, still the analysis of this power lies among considerations beyond our depth.

The ostentatiously healthy Whitman was no less committed to a mode of perception in which lilac and star and bird were the source of "long panoramas of visions," and "the shows and forms presented by Nature" were caught up into a symbolistic realm:

Out of these, and seizing what is in them, the poet, the esthetic worker in any field, by the divine magic of his genius, projects them, their analogies, by curious removes, indirections, in literature and art. (No useless attempt to repeat the material creation, by daguerreotyping the exact likeness by mortal mental means.) This is the image-making faculty, coping with material creation, and rivaling, almost triumphing, over it.

For years the easy generalization has been that American literature, in the rare intervals when it is not dull and thin-blooded, is formless and crude; and until very recently the literary historian of America has largely avoided questions of literary method. His account has been given over to bibliography, anecdote, sociology, and the history of social, economic, and political ideas; Parrington almost boasts of his freedom from "belletristic" considerations. The first large-scale attempt to define the literary quality of American writing at its best was Matthiessen's *American Renaissance,* which is "primarily concerned with *what* these books were as works of art," with "the writers' use of their own tools, their diction and rhetoric, and . . . what they could make with them." Yet even in this magnificent work, which reorients the entire subject, the sociological and political bent of studies in American literature makes itself felt indirectly. Despite Matthiessen's emphasis on literary form, his concern with the "artist's use of language" as "the most sensitive index to cultural history" tends to lead him away from specifically aesthetic problems. The "one common denominator" which he finds among the five writers treated in his book is not, in the final analysis, a common approach to the art of writing but a common theme—"their devotion to the possibilities of democracy."

It is more likely that the really vital common denominator is precisely their attitude toward their medium—that their distinctive quality is a devotion to the possibilities of symbolism. The pattern of American romanticism, which began a generation late, was something more than romantic. Edmund Wilson was the first to note the affinity between mid-nineteenth-century American writing and the symbolist aesthetic that produced modern literature. Emerson, Melville, Hawthorne, Poe, and Whitman inherited the basic problem of romanticism: the vindication of imaginative thought in a world grown abstract and material. But the problem is still before us today; and their solution—offered with the diffidence of Hawthorne or the assurance of Emerson and Whitman, in Melvillian perplexity or the desperation of Poe—is closer to modern notions of symbolic reality than to romantic egoism. Considered as pure romantics, they are minor disciples of European masters. Their symbolistic method is their title to literary independence. Whether romantic or symbolistic, they wrote no masterpieces; the relative immaturity of the American literary tradition cannot be denied. But as symbolists they look forward to one of the most sophisticated movements in literary history; however inexpert, they broaden the possibilities of literature.

That point somehow gets lost in another book which has done much to focus attention on the distinctive aesthetic qualities of American writing. The defects of *Maule's Curse* are worth noting because the book has the virtue of its defects. Winters keeps very close to "the relationship of the history of ideas to the history of literary forms" and to "the intellectual and moral significance of literary forms," which, as he says, must constitute "the very core of literary criticism and of the understanding of literature." He braves the difficult region where theoretical premises dissolve and reshape themselves into literary attitudes and structures. But in so doing he oversimplifies both terms of his equation. American thought and letters are both reduced to "American obscurantism."

To be fair to Emerson, to Hawthorne and Whitman, to Melville and Poe, one must take Winters' basic question in a more disinterested way than he himself intends. What could be made of the intellectual resources open to these writers? A great deal could be made, and symbolism was the mode of their "making." Each was preoccupied with a kind of archetypal figure, whose outline looms equally behind Usher's jittery friend and the benign Emerson tending his parsnips. This was the figure of Man Seeing, the mind engaged in a crucial act of knowledge. Beyond their obvious differences of literary theory and practice, these men were committed to a common theory and practice of perception, which entered into both the form and the content of their work. Their movement was not obscurantist but honest, an ingenuous attempt to explore a common intellectual situation.

As already suggested, the concept of symbolism is not only a key to their situation but also a link between their literature and our own. It is not my purpose merely to see how the nineteenth-century worthies look in modern dress; nor do I wish to reduce contemporary literature to the terms of a hundred years ago; least of all would I limit the meaning of "symbolism" to the special sense developed in this book. My intentions are synthetic. The general theory of symbolism here put forward is frankly derived from a particular strain in the literary history of the last two centuries. Modern literature and American literature are ways of getting at that strain. Conversely, "symbolism" is a way of getting at modern and American literature. But none of these correlations need be taken in a restrictive sense. The following study has been written, and I hope it will be regarded, in something like the experimental spirit that it chronicles—as a schema, an intellectual form, a set of possibilities. It defines a point of view. The well-disposed reader will make his own qualifications and extensions. To the less well disposed I can only say by way of placation that even so speculative an approach is not without its inner check. I have tried to let the materials speak for themselves as much as possible; and my end is not pure theory but practical criticism.

I *Four American Symbolists*

I remember them with the sunlight breaking through overshadowing branches, and they appearing and disappearing confusedly ... as if the every day laws of Nature were suspended for this particular occasion.

HAWTHORNE, *The American Notebooks*

Hawthorne had enormous respect for the material world and for common-sense reality; he admired the novels of Trollope, "solid and substantial, ... and just as real as if some giant had hewn a great lump out of the earth." Even in his own writings, as he pointed out, the style is public. There is "none of the abstruseness of idea, or obscurity of expression, which mark the written communications of a solitary mind with itself.... It is, in fact, the style of a man of society." Yet this devotee of Trollope began his literary career by a ten years' retreat, and his books are precisely the expression of the solitary and the mental. Or, rather, they might be considered the resultant of the two quite opposite forces within Hawthorne; they establish "a neutral territory, somewhere between the real world and fairy-land, where the Actual and the Imaginary may meet, and each imbue itself with the nature of the other." Unable to feel any confidence in the reality of the subjective, and unable, despite the long effort of his notebooks, to come to grips with the solid earth, Hawthorne evolved his conception of the "romance." Whereas the novelist was limited to "the probable and ordinary course of man's experience," the romancer tried to create a realm midway between private thought and the objective world. This doctrine, which is the burden of the prefaces to *The House of the Seven Gables, The Blithedale Romance,* and *The Marble Faun,* betrayed an intellectual as well as a literary problem. Hawthorne was anxious not merely to draw the literary distinction between the novel and the romance, and to enter apologies for the latter, but also, and more fundamentally, to fix the status of the romance in an almost metaphysical sense. While he was granting or even insisting that "reality" belonged to Trollope, he was trying, in effect, to say what kind of reality his own work had. For the fact is that what seems at first a wholly personal problem, resulting from Hawthorne's peculiar temperament, turns out to be a reflection of the problem of the times. The Actual and the Imaginary can meet only in a theory or habit of perception. Hawthorne's comment on *Twice-Told Tales* is true of all his books: they were "attempts, and very imperfectly successful ones, to open an intercourse with the world."

The imperfect success may be attributed at least partially to the way he put the question. Hawthorne, who was contemptuous of abstract speculation, was caught willy-nilly in a speculative dilemma, and his approach to it was oversimplified. He believed that he had only to discover suitable materials: he chose Brook Farm as the subject of *The Blithedale Romance* because that social experiment in itself had been "essentially a day-dream, and yet a fact, ... thus offering an available foothold between fiction and reality." But the problem before him actually involved the relationship of the imagination to *any* fact, and it could be solved only by a fundamental adjustment of the mind and things, not by seeking out ready-made solutions. It was inevitable that Hawthorne should find, as he complained in preface after preface, that materials with the proper "atmosphere" were hard to come by. This faulty conception of his problem was complicated by his prejudice in favor of the physical and the rational, a bias which, if followed through, would have made any valid union of the Actual and the Imaginary not only impossible but undesirable. While he stated clearly enough that he sought to mediate between the private vision and the common-sense objective world, he was likely at the same time, adopting an apologetic tone, to speak of his work as "fancy-pictures" and "castles in the air," as though his aim were simply the amusement of cutting himself loose from any reality.

The natural outcome of this theoretical indecisiveness was Hawthorne's allegorical method; by this means, consciously or not, he evaded the issue with which he was confronted. For it is in the nature of allegory, as opposed to symbolism, to beg the question of absolute reality. The allegorist avails himself of a formal correspondence between "ideas" and "things," both of which he assumes as given; he need not inquire whether either sphere is "real" or whether, in the final analysis, reality consists in their interaction. Hawthorne's initial notes for his tales are for the most part abstract formulas, equally remote from the subjective and the objective world: "Personify the Century—talk of its present middle-age—of its youth, and its adventures—of its prospects." Such schemata point to a parallelism between the two worlds, but hardly would lead to richness either of imagination or of physical substance, and certainly would never produce a meeting in which each might "imbue itself with the nature of the other." If Hawthorne's writings tend to be thin in both respects, it is because he never fully faced the problem of knowledge which his own situation raised.

Yet his underlying purpose was always "to open an intercourse with the world," and out of this purpose arose not allegory but symbolism. The "Custom House" essay, introductory to *The Scarlet Letter,* is a portrait of the artist as symbolist in spite of himself. Of course Hawthorne indulges in his usual *peccavi:* "It was a folly, with the materiality of this daily life pressing so intrusively upon me, to attempt to fling myself back into another age; or to insist on creating the semblance of a world out of airy matter. . . . The fault was mine." But this reverence for the material present and trivial view of the imagination do not obscure the central theme of the sketch—the theme implicit in the vignette of Hawthorne poring over the scarlet letter. That self-portrait—which, be it noted, is a self-projection, since Hawthorne in point of fact came upon his subject quite otherwise—amounts to a dramatic definition of the following "romance" and of the author's relation to it. The author's *donnée,* as James would call it, is neither Imagination nor Actuality per se but a symbol whose inherent meaning is *The Scarlet Letter.* The world that the writer seeks is generated by contemplation of the symbol, not by the external yoking-together of two realms which by definition are different in kind. This integral act of perception effectually "opens" an imaginative reality. That it is not the material reality of nineteenth-century Salem becomes wholly irrelevant, since the meaning of the symbol, accreted by generations who have lived with it and in it, is continuous in time.

Such would seem to be the implication of the essay as a whole. The Custom House itself, with Hawthorne as Surveyor of the Customs, is the stage for potential commerce or "intercourse with the world." The Custom House is at once the Surveyor's ally and his enemy. As enemy, it destroys his creative power by involving him in material commerce, in weighing and gauging, in all the mechanistic ways of thinking which, as Melville said, make "the round world itself but an empty cipher, except to sell by the cartload." On the other hand, business at the Salem wharf is virtually at a standstill, and the Custom House actually imposes very few practical duties on the Surveyor. As his ally, it embodies, like its aged inhabitants, the residue of past experience; it is the analogue of the Surveyor's own consciousness, in which, though a mere "writer of story-books," he feels a continuity with his Puritan and seafaring ancestors. Thus the Custom House makes possible another kind of commerce and another kind of revenue: a traffic with the world by means of the significance vested in a traditional symbol. The discovery of the scarlet letter amid the old documents of the Customs—lists of wrecked or rotten ships and dead merchants—signalizes not a retreat into the past but a penetration into persistent meaning.

In this way "The Custom House" throws light on a theme in *The Scarlet Letter* which is easily overlooked amid the ethical concerns of the book. Every character, in effect, re-enacts the "Custom House" scene in which Hawthorne himself contemplated the letter, so that the entire "romance" becomes a kind of exposition of the nature of symbolic perception. Hawthorne's subject is not only the meaning of adultery but also meaning in general; not only *what* the focal symbol means but also *how* it gains significance. This aspect of the book is emphasized by Hawthorne's pointed use of the most problematic kind of symbol, a letter, and by his method of circling interpretation through the minds of various characters. In the opening chapters the scarlet "A" is the object of hundreds of eyes; Hester is not the only one who wears the symbol, if "wearing" it is synonymous with discovery and absorption of its meaning. As Mr. Wilson delivers his "discourse on sin . . . with continual reference to the ignominious letter," the minds of the populace are confirmed in the mold of Puritan thought, and the real Hester for them is the Adulteress. Hester, standing before them, is caught in their vision of the world. Looking down at the letter on her bosom and touching it with her finger, she feels that this hostile society and its judgment upon her are "her realities." Yet, at the same time, "the scaffold of the pillory was a point of view," and one wholly different from that of her judges. Although the pageant of her past life which presents itself before her cannot withstand the pressure of the surrounding Puritan vision, the independent view that she will later attain is foreshadowed by this "mass of imperfectly shaped and spectral images." As the years pass, the symbol has a "powerful and peculiar" effect upon her being; Hester escapes the Puritan world by taking the letter to herself, extending the "lawlessness" of adultery into all her habits of thought, and reshaping conventional values into her own reality. "The world's law was no law for her mind. . . . She assumed a freedom of speculation . . . which our fore-fathers, had they known it, would have held to be a deadlier crime than that stigmatized by the scarlet letter." For all her seeming compliance with the doctrines of the Puritans, the symbol has rendered to her, and she inhabits, a realm quite different from theirs.

More important than this divergence, however, is the fundamentally similar process by which Hester and the Puritan populace come to terms with the symbol of adultery. In both cases the "A" is psychophysical, entering into and shaping the perceiving mind and the objective scene. This notion is applied with variations to the other principal characters. Pearl, as Hawthorne reiterates at tiresome length, *is* the scarlet letter both physically and mentally. Her function in the book is more than to symbolize the union of Hester and Dimmesdale; she is actually a kind of commentary on the symbol itself. As "the scarlet letter in another form" she reveals what the letter is—the psychophysical presence of "adultery," whatever meaning that word may take. In Dimmesdale the symbol is diverted from its normal course and emerges obliquely as the psychosomatic mark on his breast. Dimmesdale is constrained from accepting either the popular version of adultery or Hester's. He cannot believe for long that what they did "had a consecration of its own," but he cannot repent and thereby take his destined place in the world projected by the Puritans. Thus his agony is not only moral but intellectual. As he tells Hester, he is cut off from any reality, conventional or otherwise. The "strange sympathy betwixt soul and body" which characterizes his disease is the indirect satisfaction of his frustrated yearning for "substance."

Chillingworth, who discovers the psychosomatic malady of Dimmesdale, is himself afflicted in the same way: his aspect changes, just as his mind is transformed, from the scholar to the devil. But in his case the effect of the symbol on body and mind is complete, because Chillingworth has totally submerged himself in a symbolic role. His interpretation of the letter is a heterodox Calvinism: embarking on his obsessive quest for the "A" in Dimmesdale, he is unconsciously throwing himself into the character of Satan in the Puritan myth of the Fall. Naturally enough, after he becomes aware of what has happened to him, he turns to Calvinism for comfort, asserting that "a dark necessity" beyond the human will has determined the whole action: "Ye that have wronged me are not sinful, save in a kind of typical illusion; neither am I fiend-like, who have snatched a fiend's office from his hands. It is our fate." Again, however, his view is heretical, since it denies moral responsibility, and his statement actually has a rather aesthetic turn. Chillingworth holds that he and the others are committed to roles in a symbolic drama, the "typical illusion" of which he speaks; in effect, their lives, both mental and physical, are a function of the meaning of the scarlet letter, which alone remains real amid the appearances that it generates. While Hawthorne obviously regards this speech as the misguided speculation of a lost soul, the unusual vigor of the language indicates the appeal which he found in these ideas. With the reservation that human lives do not become illusory, but gain reality, through the operation of the symbol, he himself could have subscribed to the sweeping theory of Chillingworth. Something like it is implicit in the tableau of Hester, Dimmesdale, and Pearl on the scaffold, with the immense letter "A" shining above them in the sky. The celestial letter transmutes the everyday objects of the scene: "All were visible, but with a singularity of aspect that seemed to give another moral interpretation to the things of this world than they had ever borne before." The world thus illuminated is at once physical and ideal. At its center are human beings who perceive the world by wearing the symbol in mind and body:

And there stood the minister, with his hand over his heart; and Hester Prynne, with the embroidered letter glimmering on her bosom; and little Pearl, herself a symbol, and the connecting link between those two.

With respect to symbolism, as in every other way, *The Scarlet Letter* is a special case among Hawthorne's works. Here, since the very focus of the book is a written sign, he has no difficulty in securing a symbolistic status for his material. The symbolistic method is inherent in the subject, just as the subject of symbolism is inherent in the method. This is only partially true of the other romances. In *The House of the Seven Gables, The Blithedale Romance,* and *The Marble Faun,* Hawthorne's effort to establish a symbolistic standpoint has an air of contrivance; he falls back on *ad hoc* devices. Donatello in *The Marble Faun,* for example, is associated with the Faun of Praxiteles, and he is apprehended by Miriam, Hilda, and Kenyon in much the same way as they perceive a work of art. The imputed identity of the man and the statue serves to abstract Donatello from any objective existence and, without relegating him to the realm of sheer fancy, to locate him in the middle ground that Hawthorne wanted. Similarly, the "sylvan dance" of Miriam and Donatello is treated as "the realization of one of those bas-reliefs where a dance of nymphs, satyrs, or bacchanals is twined around the circle of an antique vase." Although Hawthorne's judgments on statuary and painting are crude and often amount to no more than sheer padding, the constant allusion to these arts in *The Marble Faun* has an over-all function. Hawthorne is trying to suggest a situation in which everything perceived has the symbolic status of an aesthetic object. "The Bronze Pontiff's Benediction," conferred on the three friends in the market place at Perugia, is typical of a mode of perception that recurs throughout the book. The statue of the Pope seems "endowed with spiritual life" because all things can become significant in the "unexpected glimpse" which removes them from the customary world:

There is a singular effect oftentimes when, out of the midst of engrossing thought and deep absorption, we suddenly look up, and catch a glimpse of external objects. We seem at such moments to look farther and deeper into them, than by any premeditated observation; it is as if they met our eyes alive, and with all their hidden meaning on the surface, but grew again inanimate and inscrutable the instant that they became aware of our glances.

In *The Blithedale Romance* Hawthorne makes use of another expedient. Miles Coverdale, the ill-natured aesthete who serves as narrator, views the entire action as a kind of play enacted before him. For him, the three leading figures—Hollingsworth, Zenobia, and Priscilla—form a "knot of characters, whom a real intricacy of events, greatly assisted by my method of insulating them from other relations, ... kept ... upon my mental stage, as actors in a drama." Again Hawthorne's purpose is to place the story in terms of aesthetic perception. But neither the imagination of Coverdale nor the artistic analogy of *The Marble Faun* can actually carry that weight, since neither is maintained fully and consistently enough. In both cases the net effect is one of coy excuse; Hawthorne is not sure of his own stand. Perhaps his books are to claim an aesthetic reality; perhaps they merely constitute an "unreal" opposite of the physical world; perhaps they must take refuge in a noncommittal parallelism between Imagination and Actuality. He himself was well aware of one aspect of this indecision—the split within him between the man of "fancy" and the admirer of Trollope. He did not see so clearly that this opposition was transected by another, more debilitating conflict—between the symbolist and the allegorist.

The truth is that symbolism at once fascinated and horrified him. While it spoke to his "sensibilities," it evaded "the analysis of [his] mind." On the one hand, the symbol was valuable precisely because it transcended analytic thought; on the other hand, that very transcendence, with its suggestion of the unconventional, the novel, the disorderly, was potentially dangerous. The letter had "deep meaning," but the letter was scarlet, and Pearl, its embodiment, had no "principle of being" save "the freedom of a broken law." Hawthorne dwells on the elusiveness, the rationally indefinable quality of Pearl, who "could not be made amenable to rules, ... whose elements were perhaps beautiful and brilliant, but all in disorder; or with an order peculiar to themselves, amidst which the point of variety and arrangement was difficult or impossible to be discovered." Allegory was the brake that Hawthorne applied to his sensibility. For allegory *was* analytic: allegory was safe because it preserved the conventional distinction between thought and things and because it depended on a conventional order whose point of arrangement was easily defined. The symbolistic and the allegorical patterns in Hawthorne's books reach quite different conclusions; or, rather, the symbolism leads to an inconclusive luxuriance of meaning, while allegory imposes the pat moral and the simplified character. This predicament comes to the surface in an absurd conversation between Kenyon and Miriam toward the end of *The Marble Faun.* Since Donatello has been symbolically identified with the statue of the Faun, in which "the characteristics of the brute creation meet and combine with those of humanity," his crime, from this point of view, is a necessary step in his attainment of fully human qualities. At the same time, Donatello has been associated with Adam, and his crime with the Fall of Man. The combination of these two meanings in the one character forces a reinterpretation of orthodox Evil. "Was the crime," Miriam asks, "in which he and I were wedded—was it a blessing, in that strange disguise?" This is more than Kenyon can stomach: "You stir up deep and perilous matter, Miriam. . . . I dare not follow you into the unfathomable abysses whither you are tending. . . . It is too dangerous." And Hawthorne himself repudiates "these meditations, which the sculptor rightly felt to be so perilous." He falls back on the simple morality of Hilda, a purely allegorical creature equipped with white robe, tower, lamp, and doves.

Yet there can be no doubt that Hawthorne experienced the attraction of inverted values—the extreme form of that anticonventional impulse which is inherent in symbolism. In the Roman Eden, he ventures to say, "the final charm is bestowed by the malaria. . . . For if you come hither in summer, and stray through these glades in the golden sunset, fever walks arm in arm with you, and death awaits you at the end of the dim vista." The "piercing, thrilling, delicious kind of regret" which these thoughts arouse in him points in an obvious direction: "Aux objets répugnants nous trouvons des appas." Baudelaire stood at the end of the dim vista. If Hawthorne was unduly anxious about the freedom of symbolic meaning, it may be to his credit that he had some inkling of how far that method could go.

One cannot say as much for Emerson and Whitman, whose faith in symbolic reality quickly disposed of awkward questions. The symbolism which for Hawthorne was no more than a sporadic intuition became for them an explicit metaphysical principle. Hawthorne's conscious philosophy belonged to the eighteenth century; his symbolic imagination to the nineteenth. His critical vocabulary, with its perpetual contrast between "fiction" and "reality," "fancy" and "fact," "imagination" and "actuality," was an eighteenth-century formula applied to a nineteenth-century art, just as his allegorical technique was the product of eighteenth-century reason at work on an antirational sensibility. But empirical fact and rational form had no hold on Emerson and Whitman, whose "transcendentalism" was specifically opposed to neoclassic doctrine and method. While Hawthorne's figure of Man Seeing largely preserves the static mold of the Lockian theory of perception, Emerson recreates that archetype in the image of the Voyager:

But man thyself, and all things unfix, dispart, and flee. Nothing will stand the eye of a man,—neither lion, nor person, nor planet, nor time, nor condition. Each bullies us for a season; but gaze, and it opens that most solid seeming wall, yields its secret, receives us into its depth and advances our front so much farther into the recesses of being, to some new frontier as yet unvisited by the elder voyagers.

If man is by nature an explorer, the "eyes, and ears, and skin" are actively poetic, not merely registers of sense data. The "symbolical" meaning of rails and barns and dung forks—a significance which we do not "understand" or "know" in the accepted fashion—is generated by the advance of the mind into the recesses of being.

"No one will get at my verses," Whitman declared, "who insists upon viewing them as a literary performance, or attempt at such performance, or as aiming mainly toward art or aestheticism." In his conscious literary theory literature is subordinate to sociology, "the United States themselves are essentially the greatest poem," the poet must "tally" the American scene, and the function of poetry is the creation of heroic citizens. Yet it is obvious that a larger principle governs both his poetic and his sociological doctrine; no one will get at his verses who insists upon viewing them as a sociological performance. Whitman intimates that the link between his poems and American life is actually a new method exemplified by both:

One main contrast of the ideas behind every page of my verses, compared with establish'd poems, is their different relative attitude towards God, towards the objective universe, and still more (by reflection, confession, assumption, &c.) the quite changed attitude of the ego, the one chanting or talking, towards himself and towards his fellow-humanity. It is certainly time for America, above all, to begin this readjustment in the scope and basic point of view of verse; for everything else has changed.

The distinctive quality of Whitman's poetry depends on this change of standpoint. In his effort "to articulate and faithfully express . . . [his] own physical, emotional, moral, intellectual, and aesthetic Personality, in the midst of, and tallying, the momentous spirit and facts of its immediate days," his interest is not so much in the Personality or the environment per se as in the "changed attitude of the ego." The new method is better defined in the poems themselves than in the critical prose. The ego appears in the poems as a traveler and explorer, not as a static observer; its object is "to know the universe itself as a road, as many roads, as roads for traveling souls." The shift of image from the contemplative eye of "establish'd poems" to the voyaging ego of Whitman's poetry records a large-scale theoretical shift from the categories of "substance" to those of "process." Whitman's "perpetual journey" is not analogous to a sight-seeing trip, though his catalogues might give that impression; the mind and the material world into which it ventures are not ultimately different in kind. Instead, what seems at first a penetration of nature by the mind is actually a process in which the known world comes into being. The "child who went forth every day, and who now goes, and will always go forth every day," is indistinguishable from the world of his experience: "The first object he look'd upon, that object he became, / And that object became part of him." The true voyage is the endless becoming of reality:

> Allons! to that which is endless as it was beginningless,
> To undergo much, tramp of days, rests of nights,
> To merge all in the travel they tend to, and the days
>   and nights they tend to,
> Again to merge them in the start of superior journeys. . . .

Here there is no clear distinction among the traveler, the road, and the journey, for the journey is nothing but the progressive unity of the voyager and the lands he enters; perception, which unites the seer and the seen, is identical with the real process of becoming. God, in this context, is a "seething principle," and human society is a flow of "shapes ever projecting other shapes." Whitman's "readjustment in the scope and basic point of view of verse" is actually a transmutation of all supposed entities into events.

A poem, therefore, instead of referring to a completed act of perception, constitutes the act itself, both in the author and in the reader; instead of describing reality, a poem is a realization. When Whitman writes, "See, steamers steaming through my poems," he is admonishing both himself and his audience that no distinction can be made between themselves, the steamers, and the words. Indeed, no distinction can be made between the poet and the reader: "It is you talking just as much as myself, I act as the tongue of you." His new method was predicated not only on the sense of creative vision—itself a process which renders a world in process— but also, as part and parcel of that consciousness, on the sense of creative speech. The "I" of Whitman's poems speaks the world that he sees, and sees the world that he speaks, and does this by *becoming* the reality of his vision and of his words, in which the reader also participates. Most of Whitman's poems, more or less explicitly, are "voyages" in this metaphysical sense. This was Whitman's genre, his "new theory of literary composition for imaginative works." Even in the most personal lyrics of *Children of Adam* and *Calamus*, the "one chanting or talking" is not simply the poet; the chant is neither pure self-expression nor pure description; what is talked about is oddly confused with the talker and the talking; and the audience is potentially both the subject and the writer. "Song of Myself," though it breathes the personal egotism of Whitman, makes sense as a whole only when the self is taken dramatically and identified with "the procreant urge of the world."

Consider the last four sections of "Starting from Paumanok"— the entire poem being the "Song of Myself" in miniature. Here at the end of the poem it appears that to start from Paumanok is to start far back of the speaker's birth in the opening line. The beginnings (of the speaker, of America, and of the world) are "aboriginal," as typified by the Indian name; the beginnings, indeed, by a leap of thought, become the perpetual genesis of "a world primal again," announced by the poet's voice. In the following section, with its images of incessant motion, the announcement itself is the genesis of the world; the voice is equated with the becoming of reality. Retrospectively, one sees that the preliminary statement of the poem—"Solitary, singing in the West, I strike up for a New World"—has ushered in a song which not only is addressed to and descriptive of America but also is the vehicle, at once product and creator, of a metaphysical "newness." In the course of the poem the solitary voice of the individual poet has expanded into the presence of an all-inclusive Word—"a word to clear one's path ahead endlessly." And the speaker's union with his hearer is imaged in the final section as the love relationship of "camerados" on the journey. The method of "Starting from Paumanok" does not palliate Whitman's diffuseness and arbitrary choice of material; rather, by depriving him of a static point of view, it is the immediate cause of these defects. Yet the principle behind this poem, the exploitation of Speech as the literary aspect of eternal process, is the source of whatever literary value resides in *Leaves of Grass*.

"This subject of language," Whitman confided to Horace Trau-bel, "interests me—interests me: I never quite get it out of my mind. I sometimes think the Leaves is only a language experiment." *An American Primer*, Whitman's fragmentary lecture on language, reveals a mind that fed upon words: "*Names* are magic.—One word can pour such a flood through the soul." The sense of language as inherently significant is his meeting ground with Hawthorne, for whom a "deep meaning . . . streamed forth" from the scarlet letter. In both cases attention is deflected from "ideas" and "objects" to a symbolic medium; and in both cases the perception of a meaningful symbol is opposed to another kind of perception, which Hawthorne calls "analysis." Hawthorne would like to reduce the meaning to the rational terms of logical construct or empirical fact; he is plainly uncomfortable at the disturbance of his "sensibilities." In practice, he not only translates symbolism into allegory but also affects a rational style which ties his language down to the common-sense world. Whitman's awareness of words in themselves is stronger, and he is militantly hostile to reason. He proposes "new law-forces of spoken and written language—not merely the pedagogue-forms, correct, regular, familiar with precedents, made for matters of outside propriety, fine words, thoughts definitely told out." He is indifferent to dictionary words and textbook grammar, which he associates with a barren formalism and externality. Fully accepting the intuition at which Hawthorne boggled, he takes his departure from a denial of conventional distinctions: "Strange and hard that paradox true I give, / Objects gross and the unseen soul are one." Since Whitman regards meaning as an activity of words rather than an external significance attached to them, language, together with the self and the material world, turns out to be a process, the pouring of the flood. "A perfect user of words uses things," while at the same time he *is* both the words and the things:

Latent, in a great user of words, must actually be all passions, crimes, trades, animals, stars, God, sex, the past, might, space, metals, and the like—because these are the words, and he who is not these, plays with a foreign tongue, turning helplessly to dictionaries and authorities.

This kind of speech "seldomer tells a thing than suggests or necessitates it," because to "tell" something would be to suppose something outside the language. The reader is not given statements but is set in action, "on the assumption that the process of reading is not a half-sleep, but, in highest sense, an exercise, a gymnast's struggle." The poem necessarily works "by curious removes, indirections," rather than direct imitation of nature, since "the image-making faculty" runs counter to the habit of mind which views the material world as separable from ideas and speech. Whitman's running battle with the rational assumptions of conventional thought reaches its peak in the hyperbolical "Song of the Rolling Earth," where he identifies all "audible words" with the marks on the printed page and glorifies, by way of contrast, "the unspoken meanings of the earth." In deliberate paradox he asserts that true poems will somehow be made from these inaudible words. The poem expresses the bravado of his conscious attempt to create a wholly symbolic language in the face of intellectual convention. For that is his purpose: the "tallying" of things and man, to which he often alludes mysteriously, is simply the presence of language in each and the presence of each in language. The "language experiment" of *Leaves of Grass*—its promise of "new potentialities of speech"—depends on the symbolic status claimed by the book as a whole and in every part. "From the eyesight proceeds another eyesight and from the hearing proceeds another hearing and from the voice proceeds another voice eternally curious of the harmony of things with man."

The patent symbols of Whitman's best poem, "When Lilacs Last in the Dooryard Bloom'd," are conditioned by the thoroughgoing symbolism of his poetic attitude. As in most elegies, the person mourned is hardly more than the occasion of the work; but this poem, unlike *Lycidas* or *Adonais*, does not transmute the central figure merely by generalizing him out of all recognition. Lincoln is seldom mentioned either as a person or as a type. Instead, the focus of the poem is a presentation of the poet's mind at work in the context of Lincoln's death. If the true subject of *Lycidas* and *Adonais* is not Edward King or John Keats but the Poet, the true subject of Whitman's "Lilacs" is not the Poet but the poetic process. And even this subject is not treated simply by generalizing a particular situation. The act of poetizing and the context in which it takes place have continuity in time and space but no particular existence. Both are "ever-returning"; the tenses shift; the poet is in different places at once; and at the end this whole phase of creation is moving inexorably forward.

Within this framework the symbols behave like characters in a drama, the plot of which is the achievement of a poetic utterance. The spring, the constant process of rebirth, is threaded by the journey of the coffin, the constant process of death, and in the first section it presents the poet with twin symbols: the perennially blooming lilac and the drooping star. The spring also brings to the poet the "thought of him I love," in which the duality of life and death is repeated. The thought of the dead merges with the fallen star in Section 2; the thought of love merges with the life of the lilac, from which the poet breaks a sprig in Section 3. Thus the lilac and the star enter the poem not as objects to which the poet assigns a meaning but as elements in the undifferentiated stream of thoughts and things; and the spring, the real process of becoming, which involves the real process of dissolution, is also the genesis of poetic vision. The complete pattern of the poem is established with the advent of the bird in the fourth section. For here, in the song of the thrush, the lilac and star are united (the bird sings "death's outlet song of life"), and the potentiality of the poet's "thought" is intimated. The song of the bird and the thought of the poet, which also unites life and death, both lay claim to the third place in the "trinity" brought by spring; they are, as it were, the actuality and the possibility of poetic utterance, which reconciles opposite appearances.

The drama of the poem will be a movement from possible to actual poetic speech, as represented by the "tallying" of the songs of the poet and the thrush. Although it is a movement without steps, the whole being implicit in every moment, there is a graduation of emphasis. Ostensibly, the visions of the coffin and the star (Sections 5 through 8) delay the unison of poet and bird, so that full actualization is reserved for the end of the poem. On the other hand, the verse that renders the apparition of the coffin *is* "death's outlet song of life." The poetic act of evoking the dark journey is treated as the showering of death with lilac:

> Here, coffin that slowly passes,
> I give you my sprig of lilac. . . .
> Blossoms and branches green to coffins all I bring,
> For fresh as the morning, thus would I chant a song for you,
>   O sane and sacred death.

Even as the poet lingers, he has attained his end. And the star of Section 8, the counterpart of the coffin, functions in much the same way. The episode that occurred "a month since"—when "my soul in its trouble dissatisfied sank, as where you sad orb, / Concluded, dropt in the night, and was gone"—was a failure of the poetic spring. The soul was united with the star but not with the lilac. Yet the passage is preceded by the triumphant statement, "Now I know what you must have meant," and knowledge issues in the ability to render the episode in verse. The perception of meaning gives life to the fact of death; the star meant the death of Lincoln, but the evolution of the meaning is poetry.

The recurrence of the song of the thrush in the following section and in Section 13 is a reminder of the poetic principle which underlies the entire poem. In a sense, the words, "I hear your notes, I hear your call," apply to all that precedes and all that is to come, for the whole poem, existing in an eternal present, is the "loud human song" of the poet's "brother." But again Whitman delays the consummation. He is "detained" from his rendezvous with the bird—although he really "hears" and "understands" all the time— by the sight of the "lustrous star" and by the "mastering odor" of the lilac. Since both the star and the lilac are inherent in the song of the bird, he actually lingers only in order to proceed. While the song rings in the background, the poet puts the questions presupposed by his own poetizing. How can the life of song be one with the fact of death?—"O how shall I warble myself for the dead one there I loved?" And what will be the content of the song of death?—"O what shall I hang on the chamber walls . . . / To adorn the burial-house of him I love?" The questions answer themselves. The breath by which the grave becomes part of his chant is the breath of life; within the poem the image of the "burial-house" will be overlaid with "pictures of growing spring." The delay has served only to renew the initial theme: the poet's chant, like the song of the thrush, is itself the genesis of life and therefore contains both life and death.

The final achievement of poetic utterance comes in Section 14, when the poet, looking forth on the rapid motion of life, experiences death. More exactly, he walks between the "thought" and the "knowledge" of death, which move beside him like companions. Just as his poem exists between the "thought" of the dead, which is paradoxically an act of life, and the actual knowledge of the bird's song, which embodies both dying star and living lilac, the poet himself is in motion from the potential to the actual. From this point to the end of the poem, the sense of movement never flags. The poet's flight into the darkness is a fusion with the stream of music from the bird:

> And the charm of the carol rapt me,
> As I held as if by their hands my comrades in the night,
> And the voice of my spirit tallied the song of the bird.

As the motion of the poet is lost in the motion of the song, the latter is identified with the "dark mother always gliding near," and in the "floating" carol death itself becomes the movement of waves that "undulate round the world." In effect, poet and bird, poem and song, life and death, are now the sheer process of the carol; as in "Out of the Cradle Endlessly Rocking," reality is the unfolding Word. The presented song merges into the "long panoramas of visions" in Section 15, and then the inexorable process begins to leave this moment behind:

Passing the visions, passing the night,
Passing, unloosing the hold of my comrades' hands,
Passing the song of the hermit bird and the tallying song
  of my soul....
Passing, I leave thee lilac with heart-shaped leaves, ...
I cease from my song for thee, ...
O comrade lustrous with silver face in the night.

But the poetic activity is continuous; the passing-onward is not a rejection of the old symbols. "Lilac and star and bird twined with the chant of ... [the] soul" also pass onward because they are activities and not finite things. The conclusion of this poem dramatizes what Whitman once stated of *Leaves of Grass* as a whole—that the book exists as "a passage way to something rather than a thing in itself concluded." Taken seriously, in the sense in which there *can* be no "thing in itself concluded," this notion is not, as Whitman sometimes pretended, a mere excuse for haphazard technique but the rationale of a symbolistic method.

Yet "When Lilacs Last in the Dooryard Bloom'd" is a successful poem only because it does not fully live up to the theory which it both states and illustrates. The poem really presupposes a static situation, which Whitman undertakes to treat as though it were dynamic; in the course of the poem the death of Lincoln, of which we always remain aware, is translated into Whitman's terms of undifferentiated flow. His other long poems generally lack this stabilizing factor. Whatever the nominal subject, it is soon lost in sheer "process"; all roads lead into the "Song of Myself," in which the bare Ego interacts with a miscellaneous world. The result is Whitman's characteristic disorder and turgidity. When the subject is endless, any form becomes arbitrary. While the antirational conception of a poem as the realization of language gives a new freedom and a new dignity to poetry, it apparently leads to an aimlessness from which the poem can be rescued only by returning to rational categories. Otherwise, the best that can be expected from Whitman's poetic principle is the "long varied train of an emblem, dabs of music,/Fingers of the organist skipping staccato over the keys of the great organ."

And much worse can be expected. In the last section of "Passage to India," Whitman's most deliberate statement of the process theory, the tone is frenetic even for him:

> Sail forth—steer for the deep waters only,
> Reckless O soul, exploring, I with thee, and thou with me,
> For we are bound where mariner has not yet dared to go,
> And we will risk the ship, ourselves and all.

What begins in Emerson as a mild contravention of reason—a peaceful journey "to some frontier as yet unvisited by the elder voyagers"—becomes in Whitman a freedom from all "limits and imaginary lines,"

> . . . from all formules!
> From your formules, O bat-eyed and materialistic priests.

Thus the looseness of form in Whitman's verse is not merely a technical defect; it is the counterpart of an intellectual anarchism designed to overthrow conventional reality by dissolving all rational order. Moreover, like Hawthorne in the malarial gardens of Rome, Whitman has his *frisson* at this inversion of established values—and without Hawthorne's reservations: "I know my words are weapons full of danger, full of death, / For I confront peace, security, and all the settled laws, to unsettle them." Mixed with the obtrusive health of the *Calamus* poems is a daredevil flouting of convention:

> The way is suspicious, the result uncertain, perhaps destructive, . . .
> The whole past theory of your life and all conformity to the lives
>   around you would have to be abandon'd, . . .
> Nor will my poems do good only, they will do just as much evil,
>   perhaps more. . . .

Nowadays we are too much in the habit of blaming "romanticism" for any irrationality in literature. Certainly the romantic spirit was enamored of a fluid reality, which could not be contained in the old channels, and the romantic often opened the dikes deliberately, just to see what would happen. The Voyager is a romantic figure, the ocean a romantic realm. Yet a distinction is in order. The antirationalism of the romantic voyage is a wilful pro-

jection of feeling; the romantic sea is the image of a world subservient to emotion. But the symbolistic voyage is a process of
becoming: Whitman is less concerned with exploration of emotion
than with exploration as a mode of existence. Similarly, his poems
not only are *about* voyaging but also enact the voyage, so that their
content (the image of the metaphysical journey) is primarily a
reflection of their literary method, in which the writer and his subject become part of the stream of language. It follows that Whitman's hostility to reason has another, more complicated source
than the romantic vision of a world suffused with feeling. Like
Emerson, he finds the antonym of reason not in emotion but in the
"symbolical"; like Hawthorne and Melville, he contrasts "analysis" with "meaning," arithmetic with "significance." For his object is not so much to impose a new form on the world as to adopt
a new stance in which the world takes on new shapes. His difficulty is that his method works too well: the shapes proliferate endlessly, and, having deprived himself of an external standpoint, he
has no means of controlling them. On the other hand, the occasional violence of his antirationalism is the result of an opposite
difficulty: while he would like to be sublimely indifferent to established distinctions, reason fights back as he seeks to transcend it,
and he is forced into the position of the iconoclast.

The mood of Whitman's reckless address to his soul is the mood of
Ahab, who also is willing to risk the ship in order to go where no
other mariner dares. Ahab's voyage is an intellectual experiment
like Whitman's "passage to more than India":

> Passage to you, your shores, ye aged fierce enigmas!
> Passage to you, to mastership of you, ye strangling problems!
> You, strew'd with the wrecks of skeletons, that, living, never
>   reach'd you.

The difference is that Whitman does not really believe in the possibility of wreck. For him the "deep waters" are, after all, the "seas
of God," and his "daring joy" is "safe." Besides, although Whit-

man talks a great deal about his freedom from all formulas, and although this freedom can lead to the destructiveness which he often likes to imagine, he largely takes it out in talk. His own associations of thought are actually not very subversive. He simply does not bring his antirational method to bear on really "fierce enigmas" or "strangling problems," and his results give him little occasion to question his own proceedings. Ahab, on the other hand, is involved in a genuine dilemma. While he is as much committed to the voyage as Whitman, he is fully aware, at the same time, that his defiance of reason can lead to strange perversions of outlook; and he knows that instead of passing through the "most solid seeming wall" of appearances, as Emerson happily prophesied, he may wreck the ship on the "solid white buttress" of Moby Dick's forehead. In Ahab the image of the voyager—the signature of transcendentalism—is at odds with itself. Ahab is the disappointed transcendentalist, knowing no other way of proceeding but shadowed by imminent failure. Whereas Whitman can proclaim that the poet's "passage to India" will unite a supposedly "separate Nature so unnatural" with the thoughts of man, Nature has apparently turned against Ahab, and he has no confidence that "the divine ship sails the divine sea." At the same time he cannot go back to the security of land. He persists in the voyage, but it is transformed into a desperate battle, which is only intensified by the haunting thought that his whole approach may be wrong.

Like Hawthorne and Whitman, Melville in his way is deeply concerned with this question of "approach." The first chapter of *Moby-Dick* is the statement of a point of view. Ishmael opens his narrative by identifying voyage with vision: the field of man's vision is the sea. Like the island city whose avenues all radiate "waterward" and whose shores are thronged with "crowds of water-gazers," the sensibility of the individual man opens onto the ocean. And the "thousands upon thousands of mortal men fixed in ocean reveries," who come from far inland, "north, east, south, and west," are united in their silent brooding upon the waters. Beneath the jocular tone these initial paragraphs create an effect of irrepressible need. The attraction of the mind to the sea is life itself as a quest for knowledge. "Why did the old Persians hold the sea holy? Why did the Greeks give it a separate deity, and own brother of Jove? Surely all this is not without meaning." The meaning is rendered more fully at the end of the chapter on "The Mast-Head," where another water-gazer, lulled into reverie "by the blending cadence of waves with thoughts,"

at last . . . loses his identity; takes the mystic ocean at his feet for the visible image of that deep, blue, bottomless soul, pervading mankind and nature; and every strange, half-seen, gliding, beautiful thing that eludes him; every dimly-discovered, uprising fin of some undiscernible form, seems to him the embodiment of those elusive thoughts that only people the soul by continually flitting through it.

Here the voyaging mind is fused with the world in a flux of wave-like forms; the identity of the self is lost in a pantheistic sea. Yet this attainment of sheer vision—in which, as Emerson described it, "I become a transparent eye-ball; I am nothing; I see all"—is suddenly dangerous. As your foot slips on the masthead, external things become alien, the empty spaces between man and nature spread to infinity, "and your identity comes back in horror." To submerge in the sea is to drown; the self and the world are two, not one. The voyage of Ishmael, though it lacks the desperation of Ahab's outlook, is crossed by a doubt similar to his. Water-gazing is a paradoxical activity—a search for absolute unity with the objects of thought, only to discover that immediate knowledge destroys the thinker. This is the "still deeper . . . meaning" of the story of Narcissus—to return to the first chapter. "Because he could not grasp the tormenting, mild image he saw in the fountain, [he] plunged into it and was drowned. But that same image, we ourselves see in all rivers and oceans. It is the image of the ungraspable phantom of life; and this is the key to it all." The image is not merely a self-reflection but the embodiment of thought, the matching phantom in the sea of forms. The phantom is ungraspable as long as we stand on the bank; and the ocean is annihilative once we dive into it.

Whatever hazards Ishmael may perceive in the alliance of "meditation and water," the impossibility of resolving the dilemma by simply returning to land is even more obvious in his case than in Ahab's. To send the visionary back home would be to invalidate the whole book. Ishmael is at once a character and the narrator of *Moby-Dick*, and he is a "voyager" in both respects. The concluding paragraphs of the first chapter are not only an explanation of the sailor's motives in going to sea but also a kind of rationale of the book itself as a "voyage." The narrator is immersed in a drama of which the Fates, in a manner of speaking, are the "stage managers," since he performs a part having nothing to do with his own "unbiassed free will and discriminating judgment." Will is the essence of self, and judgment is objective knowledge; but he is governed by the symbolic imagination, which moves in still another plane. Before him swims "the overwhelming idea of the great whale." In the sea, which is the field of his vision, the White Whale is the mightiest image, the summation of all the myriad shapes that succeed one another through infinite change:

The great flood-gates of the wonder-world swung open, and in the wild conceits that swayed me to my purpose, two and two there floated into my inmost soul, endless processions of the whale, and, midmost of them all, one grand hooded phantom, like a snow hill in the air.

The "endless processions of the whale" are transitive forms that issue out of a fecund center; each procession comes "two and two," for each shape implies an opposite. To go whaling is to entertain these symbolic perspectives. It is significant that the narrator himself is flooded as he sets out to invade the sea. For, properly speaking, the moment of imagination is a state of becoming, and the visionary forms simultaneously are apprehended and realize themselves.

In "The Whiteness of the Whale" the ambiguity of whiteness—its mingled beauty and horror, as exemplified in countless ways—repeats the doubleness of the "endless processions," and "whiteness" becomes a synonym for fluid reality, like the "grand hooded phantom" of the earlier account. In this chapter Ishmael solicits the reader's understanding of his method; he must explain himself, he says, "else all these chapters might be naught." He is trying to define not only "what the White Whale . . . was to me" but also the kind of thinking which generates that ambiguous creature: "How is mortal man to account for it?" The apparent answer is that the double meaning of whiteness is a product of imaginative perception: "To analyze it would seem to be impossible. . . . In a matter like this, subtlety appeals to subtlety, and without imagination no man can follow another into these halls." He who would follow Ishmael must exert the symbolic imagination, for Ishmael's "pursuit" of the whale is the evolution of an image. Although the meanings that develop are disquieting, and the whole process tends to become a "fiery hunt," he has no other approach.

Ishmael, unlike most fictive narrators, is not merely a surrogate for an absentee author. Behind him, always present as a kind of *Doppelgänger*, stands Herman Melville. As Ishmael the narrator enters more deeply into his symbolic world, he increasingly becomes a presence, a visionary activity, rather than a man; we lose interest in him as an individual, and even Ishmael the sailor almost drops from the story. Ishmael the visionary is often indistinguishable from the mind of the author himself. It is Melville's own voice that utters the passage on the heroic stature of Ahab. This apparent violation of narrative standpoint is really a natural consequence of the symbolic method of *Moby-Dick*. The distinction between the author and his alter ego is submerged in their common function as the voyaging mind. In fact, the whole book, though cast in the form of historical narrative, tends to the condition of drama, in the sense that it is a presentation, like Ishmael's vision of the whale processions, in which both Melville and Ishmael lose themselves. The frequent references to drama and the actual use of dramatic form in a number of chapters reflect the visionary status of the entire action. In the sequence of chapters (xxxvi–xl) from "The Quarter-Deck" to "Midnight, Forecastle," there is no narrator, to all intents and purposes; Ishmael has to re-establish his own identity at the beginning of chapter xli. At the same time the drama does not take place *in vacuo;* the symbolic nature of the action depends on its being perceived. This is the reason why Ishmael is necessary in the book, despite the fact that he and Melville often merge into one. Ishmael is the delegated vision of Melville: he can enact the genesis of symbolic meaning, whereas Melville, speaking solely as an omniscient author, could only impute an arbitrary significance. Unlike Hawthorne, the Melville of *Moby-Dick* does not verge toward allegory, because he locates his symbols in a unitary act of perception. Moreover, the symbolic vision of Ishmael is repeated by the dramatis personae. From Father Mapple's interpretation of Jonah to Ahab's blasphemous rituals, the symbols take on meaning in the course of perception. The pattern of "The Doubloon" is the scheme of the book: under the overhanging consciousness of Ishmael, with Melville looking over his shoulder, the several characters envisage the meaning of the coin. As the various meanings multiply, we hear the chant of Pip: "I look, you look, he looks; we look, ye look, they look."

Melville, first and last, assumes that "some certain significance lurks in all things." There is no other justification for the survival of Ishmael at the end of *Moby-Dick.* "The drama's done. Why then does anyone step forth?" Ishmael survives as the voyaging mind, the capacity for vision, the potentiality of symbolic perception. He floats on the ocean to which he is dedicated, just as the entire narrative assumes the necessity of water-gazing. The white shroud of the sea, the plenum of significance, remains an eternal challenge. Yet the very fact that Ishmael and the sea are left as mere potentiality indicates the deep distrust interwoven with Melville's faith. The translation of man and the world into sheer process, which satisfies Emerson and Whitman, does not content him. The doubloon is evidence of the reality of symbolic meaning; the significance is *in* the world, and the significant world is generated by "looking." But the meaning suffers a fragmentation as it comes into being, and Pip's commentary is an assertion of real multiplicity. The diversity that Emerson and Whitman easily accept as new "frontiers" of exploration presents itself to Melville as a network of paradox.

Traveling with Whitman down the open road, "the earth expanding right hand and left hand," Melville notes that right and left are opposites.

Not only does symbolism imply a complex of logical oppositions but it also tends to obscure these real and important differences. While Melville hardly contemplates, except as a lost hope, any return to the substance of the land, he is uncomfortably aware of the irrationality of the fluid sea. The ultimate horror of whiteness is "its indefiniteness," the merging of distinctions in the insubstantial medium. For "whiteness is not so much a colour as the visible absence of colour, and at the same time the concrete of all colours," so that a snowy landscape, though "full of meaning," is "a dumb blankness, . . . a colourless, all-colour of atheism from which we shrink." The totality of symbolic meaning is intensely present, but destroys individuality; its "atheism" is that of transcendentalists like Whitman, who, in order to become God-possessed, deny a personal God. By the same token, in order to unite themselves with nature, they also deny personal identity. Melville follows in evident dismay. Seen rationally, as an object, the world is inaccessible; but, seen as accessible, the world swallows up the visionary. Ishmael's presentiment of the danger of water-gazing is verified by the fate of the "Pequod," which disappears into the ambiguity and formlessness of the sea. Only by self-annihilation does the "Pequod" penetrate the whiteness, which closes above it in "a creamy pool." Ishmael, as though to epitomize Melville's position, almost follows, but does not. He is drifting toward the "vital centre" of the swirling vortex when the "coffin life-buoy" suddenly emerges. Ishmael's status remains provisional. He accepts ambiguity and indefiniteness—he is "buoyed up by that coffin"— and yet somehow manages to retain his own "identity."

If the inconclusive fate of Ishmael evinces a double attitude in Melville—an acceptance of "voyaging" and a fear of its full implications—the fate of Ahab results from a refusal to remain in suspense. Ahab's motives, which are dramatized as vengeance against nature and revolt from God, lie deeper than mere satanic pride. Beneath his ferocious mood is the "little lower layer" which he confides to Starbuck: he seeks a kind of value not to be measured by the arithmetical methods of accountants. Money, the medium of exchange, is for him a symbolic medium; and his repudiation of the "Nantucket market" is a rejection of rational thought, just as Melville's doubloon is opposed to the commerce of Boston. When Starbuck continues to protest this irrational "profit," Ahab counters with a still "lower layer." He draws a contrast between "visible objects" and the world in process—the "event," the "living act," the "undoubted deed." Ahab has taken quite seriously Emerson's dictum, "But man thyself, and all things unfix, dispart, and flee." The visible object is only a "pasteboard mask"; the wall should open, as Emerson says, "into the recesses of being"; the living act is fraught with meaning. And in one sense the death of Ahab is the necessary outcome of these premises. For him "the White Whale is that wall, shoved near." He does manage to penetrate, hurling his harpoon, and he disappears into the sea, "still chasing ... though tied to" the whale. In another sense, indicated by the wreck of the "Pequod," Ahab dies because the object is impenetrable and his assumptions are wrong. As he remarks long before the final chase, "the dead, blind wall butts all inquiring heads at last." He simultaneously carries the voyage to an extreme, losing himself to gain reality, and is forced to accept the rational distinction between the human intellect and the world it explores. In either case he is faced with an "inscrutable" world: a mask whose meaning is enticing but destructive, or a wall without any human significance. "That inscrutable thing," he declares, "is chiefly what I hate." He hates both the ambiguity of the meanings that lure him on and the resistance of objects to the inquiring mind. As the mood of the voyager alters, from love to hate, the world of the Emersonian journey changes from hospitality to malice, and the "living act" becomes an act of defiance.

All this does not imply, however, that Melville washes his hands of Ahab. If Ahab persists in the face of an obvious dilemma, and is thereby destroyed, the dilemma is the same as Melville's own, and Melville has not resolved it for himself. Melville can reprobate Ahab only as part of his self-reprobation, for Ahab's fury is the last stage of Melville's malaise. Actually, no final condemnation is possible. The largest paradox in *Moby-Dick*, prior to any moral judgment, is the necessity of voyaging and the equal necessity of failure. The voyage can accommodate the benevolence of Father Mapple; it is the "apotheosis" of Bulkington, the perfect transcendentalist, who is present as a "sleeping partner" throughout the book; but it issues in the satanism of Ahab, the wilfully destructive pursuit of a knowledge that dissolves into nothingness. Melville feels involved in what happens to Ahab. That is why he could write Hawthorne that Ahab's greatest blasphemy was "the book's motto (the secret one)": "Ego non baptizo te in nomine patris, sed in nomine diaboli!"

The diabolism of *Moby-Dick* is more an effect than a cause of Melville's method. Pursuing the symbolic voyage to the utmost, but realizing at the same time its ineffectuality, Ahab is ruined, and Melville discovers that he is potentially an Ahab, the devil's partisan, the nihilist. Poe begins where Ahab leaves off. His primary aim is the destruction of reason, and he takes pleasure in the very horror of the task. The gentleman who comes riding up to the house of Usher is the personification of rational convention. Like all Poe's narrators, even the most unbalanced, he would like to cling to logic and to the common-sense material world. But he has set out on a journey which is designed to break up all his established categories; reason is deliberately put through the mill and emerges in fragments. The story concerns not only the fall of Usher's house—itself a symbol of the end of rational order—but also the shock to the narrator's assumptions, the dissolution of his house. The writer of the "MS. Found in a Bottle" is a similar type. His "habits of rigid thought," "deficiency of imagination," and "strong relish for physical philosophy" lay him open to an extraordinary agitation as he voyages into a region of eccentric thought and anomalous things. Moreover, despite his intense rationalism, the abnormal appeals to something within him. At the beginning of the story he is estranged from country and family, and he goes voyaging out of "a kind of nervous restlessness." The secret aim of his journey, hidden from his own conscious thought, is the creation of a new world by the destruction of the old. Meditating his fate, he unconsciously daubs "the word DISCOVERY" upon a sail that lies on the deck. But this Emersonian motive takes on an exaggerated air because of the tension within him. Irrationality is the main characteristic of his discoveries:

A feeling, for which I have no name, has taken possession of my soul—a sensation which will admit of no analysis, to which the lessons of by-gone times are inadequate, and for which I fear futurity itself will offer me no key. To a mind constituted like my own, the latter consideration is an evil. I shall never—I know that I shall never—be satisfied with regard to the nature of my conceptions. Yet it is not wonderful that these conceptions are indefinite, since they have their origin in sources so utterly novel. A new sense—a new entity is added to my soul.

The new sense of the narrator is cultivated by the immeasurably ancient, swollen ship, hovering, like the house of Usher, on the verge of annihilation; by the incomprehensible mariners, whose eyes have "an eager and uneasy meaning"; and by the chaotic sea, stretching away to ramparts of ice that look like "the walls of the universe." The horror that his old sense feels at impending extinction is balanced by "a curiosity to penetrate the mysteries of these awful regions." He comes to see that the horror and the extinction are the necessary means to the new vision: "It is evident that we are hurrying onward to some exciting knowledge—some never-to-be-imparted secret, whose attainment is destruction." The ship whirls round a gigantic amphitheater of whiteness and plunges into the vortex. The narrator makes his "Discovery" through a discipline of horror, finds a new reality through the violation of the old, and attains "exciting knowledge" through the loss of his own identity.

Just as the reason of Poe's narrator is conquered not only by the situation in which he is caught but also by something within him, Poe himself was divided between extreme rationalism and extreme hostility to reason. Together with the stories that destroy the rational mind and world, he produced the tales of ratiocination. The advocate of "indefiniteness" as a poetic principle was also the author of "The Philosophy of Composition," in which the poetic process is treated as a mathematical problem. Poe's extreme degradation of reason resulted from the presence of both factors inside him. He was not, like Emerson and Whitman, primarily in conflict with a rationalistic society; he was at war with himself. In addition, his ability to take a purely objective view gave a new twist to their theory of poetry. While he held with them that poetry is "indirect" and "suggestive," he considered the poet a craftsman, deliberately constructing the vehicle of irrationality. Again, the result was extremism.

For the rest, Poe's conception of literature was basically similar to theirs and had a similar origin. The ambiguity of Poe's metaphysics, which constitute a kind of materialistic idealism, exactly corresponds to the paradox of "process." The psychophysical world projected by the transcendentalists might be called an idealistic materialism. But, instead of attempting to describe the unity of thought and things from the side of "spirit," Poe carries out the same unification in terms of matter, infinitely rarefied "until we arrive at a matter *unparticled*—without particles—indivisible— *one*." His purpose is not reduction of one term to the other but reconciliation: "The matter of which I speak is, in all respects, the very 'mind' or 'spirit' of the schools ... and is, moreover, the 'matter' of these schools at the same time." Whether phrased in idealistic or materialistic language, the paradox is the consequence of a new category, creative motion. Poe continues: "The unparticled matter, in motion, is thought. ... This thought creates. All created things are but the thoughts of God." As applied to poetry, creative motion becomes "the *physical power of words*." The thought and the thing are spoken into birth in the course of that incessant modification of form which is reality. Although Poe's God is still the unmoved mover, everything else is translated into continuous activity.

These ideas, which Poe sets forth only in a half-poetic style, lie behind the ambiguity of his formal literary theory. His well-known literary doctrines hover between materialism and idealism, which cut across his odd mixture of psychological and philosophical principles. According to his psychological doctrine, beauty is "not a quality ... but an effect," a state of mind produced by a certain collocation of words. According to the philosophical doctrine, a poem is the reflection of "supernal" Beauty, "of which *through* the poem ... we attain to but brief and indeterminate glimpses." Both views were disastrous in practice: the theory of effect led to crude effects; the theory of supernal beauty led to the romantic claptrap which was Poe's stock in trade. But the two doctrines met in a conception which was potentially a good deal more profitable. The reflection of supernal beauty is attained "by multiform combinations among the things and thoughts of Time"; these combinations, in various mediums, create the psychological beauty of "effect." In both cases the key to poetry is the meaningful medium, which is at once a material and a spiritual reality. In both cases poems are made by novel structures of the medium, "modifications of old forms—or in other words ... *creation of new.*" It is this conception of a distinctively aesthetic method and content that makes Poe so hostile to the poetizing of science and ethics. He wants a free hand with his "multiform combinations," unhampered by determinate rational form. Like the French Symbolists who admired him, Poe takes music as the prototype of all art, because here, in the medium that is least distinguishable from its subjective or objective reference, he finds the perfect antithesis to the language and methods of reason. His emphasis on the sound of words to the detriment of their meaning is a relatively superficial point. He aims at a much more sweeping musicality: the treatment of meaningful words as though they were the autonomous notes of a musical construct, capable of being combined without regard to rational denotation. And as he persists in his elaboration of the pure poem ("this poem *per se*—this poem which is a poem and nothing more—this poem written solely for the poem's sake"), his mood becomes not merely indifferent to reason but actively antirational. In order to live in the reality of creative motion, the old static reality must be destroyed; the new forms can arise only through a drastic modification of the old.

The advocate of new form is Mallarmé's Poe, born to invent: "Donner un sens plus pur au mots de la tribu." This Poe failed in practice. Although "indefiniteness" could mean the power to transcend the finite words of the mob, it actually produced sloppy poems. He succeeds better in his stories, which do not carry out, but portray, his aspirations. Most of the tales play upon the wonders that lie beyond the confines of reason and upon the concurrent horror of the aberration necessary to attain them. This is Baudelaire's Poe, "l'écrivain des nerfs." The narrator of "The Tell-Tale Heart" grants that he is "very, very dreadfully nervous" but insists that his disease has "sharpened ... not dulled" his senses. This story, like many others, is a variation on the theme of "perverseness," which Poe defines as "a perpetual inclination, in the teeth of our best judgment, to violate that which is *Law*, merely because we understand it to be such." The center of interest in these stories is not simply the emotion of horror but the irrational state of mind, terrified at itself, yet oddly prolific. In a sense, the unnatural violation of law is a natural capacity. Perverseness, though abnormal from the standpoint of reason, is "an innate and primitive principle of human action."

The most general treatment of this theme is "The Fall of the House of Usher," the subject of which is aesthetic sensibility. Poe strikes a balance between the wonder and the horror of the images that assail the narrator and preoccupy Roderick. The first glimpse of the mansion "unnerves" the visitor in a manner wholly beyond analysis; try as he may to explain his melancholy as the result of "very simple natural objects" in peculiar combination, he cannot make out the formula. At the same time, his gloom has nothing in common with the romantic love of ruin: "no goading of the imagination could torture [it] into aught of the sublime." As he proceeds into the house, his unnerved sensibility becomes increasingly aware of novel possibilities. "I . . . wondered to find how unfamiliar were the fancies which ordinary images were stirring up."

Throughout the story the narrator, like the house, is "falling"; he exists in a kind of suspended motion between the perception of "simple natural objects" and the neurotic perception of an aberrant world. The house itself is described as utterly decayed in every stone, yet possessed of a "specious totality." It exists on the verge of complete disintegration and transformation, standing on the brink of the dark lake where the narrator sees its "remodelled and inverted" image. The zigzag fissure that is "barely perceptible" in its front points downward into the tarn. The house is poised between objective reality and a symbolic status that can be attained only by its immersion in the reflecting water and simultaneous dissolution. Usher's belief in the "sentience" of the house is another way of stating the same idea. For generations this psychophysical quality has been growing, occasioned not only by the structure of the building ("the method of collocation" of the stones) but also by "its reduplication in the still waters of the tarn." The mansion and the lake together create a distinctive world, whose evidence, verified by the narrator, is "the gradual yet certain condensation of an atmosphere of their own about the waters and the walls." Usher and his family have long inhabited this world, which exerts a "silent, yet importunate and terrible influence" upon them. Their "peculiar sensibility of temperament" is inseparable from their peculiar environment, just as the name "House of Usher" includes "both the family and the family mansion." But they are victims of their environment only in the sense that they have made their own milieu. The strange atmosphere is the kind of reality created by their strange habits of thought—the product, as its psychophysical quality testifies, of a fusion between the mirror of their minds and the material world. The "host of unnatural sensations" that afflicts Roderick and all his clan is synonymous with the decay of their mansion. The imminent disintegration of the house is Roderick's own moment of transition between the vestiges of reason and the "exciting knowledge whose attainment is destruction."

His terror is the measure of his adherence to the old reality; his art is the reward of the new. For behind the whole story is the conception of an antirational art. He produces music of "singular perversion," abstract paintings of an indescribable eccentricity, and poems that are "wild fantasias." He is the artistic mind *in extremis* but profiting by its own extremity. Although the specimen verses that Poe offers are unfortunate, the allusions to unorthodox music and to "pure abstractions" in painting make his point well enough. Usher's art is the last stage of the quest for novelty which begins when all art is conceived in the image of music. Antirational in genesis, it is doubly antirational in form and terrifying in its escape from the canons of reason: "The paintings over which his elaborate fancy brooded ... grew, touch by touch, into vaguenesses at which I shuddered the more thrillingly, because I shuddered knowing not why."

The denouement comes in "a tempestuous yet sternly beautiful night ... wildly singular in its terror and its beauty." The shifting winds, the careering clouds, and the "unnatural light" appeal to Roderick Usher; his disorder is one with the external chaos, which announces the final disintegration that has been impending throughout the story. The movement of "The Fall of the House of Usher" is like that of "The City in the Sea," from expectation to fulfilment; and in both cases it is Death that is pending and realized. Death broods over the luxuriant art of the city, and death is implicit in the crumbling house and deranged mind of the Ushers. Poe associates death, the opposite of life, with the inverted world, the opposite of reason. In "The Masque of the Red Death" the bizarre taste of the duke is the counterpart of the pestilence which his walls cannot shut out; the "spectral image" of death takes over the masquerade. In "The Assignation" the hero, who is dedicated to artistic incongruity, dies in order to achieve the last full measure of eccentricity: "Like these arabesque censers, my spirit is writhing in fire, and the delirium of this scene is fashioning me for the wilder visions of that land of real dreams whither I am now rapidly departing." In "The Colloquy of Monos and Una" the process of dying is a revelation: "The senses were unusually active, although eccentrically so—assuming often each other's functions at random. The taste and the smell were inextricably confounded, and became one sentiment, abnormal and intense."

Yet if death, like mental derangement, creates through disorganization, it is also the loss of personal identity. Just as Usher simultaneously exploits and loathes his disease, he longs for death and fears it—longs for the state of "real dream" to which he tends and fears the annihilation which that entails. This is the meaning of the relationship between Roderick and his twin sister Madeline, between whom "sympathies of a scarcely intelligible nature had always existed." They are hardly distinguishable, except that Madeline is less substantial, and they come to stand for two aspects of the same individual. Although Roderick laments her seeming death, he puts her living in the tomb and cannot bring himself to rescue her; she, who when living seemed almost dead, struggles to return to life. The issue here is what Poe learnedly refers to in "Morella" as "the *principium individuationis*—the notion of that identity *which at death is or is not lost for ever.*" And the issue is decided by the loss of identity, since Roderick is unable to desire that she live, and her will is unable to survive. The two collapse together; derangement is completed by dissolution. With them their world collapses into eternal flux—amid "a long tumultuous shouting sound like the voice of a thousand waters." The lake which formerly presented the "remodelled and inverted" image of the mansion now actually closes over "the fragments" of the house of Usher.

At a time when English literature was living on the capital of romanticism and increasingly given over to unambiguous narrative and orthodox meditation, American literature had turned toward a new set of problems, growing out of a new awareness of symbolic method. In the central work of Hawthorne, Whitman, Melville, and Poe, symbolism is at once technique and theme. It is a governing principle: not a stylistic device, but a point of view; not a casual subject, but a pervasive presence in the intellectual landscape.

Literary fashions and influences alone cannot account for the rise of symbolism in America, its differentiation from romanticism, and its continuity with modern literary aesthetics. The significant causes lie deeper. Symbolism is the coloration taken on by the American literary mind under the pressure of American intellectual history. Modern symbolism is a parallel response to closely related conditions; it is the literary consequence of certain basic problems of modern thought. The aim of the two following chapters is to define this perspective, theoretically and historically. Theory first: the next chapter is concerned with symbolism in general and modern symbolism in particular. It would propose a rationale for what has happened in literature since the decline of romanticism and in this way would point out the family resemblance between the American symbolists and their unwitting relatives.

Of course, one must make due reservations. Nothing to approach the conscious craftsmanship of modern writing is apparent in the most obviously symbolistic of American writers. Emerson, Melville, and Whitman, in this respect, may seem sufficiently romantic and clearly alien to the modern spirit. But the question may at least remain open whether craftsmanship, after all, is the differentia of modern taste—whether this concept may not be subordinate to another, in which Eliot is closer to Emerson than to Pope.

II *The Symbolistic Imagination*

*Je n'ai plus d'autre personnalité que celle qui
convient à cette œuvre—objective? subjective?
Ces mots perdent ici tout leur sens. ...*

GIDE, *Journal*

A distinctive strain of method and assumption runs through much
twentieth-century criticism, centering in the idea of "structural
analysis." Moreover, the critical ideals and literary practice of
modern literature are often remarkably close together, so that the
"structural" emphasis of the critics corresponds directly to a certain experimentation with language by poets and novelists. Empson's *Seven Types of Ambiguity* and Joyce's *Finnegans Wake* suggest at once a new departure in taste and a close kinship of theory
with practice. Empson investigates "ambiguity" as a principle by

which poetic meanings are related to each other in poetic language. Joyce assumes the intrinsic ambiguity of words as the chief resource of his art. What movement of thought, what basic shift of conception, lies at the bottom of this development? What has been the intellectual genesis of modern taste? When the literary history of the twentieth century is ultimately written, it is likely that the distinctive spirit of the literature of our day, both in theory and in practice, will be found to depend on two factors: the emphasis on literary structure already mentioned and an unusual awareness of the linguistic medium itself. The preoccupation with the medium is actually prior. Critical analysis of structure and creative experimentation with language are characteristic of our time because critics and writers tend to conceive of the literary work—the *real* poem or story or novel—as residing primarily in language and as consisting primarily of word arrangements. The strategy of modern criticism is to give "language" a kind of autonomy by conceiving it as a realm of meaning, and the structure explored is discovered *in* the language, not *behind* the poem in the writer's mind or *in front of* the poem in an external world. "In criticizing poetry," says Eliot, we must begin "with poetry as excellent words in excellent arrangement and excellent metre," and to say this is to imply that "a poem, in some sense, has its own life." For Pound, "great literature is simply language charged with meaning to the utmost degree."

This focusing of attention on the medium amounts to a good deal more than the universal interest of the artist in his craft. To the true romantic, however faithful an artist he might be, the language of a poem could never take on this autonomous quality. However carefully elaborated, the words remained a *self*-expression, the vehicle of personal ideas or emotions; the literary work was formed in the writer's soul, and language was merely the instrument of expression. For Wordsworth, "all good poetry is the spontaneous overflow of powerful feelings"—an emanation, generalized by the poet's basic resemblance to all other men, from the personality of the poet. For Eliot, on the other hand, the prime fact is that "the poet has, not a 'personality' to express, but a particular medium, which is only a medium and not a personality, in which impressions and experiences combine in peculiar and unexpected ways." Here the romantic concept of self-expression has passed into a totally different ideal: exploitation of the medium. Eliot's position rules out naturalism as well. He is no more concerned with a supposedly external reality than with a purely personal experience. Zola would have the writer simply "feel nature and render it as it is"; he supposes that out of an accumulation of objective facts a work of art will arise almost automatically, the facts themselves establishing the form. But Eliot's eye is on the peculiar and unexpected forms delivered to him by a medium that shapes the data of experience. Richards, in his later writings, holds that the medium of language is not merely instrumental but in a large measure creative:

Words are the meeting points at which regions of experience which can never combine in sensation or intuition, come together. They are the occasion and means of that growth which is the mind's endless endeavour to order itself. That is why we have language. It is no mere signalling system.

R. P. Blackmur describes the imaginative act entirely in terms of a manipulation of language that brings a meaning into existence; there is no longer any question, in his account, of a self to be expressed or an external reality to be described but only of a medium to be exploited:

Words, and their intimate arrangements, must be the ultimate as well as the immediate source of every effect in the written or spoken arts. Words bring meaning to birth and themselves contained the meaning as an imminent possibility before the pangs of junction. To the individual artist the use of words is an adventure in discovery; the imagination is heuristic among the words it manipulates. The reality you labour desperately or luckily to put into your words . . . you will actually have found there, deeply ready and innately formed to give an objective being and specific idiom to what you knew and did not know that you knew.

The modern creative process is greatly influenced by this redefinition of the status of literature. The typical modern writer views the task before him neither as the expression of his own feelings nor as the description of given things but rather as an adventure in discovery among the meanings of words. As someone has said of Joyce, "his writing is not *about* something; *it is that something itself.*" "Words bring meaning to birth" in the elaborate punning of *Finnegans Wake*—an attempt to give words their head and to make the most of the path they follow. This conception was growing upon Joyce quite early in his career. In the *Portrait of the Artist* he relates how Stephen "read the word *Foetus*" cut into the wood of a desk and at once "seemed to feel the absent students of the college about him and to shrink from their company. A vision of their life . . . sprang up before him out of the word cut in the desk. . . . His monstrous reveries came thronging into his memory. They too had sprung up before him, suddenly and furiously, out of mere words." Later Stephen found himself walking in a lane "among heaps of dead language." Then he observed that "his own consciousness of language was ebbing from his brain and trickling into the very words themselves which set to band and disband themselves in wayward rhythms." The word *ivory* "shone in his brain"; he thought of its form in French, Italian, and Latin. Recalling the Latin examples he had learned in school, he reflected that the vicissitudes of Roman history "were handed on to him in the trite words *in tanto discrimine*" and that "he had tried to peer into the social life of the city of cities through the words *implere ollam denariorum.*" Frank Budgen describes Joyce's enthusiasm for the word *Leib*. "It was a sound that created the image of a body in one unbroken mass. . . . He spoke of the plastic monosyllable as a sculptor speaks about a stone."

Joyce's obvious fascination with the reality that the artist at once makes and finds in language may seem rather a special case. But the point of view of a writer like Henry James is roughly parallel. James found himself in the position that Eliot, much later, was to make explicit, and he took a similar course. "Between the deterioration of romantic sentiment," on the one hand, and of "realism," on the other, he became aware that "there survived one certain mediator—the proving discipline of technique." The Jamesian technique is discovery as well as construction; it is the exploitation of a prolific medium. In his prefaces and notebooks James clearly assumed that his work lay in a realm of meaning equally distinct from his own ego and from the world of objective experience. His work *presented itself* to him. The characters of *The Portrait of a Lady* "simply, by an impulse of their own, floated into my ken, and all in response to my primary question: 'Well, what will she *do?*' Their answer seemed to be that if I would trust them they would show me." Technique was the art of eliciting the answer. In his notebooks James often referred to this process as "ciphering out." To "cipher out" was to discover all the ramifications of what was presented to him, "to let one's self go to it." What these ramifications will be "one doesn't know—ideally—till one has got into real close quarters with one's proposition ... by absolutely putting to the proof and to the test what it will give." James's account of "the act of revision," which he carefully defined as "the act of seeing it again," shows how he went about the extrication of meaning. Revision "caused whatever I looked at on any page to flower before me as into the only terms that honourably expressed it." Revision, in the very act of reseeing, was a rewording, and a rewording that had its own principle of growth; the autonomous flowering of words revealed to the artist (as Blackmur says) what he knew and did not know that he knew:

> The term that superlatively, that finally "renders," is a flower that blooms by a beautiful law of its own (the fiftieth part of a second often so sufficing it) in the very heart of the gathered sheaf; it is *there* already, at any moment, almost before one can either miss or suspect it—so that, in short, we shall never guess, I think, the working secret of the revisionist for whom its colour and scent stir the air but as immediately to be assimilated.

The "it" that had been seen again and "honourably expressed" was not defined by James, and he used the verb "renders" without an object, because "it" existed only in the expression, and *what was rendered* could not be distinguished from the language of rendering.

To consider the literary work as a piece of language is to regard it as a symbol, autonomous in the sense that it is quite distinct both from the personality of its author and from any world of pure objects, and creative in the sense that it brings into existence its own meaning. This is obviously not a formula to which all modern theorists and writers—even the most determinedly "structural" of critics and the most experimental of poets—would subscribe without reservation. But it represents the inherent direction of the interest in language that they evince.

The symbolistic outlook involves much more than the stylistic device which is ordinarily called "symbolism"; the physics of symbolistic literature depends on its metaphysics. It is not surprising to find that the idea of symbolism has a kind of prestige in contemporary philosophy. According to Mr. Urban, this concept is a turning point in almost every "characteristic philosophic movement of our time." Mrs. Langer concludes that "the study of symbol and meaning" has shifted philosophy into "a new key"; that the idea of symbolism has actually changed the very questions of philosophy. When the philosopher changes his problems, the literary critic changes his method, and the writer also begins to approach the world with new questions. He asks the questions by assuming a new stance vis-à-vis the world, and he receives the answers in a new literary structure. The symbolistic poem or novel gives the world a distinctive shape—which we try to describe in our current theories of paradox, ambiguity, metaphor, tension, and the like—because the writer is confronting the world in a particular fashion, and the work itself thus comes into being by a particular path.

Of course, every philosophic revolution in a sense changes the questions of philosophy. At a certain point in intellectual history the philosopher stops looking for new solutions to old questions and discovers a new question, a new set of terms, that makes possible a new knowledge of the world. For the philosophy of symbolism, however, this change is doubly important, because the theory of symbolism is really a theory of knowledge. The textbooks all point out that knowledge became a "problem of philosophy" as a result of metaphysical dualism, the Cartesian division of reality into extended and thinking substances. The double consciousness that has dogged our thinking since the seventeenth century divides not only reality but the very act of knowing. In this light, knowing becomes a relation between given ideas and given things, the subject and the object, the conception and the fact, so that the question arises how there can be any integral act of knowledge at all. And the question carries its own answer: there cannot be, as long as we maintain the dualism assumed by the question. Idealism and materialism, each in its own fashion, have proposed remedies, but the starting point of each remains within the inherited framework. As Whitehead says, perhaps too bluntly, the idealists merely "put matter inside mind," and the materialists "put mind inside matter." These, in short, are drastic solutions and not total revisions of the problem itself. The philosophy of symbolism (like Whitehead's own philosophy) is an attempt to find a point of departure outside the premises of dualism—not so much an attempt to solve the old "problem of knowledge" as an effort to redefine the process of knowing in such a manner that that problem never arises.

During the nineteenth century the full impact of philosophic dualism was experienced in literature, not only as a theory but as a process of thought. The romantic and the naturalist, in their respective emphasis on individual feeling and material nature, were equally and overwhelmingly aware of the distinction between the mind and things. Both, like the idealist and the materialist in philosophy, found their starting points within the inherited philosophic structure of thinking ego and brute fact; each was therefore committed in practice to a given reality that must be put into language and was knowable apart from the language. In *Axel's Castle* Edmund Wilson pictured the modern symbolist movement as an extreme recurrence of the romantic method in reaction from naturalism, a "second swing of the pendulum," as he calls it, that tended "to make poetry even more a matter of the sensations and emotions of the individual than had been the case with Romanticism." This has become the official view. But the truth is that the center of symbolism is not in private feelings any more than in the objective world of science. Eliot's "peculiar and unexpected" forms, whatever difficulty they may present to the reader, belong to the public medium of language, not to the private world of the poet. The aim of literature for Mallarmé, as Valéry says in a passage that Wilson himself quotes, was "to emphasize, to conserve, and to develop the forms of which language is capable." For the symbolist, both romanticism and naturalism are uses of language that place the focus of reality outside language—romanticism, as Allen Tate puts it, is "not qualitatively different from the naturalism it attacked, but identical with it, and committed in the arts to the same imperfect inspiration." In both cases, from the symbolistic point of view, the literary process is weighted by an ulterior motive, and the writer's eye has a cast induced by a conflicting habit of mind. Symbolism is neither one nor the other but a new departure, a revision of the literary question.

The new starting point, both philosophic and literary, is designed to recapture the unity of a world artificially divided. According to R. M. Eaton,

The truly significant tendency in modern metaphysics . . . is toward breaking through the old fixed categories of the mental and the physical. We are returning to the point of view of the ancients, having suffered for three centuries from the blindness of the Cartesian dualism. If a chasm is opened, as it was by Descartes, between the physical and the mental, there is no way of closing it. . . . *Mind and body are aspects of, abstractions from, a known reality which is wider and richer than either.*

Eaton has rejected not only absolute dualism but also both forms of monism that stem from it: absolute idealism and absolute material sm. He avoids the "juggling of abstractions" which Whitehead blames on seventeenth-century metaphysics by returning to a "known reality" from which the abstractions were derived to begin with. A literary study like Owen Barfield's *Poetic Diction* sets out from a similar position, postulating a "concrete thinking" in the light of which "the time-honoured 'subjective-objective' dichotomy vanishes." The word "concrete," Barfield says, "can perhaps best be defined as 'that which is neither objective nor subjective.' " These writers do not deny the validity of a provisional dualism, but they aim at a formula which will dig beneath it. Like Whitehead, they are opposed to a "*misplaced* concreteness" and envisage a "concrete fact" into which both mind and matter enter as relative terms. Mrs. Langer's "new key" has the same function. It undercuts "the dichotomy of all reality into *inner experience and outer world*, subject and object, private reality and public truth," thus serving to "overcome the checkmated arguments of an earlier age by discarding their very idiom and shaping their equivalents in more significant phrase."

Whitehead refuses to make the step from "concrete" to symbolic fact. Although he merges mind and matter, he continues to hold that language is external to reality. Yet it is obvious that the conception of a "known reality" tends to give language a new and more important status; it might even be said that the new metaphysics is made possible by a new theory of language. If absolute dualism is abandoned, there is no longer any question of subjective expression or objective description; instead, as Eaton says, "the three elements, symbol, attitude, and object, are united in a whole which is the presentation of the object." From this standpoint the symbols of language are not mere signs, "proxy for their objects," but rather "vehicles for the conception of objects"; all three terms are to be felt as aspects of a single process of meaning. The real world, therefore, is known in symbolic form; to know is to symbolize in one way or another. "Language, which . . . is inseparable from thought and knowledge, is not moulded on reality. It is rather the mould in which reality as significant is first given." The word "mould," however, suggests a static quality that is alien to the philosophy of symbolism. If the meaning of a symbol is not an idea or thing for which the symbol arbitrarily stands, it is a productive activity, "the mean*ing* rather than the meant." In Cassirer's view "myth, art, language, and science appear as symbols; not in the sense of mere figures which refer to some given reality by means of suggestion and allegorical renderings, but in the sense of forces each of which produces and posits a world of its own." As he goes on to say, "the question as to what reality is apart from these forms, and what are its independent attributes," simply "becomes irrelevant here." For, instead of assuming that "the reality of objects ... [is] something directly and unequivocally given," so that symbols become "mere copies of something else," Cassirer begins with the idea that each symbolic form contains "a spontaneous law of generation, an original way and tendency of expression, which is more than a mere record of something initially given in fixed categories of real existence." In the philosophy of Cassirer subject and object fade before the unitive reality created by the symbolic medium:

Man lives with *objects* only in so far as he lives with these *forms;* he reveals reality to himself, and himself to reality, in that he lets himself and the environment enter into this plastic medium, in which the two do not merely make contact, but fuse with each other.

At the opposite extreme from Cassirer is the logical positivist, who has fathered most of the current popular expositions of "semantics." While the positivist adopts an air of metaphysical neutrality, he perpetuates the old dualism as a distinction between factual statement and emotional utterance. "Certain expressions in our language," according to Carnap, "assert something, and are therefore either true or false. Such expressions exercise a *cognitive function* and have a cognitive meaning. On the other hand, certain expressions express the emotions, fancies, images, or wishes of the speaker, and under proper conditions evoke emotions, wishes, or resolutions in the hearer. Such expressions will be said to exercise an expressive function." Semantics was applied to literature in Richards' *Principles of Literary Criticism* and *The Meaning of Meaning*, where the "scientific" use of language ("for the sake of the *reference*, true or false, which it causes") is distinguished from the "emotive" use ("for the sake of the effects in emotion and attitude produced by the reference it occasions"). Literature is subordinate to scientific reference; it is an affective by-product of cognitive statement or, as Richards later suggested, of "pseudo-statement." The psychological terms of positivist semantics cannot disguise the philosophical pattern: the catch-all of "emotive" language has the same purpose as the older notion of "mental substance"—to take care of everything in experience for which the scientist has no use. But, as soon as a real effort is made not merely to ignore but to transcend the premises of dualism, the two relations of language merge in the process of *meaning*. The subsequent career of Richards has shown how a philosophy of signs, when fully developed, tends to become a philosophy of symbols. In *Coleridge on Imagination* he proposes a scale, through which he himself seems to have passed, "between words taken as bare signs and words into which some part or the whole of their meaning is projected." In the end, the "interactions of words" take place in a realm, frankly metaphysical, where subject and object are fused:

It is itself that thought (or intellect) thinks, on account of its participation in the object of thought: for it becomes its own object in the act of apprehending it: so that thought (intellect) and what is thought of are one and the same.

Symbolism in modern literature is the symbolistic theory of knowledge put into practice. F. W. Bateson has suggested that the history of poetry is part of the history of language and that changes in poetic style merely reflect changing tendencies in the use of language. But the differentia of modern taste is more than a new application of the medium. It is an unusual awareness of the medium per se, a feeling that "symbols . . . are the sources as well as the reminders of meaning, and, . . . once recognized, are inexhaustible, and are, so to speak, fertile in themselves."

In working out the implications of this standpoint, the modern literary symbolist is potentially more radical than the philosopher of symbolism. The symbolistic outlook of Cassirer is most apparent in his general statements, as when he remarks that "instead of defining man as an *animal rationale,* we should define him as an *animal symbolicum.*" Even science, in this larger view, is a symbolic version of the world, a force "which produces and posits a world of its own." Yet Cassirer emphasizes the fact that language can "grow into . . . an expression of concepts and judgments . . . only at the price of foregoing the wealth and fullness of immediate experience." In logical discourse "words are reduced more and more to the status of mere conceptual signs," and language no longer possesses "its original creative power." In short, rational speech tends away from the condition of symbolism; man, after all, is an *animal rationale* as well as an *animal symbolicum.* It is here that literary theory is likely to give another turn to the argument. Although Cassirer represents poetry as the regeneration of the creative power of the word, "a sort of constant palingenesis," he is ultimately loyal to reason. Truth is the province of the "conceptual sign," and poetry, however valuable, is "a world of illusion and fantasy." But the same premises can lead to other conclusions. It is quite possible to take poetry as the norm and to regard logical statement as the fantasy; this, indeed, seems the more natural outcome of a philosophy which begins in a contrast between logical sign and creative symbol. The literary symbolist is inclined to consider poetry as *peculiarly* symbolic, in that poetry (and, by extension, all literature) holds to the creative speech from which logic tends to depart. From this point of view, the symbolic status of literature constitutes a positive victory over logic, the reinstatement of "concrete fact" in the face of abstract fiction.

Given the same alternatives, the romantic made the same choice, but he meant something quite different and a good deal less fundamental. Riding in on the high tide of the Kantian revolution, he extended the transcendental forms to include all the felt relationships which Kant's predecessors, in their effort to isolate an absolutely knowable object, tried to eliminate, and in which Kant himself had little interest. Yet the antirationalism of romantic literature pertained to subject matter more than to method. Although the romantic was bent on expressing the complex mental content that escapes the net of logic, for the most part he did not challenge the essentially rationalistic metaphysics which left literature only two possibilities—expression and description. He was content to accept the greater elbow-room which idealism gave him within the traditional framework. The symbolist, on the other hand, redefines the whole process of knowing and the status of reality in the light of poetic method. He tries to take both poles of perception into account at once, to view the subjective and objective worlds as functions of each other by regarding both as functions of the forms of speech in which they are rendered. Here is the sum of his quarrel with reason. Meaning for him, as Mrs. Langer puts it, is "a function of a term," not an external relation between word, thought, and thing. "A function is a *pattern* viewed with reference to one special term round which it centers; this pattern emerges when we look at the given term *in its total relation to the other terms about it*." Once we refuse to contemplate a separate reality "meant by" the word, meaning becomes an activity that generates a pattern. By turning away from the old dichotomy, the symbolist uncovers a new variety, what Richards calls "the fabric of our meanings, which is the world."

This texture is antirational, like the method that produces it. Whereas the formal innovations of romanticism were a loosening of traditional boundaries, the symbolism of modern literature is a deliberate experiment with alogical structures of multiple meaning, and our latter-day analysis of metaphor and other poetic figures is an effort to define the complex structure of symbolism as distinguished from logic. As the partisan of poetic method, the symbolist is faced with a kind of literary problem that remains latent for other writers: the problem of the relationship between poetic and logical language. What, therefore, is this relationship as he is confronted with it? And do the theory and practice of symbolism have a real basis in the structure of language?

Logical language is built upon the principle of discreteness. Although in an ultimate sense logical statements may be purely symbolic, in practice they seem to entail a distinction between the speaker, his words, and what he talks about. Logical structure is typically atomistic. As Cassirer expresses it, "every [logical] concept has a certain 'area' that belongs to it and whereby it is distinguished from other conceptual spheres. No matter how much these areas may overlap, cover each other, or interpenetrate—each one maintains its definitely bounded location in conceptual space." We usually assume that the atoms of logical meaning antedate the proposition in which they occur. But even if the meaning is held to be, in a sense, symbolic, and therefore created simultaneously with the statement, its elements are created in a discrete form. Even if we suppose that there is some difference in meaning between the "Socrates" who "is a man" and the one who "drinks hemlock," Socrates in either case is an inherently distinct segment of meaning. In poetry we feel no compulsion to refer outside language itself. A poem delivers a version of the world; it *is* the world for the moment. And just as the language of a poem is a plastic symbolic medium in which subjective and objective elements are presented as an integral whole, so within the poem each word is potentially a standpoint, a symbolic crossroad, from which the whole poem may be viewed. Whereas "two logical concepts, subsumed under the next higher category, as their *genus proximum*, retain their distinctive characters despite the relationship into which they have been brought," poetic structure depends upon fusion. Two poetic words, brought into metaphorical relationship, actually lose their distinctive characters in the light of the whole metaphorical meaning.

Poetry and logic are different modes of language, different ways in which language exists. The two are incommensurable: "the logic of poetry," as Dewey says, "is super-propositional even when it uses what are, grammatically speaking, propositions." Moreover, the exercise of the alogical language of poetry is necessarily antilogical. Existing in the same medium, literature supersedes, manipulates, and recasts logical structure. Figures of speech fly in the face of logic; their structure is ordered on a different plan. They cast through the body of language a light that erases the lines drawn by logical discourse and creates new contours in the same stuff. Literature can exist only *à rebours*. Its alogical form is not simply a return to primitive "undifferentiated" modes of perception. Whatever theory we adopt concerning the prehistoric origins of speech—whether we emphasize the logical tendency in the use of words to isolate separate and distinct things, or the poetic tendency in the "radical metaphor" that seems to precede conscious discrimination between things—all literary documents date from a period when logical statement and poetic figure were equally well established in language. In civilized language at least, literary structure is a reshaping of the logical form into which words may also fall. It is neither purely "emotive" nor, as a sort of halfway house, an ornamentation of a logical pattern but has a cognitive value quite on a level with the logical use of words and actually reshapes the body of speech from inside out and from head to toe. When all language is viewed as an autonomous realm, the structure as well as the status of poetic language takes on an essential autonomy. A figure of speech is as absolute a form of language as logical categories like class and member.

Aristotle's description of metaphor—still the dictionary definition—implies a quite different assumption:

> Metaphor consists in giving the thing a name that belongs to something else; the transference being either from genus to species, or from species to genus, or from species to species, or on grounds of analogy.

The very notion of "transference" of "a name that belongs to something else" presupposes a scheme of atomistic words and phrases which may be substituted for one another by a kind of code. The terms retain their logical discreteness, and the metaphor is only a conventional device for summarizing a logical relationship, founded ultimately on resemblance between things. But does the relationship of terms in a poetic metaphor, or even a simile, remain logical, and do the terms themselves remain logical atoms? Does the figure really use logical classification, based upon resemblance, at all? If we say that Scott is like Boswell in that both are Scotsmen, the function of the statement is to place a middle term between Scott and Boswell (the "basis of the comparison"), and the remark is logically equivalent to saying that there is a class or category called Scotsmen of which Scott and Boswell are members. A simile often has the same grammatical form as a statement of resemblance, and even the "basis of comparison" is sometimes made explicit:

> As flies to wanton boys, are we to the gods;
> They kill us for their sport.

But plainly this figure involves something more than a logical resemblance. The stated "basis of comparison" does not exhaust the relationship between ourselves and flies, wanton boys and the gods; "They kill us for their sport," instead of defining this relationship, serves to complicate it. And the ground of comparison is not even ostensibly stated in most figures, because it cannot be stated fully or accurately. Resemblance is a function of logical, not metaphoric, structure. The terms of any metaphor are susceptible of logical form; a paraphrase of the figure will place them in logical form; the paraphrase, unless very carefully worded, will represent them as possessing various kinds of logical resemblance (or difference). But in their actual functioning these terms violate logical form and enter into the characteristic structure of metaphor, so that any logical account must necessarily remain incomplete. No logical relation is quite applicable to a poetic figure, not merely because logic is unpoetic, but, even more fundamentally, because poetic structure is not logical.

The result of poetic recasting is a different and more intricate kind of order. Marvell's phrase, "the iron gates of life," does not "point out" or "play on" a pre-existing similarity between the logical elements, life and iron gates. It is not sufficient to add, as does Richards, that the relation between "tenor" and "vehicle" is "even more the work of their unlikenesses than of their likenesses." The phrase, taken as a whole, establishes the idea of life *under the aspect of* iron gates, and of iron gates under the aspect of life. If emphasis is laid upon "iron gates," the phrase "of life" serves to place "iron gates" in a certain light; and if emphasis is laid upon "life," the phrase "iron gates" compels a special meaning upon it. From this standpoint, both the similarities and the differences between tenor and vehicle become irrelevant. If the two terms are seen under the aspect of each other, the *real* tenor is a meaning produced by the interaction of the two terms, which together form the vehicle. The tenor is at once the special kind of life that we can entertain under the aspect of iron gates, and the special kind of iron gates that are capable of being thought under the aspect of "life." On the other hand, a phrase like "the iron gates of the park" cannot be construed in this manner. We may shift the emphasis from one term to another, but the logical structure remains logical and remains the same. "Iron gates" are a part of the whole called "the park": no change of emphasis can alter that relation. Logical structure is mechanism: the parts are independent; their relationship is additive; and neither a part nor the relation between parts is retroactively affected by the whole into which they may enter. To say that literary structure, by way of contrast, is "organic" implies that the relationship of part to part involves a relationship of part to whole. The elements of a metaphor have meaning only by virtue of the whole which they create by their interaction; a metaphor presents parts that do not fully exist until the whole which they themselves produce comes into existence.

Literary structure, therefore, is logically circular. Any attempt to describe it must end in paradox.

The counterlogical quality of literary form is only one instance of a rule that obtains throughout language. Language is a kind of protoplasm that is capable of falling into four principal shapes: the collocation of words, grammar, logic, and rhetoric. These several claimants are eternally at war with one another. As Richards has pointed out, grammar often violates logic (which, in his terminology, is a "form of thought"):

> It is not true that the rules of syntax of any language correspond to the forms of thought. . . . The most obvious examples disprove it: "I see a tiger" and "I kick a tiger" are syntactically the same; the forms of the thoughts that they express are extremely different. . . . When I kick a tiger I do something to him, but not when I see him.

The collocation of words, similarly, has little effect on logical structure:

> We use one word-pattern with many different thought-forms; and conversely, can put one thought-form into many different word-patterns.
>
> > Socrates is wise.
> > Wisdom belongs to Socrates
>
> are two different word-patterns; the same form of thought might use either.

A certain arrangement of words is often capable of more than one grammatical interpretation. At the same time the great influence of grammar upon logic is evidenced by terms such as "copula," "subject," and "predicate" that are shared by the two, and grammatical form in a language like English often depends directly on the order of words. In general, each shape of language draws upon the prior ones, but always with some important recasting. Logic finds its chief support in grammar and is most indifferent to word patterns. Rhetoric depends on the juxtaposition of words and often is forced to circumvent the implications of grammar. The metaphorical fusion in "the iron gates of life" is made possible by the collocation of the words "gates" and "life"; the "possessive" grammatical form is quite irrelevant.

Still, we must resort to logical statement in order to analyze literature. We must impose a logical grill upon the literary fact. Paradox and multiple meaning are the reflection of literary structure in the mirror of logic. Even so classic a device as the Homeric simile introduces flagrantly disparate elements into a poem. The flight of the Tyrian trader at the conclusion of "The Scholar Gipsy" has little analogy to the hero's escape from the infected world of mental strife. The intruders turn out to be lighthearted Greeks, not at all resembling Arnold's modern men, and the flight is full of details that do not correspond in the least to what the Scholar might encounter in Oxfordshire. To contend that the figure is merely ornamental is a denial of all coherent structure. Actually, the Homeric simile, though cast in the grammatical form that also serves for logical analogy, manipulates logic for a literary end. The logical disparity between the Tyrian trader and the Scholar is resolved by their metaphorical union, in which each is conceived under the aspect of the other; our awareness of their difference is the result of translating the metaphor into logical language. In this sense the Homeric simile is just as paradoxical as the most extreme conceit of metaphysical verse. A logical statement of resemblance avoids paradox by ruling out all qualities except those that have logical relevance: the fact that Scott was an upright man and Boswell a scapegrace does not enter into the question of their being Scotsmen. But a metaphor insists upon including as many qualities as possible, thus introducing elements unassimilable by logic. The most harmonious metaphors potentially contain elements of logical difference which, when paraphrased into statements, become logical oppositions and therefore logical paradoxes. And in many metaphors opposition is at least as strong as any "basis of comparison":

> Dost thou not see my baby at my breast
> That sucks the nurse asleep?

The stark contrast between the asp and an infant is resolved not by any logical equation but by the poetic process of conceiving the serpent and the baby in terms of each other. The metaphysical conceit, which Johnson defined as "the most heterogeneous ideas ... yoked by violence together," was a deliberate exploitation of the paradox implicit in all metaphor; its function was to place heterogeneous ideas in the same literary framework. Johnson, with the quasi-logical ideal of the eighteenth century, looked for and could not find an adequate "basis of comparison."

Poetic multiplicity of meaning is the universe of paradox. The closest logical equivalent to a literary figure is an infinite series of statements; literary structure, from the standpoint of logic, is inherently ambiguous or equivocal. Merely singling out an analogy does not in the least render the meaning. Nor do we make much progress by marking out a core of resemblance and treating all that cannot be forced into the analogy as an aura of "suggestion" or "association." If a metaphor has a distinctive structure of terms acting upon each other, a paraphrase must be, as it were, a cross-section of the whole. It must be worded so as to cut through logical divisions, just as the metaphor itself gives those divisions an alogical relationship, and to reflect the full meaning of the parts of the figure as they are seen under the aspect of each other. But such a cross-section may be projected at many angles, and no single statement or single critic will serve for the task. Each critical version will reproduce the shape of the whole, but only in one dimension; there is no end to the process of paraphrase. It follows that ambiguity is not an accident of poetry. We recognize literary structure as such by the necessity of multiple statement when we try to render the meaning in logical terms. As Michael Roberts says, "The meaning is not any of these readings, nor is it their arithmetical sum; it is the result of having all these in mind at one time; it is something of which these, together with the sound of the passage, are aspects." Multiple statement is the effort of the univocal terms of logic to measure the equivocal language of literature.

Any literary term is a literary symbol, issuing in a paradoxical ambiguity. It has a categorizing function which cuts across logical categories. The "iron gates of life" and the "voyage of life" are both under the aspect of "life," and a literary relation exists between these two things that have been, and may be, seen under the same aspect. Terms like "life," which are usually said to be highly "connotative," are really words that have been repeatedly used in this metaphorical way. Their "associations" consist of the range of other terms with which they have metaphorical relation. The literary symbol proper is a key term, the center of many overlapping circles of metaphorical meaning. "Kingship," for instance, is a focal term in *Paradise Lost*. The word "King" exists on a number of levels, which are often logically inconsistent:

> What precisely . . . is the meaning, the reference value, of royalism in *Paradise Lost?* God is King. He is not to be confused with the kings of earth. *He is precisely like the kings of earth.* He is not king at all! Kingship is the tyranny of the wicked over the wicked. Kingship is the power of God. Kingship is not desirable in itself, and will cease to exist *even metaphorically* in the final dwelling-place of the blessed spirits.

But the logical inconsistency is beside the point, for as a symbol Kingship has no "reference value." God and Satan are viewed under the aspect of King, which is inherently and simultaneously both divine and diabolic, and the meaning of each necessarily shifts as different aspects of Kingship are set forth. To those who would say that Kingship is simply the power of God and to those who would say that it is merely the tyranny of the wicked over the wicked, the poem replies by presenting it as both at once. "King God" and "King Satan" belong to the category of things which for the purposes of the poem are Kingly. A symbolic category is formed by the metaphorical history of the symbol.

Thus the symbol stands as a kind of synecdoche for the metaphors into which it has entered. Synecdoche is not the logical substitution of a part for its whole: the part is not extracted, as if it were a building brick, and used as a sign. Instead, the part retains its organic character as *part of a whole*. This figure, as Cassirer has pointed out in the case of "mythic" synecdoche, implies "the leveling and extinction of specific [i.e., logical] differences":

Every part of a whole is the whole itself; every specimen is equivalent to the entire species. The part does not merely represent the whole, or the specimen its class; they are identical with the totality to which they belong; not merely as mediating aids to reflective thought, but as genuine presences which actually contain the power, significance, and efficacy of the whole.

The language of literature is a body of terms whose significance has been built up by metaphor and whose power is the power of synecdoche. The total pattern of literary speech has much in common with Whitehead's picture of the organic structure of reality: "Every actual thing is something by reason of its activity; whereby its nature consists in its relevance to other things, and its individuality consists in its synthesis of other things so far as they are relevant to it." A literary term *is* a term by virtue of being under the aspect of other terms, and it is focal by virtue of placing other terms under its aspect. This structure, as Whitehead says, is possible "by reason of ... activity." The ultimate difference between literary and logical structure is that the former transmutes all static entities into functions. For in the final analysis the structural difference is another way of viewing a difference in method; in contrast to the external relation of static subject and object, which is the product of rational speech, literature renders the idea and the thing as interdependent factors in a creative movement of experience. To quote Whitehead again, "an occasion of experience is an activity, analysable into modes of functioning which jointly constitute its process of becoming. Each mode is analysable into the total experience as active subject, and into the thing or object with which the special activity is concerned." Metaphor and synecdoche are the formal side of reality as process. Their instability is at once cause and effect of the fluid experience they deliver.

As the exploration of this general picture, modern symbolism has all the vitality of a return to the foundations of literature. It is not only feasible but profitable to regard all speech as an autonomous realm of meaning where subject and object are relative factors produced by logical method and finally resolvable by poetic apprehension. Within language, so regarded, poetry constitutes a complete and self-consistent structure, and this peculiarly symbolic structure of poetry can exist only at the expense of logical form. When we think in metaphor and synecdoche, reshaping the logical entities of the conventionally real world, we are not performing a verbal trick but exercising a flexibility proper to language itself; we are seeking to discover all that our medium is and thereby all that it can render.

But there would seem to be a crucial difference between generic and deliberate symbolism—between the symbolistic principle and a symbolistic program. What is the theoretical connection between these two manifestations of symbolism? And what will be the practical consequences when unconscious method becomes conscious end?

Symbolism and logic, though incommensurable, are not discontinuous. The concepts formed by the terms of a rational doctrine are implicit in the corresponding symbol, which "contains them, but encompasses them within a wider frame—and as so encompassed, they act entirely differently than they would if 'efficiently' isolated in their 'purity.' " It is when logical opposition becomes acute that the movement from generic to deliberate symbolism begins. To take an example from medieval symbolism, the Arian and Athanasian doctrines of the Trinity were at odds. Arius held the heretical view that Christ was not coeternal with God the Father; Athanasius held the opposite. The two doctrines were logically irreconcilable. Yet the origin of Arius' view was not logical at all. Arius asserted that Christ was not coeternal with God the Father because he was accustomed to think of Christ as Son— to see Christ, that is to say, under the aspect of a Son. His doctrine was a logical rendering of this symbolic expression, a paraphrase, partial as all paraphrases must be, to which he gave an absolute validity. Athanasius met the difficulty by deliberate return to symbolism. Without abandoning the metaphorical identification of Christ with a Son, he added a new metaphor to the Christ-symbol; he spoke of Christ in terms of solar radiance, which is necessarily coeternal with its source:

> The radiance also is light, not second to the sun, nor a different light, nor from participation of it, but a whole and proper offspring of it. And such an offspring is necessarily one light; and no one would say that they are two lights, but sun and radiance two, yet one the light from the sun enlightening in its radiance all things. So also the Godhead of the Son is the Father's; whence also it is indivisible; and thus there is one God and none other but he.

If Christ is conceived simultaneously as a Son and as a Radiance, and God as at once a Father and the Sun in heaven, the impasse of the Arian and Athanasian doctrines no longer exists. The opposing concepts remain potential, but their opposition is suspended, for the central terms of the problem—Christ, God, Son, Father, Radiance, Sun—cease to be logical entities and enter into symbolic structure. Athanasius warned that a rational analysis of the Christ-symbol would destroy its efficacy as a symbol: "He [Christ] is the Father's Radiance, and as the Father is, but not for any reason, neither must we seek the reason of that Radiance."

Less conclusively and less economically, dilemmas of this kind are often reconciled by logical "dialectic," which aims at reuniting strands of thought that logic itself has separated. A course of rational thought is governed by the basic terms from which it sets out. In any given era "there will be some fundamental assumptions which adherents of all the variant systems within the epoch unconsciously presuppose." These assumed terms can be run, as it were, through a fixed series of permutations. By existing together, they at once pose a question and suggest possible answers, which may be quite divergent. The terms of absolute dualism generated answers as far apart as absolute materialism and absolute idealism, which are not only opposed but actually contradict one another.

Yet the fact that these variant answers all derive from a common ground indicates that they are mutually supplementary. Dialectic works backward from logical dilemmas by finding the more inclusive statement under which opposing concepts may be reconciled. It assumes that the conflict is entirely within the universe of discourse, that the problem is produced by the relationship of terms and does not involve a "question of fact." If one man asserts that a certain table is elliptical in shape, and another that it is round, they may examine, in order to resolve their dispute, either the table or their statements. If they examine the table, they treat the matter as a question of objective fact, and no dialectic can occur. But, if they try to reconcile their statements, they engage in a dialectic process, based on the assumption that there exists a larger unity of language beyond the apparent contradiction. They might discover in this fashion that the first man was speaking of the appearance of the table from his position, and the second of the "real" shape of the table. Dialectic arises in an opposition of meanings which have been shaped by a structure of terms, and it resolves the opposition by a further meaning. The process is endless, for each resolution contains within itself the possibility of a new conflict. A new controversy is sure to arise as to the meaning of a "real" table.

The dialectician closely approaches the symbolistic point of view. The language in which he works is an autonomous realm of meaning; place the focus of attention in objects outside the medium, and his function simply disappears. Confronted with the divisiveness of logic, the fact that we can define a word only as meaning *this, not that,* he assumes that "opposition can occur only between the parts of a *whole.*" His search for the inclusive statement is an act of faith in a unity which is prior to logical exclusion and which appears in the human capacity to entertain contradictory propositions:

The universe of discourse may comprise statements as antagonistic in their intent as water is nihilistic of fire; and yet those statements also may get along together in peace, together only in the sense of a relatedness potentially provocative of consequences, though not actually so. Water must be poured upon fire, and statements must be submitted to question before the universe of discourse becomes alive with confusion.

But dialectic can only partially counteract the inherent disputatiousness of logical method. Each reconciling statement excludes far more than it entails; once the opposition becomes explicit, a new reconciliation is necessary; and dialectic proceeds through wider and wider generalizations. In the very act of resolving an opposition, it must always respect the law of opposition, the "either-or" of logic. In· symbolism no "either-or" can arise. "Beatrice is not *either* a real girl *or* a symbol of Love, but a real girl *and* a symbol of Love *and* of the Holy Spirit *and* of the Divine Sun." Unlike the structure of symbolism, which presents opposed elements in absolute unity, the structure of dialectic asserts the unity as a logical proposition, thereby continually undermining itself.

Having the structure of logic and the status and purpose of symbolism, dialectic is a kind of transitional stage between the two. Its hybrid nature points back to the intellectual discord which is the matrix of symbolism and forward to the harmony which is brought about by symbolic recasting. Dialectic and symbolism are products of intellectual strife, which forces attention away from "fact" to the medium of knowledge, and from the external correspondence of the medium to its internal coherence. Urban has pointed out that a concern with language is characteristic of the watersheds in the history of philosophy, the eras of the great dilemmas. The resulting philosophy of language may be confined to an instrumental view—as in medieval nominalism, the "semeiotic" of Locke, or modern logical positivism, where the word remains a sign of putative fact. But the tendency is to go further. In a logical impasse, as Mill said of Coleridge amid the jostling of the empirical and idealist traditions, the thinker does not ask "Is it true?" but "What is the meaning of it?" This is the form in which any problem is cast by dialectic. Whatever the issue, it can

be translated not only from a question of fact to one of signification (the method of "semantics") but also from a question of objective truth to one of coherent meaning. Ultimately, the whole
movement from intellectual conflict to a philosophy of language,
and from logic to dialectic, gravitates toward symbolism, which is
continuous with the rational world and completes it.

What gives a distinctive coloring to modern symbolism is the
particular issue that lies behind it. The problem here, like the doctrine of the Trinity or any other, can be translated into a dialectical question of meaning and thence into symbolism; but it also
directly involves the conception of meaning, the relationship between thought, word, and object. The whole seesaw movement
from Descartes through the English empiricists to Kant, issuing
in the nineteenth-century split between materialism and idealism,
is precisely the kind of intellectual situation which would lead to
the dialectical standpoint; at the same time, the fulcrum of the
movement was the problem of mediation, which led to the problem of language. Dualism invites a philosophy of language, "for,"
as Locke said, "since the things the mind contemplates are none
of them, besides itself, present to the understanding, it is necessary
that something else, as a sign or representation of the thing it con-
siders, should be present to it." Within the formula of Coleridgean
dialectic—"What is the meaning of it?"—lurks the more general
problem, "What is meaning?" The modern mind has inherited
both questions, and the modern symbolistic method, having a
double motive, is doubly pronounced. Modern writing, which from
one point of view is a return to the premises of all literature, is a
notably *conscious* return because it reconsiders the premises of
dualism.

The conscious symbolist will find himself in a curious position.
He is committed to carrying out in an especially elaborate way
what all writers, as he sees it, practice more or less. He must exploit his language where another would be content to take what
language gives. In this lies his strength and his weakness. On the
one hand, his *raison d'être* is the extent to which he inhabits the

reality generated by words. What he finds and makes in his words will be at once himself and the world about him; the meaning that his words bring to birth will be a realization of his own being and of his environment. On the other hand, though the differentia of poetry may well be its peculiarly symbolic status—though science itself, in the largest view, may approach the status of poetry—the symbolic realm is definable only in the rational terms of subject and object. Poetic form presupposés the rational world at every point. And the more thoroughly the symbolist conceives of language as symbol, the more likely it is that he will lose touch with language as sign; to the extent that he attains his aim, it would seem that his sense of direction must waver, since he cannot locate his work with reference to himself or an external world. Deliberate symbolism is hazardous in its quest for a pure poetry, for poetry can be pure only by virtue of the impurities it assimilates. In the degree that the poem shakes loose from the poet himself and from the world of objects, in the degree that the poetic word is freed from logical bonds, poetry will be deprived of material; in performing its function, it will destroy its subject matter. At the same time every attempt to grapple once more with rational multiplicity can only lead the symbolist back to his starting point. It is the divisiveness of logic that occasions his effort to live in the unitive world of language. In practice the symbolist will be caught between the consequences and the necessity of his method—between a sort of pathless void, pregnant with significance, and a radically unknowable world of absolute distinctions.

The same antinomy appears in other ways. The whole attempt to make the inherent *method* of literature an *aim* is equivocal. Though the symbolic process as such is simply a becoming, the cultivation of symbolism must make for an ambiguity of attitude, between the passive reception and the active formation of meaning. To "exploit" language is both to discover meaning and to create it. The ambiguity is blurred, not disposed of, by Auden's comment:

The poet is the father who begets the poem which the language bears. At first sight this would seem to give the poet too little to do and the language too much, till one remembers that, as husband, it is he, not the language, who is responsible for the success of their marriage, which differs from natural marriage in that in this relationship there is no loveless lovemaking, no accidental pregnancies.

This equivocation on "making"—objective craftsmanship—and "finding"—receptive apprehension—can produce extremes of classical formalism and surrealistic unconsciousness. In effect, the very kind of opposition that symbolism aims at overcoming will cast its shadow within the symbolistic framework. Parallel to this double potentiality is another ambivalence, between conscious antirationalism, which would entail utter inconclusiveness, and the practical need for finitude, which is actually the invocation of rational limits. While the poetic term may be distinguishable from the logical by its endless expansion of meaning, the cultivation of endlessness is hardly feasible. As a theory of literature, symbolism is potentially valid; it strikes through to a deeper principle than romantic or naturalistic doctrine. But, when it becomes a literary program, it will raise serious difficulties and revive in another form the problems that it is able to settle in theory.

Something like this could probably be said of any literary school, for in each the initial doctrine more or less fails in practice. In each the doctrine is a kind of question that the writer wants to answer; the form of his work to some extent *is* an "answer"; but he soon encounters other questions, not contemplated by his doctrine, with which his work must contend. In symbolism, however, quality and defect are more closely related. While the failings of romanticism and naturalism are sins of omission, symbolism will get into difficulties through the all-inclusiveness of the problem it sets, which at the same time will account for the richness of its possibilities. Its basic question is meaning per se—"the meaning of meaning"—and its working principle, the implied "answer," is that meaning is autonomous. "How can I know what I think till I see what I say?" asks Auden, implying that "what I say" is prior to what I think and know and see. But who am "I" in this context?—and what is "what"? These latent questions will rise in the way of the practicing symbolist.

Since he cannot avoid them, he must accept them. Symbolism as a literary school is distinctively *problematic,* not merely in the sense in which every literary symbol is indeterminate, but more specifically in the sense that its characteristic subject is its own equivocal method. The problematic work is self-critical. In the poems of Wallace Stevens poetic speech is its own best theme:

> It was her voice that made
> The sky acutest at its vanishing.
> She measured to the hour its solitude.
> She was the single artificer of the world
> In which she sang. And when she sang, the sea,
> Whatever self it had, became the self
> That was her song, for she was the maker. Then we,
> As we beheld her striding there alone,
> Knew that there never was a world for her
> Except the one she sang and, singing, made.

The involuted structure of *Les Faux-monnayeurs,* which plays upon the dubious standpoint of the modern writer, makes the author's own self-questioning the most inclusive ambiguity of the ambiguous realm in which he deals. *Finnegans Wake,* which ends as it begins, is itself a symbol of the tension between the infinity of symbolic aspiration and the conclusiveness which the objective work entails. These devices cannot be dismissed as a peripheral kind of romantic irony. They are central. When the symbolistic method becomes the theme of symbolism, the literary work is attaining the immediate reality of symbol by acknowledging that language, after all, is at the same time mediate. While dramatizing the conscious effort of its author, it enjoys an autonomy to which the person of the author is irrelevant. Insisting on its own finite nature, it embraces the infinity of poetic meaning. In general, the problematic work saves symbolism by symbolizing all that can be said for and against the symbolistic method. While it aspires to the status of pure symbol, it acquires that status by depicting the genesis of the symbol. At once denying and affirming its own validity, it is utterly inconclusive; and yet it escapes the penalties of inconclusiveness, for it furnishes a stage where the lost worlds of self and nature are reborn as actors in a drama of meaning.

The great danger of such an approach is not preciosity, as might be supposed, but intellectual suicide. There is only a slim margin of difference between a completely noncommittal and a nihilistic mood. Within that difference the problematic writer leads a precarious life, fostering the mutual criticism of reason and imagination and a provisional trust in both. He runs the danger of finding himself convinced by both and therefore unable to trust either. Yet even this impending fate can enter into his subject. The nemesis that hangs over him is also the final paradox which he must admit and turn to account—the possibility of the meaninglessness of meaning. In effect, he reaches, within his own frame of reference, the same sense of the ineluctable tension of human life as others put in terms of the distance between man and the supernatural. His God is the present reality of his work, the process that unifies all contradictions. His Devil is the potentiality of illusion and disunity. In so far as he succeeds, he is a kind of Manichee: his God comes into being by acknowledging the Devil. In so far as he fails, he allows the Devil to put an end to the inconclusive battle whereby his God exists. His heaven is the meaningfulness of meaning; the tragic theme of his work is the imminent loss of meaning which is the modern version of hell.

The symbolistic strain has no clear-cut *terminus a quo*. Precipitated by the continued pressure of intellectual conditions, it began to appear long before romanticism was spent, cropping up not only in Coleridge but in Blake, Carlyle, and Wordsworth; in Blake, and to a lesser extent in Carlyle, it is a method as well as a theory. Parallel to their speculations was the *Sprachphilosophie* of Germans like Wilhelm von Humboldt:

The most general and characteristic function of language is that it is a medium or link of communication. . . . It bears the imprint of the double nature of man blended into a symbol. In language our spontaneity and receptivity act together, and the subjective unites itself with the objective. By the act of speech the external world becomes converted into an internal one; and it is thus that nature, its individual objects as well as the laws by which we conceive it regulated, becomes translated into something that is human. Language is thus a perpetual prosopopoeia. As the isolated sound establishes a relation between the object and ourselves, so language, as a totality, constitutes a medium between us and nature, as the latter produces its impressions on us either from without or within. It is an intellectual world linked to sounds and occupies a sort of middle ground between man and the external; and it not only represents objects to the mind's eye, but it also gives us the impression produced by them, thus blending and uniting our receptivity with the self-determining, active energy of our being.

Seeking to avoid the conception of words as "arbitrary signs," Coleridge proposed that they be regarded as intrinsic to the organic growth of the mind—"parts and germinations of the plant"—while he also "would endeavour to destroy the old antithesis of Words and Things; elevating, as it were, Words into Things and living things, too." In this sort of emphasis on the act of speech as the realization of organic unity one can detect the rudiments of a modern symbolist tradition, carried on not so much by a chain of literary influence as by a growing intellectual need. It is a tradition not of subject matter or convention but of aesthetic standpoint; not of dogma but of method.

The symbolism of Emerson and his colleagues is a chapter in the history of modern taste. It is part of the symbolist tradition that culminates in modern literature. Hawthorne's indecision, Whitman's diffuseness, the complication of Melville's attitude, and the exaggerated unreason of Poe reflect the hazards of symbolism together with its possibilities, for each sets out from the question of *meaning*. These writers anticipated modern symbolism because they lived in the midst of the same intellectual forces: mid-nineteenth-century America was a proving ground for the issues to which the method of modern literature is an answer. They envisaged the symbolistic program to an extent that few of their English contemporaries even thought possible, because the crux of modern thought was oddly accentuated by the provincial culture they inhabited. Thus they stumbled upon many of the literary resources which recent symbolism has developed, and they were forced to contend with similar difficulties. The issues, moreover, were not entirely new. The American mind from its beginning was harassed by a problem of expression. The stage was set long before Emerson, among men who owed nothing to Descartes, but whose way of thinking embraced both the symbolism of the transcendentalist and the farthest extreme of rationalism.

III *An American Tradition*

*What could become of such a child of the
seventeenth and eighteenth centuries, when he
should wake up to find himself required
to play the game of the twentieth?*

The Education of Henry Adams

John Winthrop records in his journal that in the midst of a sermon
before the synod at Cambridge a snake appeared behind the pulpit
and was killed by one of the elders. Winthrop's comment, with its
queer leap from fact as fact to fact as meaning, embodies a kind
of symbolic perception that pervaded the life of the American
Puritans:

This being so remarkable, and nothing falling out but by divine
providence, it is out of doubt, the Lord discovered somewhat of his

mind in it. The serpent is the devil; the synod, the representative of
the churches of Christ in New England. The devil had formerly and
lately attempted their disturbance and dissolution; but their faith in
the seed of the woman overcame him and crushed his head.

What John Winthrop felt in the Cambridge meeting-house was
neither a historical event nor an allegorical fancy but an experience that united the objectivity of history with the meaningfulness
of Scripture. The deviltry of the serpent was as present as its
scales; to name the creature as a serpent was to imbue it with the
quality of Satan. The destruction of the serpent was a symbolic
act, grounded in biblical speech and in the heroic dreams of the
New England theocracy. A similar passage occurs in the diary of
Samuel Sewall. Cotton Mather was visiting Sewall's house during
a hailstorm and "had just been mentioning that more Ministers
Houses than others proportionably had been smitten with Lighten-
ing; enquiring what the meaning of God should be in it." A moment later the hail had broken the windows; Mather "told God He
had broken the brittle part of our house, and prayd that we might
be ready for the time when our Clay-Tabernacles should be
broken." Within, not superadded to, such happenings was a constitutive language; the devil-serpent and the body-house took
shape and were experienced as radical metaphors made by God.
As Joshua Moody stated, the practical activities of life were capable of being transmuted, "spiritualized," by being conceived under the aspect of scriptural usage: "All our Relations and Conditions, as well as Imployments, are ... improved to our Hands by
the Spirit of God in his Word. ... From the King upon the Throne
to the Hewer of wood and drawer of water, the Lord is in his
word teaching us by such familiar and known *Metaphors* taken
from those Callings that we are versed in."

The symbols themselves were meager, for the mental economy
of the Puritans gave little scope for aesthetic realization of the
natural world. These men narrowed "the meaning of God" to the
meanings of a crabbed schoolmaster. Yet the symbolizing *process*
was constantly at work in their minds. For them, the word "wilder-

ness" inherently united the forty years of the ancient Hebrews with the trials of the New England forest. "When they wandered in the deserte willdernes out of the way, and found no citie to dwell in, both hungrie, & thirstie, their sowle was overwhelmed in them." Here for a moment Bradford is not merely narrating the facts of Plymouth history; he is invoking an image which colored that history as it was actually experienced. And the symbol took on another aspect in the words of Thomas Shepard: "Wee cannot see but the rule of Christ to his Apostles and Saints, and the practise of Gods Saints in all ages, may allow us this liberty as well as others, to fly into the Wildernesse from the face of the Dragon." When Edward Johnson urges all who long for the destruction of Antichrist to "pray continually with that valiant worthy Joshua that the Sun may stand still in Gibeon, and the Moone in the vally of Aijalon," persons and places like Joshua, "Gibeon," and "Aijalon" are drawn out of the realm of biblical history and become parts of a living language through which he perceives the world. Johnson has a vision of Christ as an oriental monarch, in which the terms of kingship permeate the conception of God, and a complete fusion, based on the language of Scripture, takes place:

See, ther's their glorious King Christ one [on] that white Horse, whose hoofes like flint cast not only sparkes, but flames of fire in his pathes. Behold his Crown beset with Carbunkles, wherein the names of his whole Army are written. Can there be ever night in his Presence, whose eyes are ten thousand times higher [brighter] than the Sun? Behold his swiftnes, all you that have said, where is the promise of his comming?

In the everyday life of New England images like the "Holy Commonwealth" and the "Wars of the Lord" converted human activity into a symbolic drama. New England was "the place where the Lord will create a new Heaven, and a new Earth in, New Churches, and a new Common-wealth together." The unfolding drama was at once human and divine; physical life was simultaneously spiritual. Every passage of life, enmeshed in the vast context of God's plan, possessed a delegated meaning. Under the aspect of the Holy Commonwealth, the crude huts and muddy streets were transmogrified into a focal symbol of God's emerging idea: "Wee are as a City set upon an hill, in the open view of all the earth, the eyes of the world are upon us." As the colonies became more worldly, and the gap between practical life and its symbolic aura widened, the ministers insisted the more strongly that New England was an emblem of God's thought, not a commercial enterprise:

'Tis possible that our Lord Jesus Christ carried some thousands of Reformers into the retirements of an American desart, on purpose that . . . He might there, *to* them first, and then *by* them, give a *specimen* of many good things, which He would have His Churches elsewhere aspire and arise unto; and *this* being done, he knows not whether there be not *all done*, that New-England was planted for; and whether the Plantation may not, soon after this, *come to nothing*.

Just as the Heavenly City was implicit in the Colonial villages, the conflict of good and evil in New England was an epitome of the war of Heaven and Hell, not merely in the sense of representing it but as an organic part of it, a true synecdoche. The Old Testament battles were at one with the slaughter of the Indians, the rooting-out of heresy, and the execution of witches. In Edward Johnson's *Wonder-working Providence* King Christ sends out his heralds to enlist soldiers:

For the Armies of the great Jehovah are at hand. See you not his Enemies stretched out on tiptoe, proudly daring on their thresholds, a certaine signe of their sudden overthrow? be not danted at your small number, for every common Souldier in Christs Campe shall be as David, who slew the great Goliah, and his Davids shall be as the Angels of the Lord, who slew 158000. in the Assyrian Army.

Satan was present in the Indians, "their quarrell being as antient as Adams time, propagated from that old enmity betweene the Seede of the Woman, and the Seed of the Serpent, who was the grand signor of this war in hand"; and it seemed to some of the soldiers, quite literally, that the Indians' bodies were impervious to swords because the devil was in them. The Wars of the Lord, which included all the "manifold afflictions and disturbances of the churches in New England," were radically metaphoric, a mode of perception that united past and present, idea and material fact, in the objectively given. Satan, the age-old Enemy, was an embodied idea. In the days of Moses, says Cotton Mather, wildernesses "were counted very much an habitation of devils"; indeed, he adds emphatically, they "really were what they were counted." And Moses lived on in the diabolic wilderness, for "the Christians who were driven into the American desert, which is now call'd New-England, have to their sorrow seen Azazel dwelling and raging there in very tragical instances."

The wearisome reiteration of "providences" in the Puritan writings is actually a record of symbolic experience that never attained formal literary structure. The commissioning of a history of Massachusetts Bay in order "to take due notice of all occurrances & passages of Gods providence towards the people of this jurisdiction since their first arrivall in these parts" reflected a popular mind that could grasp events only in terms of a totality, the mind of God, presupposed by every occurrence. Memoirs were cast so as to reveal God's intention at every juncture. A favorable wind was God's answer to prayer, the death of a profane young man was "a spetiall worke of Gods providence," and the triumph of the Pilgrims over hardship was an example to the indifferent world. Cotton Mather gathered such "significant" events by the score, and in 1694 the president and fellows of Harvard College proposed a systematic collection:

The things to be esteemed *memorable,* are especially all *unusual accidents,* in the heaven, or earth, or water: all wonderful *deliverances* of the distressed: *mercies* to the godly; *judgments* on the wicked; and more glorious fulfilment of either the *promises* or the *threatnings* in the Scriptures of truth; with *apparitions, possessions, inchantments,* and all extraordinary things wherein the existence and agency of the *invisible world* is more sensibly demonstrated.

Trivial and grotesque as the individual "providences" and mechanical compilations often appear, in them a powerful imaginative capacity was haltingly exercised. Behind the "providences," and referred to in each, was Providence, the eternal "concurrence" of God sustaining the order of things and giving to divine and human acts a perpetual unison. In government, for instance, "there are not two several and distinct actings, one of God, another of the People: but in one and the same action, God, by the Peoples suffrages, makes such an one Governour, or Magistrate, and not another." By "special providences" God gave a particular direction to the process of natural events, thereby creating an effective sign of one of his ever present purposes. And miracles, in which God interrupted the natural order, were like exclamations in the divine discourse, eruptions of the force which motivated all things: "He can stop the Sun in its course, and cause it to withdraw its shining; He can give check to the Fire, that it shall not burn; & to the hungry Lions, that they shall not devour." The "reading" of events was the inadequate form taken by a basically symbolic vision; the Puritans saw the world as instinct with meaning by reason of God's concurrence and susceptible of interpretation by reason of God's salient acts.

They did not understand the gift. The fusion of serpent and devil, Hebrew and New Englander, Christ and king, which followed from their basic apprehension of a world permeated with God's ideas, seldom entered their literature as functional metaphors with a symbolic structure. Instead, their practice was to "open" a figure, to render it illustrative or decorative by analytic presentation. When Edward Johnson set out to portray Anne Hutchinson as Sisera, he proceeded by logical steps:

And now to follow our first simile of a Souldier, the Lord Christ having safely landed many a valiant Souldier of his on these Westerne shores, drawes hither also the common enemies to Reformation, both in Doctrine and Discipline; But it was for like end, as the Lord sometime drew Sisera the Captaine of Jabins army to the River Kishon for their destruction, onely herein was a wide difference; there Sisera was delivered into the hands of a Woman, and here Sisera was a woman; their weapons and warre was carnall, these spirituall; there Jabin was but a man, here Jabin was the common enemy of mans salvation.

Johnson produced the bare bones of a metaphysical conceit, a paraphrase of a complex figure that never came into actual existence. The same kind of logical analysis vitiates the elaborate similes of Anne Bradstreet's *Meditations;* when she tries to present Christ with the saints and angels as the sun surrounded by stars, the passage reads like an exposition of some other writer's poem on the subject.

In the best Puritan writing the images are frankly illustrative, and sometimes, all unawares, they quicken into symbols as idea and illustration coalesce. The attempt to follow an opposite method —to imitate directly in literary form the metaphoric experience of every day—resulted only in the crude mannerisms of Cotton Mather. The historian of the Wars of the Lord, for whom broken windows were the appointed sign of the destruction of our "Clay-Tabernacles," awkwardly built his tales around double meanings and outright puns. He approaches the subject of Roger Williams obliquely through the figure of a windmill:

In the year 1654, a certain Windmill in the Low Countries, whirling round with extraordinary violence, by reason of a violent storm then blowing; the stone at length by its *rapid motion* became so intensely hot, as to fire the mill, from whence the flames, being dispersed by the high winds, did set a whole town on *fire*. But I can tell my reader that, about twenty years before this, there was a whole country in America like to be set on *fire* by the *rapid motion* of a windmill, in the head of one particular man. Know, then, that about the year 1630, arrived here one Mr. Roger Williams; . . . being a preacher that had less *light* than *fire* in him. . . .

Even beyond the nervous italics, there are *double-entendres:* the Low Countries were the gathering place of sectaries and swept by winds of doctrine. In Mather's account of Anne Hutchinson a "special providence" is played upon in a similar style. The "testimony of heaven" is translated into deliberate word-play and a labored pun:

> While these things were managing, there happened some very sur-
> prising *prodigies*, which were lookt upon as testimonies from Heaven,
> against the ways of those greater prodigies, the sectaries. The *errone-
> ous gentlewoman* her self, convicted of holding about *thirty* monstrous
> opinions, growing big with child, and at length coming to her time
> of travail, was delivered of about *thirty* monstrous births at once;
> whereof some were bigger, some were lesser; of several figures; few
> of any perfect, none of any *humane* shape. This was a thing generally
> then asserted and believed; whereas, by some that were eye-witnesses,
> it is affirmed that these were no more *monstrous births*, than what it
> is frequent for women, labouring with false *conceptions*, to produce.

The crudity of Mather's attempt to duplicate in literary form the overlapping structure of experience which he knew outside of literature reflects a fundamental limitation in the Puritan views of knowledge and language. A properly symbolic method was denied the Puritan writer by his assumptions on method in general. Aquinas held that things have multiple meaning and that language is at one with the symbolic structure of reality. The Puritans made a drastic break with this Catholic tradition. For Samuel Willard the only realistic form of language was logical, and logic was the way in which men necessarily apprehended the world:

> It is impossible for us to know or understand things, but by some
> rule of reason or other. *Reason is nothing else but the manner of a
> Being, whereby it is acted upon our Understanding*. We know nothing
> of God but by putting some Logical Notion upon him. *All things are
> conveyed to us in a Logical way*, and bear some stamp of reason upon
> them, or else we should know nothing of them.

Although the Puritan mind easily united Palestine and Massachusetts into a fluid realm where God's ideas were enacted, theory was all against the cultivation of this practice, and the New Englanders were governed by theory as no people before or since. According to their theory, the truth of Scripture was not aesthetic but propositional; understanding consisted in analytic interpretation:

A Scripture consequence; is a Trueth evidently & necessarily arising out of a proposition, held forth therein in express termes; So that: if the doctrine conteined in the proposition held forth in express termes be true, then is the doctrine conteined therein by consequence, also true. . . . The greatest part of Scripture-trueth is revealed in Scripture-consequences. Yea many fundamentall trueths are not held forth in express termes, but by manifest consequence.

If the real structure of language and reality was purely logical, aesthetic form was merely an ornament. The Puritan clergy possessed a sort of universal vade mecum in the philosophy of Peter Ramus, a sixteenth-century French logician and rhetorician, whose works were transmitted to them in a multitude of summaries and commentaries. Whereas Scholastic philosophy had given rhetoric virtually an equal status with logic in the scheme of things, thus providing a sanction for symbolism as a form of knowledge, Ramus treated rhetoric as decoration added to and presupposing a logical framework:

This is the true distinction between Dialectic and Rhetoric: For even if the oration be most illustrious or most ample, subtlety of invention in thinking the arguments, of truth in enunciation, of consequence in syllogism, and of order in method, is entirely, I say, a matter of dialectic and logic. But ornament and elocution in trope and figure, and pronunciation in voice and gesture is entirely a matter of rhetoric and completely pertaining to it, even if the disputation itself be mostly philosophical.

Since "trope and figure" were merely embroidery on the logical doctrine, interpretation was a simple process of reduction. A rhetorical expression was equated with some univocal logical paraphrase. The method was to find a grammatical bridge between the figure and its logical equivalent:

All Rhetorical expressions must be reduced to the Grammatical sense, and accordingly interpreted. Types and figures must be allowed to the Scriptures as well as to other writings, else God had not spoken in our mode, and this way is not too obscure, but to illustrate, and also to move the affections, but still we must reduce it to the Intention: Rhetorick is but an Ornament of Speech, and must therefore be brought to the Grammar of it.

This ornamentalism effectually destroyed the Puritan sense of artistic coherence. To the New England mind the poetry of the Psalms was extrinsic and separable from the meaning conveyed, as Richard Mather declared in his Preface to the *Bay Psalm Book*. Thomas Hooker assumed a radical distinction between the "quaintnesse of language," which serves only "to please the nicenesse of mens palates," and "the substance and solidity of the frame . . . , which pleaseth the builder." The meaning could not inhere in the poetry, or the substance in the rhetoric; the Ramistic scheme offered no ground for a functional symbolism.

The Puritan revolt from Catholicism was not only doctrinal but methodological; from one point of view it was part and parcel of the vast movement which established the scientific technique of modern thought. Whitehead has shown how the habit of picturing nature in atomistic form grew upon the modern consciousness. The scientific method devised in "the Century of Genius" prescribed a world made up of objects with "simple location" in space and time, objects lacking "any essential reference . . . to other regions of space and to other durations of time." But these objects, Whitehead points out, were devised by "high abstraction"; they are "the products of logical discernment" supervening upon the world as it is concretely experienced. In concrete reality we apprehend no "mere multiplicity of points" ordered mechanically but rather an organic whole in which "each part is something from the standpoint of every other part, and also from the same standpoint every other part is something in relation to it." Poetry since the seventeenth century has very often been an attempt either to accept the world of simple location as a kind of *pis aller* or to displace the narrowly logical habits of mind which created that vision of nature.

Calvinistic Protestantism, as Whitehead says, was the theological counterpart of the contemporary science. It too imposed upon the world the pattern of a simplistic logic, which issued in "the mechanism of God" just as scientific method issued in "the mechanism of matter." Like the scientific theory of knowledge and the scientific metaphysics, it had the effect of invalidating the organic structure of poetry and nullifying the organic world of experience that poetry claims to render. The logical methodology which the Puritans derived from Ramus mapped out a world of discrete entities—"arguments"—each with its simple location in the conceptual scheme. Anything—a substance, a quality, an action, a relation—was an "argument," and the ten Aristotelian categories were lost in this sweeping concept. Every discipline could be schematized by a succession of dichotomies so as to distinguish and put in their places the arguments of which it was composed. The syllogism was of minor importance beside this technique of dichotomizing. In some respects, as will presently appear, the Ramistic logic was more than a mechanically divisive system; but its practical effect was to convert the universe into an assemblage of logical counters, a mechanical framework of causes and effects, "subjects" and "adjuncts," whose "either-or" relationship was dramatized by the elementary principle of dichotomy. The Aristotelians against whom Ramus contended were inclined to be nominalistic, but the Ramistic logicians made their boast that the "places" of their skeletal outlines were the "places" of reality. By his revision of the Aristotelian logic—at once a bold extension of logical method and a drastic leveling—Ramus created a world which in its utter simplicity was the more plainly a "high abstraction."

Medieval Catholicism was sufficiently devoted to logic but inherited and cultivated another mode of thought as well. The Jewish theologians of Alexandria, caught between Greek philosophy and the Mosaic law, had rescued themselves by an ingenious method of biblical interpretation. The ancient words, they decided, must contain a multiplicity of meaning: "As a hammer divides fire into many sparks, so every verse of Scripture has many explanations." Rules of "allegorical" interpretation were gradually formulated. According to the "fourfold interpretation" invented by the early Fathers and accepted thereafter, the four levels of meaning in the language of the Bible ("literal," "moral," "allegorical," and "anagogical") were all equally true and mutually supplementary.

The principle of "multiplex intelligentia," although it became an artificial formula in the course of time, was actually a recognition of symbolic thinking, for it originated in an effort to use the figures of the Bible as vehicles for a variety of ideas, and it persisted as a means of unifying the complex intellectual heritage of Christianity. "Multiplex intelligentia" was no freak of words but coincident with the nature of things. Aquinas held that interpretations "are not multiplied because one word signifies several things, but because the things signified by the words can be themselves types of other things." All the interpretations grew out of the "literal" meaning, the simple designation of an object; reality had a symbolic structure, in which everything referred beyond itself. The theory bore fruit in the *Divine Comedy*, the meaning of which, Dante explained, "is not of one kind only; rather the work may be described as 'polysemous,' that is, having several meanings." The meanings all converge into the literal one, "that sense in the expression of which the others are all included, and without which it would be impossible and irrational to give attention to the other meanings." The "poetriae," the medieval literary handbooks, treated figurative language as ornamental circumlocution and afforded no basis for symbolism, but theology fostered the capacity to think and feel in figures, so that the medieval mind "moved as frequently from symbol to symbol as from fact to fact."

The Puritans gingerly preserved this Catholic tradition as the science of "typology," a system of correspondences between the Old Testament and the New. Adam and David were types of Christ, and the deliverances from Egypt and Babylon "shadowed forth" the deliverance of the Church from the Antichrist. These relationships were real, designed and instituted by God like sacraments. They were expressly distinguished from merely illustrative similes and metaphors. Yet precisely in this distinction appears the characteristic narrowness of Puritan thought. The Puritan typologist was afraid of the types, or rather of the symbolic thinking necessary to perceive them, and he consigned many figures of the Bible, and all outside it, to an "arbitrary" status. Gone were the habits of mind that produced the *Divine Comedy* out of a sense of multiple meaning inherent in real things. Although such images as "the Wars of the Lord" and "the Holy Commonwealth" were an effort to carry typology one step further, from the New Testament into the New World, a measure of the forces working to constrain the Puritan imagination is given by this warning:

> Men must not *indulge their own Fancies,* as the Popish Writers use to do, with their Allegorical Senses, as they call them; except we have some Scripture ground for it. It is not safe to make any thing a Type meerly upon our own fansies and imaginations; it is *Gods* Prerogative to make *Types.*

The obvious difficulty that one might well mistake an individual fancy for a divinely appointed type (both are "similitudes," and the rules given to discover the "Scripture ground" are hardly conclusive) did not affect the principle. The types belonged in a special and jealously guarded category; figures in general, unless plainly illustrative or decorative, became dangerous subjective fancies emulating the types. As to the particular types of Scripture, there might remain some slight difference of opinion, but "typical" thinking in literature was beyond the pale.

The intellectual stance of the conscious artist in American literature has been determined very largely by problems inherent in the method of the Puritans. The isolation of the American artist in society, so often lamented, is actually parallel to the furtive and unacknowledged role of artistic method in the American mind; both factors began in the seventeenth century with the establishment of Puritan philosophy and of a society that tried to live by it. Hence the crudity or conventionality of a great part of American literature from 1620 through the third quarter of the nineteenth century may be attributed no more surely to frontier conditions, provinciality, and industrialism than to inherited mental habits which proscribed a functional artistic form. And the symbolism of Emerson, Thoreau, Melville, Hawthorne, and Whitman was an attempt to hew out such a form in defiance of intellectual methods that denied its validity.

The effect of Puritanism, however, was not simply repressive. The early Colonial writers, in their limited fashion, did perpetuate the medieval symbolist tradition. The purpose of Mather's *Magnalia* was to bring to bear "innumerable Antiquities, *Jewish, Chaldee, Arabian, Grecian,* and *Roman,* . . . with a *sweet light* reflected from them on the *word,* which is our *light.*" In daily life the Puritans customarily evaded their rhetorical theory, and in them, as Emerson said, "the whole Jewish history became flesh and blood." What the Puritan mind bequeathed to American writing, from the standpoint of literary method, was a special and extreme case of the modern literary situation: a conflict between the symbolic mode of perception, of which our very language is a record, and a world of sheer abstractions certified as "real." The divided consciousness which Whitehead sees beginning in England in the seventeenth and eighteenth centuries under the impact of physical science, and coming into the open in romantic and Victorian literature, had an even deeper foundation in America, for here it began with Puritan rationalism.

The rationalism itself was not wholly rational. The highly wrought logic of the "Covenants" hid a symbolic pattern which bound together the theoretically distinct Covenant of Grace, Church Covenant, and Civil Covenant. These three bargains with God were the gigantic shadow cast by the new society of commercial contracts and constitutional government; more particularly, they reflect the conventicles and small group agreements under which the New England colonies were founded. The earthly covenant, such as marriage or the relation of master and servant, frequently offered by the theologian as an *example* of spiritual contract, "must in fact have been exemplar," and the Covenant idea gained its real cogency not from rational argument but from the way in which its various levels shed light on each other. This symbolic reference, which gave a kind of organic unity to the entire scheme, is the more striking in that the Covenant idea per se was a repudiation of the organic society and imputed a mechanical quality to the relationship between man and God. Puritan method was actually at odds with itself. Ramus and his followers gave an ontological status to a highly simplified version of the logic of classes; his "arguments," linked only by the concepts of formal logic, and his technique of dichotomizing every whole into radically distinct parts, evince in the most thoroughgoing fashion the effort of the modern mind to picture an atomic world. But it was possible to found upon this system a doctrine of mutually subservient disciplines, the universal organon known as "technologia":

All the Arts are nothing else but the beams and rays of the Wisdom of the *first Being* in the Creatures, shining, and reflecting thence, upon the glass of man's understanding; and as from *Him* they come, so to him they tend: the circle of Arts is *a Deo ad Deum.* Hence there is an affinity and kindred of Arts (*omnes Artes vinculo & cognatione quadem inter se continentur:* Cicer. pro Arch. Poet.) which is according to the reference and subordination of their particular ends, to the utmost and last end: One makes use of another, one serves to another, till they all reach and return to Him, as Rivers to the Sea, whence they flow.

The God who sanctioned technologia was not the Supreme Mechanic but rather a mind whose organic unity was reflected in nature and potentially in the mind of man.

From its beginning the logic of Ramus was avowedly "dialectic," a process of right thinking as well as an external description of thought. The claim was made with the utmost seriousness. The Puritan obsession with "method" was not simply a love of logical form but more fundamentally an intense concern with thought, language, and reality. Like the originators of "multiplex intelligentia," who evolved a philosophy of language at the turning point of the classic and Christian eras, the Protestant reformers in their revolt from Catholic modes of thought were thrown back on the nature of words. The language of the Bible was authority; since the Bible had been variously misinterpreted, it was necessary to know how this language worked; and, since truth was subject to controversy, one must be able to use language according to its nature. The Puritan ministers spent their lives immersed in the meaning of words. They were quick to grasp the value of any nuance and to turn it to their own purposes:

> Bernard, upon that clause in the Canticles ["O thou fairest among women!"], has this ingenious gloss: *Pulchram, non omnimode quidem, sed pulchram inter mulieres eam docet; videlicet cum distinctione, quatenus ex hoc amplius reprimatur, et sciat quid desit sibi* ["Fair, not in an absolute sense, but fair *among women;* implying a distinction, in order that his praise may have due qualification, and that she may apprehend her deficiencies"]. Thus, I do not say, that the Churches of New-England are the most *regular* that can be; yet I do say, and am sure, that they are very like unto those that were in the first ages of Christianity.

Although, in his hostility to Catholic methods and in the manner of his age, the Ramist assumed that language is essentially logical and that "all things," as Willard said, "are conveyed to us in a Logical way," his very concern with language as *the way things are conveyed* gave a peculiar quality to his logic. Puritan rationalism, unlike the scientific world view that supplanted it and to which it is in some ways cognate, predicated an indivisible unity of thought, word, and thing. The Ramistic "argument" did not "refer to" an external thing, nor did it "signify" a subjective idea. "Had Ramists known the terms, they would have allowed no distinction between the idea and the 'ding-an-sich,'" or at any rate very little. "The argument was the thing, or the name of the thing, or the mental conception of the thing, all at once." The Puritans were not troubled by modern epistemological difficulties. Willard's faith in logical language depended upon his belief that "knowledge is made by an assimilation between the Knower, and the thing known," that "the object known must be (some way) in the faculty knowing," and that the word is part of a unit which *is* knowledge.

Dialectic is a logic that moves in the realm of symbolism, where there are no things or ideas apart from the language that makes them, and the criterion of truth is coherence, not correspondence to external fact. The very term "argument," for which there is no modern equivalent, expresses this conception. Arguments were "invented" by the mind in the sense that they became present to it, just as the eye perceived colors, and no other demonstration was necessary to prove them true. Laid side by side, arguments built up axioms, which were similarly validated: "The light of nature ... reveals itself in the observer, and a natural assent follows when an arrangement of this kind is perceived." Similarly, a complete discourse was constructed by the juxtaposition of axioms containing within themselves an evident connection and order. Although arguments and axioms were the terms and propositions of discursive thinking, at once the instruments and products of abstraction, another force was operating on this logic. While the argument was basically an atomistic logical entity, prior to all combinations into which it entered and remaining unaltered by them, at the same time it was inherently relational, as is shown by Ramus' definition: "An argument is whatever is affected to the arguing of something else." The axiom was simply a proposition, but the Ramists pointedly minimized the process of inference (the syllogism was a means of checking, not the essence of method) and depended on juxtaposition to reveal a pattern in thoughts and things. Working to modify the mechanistic tendency to which any logic is prone, and of which the Puritan method had more than its share, was a sense of organic unity—not only between the mind and objects but also, growing out of that, among all things in the given world. The arguments were "glued together," said Alexander Richardson, in the nature of things, and each axiom, according to Nathaniel Ward, contained some tincture of the whole of God's truth:

The least Truth of Gods Kingdome, doth in its place, uphold the whole kingdome of his Truths; Take away the least *vericulum* out of the world, and it unworlds all, potentially, and may unravell the whole texture actually, if it be not conserved by an Arme of extraordinary power.

It was not merely a desire to popularize, therefore, which led Ramus to illustrate his method by quotations from poets and orators. As dialectic, his logic was germane to the organic forms of aesthetic experience and partially modified by them. Nor did the vogue of Ramus among the seventeenth-century poets, which has recently been explored, result only from a common desire to make poetry logical. On the contrary, his method was accessible to the poetic mind because it was also inclined to poeticize logic and thus, however flimsily, to bridge the gap between abstract and concrete thinking. The American Puritans fastened upon another, more obvious aspect of the system: its apparent elimination of aesthetic form from the structure of reality. But a quasi-aesthetic, dialectical strain belonged to the method, little as they were aware of it. It crops up again in Emerson, both as theory and as practice, and Emerson consciously relates it to the theory and practice of symbolism.

Meanwhile, the Puritans, who longed for a stable, timeless order, found that dialectic has its own momentum, which cannot be halted arbitrarily. Emerson was prepared to accept the incompleteness of any logical statement; he saw that every proposition aims at an absoluteness which its very nature precludes, since "we cannot strongly state one fact without seeming to belie some other." But his seventeenth-century ancestors thought they had captured the whole of reality in the texture of a rational language, and they were doomed to pay for their mistake. They were plagued by controversies over the meaning of words; their vocabulary concealed logical oppositions that could only jar against each other and draw apart. Since word, thought, and thing were one, the controversialist could appeal only to immediate apprehension by the "natural light" of reason and try to convince by demonstrating a necessary meaning. To gain acceptance became increasingly difficult. At the trial of Anne Hutchinson a quarrel arose over the relation of the Holy Ghost to the believer. In desperation, "it was earnestly desired, that the word person might be forborn, being a term of human invention, and tending to doubtful disputation in this case." The same sort of difficulty persisted, the lady and her judges differing over the meaning of a "rule." John Cotton summed up the whole controversy as a dispute "about magnifying the grace of God; one party seeking to advance the grace of God *within us,* and the other to advance the grace of God *towards us,* (meaning by the one justification, and by the other sanctification)." The latent tensions of Puritanism, lacking any vehicle for symbolic unity, emerged in equivocation on terms like "person," "rule," "within us," and "towards us." Moreover, the terms were continually being spirited away into a new context that utterly changed their sense. The arbitrary God who had bound himself by "covenant" was at once a medieval seigneur and a modern businessman with a contract. The balance of this conception was hard to maintain by logic alone: if the arbitrary God was bound by law, it might seem logical to consider the law more important than God. In the eighteenth century, when a society of contract had largely replaced the medieval society of status, the Calvinistic balance was lost, and the doctrine that laws were good because God made them verged easily into the quite opposite belief that God made them because they were good. The shift was already taking place in the logical exercises of mid-seventeenth-century divines:

It is his [God's] will and good pleasure to make all laws that are moral to be first good in themselves for all men, before he will impose them upon all men. And hence it is a weakness for any to affirm, that a moral law is not such a law which is therefore commanded because it is good, because (say they) it is not the goodness of the thing, but the sovereign will of God, which makes all things good; for it is the sovereign will of God (as is proved) to make every moral law good, and therefore to command it, rather than to make it good by a mere commanding of it.

There are not many steps between this bit of reasoning and the completely secularized opinion of Benjamin Franklin:

Revelation had indeed no weight with me, as such; but I entertain'd an opinion that, though certain actions might not be bad *be-*

cause they were forbidden by it, or good *because* it commanded them, yet probably these actions might be forbidden *because* they were bad for us, or commanded *because* they were beneficial to us, in their own natures, all the circumstances of things considered.

The logical marches and countermarches of the New England theologians, in their effort to stabilize a dissolving system, were farther and farther removed from experience. Language was tortured until "regeneration became merely an 'X,' which filled a gap in a theological structure; a mere postulate in an ideology." When Nathanael Emmons defined visible saints as "those who *appear to profess real holiness*," he precipitated endless discussions in which all the permutations of "appear," "profess," and "real" were paraded like speculative geometries that no one could live by. It was as though, betrayed by the logical method of their fathers, the later Calvinists had no recourse save to further, increasingly mechanical juggling of terms. At length, the Unitarians dissolved the Trinity itself by uncompromising logic. According to Andrews Norton:

When it is affirmed that "the Father is God, and the Son is God, and the Holy Ghost is God; and yet there are not three Gods, but one God"; no words can more clearly convey any meaning, than those propositions express the meaning, that there are three existences of whom the attributes of God may be predicated, and yet that there is only one existence of whom the attributes of God may be predicated. But this is not an incomprehensible mystery; it is plain nonsense.

Norton had completely lost the capacity for symbolic thinking. Whereas the original Puritans had retained a vital symbolism in everyday experience and even, however unconsciously, in the structure of their system, meaning for their descendants was either rational or nonexistent. Norton recognized "the intrinsic ambiguity of language"—indeed, he devoted many pages to the subject —but he insisted that interpretation must "distinguish among *possible* meanings, the *actual* meaning" of a passage. Just as the doctrines of Calvinism gravitated into eighteenth-century benevolence, the old rational method drifted into the rationalism of deists and infidels. There is not much to choose, as far as habits of thought are concerned, between Norton and the *philosophe* Thomas Jefferson, to whom "the Trinitarian arithmetic, that three are one, and one is three," was an "incomprehensible jargon," or the infidel Thomas Paine, whose attack on "the Christian system of arithmetic, that three are one, and one is three," was only part of a general assault on the whole of Christian symbolism.

In this harsh intellectual climate, brought on by the Puritans' commitment to a dialectic which they did not fully understand, men like Emerson were born. They proposed to rescue the intellect by showing that controversy grew out of the nature of logical language. The supplanting of one creed by another, they declared, was the normal course of dialectic; through the jostling of formulas wider generalizations became possible; and the full substance of theology could never be rendered in creeds at all, but only in complex symbols. Running counter to the Calvinistic orthodoxy of New England was a strain of liberalism, stemming ultimately from Luther's doctrine of the priesthood of all believers. Roger Williams set up his colony as a haven for all varieties of belief; he regarded his own creed as provisional and called himself a "seeker." The conventional Puritans condemned Williams not only for heresy but for obvious illogicality:

How all Religions should enjoy their liberty, Justice its due regularity, Civill cohabitation morall honesty, in one and the same Jurisdiction, is beyond the Artique of my comprehension. If the whole conclave of Hell can so compromise, *exadverse, and diametriall contradictions,* as to compolitize such a multimonstrous maufrey of heteroclytes and quicquidlibets quietly; I trust I may say with all humble reverence, they can doe more then the Senate of Heaven.

Actually, Williams had accepted the inevitability of logical opposition and moved on to another principle. The proliferation of dialectic—each proposition generating its opposite—had become a resource of thought for the "seeker." A century and a half later, after infinite logical acumen had failed to check the disintegration of Calvinism, Channing proclaimed that the mind needs to entertain contradictory ideas in order to encompass the truth:

> God's sovereignty is limitless; still man has rights. God's power is irresistible; still man is free. On God we entirely depend; yet we can and do act from ourselves, and determine our own characters. *These antagonist ideas, if so they may be called, are equally true, and neither can be spared.* It will not do for an impassioned or an abject piety to wink one class of them out of sight. *In a healthy mind they live together. . . .*

Out of the view that mutually exclusive ideas may be equally true and necessary came Emerson's defiance of system and Horace Bushnell's assertion that he was ready to accept as many creeds as fell in his way. For both, the answer to Puritan logic-chopping was the method of liberalism. And, for both, the ultimate expression of the liberal mind was the symbolic "language of paradox."

The history of New England theology had demonstrated what the better instinct of the New Englanders themselves had said all along—that a language to live in could not be made in the image of mathematics but must articulate the organic processes of human activity and experience. Horace Bushnell defined his main problem as "how to get a language, and where"—the question posed for American literature by the Puritan obsession with "method" and emphasized by the decline and fall of Calvinism. His answer, that language is made by giving oneself to words, not calculating upon them, was equally implicit in the tradition. Ramus had created a dialectic rather than a pure logic because he held that "not art in itself, but the exercise and practice of it, makes the artisan." The abstract and descriptive terms of theory became concrete as functions in the process of knowledge; apart from the substance of concrete experience, they were mere instrumental signs. Richard Sibbes, an English Puritan, brought out the point even more explicitly when he warned that "religion is not a matter of word, nor stands upon words, as wood consists of Trees . . . but religion is a matter of power, it makes a man able." The being of religion did not consist in dogma, which could only refer to it. The "art" (or theory) must enter into the "trade" (or activity), the words into the things they designated: "A Trade is not learned by words, but by experience: and a man hath learned a Trade, not when he can *talk of it,* but when he can *work according to* his Trade." The Puritans were aware that two very different kinds of knowledge are possible, and in the midst of their concerted effort to formulate the world in doctrines they clung to the active perception that is prior to all logical statement:

There is great ods betwixt the knowledg of a Traveller, that in his own person hath taken a view of many Coasts, . . . and by Experience hath been an Eye-witness . . . and another that sits by his fire side, and happily reads the story of these in a Book, or views the proportion of these in a Map, the ods is great, and the difference of their knowledg more than a little. . . . The like difference is there in the right discerning of sin. . . . The one sees the History of sin, the other the Nature of it; the one knows the relation of sin as it is mapped out, and recorded; the other the poyson, as by experience he hath found and proved it.

Jonathan Edwards was the most notable exponent of knowledge by experience. Although his "real sense of the excellency of God" seemed to him a "divine and supernatural light," as distinct from imagination and inspiration as from doctrines and propositions, he set it off in this way in order to save his theology from the charge of mere subjective wilfulness, and his over-all aim was to validate the language of direct perception. Theology aside, Edwards anticipated the symbolic consciousness of Emerson. He shared Emerson's conviction that "the spontaneous or intuitive principle" is superior to "the arithmetical or logical":

There is a difference between having an opinion, that God is holy and gracious, and having a sense of the loveliness and beauty of that holiness and grace. There is a difference between having a rational judgment that honey is sweet, and having a sense of its sweetness. . . . There is a wide difference between mere speculative rational judging any thing to be excellent, and having a sense of its sweetness and beauty. The former rests only in the head, speculation only is concerned in it; but the heart is concerned in the latter.

In "sense" were united the opposites that "judgment" had distinguished. God's power and his love, logical extremes on which the most diverse sects had been founded and which were turning points of Puritan controversy, were combined by Edwards in his intuition of "the glorious *majesty* and *grace* of God":

> I seemed to see them both in a sweet conjunction; majesty and meekness joined together; it was a sweet, and gentle, and holy majesty; and also a majestic meekness; an awful sweetness; a high, and great, and holy gentleness.

The language of Scripture, Edwards discovered, was not propositional at all, but a functional rhetoric:

> The design of the Spirit of God *does not seem to be to represent God's ultimate end as manifold, but as one.* For though it be signified by various names, yet they appear not to be names of different things, but *various names involving each other in their meaning;* either different names of the same thing, or names of several parts of one whole, or of the same whole viewed in various lights, or in its different respects and relations.

And finally, at his most daring, Edwards maintained that nature as well as the Bible is radically figurative. Within "those metaphors and similes, which to an unphilosophical person do seem so uncouth," were real affinities, for "there is really . . . an analogy or consent between the beauty of the skies, trees, fields, flowers, etc., and spiritual excellencies."

The "images or shadows of divine things" that Edwards collected in a notebook throughout his life were an attempt, as Perry Miller has shown, to find a ground for religious perception without denying the Newtonian universe. Edwards rehabilitated the old typology in a new context. He wished as earnestly as the most cautious of his predecessors to avoid mistaking mere personal fancy for a divinely appointed figure (his reason for this was even more compelling than theirs, since the objectivity of religion could not be established by subjective inventions). Yet at the same time he knew that the types must no longer be confined to Scripture and would have to be extended into Nature, the empirical world of eighteenth-century science, if religion were not to become an isolated mental habit. What he needed was a medium where valid ideas and the data of sense would be inseparable. To this end, he accepted the new principle that all knowledge is derived from experience but proceeded to modify Locke's theory of knowledge out of all recognition. "As Edwards read the new sensationalism, far from setting up a dualism of subject and object, it fused them in the moment of perception. The thing could then appear as concept and the concept as thing." For Edwards, real types existed in the realm of "experience":

Seeing the perfect idea of a thing, is, to all intents and purposes, the same as seeing the thing. It is not only equivalent to seeing it, but it is seeing of it; for there is no other seeing but having an idea. Now, by seeing a perfect idea, so far as we see it, we have it.

But this is only to say that Edwards was a philosophical symbolist. There can be no "doubt whether John Locke would have been altogether happy over his American disciple." The case is not essentially, as Miller would suggest, that of a man who used the philosophy of science to substantiate the philosophy of religion; rather, Edwards was trying to affirm the basic premises of symbolism, which were part of his intellectual tradition, in contemporary terms. His epistemology did not derive from Locke in any fundamental way: he reinterpreted Locke in the light of his epistemology. If he anticipated a post-Kantian like Emerson, as is certainly true, it was because he brought to the sense-world of empiricism a symbolist tradition that Emerson was to rediscover after empiricism had worked itself out. Edwards and Emerson used an old philosophy to reorient the new philosophy. After all, the issue had been defined long before and did not come as an utter novelty, since Puritan method, which embodied the groundwork of symbolism, had equally embodied and illustrated the ways of modern science.

Alexis de Tocqueville in 1831 foresaw the coming vogue of pantheism in America:

If there is a philosophical system which teaches that all things material and immaterial, visible and invisible, which the world contains are to be considered only as the several parts of an immense Being, who alone remains eternal amid the continual change and ceaseless transformation of all that constitutes him, we may readily infer that such a system, although it destroy the individuality of man, or rather because it destroys that individuality, will have secret charms for men living in democracies.

The American principle of human equality, which Tocqueville regarded as the essence of democracy, could lead in two opposite directions. While each individual was independent of all others in the land of the social contract, at the same time he was only a unit in the level mass and secretly yearned to be submerged in humanity. Tocqueville extended this pattern from politics to habits of thought and language. On the one hand, "nothing is more repugnant to the human mind in an age of equality than the idea of subjection to forms. Men living at such times are impatient of figures; to their eyes, symbols appear to be puerile artifices used to conceal or to set off truths that should more naturally be bared to the light of day." Tocqueville reported that he knew no country in which Christianity was emptier of "forms, figures, and observances" than in the United States. Yet, on the other hand, the democratic mind had a passion for generalization, which corresponded to the feeling that individuals differ little from each other, and the American language was marked by "continual use of generic terms or abstract expressions."

Tocqueville was studying *homo americanus* as modern man in his native habitat, and he traced "the philosophical method of the Americans" back to the modern rationalist tradition of "private judgment." In the atomism of society and the repudiation of intellectual forms, in majority rule and the love of generalization, America was the embodiment of ideas that began with the Protestant reformers in the sixteenth century and with Descartes and Bacon in the seventeenth. Tocqueville did not see, however, that the doubleness of American thought was more than an outcome of this rationalist tradition and actually pointed toward a revolt against it. The destruction of individuality by pantheism followed a different method from the subordination of persons to majority opinion and the grouping of ideas under abstract concepts. Pantheism, as Tocqueville's own description intimates, would substitute processes for the individual entities of eighteenth-century logic and politics; the "parts" would be related to the "immense Being" not as members to class but as functions to existence. Although, because of the prevalent individualism, symbolic forms were strikingly absent from American thought, abstract generalization was not the only means of unifying the American world. Side by side with the generic terms of American speech, Tocqueville found unusual ambiguity. One writer after another, by "giving an unwonted meaning to an expression already in use," built up an indeterminate vocabulary. American authors seemed almost never "to dwell upon a single thought" but rather "to aim at a group of ideas."

The issue (though Tocqueville could hardly have been expected to view it in this light) was not only between the extremes of individualism and conformity, the part and the whole, but also between two ways of conceiving individuals and forms, things and their relations. The two worlds over which the Puritans hovered came into open conflict in the early nineteenth century, when the abstract method of modern thought, on which the Puritans unconsciously depended, had completely entered into the texture of American life. Emerson was separated from his conservative critics by more than differences of opinion; as Margaret Fuller said, his mind worked differently from theirs:

They were accustomed to an artificial method whose scaffolding could easily be retraced and desired an obvious sequence of logical inferences. They insisted there was nothing in what they had heard, because they could not give a clear account of its course and purport. They did not see that Pindar's odes might be very well arranged for their own purpose, and yet not bear translating into the methods of Mr. Locke.

The new movement in American philosophy which was beginning about the time of Tocqueville's visit sprang up as a renewed awareness of the functions of language; it was not so much doctrinal as methodological. Emerson and his fellows contended that man was involved in society, ideas in the whole of truth, things in nature, and the mind in its objects, far more profoundly than the methods of Mr. Locke had suggested. The real form of the world was not logical, and the real use of language was not as an artificial framework. Instead, language should inhere in experience and render the fluidity of experience:

> So Speech represents the flowing essence as sensitive, transitive; the word signifying what we make it at the moment of using, but needing life's rounded experiences to unfold its manifold senses and shades of meaning. Definitions, however precise, fail to translate the sense. They confine in defining. . . .

The conventional American mind could only interpret such remarks in terms of its own Lockian nominalism: "Transcendentalism," Noah Porter declared, was "rather unbelief than disbelief. Subtle, refining, symbolizing all living truths and real facts into inert and powerless mythi." Yet to say, as Alcott did, that "the world is but the symbol of mind, and speech a mythology woven of both," was not to reduce truth and fact to a barren subjectivity but to give all the shapes of language an objectivity that men like Porter never thought possible. "Transcendentalism" in this sense could not be escaped even by writers like Melville, Hawthorne, and Poe, who were hostile to its superficial features. As a method, the new philosophy extended beyond the provincial clique which was labeled "transcendentalist" and which stated the theory most fully; for it arose as a function of American life and thought and, more generally, as a function of the modern world.

Even the orthodox rationalist was forced to admit that the issues of the day were on an utterly different plane from the interminable New England controversies of the past. "Certain it is," Francis Bowen wrote in 1837, "that a revolution in taste and opinion is going on among our literary men, and that philosophical writing is assuming a phasis entirely new." The conservatives blamed it all on alien ideas, primarily German idealism and French eclecticism, and reaffirmed their faith in "the mode of philosophizing which has for several generations prevailed among our British ancestors." But actually the new philosophy was thoroughly native, though not in a sense that cuts it off from contemporary thinking. Superficially, it is true, the mid-nineteenth-century intellectual revolution in America was a version of European romanticism and post-Kantian idealism, spiced with the local religious tradition and with Platonic, Neo-Platonic, oriental, and Swedenborgian ideas. Doubtless every speculation of the American "transcendentalists" could be paralleled from Fichte or Schelling or Hegel, from Coleridge or Wordsworth or Carlyle, not to mention the remoter analogues. The movement was proudly dependent on the "usage" of its own day: "The very time sees for us, thinks for us; it is a microscope such as philosophy never had. Insight is for us which was never for any." Yet Emerson is here defining a subtler relationship than imitation, and to put the case in terms of mere "influence" is to miss the point. The American mind fell easily into this usage, and the American writer was an agent of a world-wide process, which was as much his as another's: "Above his will and out of his sight he is necessitated by the air he breathes and the idea on which he and his contemporaries live and toil, to share the manner of his times, without knowing what that manner is." The American shared the manner of his times because his whole history was a modern instance; the intellectual situation of nineteenth-century America was a kind of epitome of modern intellectual conditions. Although Emerson and his colleagues were often simply imitative of romantic and idealistic clichés, their distinction was to have grasped a basic issue of modern thought, in which idealism and romanticism were only an episode. "The movement," Orestes Brownson emphatically declared, "is really of American origin, and the prominent actors in it were carried away by it before ever they formed any acquaintance with French or German metaphysics; and their attach-

ment to the literatures of France and Germany is the effect of
their connexion with the movement, not the cause."

The basic cause lay in a peculiarity of the whole American tradition and not least in the very "mode of philosophizing" which
the orthodox defended. Though the method of Emerson and Alcott
seemed and was a violent departure from eighteenth-century rationalism, the American brand of rationalism had set the stage
for their advent by its own distinctively methodological cast. In
1715 Samuel Johnson, the future president of King's College,
gave up Ramistic logic and was "wholly changed to the New
Learning," to the philosophy of Descartes and Locke, the natural
science of Boyle and Newton. The suddenness of his conversion,
which he noted dramatically at the end of his uncompleted "Technologia," indicates his real motive. Johnson, though in a way a
genuinely speculative man, had no notion of the potential problems raised by the modern philosophy he accepted. He was concerned with systematizing, not with metaphysics, and the first use
to which he put the new learning was to revise his Ramistic "En-
cyclopedia" into another "system of travails of the humane intellect." Jonathan Edwards, who came upon Locke a few years later,
found much more in empiricism than a new logic, but in his case
too the Puritan obsession with logical method was perpetuated
long after the Lockian "way of ideas" had replaced the dialectic
of Ramus:

> One reason why, at first, before I knew other Logick, I used to be
> mightily pleased with the study of the Old Logick, was, because it
> was very pleasant to see my thoughts, that before lay in my mind
> jumbled without any distinction, ranged into order and distributed
> into classes and subdivisions, so that I could tell where they all be-
> longed, and run them up to their general heads.

The secularization of Calvinism, which proceeded throughout the
eighteenth century, was made possible by this continuity between
the old method and the new and by the unsuspecting fashion in
which the Lockian approach was assimilated. In turn, the major
figures of the American Enlightenment were completely indifferent

to the philosophic matrix from which their thoughts emerged: Jefferson's "self-evident" truths were a means of achieving "certainty without metaphysics." By 1800 the philosophy taught in American colleges was almost entirely Lockian, and the political, social, and economic life of the New World was an embodiment of the New Learning; for Tocqueville, in the 1830's, the United States was the country "where the precepts of Descartes are ... best applied." Yet Descartes and Locke and all they stood for had been adopted chiefly as a method, both in theory and in practice; their basic assumptions, their historical derivation, and their skeptical potentialities were largely ignored.

This uncritical commitment to an abstract methodology had both positive and negative results. The uniformity of American character and opinion, which Tocqueville noted as a paradoxical counterpart to the democratic faith in "private judgment," was intensified by the lack of philosophic perspective in America. Since everyone thought in the same way, without asking why, everyone was inclined to think much the same things. Religious controversy, rich in method and poor in substance, became a conventional game. Here is the way a writer in 1839 described the New England habit of mind:

The theology of this school has always been, in a high degree, metaphysical; but the metaphysics is of a Hyperborean sort, exceedingly cold and fruitless. In the conduct of a feeble or even an ordinary mind, the wire-drawing processes of New England theologizing become jejune and revolting. *Taught to consider mere ratiocination as the grand, and almost sole function of the human mind,* the school-boy, the youth, and the professor, pen in hand, go on, day after day, in spinning out a thread of attenuated reasoning, often ingenious, and sometimes legitimately deduced, but in a majority of instances a concatenation of unimportant propositions.

Yet if the dominant strain of American thought, from one point of view, was a method without context and often without content, it was able, by virtue of that very fact, to become extraordinarily flexible. Unitarianism, the end product of New England controversy, found freedom in the exercise of uninhibited reason. The liberalizing effect of the Unitarian movement, as Parrington says, came about as much "because of" as "in spite of its eighteenth-century nurture," for the Unitarians depended so completely on a kind of autonomous rational inquiry that they deprived rationalism of any doctrinal basis:

> They had no creed, and no system of philosophy on which a creed could be, by common consent, built. Rather were they open inquirers, who asked questions and waited for rational answers, having no definite apprehension of the issue to which their investigations tended, but with room enough within the accepted theology to satisfy them, and work enough on the prevailing doctrines to keep them employed. Under these circumstances, they honestly but incautiously professed a principle broader than they were able to stand by, and avowed the absolute freedom of the human mind as their characteristic faith; instead of a creed, the right to judge all creeds; instead of a system, authority to try every system by rules of evidence.

The negative outcome of American rationality was conventional orthodoxy and empty verbalism; its positive result was a consciousness of method that freed the spirit from dogma. The Unitarians reasserted private judgment in a special sense: they emphasized the *act* of inquiry. Their children went further and emphasized the act of experience in all its multiplicity. When the older generation protested against their "mania of tolerance and many-sidedness," the reply was easy: "You must plead guilty for some part of my vagaries. You bade me be a Seeker." There is one continuous movement from the Puritan era through the new learning of Locke to the new philosophy of Emerson. As Brownson declared in his disillusionment, "Protestantism ends in Transcendentalism."

While the native rational method was being transmuted under its own momentum, a still newer new learning—German idealism —finally arrived in the United States. The blindfold was suddenly lifted from American philosophy, and there stood revealed a coherent intellectual trend of modern times which included as an integral part the long-cherished "Mr. Locke." Kantian idealism had a unique impact in America because it called attention to issues that had previously been neglected, though implicit in the very language being used. In this sense the furore of the 1830's and 1840's was not a mere provincial imitation of European transcendentalism. It was an attempt to give body to the problems of modern philosophy. To that end the New England revolutionary fed upon all the scraps of literature and speculation that came his way. Sampson Reed's *Observations on the Growth of the Mind* (Boston, 1826) had "the aspect of a revelation" to Emerson, and one revelation followed another: Coleridge's *Aids to Reflection* and *The Friend*, edited by James Marsh of Vermont (Burlington, 1829 and 1831); Carlyle's early *Edinburgh Review* articles, which were being published about the same time; Victor Cousin's *Introduction to the History of Philosophy*, translated by H. G. Linburg and published at Boston in 1832. When the excited young liberals "rushed into life, certain that the next half century was to see a complete moral revolution in the world," they were partisans not so much of a particular philosophy as of Philosophy itself, and in this respect, as Francis Bowen remarked at the time, the American situation was very different from that in England, where "the taste for metaphysical speculations" had virtually disappeared.

From Descartes to the post-Kantians, technical philosophy had had a skeleton in the closet. The abstractive intellect, whether rationalistic, empirical, or idealist, produced a world neatly divided into the two mutually exclusive categories of mind and matter. But "in between," as Whitehead has said, "there lie the concepts of life, organism, function, instantaneous reality, interaction, order of nature, which collectively form the Achilles heel of the whole system." The characteristically modern "problem of knowledge," the attempt to rejoin what Descartes put asunder, has been the oblique admission that a richer world exists than abstract reason dreams of. The suppressed reality asserted itself in a roundabout way as the question of how knowledge is possible. "Knowledge was not a problem for the ruling philosophy of the Middle Ages; that the whole world which man's mind seeks to understand is intelligible to it was explicitly taken for granted." Man, according to Ramus, who in this respect was sufficiently medieval, "has naturally within him the power to know all things." But Descartes explicitly proposed a method of doubt, since "only those objects should engage our attention, to the sure and indubitable knowledge of which our mental powers seem to be adequate." His "two ultimate classes of real things," which could not be united except externally, raised the extraordinary issue of how he could be certain of anything.

Similarly, Locke found it imperative "to examine our own abilities, and see what *objects* our understandings were, or were not, fitted to deal with," because he assumed that "observation" had two distinct fields, being "employed either, about external sensible objects, or about the internal operations of our minds, perceived and reflected on by ourselves." Locke does not name "the difficulties that rose on every side" as he and his friends sat in his chamber; but his way of resolving them—by a critique of knowledge—was the result of a particular difficulty, which was doubtless at the bottom of those he consciously felt. The Cartesian dualism made the world safe for science by creating separate repositories, called "matter" and "mind," for the scientifically relevant and irrelevant, yet at the same time made it hard to see how even the scientific object could be known. Empirical theory held that the given materials of knowledge are atomistic sensations, passively received and variously combined by the intellect, so that the fulness of subjective life becomes unreal, and, in Hume's words, the "creative power of the mind amounts to no more than the faculty of compounding, transposing, augmenting, or diminishing the materials afforded us by the senses and experience." But the creative power of the mind had its revenge when Hume proved that even the mathematical world of extension, figure, and motion had no claim to objectivity:

It is a question of fact, whether the perceptions of the senses be produced by external objects, resembling them: how shall this question be determined? By experience surely; as all other questions of a like nature. But here experience is, and must be entirely silent. The mind has never anything present to it but the perceptions, and cannot possibly reach any experience of their connexion with objects. The supposition of such a connexion is, therefore, without any foundation in reasoning.

Hume simultaneously gave away his methodology (the true source of his difficulty) and tried to avoid the question of method by declaring that the relation of mind to objects is "a question of fact." Kant's new principle, "that the objects must conform to our mode of cognition," brought the vital question of method into prominence by explicitly reversing Hume's approach. Kant maintains, moreover, that "the primary datum of knowledge is ... the single whole of experience." He is aware that "thoughts without contents are empty, intuitions without concepts are blind. . . . By their union only can knowledge be produced." Yet he sees "no reason for confounding the share which belongs to each in the production of knowledge." Although Kant, by making the mind active instead of passive, brought out in high relief the equivocal position of his forerunners, he himself was committed to a similar equivocation. As James Gibson puts it, "the Kantian theory is dominated throughout by the antithesis between the abstract universal as an object of conceptual thought and a mere manifold of sense impressions; and between these two, as thus opposed, only an artificial and external union is possible." Kant began under the old dispensation with a general picture of two elements, "that which we receive through impressions, and ... that which our own faculty of knowledge ... supplies from itself"; he ended with the conviction that "in the world of sense, however far we may carry our investigation, we can never have anything before us but mere phenomena . . . , the transcendental object remaining unknown to us."

It has never been sufficiently emphasized by historians of American "transcendentalism" that the movement was generally regarded by its exponents as a revaluation of empirical philosophy. "Now the young are oppressed by their instructors," Emerson declared. "Bacon or Locke saw and thought, and inspired by their thinking a generation, and now all must be pinned to their thinking, which a year after was already too narrow for them." Placed in a wider context, Locke seems ignorant of "the meaning of ideas," and "Hume's abstractions are not deep or wise." The founders of the "Transcendental Club," although their positive aims were so vague that they were not even sure how or why they got their name, were sure of one thing: "What we strongly felt was dissatisfaction with the reigning sensuous philosophy, dating from Locke, on which our Unitarian theology was based." Such men viewed their situation in an almost melodramatic manner. Their obsession with the evils of empiricism became a popular joke. They pictured mankind as prisoners of an outworn creed and spoke with "distrust and dread" of Locke's "iron hand":

The notion, that the human soul is but a capacity, more or less extensive, for the reception of impressions to be made upon it by surrounding objects through the external senses, seems to be the darkest, the most deathlike predicament in which humanity could be entrammelled. . . . The worst result of this error is its very general diffusion. *The notion and the language of it pervades* [sic] *all ranks. . . . We may appeal to the current language employed in every-day life,* through the mouth and through the pen, for proof to what an extent this depressing idea prevails of man being passive to surrounding objects.

It was this sense of crisis that enabled the American mind to seize upon the basic problem rather than the results of modern philosophy. Although the absolute reign of Locke had been, as James Marsh said, a "peculiar misfortune" of the United States, it created a situation in which Kant's reversal of approach would have a remarkable poignancy. In America it was startling news that "since the time of Descartes," through Locke, Berkeley, and Hume to Kant and his followers, there had been a continuous problem and that this issue had been "before all a question of the human mind itself":

Can I know? Can I know that I know? What is it, psychologically considered, to know? What is it to know that I know? How do I know? How do I know that I know? These are the problems, and problems very nearly peculiar to modern times.

Ancient philosophy, Brownson informs us, was seldom concerned with such questions, "and the scholastic philosophy, never." The American intellectual turned to Kantian idealism not as the answer to what now seemed "the fundamental problem of human science" but as its "strongest expression." German thought was most patently what the whole modern tradition had been—"not a *ratio essendi,* but a *ratio cognoscendi*"—and the premises of Locke, which had remained unexamined for so long, must now be seen in the perspective of Kant's criticism. In 1803 Locke's *Essay,* according to Samuel Miller, established "an era in the history of metaphysical science," while Kant was obscure and probably inconsistent. By 1848 J. B. Stallo could assert that "the 'Critique of Pure Reason,' though it nowise contains the sought-for axiom of the philosophy of the present, is nevertheless the cabalistic formula that has conjured it up."

The revolt from Locke reinforced the American awareness of method by affording a perspective where the language of empiricism became only a partial language. In history, it was now apparent, system was opposed to system, and one merged into another, so that no method was absolute, though method was the key to it all. At the same time, the concept of method was deepened by the new perspective of history and became something more than the free-floating rationalism of the Unitarians. The clash of Locke and Kant betrayed a basic problem of approach, and one that was still unsettled. In this light the significance of Kant was his own shift of emphasis from dogma to methodology. The American "transcendentalists" dallied with transcendental doctrine but hardly understood it in sufficient detail to become disciples; what they singled out was "the transcendental grammar of the intellect," the Kantian emphasis on form and method. The earliest American historian of modern idealism, James Murdock, noted that Kant's first *Critique* "is not properly a *system* of philosophical knowledge" but "rather an introduction to sound philosophizing." Men like Theodore Parker and Frederick Hedge echoed the distinction. Parker "found most help in the works of Immanuel Kant," but not in Kant's conclusions: "He . . . gave me the true method, and put me on the right road." Hedge attributed the flourishing science and literature of Germany not to the current idealistic theories, which were disappointing, but "to the faculty which that philosophy has imparted of seizing on the spirit of every question, and determining at once the point of view from which each subject should be regarded,—in one word, to the transcendental method."

To take German idealism in this way was to follow the same path as Coleridge, whose aim, as James Marsh pointed out, was "not so much to teach a speculative system of doctrines built upon established premises . . . as to turn the mind continually back upon the premises themselves." By explicitly putting the question of the "conformity" between subject and object, idealism focused attention on the *forming* process and led to Emerson's feeling that "the state of the world at any one time [is] directly dependent on the intellectual classification then existing in the minds of men." And, for Emerson, Kant was the philospher of "intellectual classification":

The Idealism of the present day acquired the name of Transcendental from the use of that term by Immanuel Kant, . . . who replied to the skeptical philosophy of Locke, which insisted that there was nothing in the intellect which was not previously in the experience of the senses, by showing that there was a very important class of ideas or imperative forms, which did not come by experience, but through which experience was acquired; that these were intuitions of the mind itself; and he denominated them *Transcendental* forms.

But what was the premise, the classifying form, of idealism? Emerson's faithful, though simplified, version of the Kantian scheme is chiefly important for the issue it leaves open. Forms do not "come by" experience; are they then imposed upon it externally? What is the locus of form? It was essentially this question that had secretly badgered the seventeenth- and eighteenth-century epistemologists. Kant had corrected the method of his predecessors, but he had not given up the first and most devastating principle of their approach. After all, he fell back on a form that made form itself problematic; he "left reason standing in the face of the schism between subject and object, with the dread conviction that the two were irreconcilable."

A true method must somehow escape this dilemma:

> Spiritualism and materialism both have their foundation in our nature, and both will exist and exert their influence. Shall they exist as antagonist principles? Is the bosom of Humanity to be eternally torn by these two contending factions? . . . Here then is the mission of the present. *We are to reconcile spirit and matter. . . . Nothing else remains for us to do. Stand still we cannot. To go back is equally impossible.*

Behind George Ripley's rhetoric (which was instigated by Brownson) was the feeling stated more formally by Stallo: "The whole theory of two independent factors of existence, Mind and Matter, Force and Inertia, is an absurdity." Since "between the radically hostile there can be no peace," the new point of departure would be the conception of interdependence. For Brownson, "the subject and the object are both given simultaneously in one and the same thought or act." Different systems, from this standpoint, are different forms of the integral reality, different relations between the two elements simultaneously given in all thinking. This was to make the most of the notion of "form" implicit in the Kantian idea of "conformity." Instead of absolute substances, one dealt with "modes of philosophizing" and "orders of thought." While the contemporary psychology texts invariably laid down the proposition that "all existence, as far as human knowledge extends, is either material, or immaterial; corporeal, or spiritual," in Emerson's rephrasing these alternatives become "two modes of thinking," which, since they are both natural, are possibly reconcilable:

As thinkers, mankind have ever divided into two sects, Materialists and Idealists; the first class founding on experience, the second on consciousness; the first class beginning to think from the data of the senses, the second class perceive that the senses are not final, and say, The senses give us representations of things, but what are the things themselves, they cannot tell.

The transformation of dualism into ways of thinking, which were often (in imitation of Coleridge) traced back to Plato and Aristotle, became one of the mannerisms of the time. Here was the conclusion of Alcott's lifelong quest for the "nexus" of mind and matter: "Nature and spirit are inseparable, and are best studied as a unit. . . . The idealist's point of view is the obverse of the naturalist's."

The orthodox opposition, intrenched in its Lockian dogmatism, tried to denounce "the latest form of infidelity" as a doctrinal heresy and was thoroughly bewildered by the real innovation of the movement, the basic shift of standpoint involved. Under the pressure of the conflict between idealism and empiricism, and in an effort to get beyond it, Emerson and others had developed the concept of dialectic. The locus of form was the universe of discourse; the solution to the inherited problem of method was to assume a realm where method and content were one. And dialectic tended in the direction of symbolism. By extending his principle to all points of view, Alcott was able to picture a "spherical" truth and a language constantly expanding in "manifold senses and shades of meaning" as it took on various aspects of the whole. The hostile critics noted that the new school made "little reference . . . to the distinction between matter and spirit." Its aim was to avoid the distinction by returning to a mode of knowledge prior to that separation of the knower from the known which Emerson called "the Fall of Man." To the prelapsarian mind, according to James Marsh, "all things were real." But, as reason supervened upon direct perception, the religious and poetic consciousness could at best attain only "a kind of mental vacillation between the subjective *idea,* and the objective *reality* of the thing believed." The disjunction that logical procedures necessarily make had dissolved the complete realism of the primitive mind, and the intrinsic duality of logic had been translated by modern philosophy into a metaphysical principle. Although Emerson said that this whole development was "very unhappy, but too late to be helped," he and his contemporaries were trying to rescue themselves. The central question, as they saw it, was no longer the external relation between subject and object but rather the internal transmutation of thoroughly realistic forms:

Unless . . . [the mind] have the higher power of divesting itself of all that is peculiar in its acquired forms of thought, and in those conceptions by which it takes cognizance of the objects of its knowledge, of clothing itself anew in the forms of thought peculiar to another people, and of so adopting their conceptions for its own, as to contemplate the world around them under the same relations with them, the man can never participate in their emotions, nor breathe the spirit of their poetry.

The meaning of "knowledge" had been changed from objective certainty to organic experience:

We no longer think of a truth as being laid up in a mind for which it has no affinity, and by which it is perhaps never to be used; but the latent affections, as they expand under proper culture, absolutely require the truth to receive them, and its first use is the very nutriment it affords.

To the conservative mind, Emerson's "Divinity School Address" seemed not only profane but absurdly illogical: "He tells us, that religious sentiment is myrrh, and storax, and chlorine, and rosemary; that the time is coming when the law of gravitation and purity of heart will be seen to be identical." This, perhaps, was poetry, yet a poetry that would not remain safely fanciful and that claimed some odd revelation out of its very extravagance. But to the school of Emerson it was clear that poetic forms bring together terms "which taken literally . . . would give nonsense, or at least bad sense." The habit of organic apprehension was a denial of rational method: the stuff of knowledge was a "fact of consciousness," not a fact. Organic activity issued in organic forms— "not mere *forms continent of* life, but forms which are *formed life*"—and the transmutation of form was potentially hostile to logical distinctions. Logic, from this standpoint, was a kind of slide rule for the immature. When the mind met nature immediately in the act of knowledge, rational structure was superfluous:

> Syllogistic reasoning will be superseded by something higher and better. It amounts to nothing but the discernment and expression of the particulars which go to comprise something more general; and, as the human mind permits things to assume a proper arrangement from their own inherent power of attraction, it is no longer necessary to bind them together with syllogisms.

The conscious aim of these men was to attain a language without particulars. Those who "regard each object in its individual capacity, as a separate, independent existence," are crippled by their own method; one must consider "the relation it bears to other objects, or to some indwelling principle of which it is the exponent." The transmutation of form is possible because the true coherence of divergent formulas is not that "of a merely logical arrangement, but of a natural development, and a growth." The age was beginning to perceive, according to W. H. Channing, "that through all varieties of creeds, through the thousand-fold forms of mythology and theology, through the systems of philosophers and the visions of poets, has spoken more or less audibly one Eternal Word." The new philosophy in America was an attempt to speak in consonance with that self-realizing language. Beneath "the discordant jargon of ten thousand dialects," as Reed said, it postulated "a language not of words, but of things," by which was meant a speech so devoid of artificiality that, while manifesting the mind, it would "lose itself in nature."

IV *Toward Melville: Some Versions of Emerson*

Oh you man without a handle!

H. JAMES, SR., to R. W. EMERSON

Emerson and Melville were the polar figures of the American symbolist movement. Whitman wrote poems in a form that Emerson might have adopted if he had been more consistent with his theory and less aware of its shortcomings. Hawthorne and Poe circle around Melville—not only because, like him, they are given to parading their hostility to all "transcendentalisms, myths & oracular gibberish," but also because in each case ostentatious hostility was only one aspect of a real mixture of attraction and repulsion. If we look for characteristic products of the complex tradition outlined in the preceding chapter, Whitman seems too pure a type; and Hawthorne and Poe, though more deeply involved than they knew, are too far off-center. Emerson and Melville are the poles.

Between them these two ran the gamut of possibilities created by the symbolistic point of view. Emerson represented the upsurge of a new capacity, Melville the relapse into doubt. Emerson was the theorist and advocate, Melville the practicing poet. Emerson embodied the monistic phase of symbolism, the sweeping sense of poetic fusion; Melville lived in a universe of paradox and knew the struggle to implement the claims of symbolic imagination. Yet neither was really an independent agent: their methods were reciprocal, and each entailed the other. Though Melville speaks to us today as Emerson does not, they stand on common ground, which is also common ground with our own sensibility. Melville assumed the ambient idea that Emerson made explicit, and if we feel Melville as one of ours, we must take Emerson into the bargain, whether we like it or not.

When Emerson says that the "perception of symbols" enables man to see both "the poetic construction of things" and "the primary relation of mind to matter," and that this same perception normally creates "the whole apparatus of poetic expression," he is identifying poetry with symbolism, symbolism with a mode of perception, and symbolic perception with the vision, first, of a symbolic structure in the real world and, second, of a symbolic relationship between nature and mind. The religious philosopher and the prophet of self-reliance with whom we are all acquainted was also a literary theorist greatly influenced by the problem of knowledge and a creative artist with a consciously adopted point of view. For him, both in theory and in practice, "the Imagination is Vision," poetic vision "is the perception of the symbolic character of things," and poetic structure, the form of this vision, is attained when the poet "no longer sees snow as snow, or horses as horses, but only sees or names them representatively for those interior facts which they signify."

Given due weight, this recurrent theme goes far to explain the substance and method of Emerson's work, the ultimate aim of which was to force a revision in philosophy that would justify and encourage literature, while at the same time it proposed the poetic outlook as a corrective to traditional metaphysics and epistemology. The crucial turn of his thought can be seen in a passage from *Nature* in which Kant's language is echoed but thrown into new perspective. "The sensual man," says Emerson— and he means the Lockian man—"conforms thoughts to things." But in Emerson's redaction of the Kantian tag it is the *poet* who "conforms things to his thoughts." The poet "impresses his being" upon material nature through symbolic vision, for "he uses matter as symbols" of his own feelings. What Emerson has at heart is not the old opposition of idealism and empiricism but a more general distinction between the canons of symbolism and of logic. The rationalist tradition, of whatever stripe, must make room for and profit by poetic method, which, as he said of the Platonic dialogues, "does not stand on a syllogism, or on any masterpieces of the Socratic reasoning, or on any thesis," but consists in "carrying up every fact to successive platforms and . . . disclosing in every fact a germ of expansion," so that "every word becomes an exponent of nature," and everything we look upon bears "a second sense, and ulterior senses." This world of multiple significance is thoroughly realistic. "The expansions are organic. The mind does not create what it perceives, any more than the eye creates the rose." For if "the poetic construction of things" is evinced in the ambiguity of every object, the "primary relation of mind to matter" appears in the organic experience of which both mind and object are functions.

As philosophy, these Emersonian dicta are often more naïve and create more problems than the "difficulties of a naïve dualism" against which his whole effort was directed. His theory has weight chiefly as a literary program, and his writings survive as literature. Yet his literary theory and practice were limited by the philosophic issues that led him to symbolism. While he gave a new prestige to aesthetic apprehension, he dwelt not on "the arts" but on Art itself; his subject was not the practicing poet but the human being, and Art was "nothing less than the creation of man and nature." While he urged an experimental attitude toward literary form, the "spheral" structure of his own poems and essays remained rudimentary—an immediate confirmation of his abstract monistic dream. Thus our sense of alienation from the Emersonian brand of symbolism is justified to the extent that he himself was remote from the specific possibilities of the *literary* symbol. Although the net effect of his philosophy was to give a new direction to literature by recapturing the sense of an autonomous language of poetry, he himself was more concerned with the other phase of his endeavor, the reorientation of philosophy in the light of poetic method. For him the awareness of "double . . . or . . . quadruple or . . . centuple or much more manifold meaning" did not primarily pose a literary question but suggested an answer to the rationalistic dilemma of his time.

As a result, it did not occur to him, as it did to Melville, to exploit the most exciting quality of modern symbolism—the tension between opposite meanings in paradox and the tension between logical paradox and its literary resolution—even though this very quality was implicit in his own approach. He was interested in reconciliation; and his great, though amiable, failing was too simple a confidence in the power of poetic harmony. Of course, conscious as he was of multiple meaning, Emerson necessarily lived in a universe of inconsistencies:

I affirm melioration. . . . I affirm also the self-equality of nature. . . . but I cannot reconcile these two statements. I affirm the sacredness of the individual. . . . I see also the benefits of cities. . . . But I cannot reconcile these oppositions.

Instead of going on, however, to make the most of paradox, Emerson usually beat a hasty retreat into transcendent unity. In his speculations the Over-Soul was always available in emergencies; in his poems he was seemingly undisturbed by any resistance to metaphoric fusion, being comfortable in the belief that through all diversity

> A subtle chain of countless rings
> The next unto the farthest brings.

A poem like "Brahma" illustrates the limitation of Emerson's symbolism both in substance and in method. Just as the theme asserts a facile harmony of far and near, shadow and sunlight—a world where the slayer, the slaying, and the slain lose all individuality— the technique of the poem rests on the easy assumption that any image will do, that a literary unity can exist without a fully articulated symbolic order.

When this much has been granted, what remains is impressive enough. Modern criticism has turned to Coleridge with the feeling that he aimed in our direction, that he was after something beyond the bounds of romanticism. Emerson, who did not possess Coleridge's knowledge and power of definition, throws another kind of light on the origins of modern taste. His works are like a continuous monologue in which the genesis of symbolism is enacted over and over. Though he never goes far beyond the breaking of the shell, he exemplifies in the most circumstantial way the new sensibility in the act of emergence. Emerson's failing was a lack of literary purposefulness, but his virtue was honesty. For all his absorption in the ineffable One, he was a faithful reporter of multiplicity. "A believer in Unity, a seer of Unity," he wrote, "I yet behold two." The essential drama of his work was the involuntary drama of his mind: the endless fusion and separation of the elements of his world, issuing in the "fragmentary curve" which was the characteristic structure of his essays. This adumbration of symbolic method is parallel to the concept of symbolism, which comes into being on his pages out of the pressure of the past and the needs of the present. It arises in his frank account of "the perpetual tilt and balance" of matter and mind, which urge their claims upon him like "two boys pushing each other on the curbstone of the pavement." Emerson's vision of symbolic reality was achieved out of the heart of a basic conflict of ideas. To follow the involution of his thought is one way of exploring what symbolism is.

The "inconsistency" for which Emerson is often censured was really the source of his power. The case against him has been drawn up by a recent writer as follows:

> The sum of Emerson's inconsistency from the beginning . . . is this: that sometimes the world seemed to him to have independent material existence, colored and interpreted by mind, and sometimes it seemed to him wholly dependent and ideal. He never could entirely make up his mind.

But to put the matter in this way is to miss both his problem and his way of solving it. The whimsical veerings that led him at one time to plump for absolute spirit and at another to acknowledge the independence of nature were actually, as he said, "somewhat better than whim at last," for each extreme was tacitly conditioned by a third view in which both became partial. Behind his fence-straddling was the feeling that the fence was his problem. His attitude was not so much indecisive as experimental, being founded on an acceptance of the intellectual world of his time and a willingness to immerse himself in the destructive element. Emerson was clear enough on the point that modern philosophy had been destructive, whether it led to subjective idealism or the scientific conception of matter. The abstraction of the thinking ego—"the discovery we have made that we exist"—had necessarily drifted into "study of the eyes instead of that which the eyes see," and this interest in the *how* more than the *what* of knowing would eventually be "punished by loss of faculty." To the Greek the world simply "signified . . . Beauty," but the modern, bound up in his theories of knowledge, was increasingly incapable of such direct perception, and "skepticism, alas! signifies sight." On the other hand, the projection of a purely physical nature had made even the study of the eyes irrelevant. Poetry had faltered in minds that made a sharp distinction between the "real" world of objects and the world of value:

> The ancients probably saw the moral significance of nature in the objects, without afterthought or effort to separate the object and the expression. . . . But when science had gained and given the impression of the permanence, even eternity, of nature, . . . the mountain became a pile of stones acted on by bare blind laws of chemistry, and the poetic sense of things was driven to the vulgar, and an effort was made to recal [*sic*] the sense by the educated, and so it was faintly uttered by the poet and heard with a smile.

Emerson did not suppose that the steps of intellectual history could be retraced; given the results of dualism, he tried to think through to the other side. He realized that "the problems to be solved" were "precisely those which the physiologist and the naturalist omit to state." The solution, therefore, must not be by external fiat but by trial and redefinition of the established scheme.

Nature, for instance, sets out from and constantly returns to a formula that seems almost childish in its avoidance of any novel implications:

> Philosophically considered, the universe is composed of Nature and Soul. Strictly speaking, therefore, all that is separate from us, all which Philosophy distinguishes as the NOT ME, that is, both nature and art, all other men and my own body, must be ranked under this name, NATURE.

But the simplistic dualism of this account really acts as a kind of reference point for a repeated shift of stance in which Emerson alters the whole meaning of the terms. Playing behind the commonplace disjunction is another concept, which comes to the surface in a journal entry of 1839:

> If, as Hedge thinks, I overlook great facts in stating the absolute laws of the soul; if, as he seems to represent it, the world is not a dualism, is not *a bipolar unity*, but is *two*, is Me and It, then is there the alien, the unknown, and all we have believed and chanted out of our deep instinctive hope is a pretty dream.

Put to the test, the opposition of Nature and Soul pointed toward the unsolved problem that the naturalist failed to state—"the relation between things and thoughts"—and suggested an answer that was actually a reinterpretation of the problem. The theory of "bipolar unity" transformed the conventional scheme by boring from within, "dualism" itself undergoing a change of meaning. There emerged a new basis for literature out of the wreckage of a system in which, as Emerson declared elsewhere, "poetry had been famished and false." Emerson's favorite term for the undifferentiated reality that persistently arose out of difference was borrowed from Coleridge and Wordsworth: "the marriage of thought and things." In the moment of genuine vision, "the act of seeing and the thing seen, the seer and the spectacle, the subject and the object, are one." The difficulty of maintaining the focus of this conception is obvious, since any statement of "bipolar unity" seems to postulate the very distinction that it denies. Emerson worked the sum over and over, starting from scratch every time. For, as he was perfectly aware, he was running counter to the mental habits of over two centuries, and each reprise of the "double consciousness" ended in the disintegration of two worlds that showed "no ... disposition to reconcile themselves."

This was the case not only because of his ingenuous nature but also because of the very nature of his enterprise. Although Emerson's compelling desire to reduce multiplicity to unity is evident on every page that he wrote, his arguments for identity could not escape the implication of diversity. He was trying to define organic apprehension in rational terms; more particularly, he was trying to describe an ancient way of seeing by means of a modern vocabulary which had been designed to repress it. Inevitably, therefore, he spoke more truly than he himself perhaps intended. He could rehabilitate the monistic power of the symbol only in language that was heavily conditioned by the rational universe from which he departed; he could proceed at all only by a paradoxical method of self-contradiction. Thus by force of circumstance he both stated and illustrated the demands of "concrete fact" in the strictest sense of Whitehead's phrase. The paradoxical "union of opposites" which Whitehead would substitute for the "vicious dualism" of undisciplined abstraction is evident in the interplay of "oneness and otherness" in Emerson's mind. And the theory which is gradually thrown up out of Emerson's "hide-and-seek, blindman's play of Thoughts" reads like a free paraphrase of Whitehead's doctrine. What Emerson calls "intellectual perception," which "severs once for all the man from the things with which he converses," is cognate to the abstractive strain in modern philosophy that Whitehead specifically repudiates. What Emerson calls "affection"—a mode of being in which the mental and the physical are identified without ceasing to be rationally distinguishable—is the counterpart of Whitehead's "occasion of actuality," wherein every dualism of the past is redeemed and finds its place. The focus of Emerson's speculation, and the rationale of his method, is the conception of a present reality from which subject and object are mere abstractions but which, paradoxically, can be defined only by reference to those abstract terms. What he wanted to depict as sheer unity emerged as unity in diversity: "Every fact is related on one side to sensation and on the other to morals." Fact was the keystone of the arch, the hypothetical point at which "the soul passed into nature" and nature into the soul. Through it ran the plane of reality, an "unsolved, unsolvable wonder," but a challenge to definition and an absolute presence in which the old categories became relative.

Using "fact" in another sense, Emerson said that the kind of perception he would advocate was "a continual reaction of the thought classifying the facts, and of facts suggesting the thought." His originality consisted in trying to take his stand precisely at the gateway through which these opposite movements pass. Again, his position is reminiscent of a very modern maneuver, one which would undercut the priorities assumed by idealism and materialism by maintaining that "the knowing relation is an entrance of the mind into external objects, or an entrance of external objects into the mind—whichever way one chooses to put it." By this means "concrete fact" is translated into the activity of knowing; the whole scheme of opposite substances is left behind in a shift of emphasis from substance to event; and the theory of knowledge, the need for which was symptomatic of all that was awkward in Cartesian metaphysics, is reoriented so as to destroy its own *raison d'être*. If Emerson ruefully accepted "the study of the eyes instead of that which the eyes see," he did so only to move the focus of study from the seer to the act of seeing; and from the act of seeing he worked back to the thing seen, which he reinstated as one aspect of the perceptual event. To become "a transparent eyeball" was to *be* nothing and to see all; at the same time "this manner of looking at things transfers every object in nature from an independent and anomalous position without there, into the consciousness." That may be idealism, as Emerson called it, but surely with a significant difference. What was important to him was not so much mind itself as "the habitual posture of the mind—beholding." Though Emerson often wavered, harassed by "a pernicious ambiguity in . . . the term *subjective*," his over-all accomplishment was to speak of ideas and objects in a way that did no violence to the process of vision which presupposed and anticipated both. In his own words,

he does not deny the sensuous fact: by no means; but he will not see that alone. He does not deny the presence of this table, this chair, and the walls of this room, but he looks at these things as the reverse side of the tapestry, as the *other end*, each being a sequel or completion of a spiritual fact which nearly concerns him.

With the proviso that the figures are in constant motion as the mind enters objects and objects enter the mind, it might be said that the tapestry, the field of vision, is Emerson's world. It is a realm in which "*subjectiveness* itself is the question, and Nature is the answer," where the precepts "Know thyself" and "Study nature" become a single maxim.

This is only to add that the *how* of knowledge—the process, the method, the form—is identical with the stuff of knowledge—the bipolar unity of idea and thing. The paradoxical fusion of "concrete fact" is also a unity of structure and content; equally paradoxical, since we always make the distinction, but even more fundamentally unified because mind and matter alike are instinct with form:

There is in nature a parallel unity which corresponds to the unity in the mind and makes it available. This methodizing mind meets no resistance in its attempts. The scattered blocks, with which it strives to form a symmetrical structure, fit. This design following after finds with joy that like design went before. Not only man puts things in a row, but things belong in a row.

Here the primary question is not the locus of form with relation to subject and object but rather the locus of subject and object with relation to a formative process evident in both. Since "Nature works after the same method as the human Imagination," method takes on a kind of autonomy as a becoming in which nature and the imagination participate. Emerson found in this manner of speaking the surest way to point back at the oneness of idea, expression, and object which "the ancients" enjoyed without effort and the lack of which had left the mind in an "alien, ... unknown" world. For, as he asked as though in reply to his friend Hedge, "what is classification but the perceiving that these objects are not chaotic, and are not foreign, but have a law which is also a law of the human mind?" To look at either pole of perception was to discover "the analogy that marries Matter and Mind"—the common structure that made everything in nature "an expression of some property inherent in man the observer" and that gave every "passage in the human soul," every "shade of thought," its predestined "emblem in nature." Reality was neither mental nor material substance but emerging form, and its locus, if one must give it a place, was the act of perception and the act of speech:

The constructive intellect produces thoughts, sentences, poems, plans, designs, systems. It is the generation of the mind, the marriage of thought with nature. ... It is the advent of truth into the world, a form of thought now for the first time bursting into the universe. ...

While this passage may seem to cling to the "idealistic minimum" that Urban finds in any adequate theory of symbolism, what Emerson is trying to emphasize is the symbolic construct per se, quite apart from the premises of idealism. He is concerned, in Cassirer's phrase, with man as "animal symbolicum," not as "animal rationale"; the advent of truth is the growth of a language in which man realizes himself by discovering nature:

> So must we admire in man the form of the formless, the concentrations of the vast. . . . The history of the genesis or the old mythology repeats itself in the experience of every child. He too is a demon or god thrown into a particular chaos, where he strives ever to lead things from disorder into order. Each individual soul is such in virtue of its being a power to translate the world into some particular language of its own; if not into a picture, a statue, or a dance,—why, then, into a trade, an art, a science, a mode of living, a conversation, a character, an influence.

Though human speech was obviously the prototype of this vision of reality as radical symbolism, it was only one mode of the symbolic universe and in a way the least characteristic. Taken in isolation, verbal language withstood the realistic bias of Emerson, his "endeavor to make the exchange evermore, of a reality for a name." It had an arbitrary aspect that lent a certain credibility to eighteenth-century nominalism and that often left Emerson himself with a despairing sense of the "remoteness from the line of things in the line of words." But Emerson's purpose in generalizing his conception of "language" was precisely to compensate for the pull of rationalism on words and things alike. To describe all human activities as "intertranslateable language" was to redefine both reality and speech by putting both in terms of creative activity. "Words," Emerson said, "are also actions," just as "actions are a kind of words." Meaning, in whatever mode, was like "the figure, movement and gesture of animated bodies," where the union of the spiritual with the physical and the submergence of both in sheer activity constitute a "silent and subtle language." Meaning was "not *what*, but *how*," or rather the substance via the manner, like the recapture of being in becoming which Yeats imaged as the chestnut tree, the dancer, and the dance.

Though he dealt in theory, Emerson's whole enterprise had its origin in a state of mind. He had experienced a linguistic fact that made nonsense of rationalism:

There lie the impressions on the retentive organ, though you knew it not. So lies the whole series of natural images with which your life has made you acquainted, in your memory, though you know it not; and a thrill of passion flashes light on their dark chamber, and the active power seizes instantly the fit image, as the word of its momentary thought.

Speech so experienced, as at once sensation and idea, could not be reduced to the status of the arbitrary sign. Language, the "quite wonderful city which we all help to build," was greater than the builder, claiming a kind of wisdom of its own:

Each word is like a work of Nature, determined a thousand years ago, and not alterable. We confer and dispute, and settle the meaning so and so, but it remains what it was in spite of us. The word beats all the speakers and definers of it, and stands to their children what it stood to their fathers.

Meaning was the unchangeable potentiality of a word; what we call change of meaning was an alteration of the perceiving mind and the objective world:

The great word Comparative Anatomy has now leaped out of the womb of the Unconscious. I feel a cabinet in my mind unlocked in each of these new interests. Wherever I go, the related objects crowd on my Sense and I explore backward, and wonder how the same things looked to me before my attention had been aroused.

Such passages of linguistic psychology are the trail left by a new mode of thought, which really demanded poetic utterance and could be fully conveyed only as a new poetic manner. What Emerson tried to render as metaphysical doctrine, and expressed more adequately by his very ambiguity of statement, was the resurgent capacity for symbolic experience, based on a peculiar sense of the inherent power of language.

Given this perspective, he moves back and forth from self-expression to impression, from language as the power of mind to language as the potentiality of nature. For him, "the seer is a sayer" and "that which cannot externize itself is not thought"; the word conveys "what I am and what I think ... in spite of my efforts to hold it back." On the other hand, "nature is a language, and every new fact that we learn is a new word"; nature is a network of significant relations, so that the writer is also a reader. Although once again Emerson finds it necessary to invoke "Mind" and "Nature" in order to state a view that dissolves them, each partial statement entails the whole truth: that language is both self-expression and impression, that speech fundamentally refers neither to a preconception nor to an external thing but "to that which is to be said." Thus the old landmarks are relocated in the Emersonian landscape. The section in *Nature* on "Language," which sets forth the "threefold degree" in which "nature is the vehicle of thought," assumes a point of view from which each term—"nature," "vehicle," and "thought"—gives the others a new implication. Emerson begins with words as "signs of natural facts"; but when he goes on to say that "particular natural facts are symbols of particular spiritual facts" and that "nature is the symbol of spirit," natural fact in the sense of his first proposition no longer exists, the instrumental sign becomes an autonomous symbol, and spirit is simply the meaning of fact as symbol.

This position is oddly circular, for it both entails and assumes a theory of poetry. Emerson rightly supposed that his new sense of language was a rediscovery of poetic method: the "Namer or Language-maker" was distinctively the poet. What he said of language in general could be said even more precisely of poetic speech, which expressed the poet's thought, "but *alter idem*, in a manner totally new," while at the same time the expression was "the new type which things themselves take when liberated." Just as the kind of perception in which Emerson was interested turned out to be a verbal intuition, inherently meaningful language was essentially the poetic word:

The poet names the thing because he sees it, or comes one step nearer to it than any other. This expression or naming is not art, but a second nature, grown out of the first, as a leaf out of a tree.

On the other hand, Emerson was most at home on the plane where philosophy and literature, science and art, are equally symbolic, and he justified his feeling that poetry is the essence of speech by the generalization that all true speech is poetic creation. He turned the tables on his predecessors and laid the groundwork for a conscious literary symbolism by assuming that all men, even Locke, are potential poets. The "progress of metaphysical philosophy," he suggested, was really "the progressive introduction of opposite metaphors":

Thus the Platonists congratulated themselves for ages upon their knowledge that Mind was a dark chamber whereon ideas like shadows were painted. Men derided this as infantile when they afterwards learned that the Mind was a sheet of white paper whereon any and all characters might be written.

This generalization was bolstered by the apparent fact that "poetry preceded prose, as the form of sustained thought." All language was patently "fossil poetry ... made up of images or tropes, which now, in their secondary use, have long ceased to remind us of their poetic origin." It followed that the objectivity of rational speech was an aberration, a distortion of the universal poetry. The basic division of mankind lay between those who speak "*from without*, as spectators merely," and those who "speak *from within* ... as parties and possessors of the fact"—between those, as Emerson liked to say, who "speak about things" and those who "speak the things themselves." Here was the necessary counterweight to the rational orthodoxy of the modern tradition, as well as the sanction for a thoroughgoing symbolistic method in literature. Emerson found a new philosophic standpoint in the language of poetry, one that left the rationalist out on a limb, and at the same time he gave the language of poetry a new standing by reasserting the basic poetry of language. To feel the world as "two, ... Me and It," had reduced poetry to "a pretty dream"; to turn about and feel the world as poetry gave dreams themselves "a poetic truth and integrity" as symbolic constructs: "My dreams are not me; they are not Nature, or the Not-me: they are both. They have a double consciousness, at once sub- and ob-jective."

It was just this resort to a generic symbolism that drew Emerson away from the specific problems of poetic art. In proportion as he dwelt on the heights where "all becomes poetry," thus establishing the symbolistic point of view, he lost touch with the practical conditions of poetic creation, which demand that the symbol be not only *found* but also *made*. For him, the poet's "expression or naming" was "not art, but a second nature." Instead of reflecting that the "first" nature, the material world, might well force a degree of art upon the poet, Emerson held that the "second" grows out of the "first" involuntarily, "as a leaf out of a tree." And he went on to maintain, as well as he could, that the order should be reversed—that the poet's unitary act of naming is really prior to the divisive language of common sense—although in the end he was still left with a "double consciousness, at once sub- and ob-jective." Emerson achieved his own aim only to the extent that he managed to represent the double consciousness as unified, not as a duality which must be forged into unity. While he was prepared to admit that poetic creation involves "a mixture of will, a certain control over the spontaneous states...a strenuous exercise of choice," his theory really left the poet no room for decision. The poet was a maker only in the sense that "perception makes"; the given "word" was literature itself rather than the raw material of literature; there was no need to build any tighter symbolic structure than such words impose upon themselves.

What is extraordinary about Emerson's writings is the way in which the problems he tried to ignore rose up again to dog him, lending a richer texture and content to his work. His flagrant inconsistency of method and the paradoxicality that he could never exclude from his theory were the product of his own encounter with the making of literature and with the claims of diversity upon every concrete fact. What is even more important is the seminal effect of his point of view, or of the kind of thinking illustrated by it: the way his facile generalizations, which were intended as philosophic answers, communicated a new set of questions to the literary mind. While he spoke of the world as two only in order to suggest how it might be one, he thereby acknowledged a duality which is no less real because it is conquered in each instant of poetic speech. Emerson made way for a mode of writing which would dwell on the bipolarity of unity; in which "every act, every thought, every cause, is bipolar, and in the act is contained the counteraction. If I strike, I am struck; if I chase, I am pursued." He laid the groundwork for Melville, who freely accepted the ambiguity of the process by which "the artist informs himself in efforming matter." Emerson implied Melville, not as premise and conclusion, but as intuition is pregnant with the possibilities of new experience.

Emerson's more immediate follower, Thoreau, was closer to the master's doctrine and method. Thoreau held and acted upon the Emersonian view that the perceiver and the thing perceived, the thought and the word and the object, are one in the moment of perception and speech. His characteristic form, like Emerson's, was the fortuitous order of the journal, an autonomous series of visionary events. His theory took its departure from "the marriage of the soul with Nature," as opposed to the independent mind or pure object of the scientist:

I think that the man of science makes this mistake, and the mass of mankind along with him: that you should coolly give your chief attention to the phenomenon which excites you as something independent on you, and not as related to you. The important fact is its effect on me. He thinks that I have no business to see anything else but just what he defines the rainbow to be, but I care not whether my vision of truth is a waking thought or dream remembered, whether it is seen in the light or in the dark. It is the subject of the vision, the truth alone, that concerns me. The philosopher for whom rainbows, etc., can be explained away never saw them. With regard to such objects, I find that it is not they themselves (with which the men of science deal) that concern me; the point of interest is somewhere *between* me and them (*i.e.* the objects).

Thoreau's antidote for the disease of his "conscious age" was "unconsciousness," vision per se, "the absence of the speaker from his speech." Language was not to be statement but interjection: "Essentially your truest poetic sentence is as free and lawless as a lamb's bleat." And in practice he attained something of this quality. His conversation, as Emerson noted, was "a continual coining of the present moment into a sentence." His journals, the daily record of his "vision of truth," are a kind of serial story, not so much autobiography as sheer discourse, which is always "to be continued."

Since Thoreau's "point of interest," in theory and practice, was the unity of absolute perception, and since he was ultimately indifferent, as he said, to its mental or physical conditions, he took over the Emersonian doctrine, broadly speaking, in the Emersonian spirit. Yet if Emerson himself was unable to keep the faith, Thoreau was a good deal less so. Though he advocated and tried to achieve a mode of speech from which the speaker, as such, would be absent, he found that the act of experience and utterance was always more complex:

I only know myself as a human entity, the scene, so to speak, of thoughts and affections, and am sensible of a certain doubleness by which I can stand as remote from myself as from another. However intense my experience, I am conscious of the presence and criticism of a part of me which, as it were, is not a part of me, but spectator, sharing no experience, but taking note of it, and that is no more I than it is you.

Emerson had said much the same thing: "A poem, a sentence, causes us to see ourselves. I be, and I see my being, at the same time." Thoreau's journals, though in a large sense they exist simply as a voice and a vision, are full of the independent "I," the speaker and spectator, who observes the real "I," the unconscious experience. His method is similar with respect to the independent object.

Just as Emerson locates symbolic reality by reference to an external nature which he finally denies, Thoreau can render his vision and his speech only as the perpetual conquest of an alien world. For him, "every walk is a sort of crusade ... to go forth and reconquer this Holy Land from the hands of the Infidels." He would like his progress to be "sauntering" (he derives the word from the journey "à la Sainte Terre"), but what should be unconscious action, the sheer advent of reality, becomes a purposeful program in an attempt to meet the "men of science" on their own ground. Having been invited by the Association for the Advancement of Science to fill out a questionnaire on his work, he reflects "how absurd" it is that "though I probably stand as near to nature as any of them, and am by constitution as good an observer as most, yet a true account of my relation to nature should excite their ridicule only!" This hostility affects him; his writing, explicitly or by implication, is always polemic and never, as he doubtless would wish, blandly indifferent to the assumptions of the enemy. Moreover, in trying to carry out the method of Emerson, he comes up against the inherent paradox of any symbolistic program: the fact that it must, as a program, stand outside the symbolic intuition. Thoreau really cannot deal with "the vision, the truth alone." He must also deal with the subject and object which the vision lies "between." He cannot merely feel and speak, losing himself and nature in the experience and the word. Instead, he must render the emergence of vision and the genesis of speech out of the given elements of rational method. Here, if he sees no farther than Emerson, he sees more clearly, since he is trying to give a practical form to the impractical counsels of his friend. Thoreau is extremely aware that what he can present is not absolute experience but a relative fact—"my relation to nature."

In one way this awareness probably contributed to the disintegration of his visionary power. As he knew, his later journals were increasingly those of an amateur naturalist. "Once I was part and parcel of Nature; now I am observant of her." To admit the relativity of the absolute is the first step toward a purely objective method, which "turns the man of science to stone." Taken another way, however, his relativism had a very different implication. When Thoreau ostensibly grants that the absolute of perception is after all relative, he is actually trying to maintain that the relativity of perception is the absolute. Though he could not wholly dispense with the dual substances of rationalism, he gave them a subordinate status by insisting paradoxically that the true starting point was their relationship. And his approach thus became an experiment with possible relations:

> Sometimes I would rather get a transient glimpse or side view of a thing than stand fronting to it. . . . The object I caught a glimpse of as I went by haunts my thoughts a long time, is infinitely suggestive, and I do not care to front it and scrutinize it, for I know that the thing that really concerns me is not there, but in my relation to that. That is a mere reflecting surface.

Emerson had said that "it is the angle which the object makes to the eye which imports." Thoreau tried to confute the scientist, who dared "to look at Nature directly," by varying the angle of vision and looking "with the side of his eye." At best, the scientific object was a convenient locus, reflecting the "intellectual ray" in all directions, and the scientific attitude was but one angle in the variable "intention of the mind and eye." But the realm of truth was the plenum of all angles, all the possibilities of relation to which science put an arbitrary end by isolating an unrelated thing. The poetic vision was like the reflection of the hill in the pond, which seemed to be an image that might be obtained from an external point of view but actually existed only in the relatedness of pond and hill. Poetry differed from naturalism as the relational from the substantive: "More or other things are seen in the reflection than in the substance."

Even more was to be seen in the description than in the perception. Scientific language consisted of external measurement:

> In a sense you have got nothing new thus, for every object that we see mechanically is mechanically daguerreotyped on our eyes, but a true description growing out [of] the perception and appreciation of

it is itself a new fact, never to be daguerreotyped, indicating the highest quality of the plant,—its relation to man,—of far more importance than any merely medicinal quality that it may possess, or be thought to-day to possess.

In dwelling on the priority of relation over substance, Thoreau was working toward a definition of the creative word. Poetry expressed neither the knower nor the known but their relationship, which was knowledge. The "most poetic" name of an object, he said, is given by the man "whose life is most nearly related to it, who has known it longest and best." Conversely, "with the knowledge of the name comes a distincter recognition and knowledge of the thing." Once named, "that shore is . . . more describable, and poetic even." Such formulations cut much deeper than his hyperbolical plea for a language like an animal cry. Thoreau was contending that his "affirmations or utterances," which came to him "ready-made,—not fore-thought," embodied the inherently relational essence of himself and nature. The fact that these expressions were involuntary did not make them easy: "Much verse fails of being poetry because it was not written exactly at the right crisis. . . . It is only by a miracle that poetry is written at all." But the labor of the poet consisted, as it were, in striving toward the moment when all labor is vain—when "the sense outruns and overflows the words"—when "it is not in man to determine what his style shall be" any more than "what his thoughts shall be." This moment, which was the nexus of man and nature, was greater than either. It was also greater than the individual man, for meaning was inherently social: "The lecturer will read best those parts of his lecture which are best heard." The recurrent theme of Thoreau's essay on Carlyle is the "tyrannous, inexorable meaning" which is not so much the result of Carlyle's method as identical with it and which must, in a way, be understood before the books make sense. The genesis of speech was participation in that absolute meaning, not a priori definition or inductive labeling. The true word was true to man and nature because, even as they made it by coming into relationship, it anticipated them.

Thoreau, like Emerson, gravitated toward an idealistic monism. "My thought," he said, "is a part of the meaning of the world, and hence I use a part of the world as a symbol to express my thought." Meaning was another name for the World Spirit. What is more important, however, and what Thoreau perhaps brings out more clearly than Emerson, is another side of the picture, in which the aim of their theory was not to accommodate speech to an absolute idealism but rather to establish the relativity of language as the most absolute of facts and as the resolution of all rival absolutes. When Thoreau complains that "in all the dissertations on language, men forget the language that is, that is really universal, the inexpressible meaning that is in all things and everywhere, with which the morning and evening teem," his originality lies in the very assumption that language "is" and that reality is synonymous with "meaning." In pointing out this universal symbolism, of course, it was possible to go to the other extreme and overlook the language of men. Thoreau says that the meaning is "inexpressible"; and according to him the time will come when "the present *languages,* and all that they express, will be forgotten." But he is thinking to more purpose when he identifies human speech with "the language that is," when he declares that "types almost arrange themselves into words and sentences as dust arranges itself under the magnet." For him the natural type and the human word are not simply analogous. The object becomes a symbol in being verbalized; intimate knowledge and deep experience "originate a word." At the same time, the word is meaningful through its consonance with natural fact; the Musketaquid "is no more *meandering* than the Meander is *musketaquidding.*" The whole theory of universal language was one way of putting the paradoxical relativity and absoluteness of speech, which Thoreau also described under the rubric of "correspondence." To speak of "the perfect correspondence of Nature to man" was to assert "something more than association"—was to say that objects affect the poet as language and that the linguistic relation is absolute.

It is this metaphysical bias that motivates Thoreau's more extravagant statements, which otherwise amount to no more than sheer bravado. When he says that "we have a waterfall which corresponds even to Niagara somewhere within us," his tone is exaggerated, but he will stand behind every word. The crux is the ultimate status of the "waterfall," which truly exists only when we "get rid of what is commonly called *knowledge*" and cultivate "a total apprehension." Thoreau identifies knowing and doing. "Who shall distinguish," he asks, "between the *law* by which a brook finds its river, the *instinct* [by which] a bird performs its migrations, and the *knowledge* by which a man steers his ship around the globe?" If knowing is a kind of activity, knowledge in the old sense is intrinsically false, for "a man can hardly be said to be *there* if he knows that he is there, or to go there if he knows where he is going." It follows that the waterfall is not a "literal" fact with a "figurative" meaning, since Thoreau has left no room for this traditional distinction. The waterfall is a radically symbolic fact of both nature and thought, body and mind. What Thoreau called his "point of interest," therefore, midway between subject and object, could be defined more positively as a point of meaning; "to be interesting," for him, is "to be significant." He applies this approach not only to the relation of thought and thing but also to the parallel relation between mind and body. "The poet's words are, 'You would almost say the body thought!' I quite say it." He can say it because he has come to regard both the mental and the physical as functions of "life," which in turn he identifies with poetic speech. "Whatever things I perceive with my entire man," he declares, "those let me record, and it will be poetry. The sounds which I hear with the consent and coincidence of all my senses, these are significant." The reality of significance, finally, is "mythological." The gist of Thoreau's program lies in two sentences: "I would so state facts that they shall be significant, shall be myths or mythologic. Facts which the mind perceived, thoughts which the body thought,—with these I deal." Myth is the omnibus term for the linguistic fact in which mind and matter, spirit and flesh, are forever reaching identity and which is equally distinct from scientific objectivity and romantic egoism:

> A fact truly and absolutely stated is taken out of the region of common sense and acquires a mythologic or universal significance. Say it and have done with it. Express it without expressing yourself. See not with the eye of science, which is barren, nor of youthful poetry, which is impotent.

Myth was the organic principle. Thoreau, like his master Emerson, translated knowledge, language, man, and the universe from mechanical to organic terms. He took the living process of poetic apprehension as the norm of knowledge and identified this organic awareness with reality itself. Oddly enough, such magnification of poetry could only minimize the poetic work. In its most general form the concept of organism obviated any need for literature:

> My life has been the poem I would have writ,
> But I could not both live and utter it.

Having achieved an "allegorical" life, where incidents were "like myths or passages in a myth," he seemed to have anticipated in the spontaneous language of event whatever might be haltingly rendered in the chosen words of the literary artifact.

Yet the organic world, though it led to a literary abdication, was a colossal image of the ideal poem. On this subject Emerson was more effective than Thoreau:

> See how cunningly constructed are all things in such a manner as to make each being the centre of the Creation. You seem to be a point or focus upon which all objects, all ages concentrate their influence. Nothing past but affects *you*. Nothing remote but through some means reaches *you*. Every superficial grain of sand may be considered as the fixed point round which all things revolve, so intimately is it allied to all and so truly do all turn as if for it alone.

Emerson describes a kind of existential poem, which, while in a sense it makes all lesser poems irrelevant, provides at the same time a rationale for the practicing artist. It provides him not only with a structural pattern but also with a status and function; for the man who can see the world of symbolic foci is himself an element in the universal poem—"a point or focus upon which all objects, all ages, concentrate their influence." Poetic man, the seer, is an instance of the structural principle which pervades his vision. It is by virtue of his power of vision that he occupies a unique place in the universal organism. The exercise of vision is a mode of being: "*so to be* is the sole inlet of *so to know.*" But human being is distinctive in that it is really the becoming of the entire structure of which mankind, from another standpoint, is a part. While all things are potential centers of the world, man is the center of centers. "He is placed in the centre of beings, and a ray of relation passes from every other being to him. And neither can man be understood without these objects, nor these objects without man." Man, who from one point of view is a function of the cosmic structure, is unique because through him issues the whole relational world. He is "a bundle of relations, a knot of roots, whose flower and fruitage is the world." If the organic universe is the soil in which he grows, it is also, simultaneously, the product of his growth. It is both presupposed and created by the poetic activity of man.

The argument is frankly circular. It is no less paradoxical, in the final analysis, than Emerson's other attempts to formulate a world without absolute distinctions between man and nature, subject and object, the knower and the known. It serves, nevertheless, to remove the whole problem to another realm of discourse, where old preconceptions are less of a drag. Man, on this theory, is not essentially a mind dealing with alien matter; on the contrary, the human being begins where this disjunction ends, for he is defined as "the point wherein matter and spirit meet and marry." The organic principle hinges on the conception of a total man, without whose central presence as the vehicle of all becoming the world would collapse into the opposite poles of rationalism: "A man should know himself for a necessary actor. A link was wanting between two craving parts of nature, and he was hurled into being as the bridge over that yawning need, the mediator betwixt two else unmarriageable facts." So considered, man and the universe transcend the rational categories. Though Emerson continues to speak of "mind" and "matter," his basic scheme is really independent of those antonyms, being concerned with the mutual dependence of an organic creature and its environment.

These merge into each other; the figure of man is blurred and fluctuating. What seems at first an external relation between thought and the objects of thought turns out to be a single activity, more on the order of "sex, nutriment, gestation, birth, growth." The concept of mind gives way to the concept of organic function:

> The intelligent mind is forever coming into relation with all the objects of nature and time, until from a vital point it becomes a great heart from which the blood rolls to the distant channels of things, and to which, from those distant channels, it returns.

Even when Emerson falls back on a more conventional vocabulary, the old terminology is wrenched and modified by his new assumptions. The "mind" he invokes is not mental substance but a kind of behavior: "to think is to act." Mind is not divisible into areas like perception, knowledge, and will, but appears as a process where "each becomes other." And even this functional definition is ultimately inadequate, for "it is by no means action which is the essential point, but some middle quality indifferent both to poet and to actor, and which we call Reality.... Not action, not speculation imports, but a middle essence common to both." What is common to poetry and action, though indifferent to poet and actor, is the advent of meaning. Man, whether in thought or deed, is no more than the "faculty of reporting"; the universe is "the possibility of being reported." In the report itself, in poems and arts and systems, the human faculty and the universal possibility both become actual.

Thus Emerson gave the poet a role by transforming man and the universe out of all recognition. In his effort to shake off any links with the rational world view, he projected a world in which only symbols exist. We ourselves, from his standpoint, "are symbols," and we "inhabit symbols." The poetic image is identical not only with the universe it generates but also with the human being through whom it is actualized: "The value of a trope is that the hearer is one: and indeed Nature itself is a vast trope, and all particular natures are tropes." Emerson asserts, in effect, the identity of "I mean" and "it means"; he maintains that there is no distinction between the poet's act of "meaning," the poet himself, and the "meaning" of things. According to him, "a man is a method, a progressive arrangement, a selecting principle." To symbolize is man's function, but to symbolize is to *become* a symbol, into which, as a momentary mold, "the world is poured like melted wax." In this light the radically symbolic status of a poem is merely another way of viewing the symbolic structure it exhibits. Whatever one may think of Emerson's free and easy way with logic, his theory enables him to speak with equal assurance, and simultaneously, of the *why* and the *what* of literature, for it treats both of these questions as a single question of method. Emerson's reply to *why?* and *what?* is always *how.* He always returns to the realm of form, where "this refers to that, and that to the next, and the next to the third, and everything refers"—where the end and the essence of humanity are its formation and its formative power, so that "the delight that man finds in classification is the first index of his Destiny." Prior to the individual "thought" and "object" is the formal principle, which is the same whether we move from idea to thing or from one thing to another:

I notice that I value nothing so much as the threads that spin from a thought to a fact, and from one fact to another fact, making both experiences valuable and presentable, which were insignificant before, and weaving together into rich webs all solitary observations.

145

The real implication of the organic theory, and, by the same token, the only scheme that would fully undercut the assumptions of rationalism, was a world of form, for this radical formalism did away with all static individuals. Here there was no substance upon which a form might be *imposed;* no thinking subject or isolated object of thought. Instead, one dealt in a web of meaning where the symbol—thought, word, or thing; the knower or the known—was a momentary point round which a whole took shape and which, in turn, received the delegated efficacy of the whole:

> The metamorphosis of Nature shows itself in nothing more than this, that there is no word in our language that cannot become typical of us of Nature by giving it emphasis. The world is a Dancer; it is a Rosary; it is a Torrent; it is a Boat; a Mist; a Spider's Snare; it is what you will; and the metaphor will hold, and it will give the imagination keen pleasure. Swifter than light the world converts itself into that thing you name, and all things find their right place under this new and capricious classification.

The sphere of meaning, perpetually redefined by its evanescent center, was simultaneously the milieu and the content of the work of art. In one dimension the artifact was itself a symbol, source and product of universal form: "A work of art is an abstract or epitome of the world." In another dimension it was the plenum of all symbols, since its meaning was unrestricted short of the entire universe.

This is the heart of Emerson's theory, the basic formula from which stem both its defects and its possibilities. By leveling the distinction between the "internal" structure and the "external" relations of the poem, so as to picture a spontaneous dance of self-determining and autonomous symbols, he left no means of control, evaluation, or limitation. On the other hand, his primary motive was certainly not the encouragement of artistic irresponsibility. He wanted to account for the psychological facts of creation, which otherwise he could only point at by alleging "the identity of the observer with the observed." It is a matter of experience that the poet *entertains* his vision of reality; he "suffers the intellect to see"; he undergoes "not instruction, but provocation." This is the differentia of the poetic attitude, and it seems to presuppose a distinctive kind of world. What that world might be is suggested by the further fact that such entertainment occurs as a formative process. Indeed, it could be defined as a state to which the two elements predicated by reason, the subject and the object, are inapplicable because they are always in process of formation; the growth of the vision is precisely the growth of the seer and the seen. "A man never sees the same object twice: with his own enlargement the object acquires new aspects." Emerson's theory is the metaphysical statement of this poetic psychology—the projection of a world of form to explain the formative essence of poetry.

It follows that there is little point in asking whether his doctrine is ontologically true. The useful question to ask is where the doctrine leads. Emerson is the appointed apologist of the symbolistic writer. His theory, partial as it is, establishes certain assumptions which any writer makes to a greater or lesser degree; it corresponds, by virtue of its very partiality, to the symbolist's obsession with the differentia of literature. The metaphysical structure which Emerson projects, circling round the figure of a man who "cannot help seeing everything under its relations to all other things and to himself," is readily translated into stylistic terms. When he declares that "there is no fact in nature which does not carry the whole sense of nature," that "the entire system of things gets represented in every particle," he is defining synecdoche. When he says that "experience identifies," that nature is "*one thing and the other thing,* in the same moment," he is describing metaphor. In practice, the self-realization of the symbolic universe is "Rhetoric, or the Building of Discourse."

The house of Rhetoric is built without logical mortar. Emerson postulates another binding force, which works through the collocation of words and thereby "gives . . . value to all the stones." He calls for a poem that shall thrill the world by the mere juxtaposition and interaction of lines and sentences that singly would have been of little worth and short date. Rightly is this art named Composition, and the composition has manifold the effect of the component parts. . . . The collated thoughts beget more, and the artificially combined individuals have in addition to their own a quite new collective power. The main is made up of many islands, the state of many men, the poem of many thoughts, each of which, in its turn, filled the whole sky of the poet, was day and Being to him.

As the last sentence suggests, the rhetorical unity of one part with another presupposes and makes possible the inherent reference of each part to the whole. Juxtaposition is a way of indicating a basic continuity, whereby every element is subject to a complete redefinition in the light of each of the others, so that (and because) each is a means of stating the whole. Or, to put the matter in another way, rhetorical structure has no finite elements. What is given in rhetoric is not a logical term, a "bounded fact," but a symbol which is really an expanding sphere presented at a "point where its rays converge to a focus." So regarded, each "noun of the intellect" or "fact of nature"—however one chooses to describe it—possesses "a double, treble, or centuple use and meaning." (This need not be consciously recognized in order to exist: "A man may find his words mean more than he thought when he uttered them, and be glad to employ them again in a new sense.") Art is habitual concentration on symbols, each of which is "the absolute Ens seen from one side":

It is the habit of certain minds to give an all-excluding fulness to the object, the thought, the word they alight upon, and to make that for the time the deputy of the world. These are the artists, the orators, the leaders of society. The power to detach and to magnify by detaching is the essence of rhetoric in the hands of the orator and the poet. This rhetoric, or power to fix the momentary eminency of an object . . . depends on the depth of the artist's insight of that object. . . . For every object has its roots in central nature, and may of course be so exhibited to us as to represent the world.

Thus there is, as it were, no real question as to how the "parts" of a literary work become coherent. The literary term, by nature, includes and is included by its context, so that it is not a "part" in the same sense as a logical entity. Synecdoche is the principle by which the whole is vested in one of its aspects, and the term exists; metaphor is the principle by which "the world converts itself into that thing you name," and the whole exists. As Emerson notes, "poetry seems to begin in the slightest change of name," for this is the beginning of the combined detachment and magnification, derivation and imposition of meaning, which simultaneously establish the rhetorical unit and the rhetorical whole. The completed poem is a kind of movement, a progressive metamorphosis, of the total work and of each constituent term.

"Why should we write dramas, and epics, and sonnets, and novels in two volumes? Why not write as variously as we dress and think?" In setting forth the symbolistic ideal of a language where "every word . . . is million-faced," Emerson was proposing not an escape from form but an exploitation of the distinctive formal resources of literary speech. Yet Emerson had a theory of poetry which eliminated the particular poem, since it provided no means of halting the proliferation of metaphor and synecdoche. The poem he described, constructed wholly on the principles of multiple meaning, was chimerical. He himself could believe in its existence only because he was always able, given his premises, to slip from the "world" of the poem to the world at large. In any individual case, for the very reason that it *was* individual, an attempt to live up to his doctrine necessarily would lead to the difficulty he seems to have experienced—where, "if we go to affirm anything, we are checked in our speech by the need of recognizing all other things, until speech presently becomes rambling, general, indefinite, and merely tautology." In practice the most radically formalistic of literary doctrines was conducive to literary anarchy. Emerson would have liked to contend that, although "our tuition is through emblems and indirections, . . . there is method in it, a fixed scale and rank above rank in the phantasms." But nothing in his doctrine gave him a right to say this. He had destroyed the concept of fixity and with it the concept of hierarchy: his poet "derives as grand a joy from symbolizing the Godhead or his universe under the form of a moth or a gnat as of a Lord of Hosts." As an attack on the idea of intrinsically "poetic" material, this notion has its measure of validity. It implies a fundamental theme of modern aesthetics—that the work of art establishes a scale of value through formal means and does not depend on any external standard. Emerson, however, tries to do without the very concept of externality. He goes further and maintains that "the truth-speaker may dismiss all solicitude as to the proportion and congruency of the aggregate of his thoughts, so long as he is a faithful reporter of particular impressions." On this showing, the poem can establish no scale of value because it is wholly fluid, changing its shape as it moves from point to point. The symbolistic work is saved from such complete indeterminacy by the struggle to melt and reorder accepted distinctions; this intrinsic bond with the rational world gives the poem a focus. When Emerson projects a totally poetic universe, he deprives himself of any brake on the transmutation of form.

In general, then, while Emerson defines the presuppositions of a symbolistic literature, he does so in such a way as to make any literature impracticable. Thoreau's ultimate preference for the art of life over the life of art is only one symptom of the basic inadequacy of a purely symbolistic doctrine, which aims at creating a literature faithful to the status and form of sheer experience, but must finally settle for experience, not literature. Matthew Arnold's commendation of Emerson might be modified to read that "he is the friend and aider of those who would live in the symbol." But he is a friend whose aid must be suspect, as Melville perceived. What he gives with one hand he takes away with the other.

In this connection an interesting exhibit is Horace Bushnell (1802-76), clergyman and theologian, who in 1849 set all New England on edge with a theory of language. In that year his "Preliminary Dissertation on the Nature of Language, as Related to Thought and Spirit" was published as an introduction to three sermons which had already created a great stir. Bushnell was attacked from every side and was forced to defend himself before the Hartford Central Association of Congregationalist Ministers. His defense, published in 1851, contained an elaboration of his theory, entitled "Language and Doctrine."

The crux of Bushnell's theory was not, as in the case of Emerson, the metaphysical status of language, although he could neither solve nor even state his problem without invoking a good deal of very Emersonian philosophy. He originally took up the subject in the form of a personal difficulty: "I had no language, and if I chanced to have an idea, nothing came to give it expression. The problem was, in fact, from that point onward, how to get a language, and where." This, as he eventually saw, was a particular aspect of the more general problem raised by the barren controversies of New England religion. What was lacking in each case was a true sense of how language worked. Bushnell's aim was to differentiate the logical and the poetic modes of language, to define the function of each, and to demonstrate the priority of poetic method.

He contended that New England theology had overestimated logical method through ignorance of linguistic method in general. "Without being at all aware of the fact, as it would seem, our theologic method in New England has been essentially rationalistic. . . . The possibility of reasoning out religion, though denied in words, has yet been tacitly assumed. . . . No real doubt has been held of the perfect sufficiency of formulas; or of natural logic, handled by the natural understanding, to settle them." This failing was characteristic of Protestantism, which had always been "organized in and by the strong ligaments of formulas, taken as . . . the very essence and literal being of the truth."

The ironic outcome of such purblind rationalism was a multiplica-
tion of doctrines, each claiming logical finality, and each, for that
very reason, doomed to decay:

> How many systems of new theology, so called, have we had in
> New England, within our own short memory. We complain that the
> Protestant world is falling into endless subdivisions. . . . This we lay
> to the evil manner of the times; but really it is due to the original
> defect of the organizing power itself. A pure dogmatic organization
> has a necessary law of limitation in its own nature. . . . And so it
> comes to pass that, while there is but one truth, we have many theolo-
> gies—little finite universes all. . . .

The only way out of this predicament was to start from other
premises, which he began to define in the course of his private
quest for speech:

> I discovered how language built on physical images is itself two
> stories high, and is, in fact, an outfit for a double range of uses. In
> one it is literal, naming so many roots, or facts of form; in the other
> it is figure, figure on figure, clean beyond the dictionaries, for what-
> ever it can properly signify. . . . Writing became, in this manner, to
> a considerable extent, the making of language, and not a going to the
> dictionaries. . . . The second, third, and thirtieth senses of words—all
> but the physical first sense—belong to the empyrean, and are given, as
> we see in the prophets, to be inspired by. Of course they must be
> genuinely used—*in* their nature, and not *contrary* to it. We learn to
> embark on them as we do when we go to sea; and when the breeze of
> inspiration comes, *we glide*.

Bushnell would replace a scientific, logical, mechanistic, or abstractive ideal of language with an aesthetic, symbolic, organic,
literary one. The vast body of meaning which lies beneath and
around logic is not, he would say, a source of error and confusion but the means of the greater part of our knowledge. Rational speech is not the rule of language but a special case, and
it goes wrong when it tries to be anything more.

The rule, as he says, is "figure, figure on figure." Bushnell
takes this word in its most general sense of "shape" or "form."
He supposes that language has two "departments," physical and
intellectual. In the former, names act as mere signs of external

objects. Whether or not the external world is absolutely real—
and Bushnell does not raise the question—we inhabit a common world of objects designated by a common set of terms; even
animals may learn such "simple representatives of things." But
in the "intellectual department," where "names of things are
used as representatives of thought," the word and its object
together begin to function as symbols. What occurs, according
to Bushnell, when words become "vehicles of thought and of
spiritual truth," is a formative process. In language the essential
formlessness of thought and truth is subject to the conditions
of form. He illustrates "the universal presence of the form-
element" by the phrase "faith in God":

The particle *in* is a word of palpable form, and we shall find, if we
narrowly inspect our consciousness, that our thought in the expression
is completely immersed in form, under and by means of this little
particle.

In this sense, all intellectual language is figurative. "Thinking,
in fact, is nothing but the handling of thoughts by their forms."
The language of reason and the language of poetry are equally
symbolic, since both constitute patterns of the intellectual world.
But what is the ground of these patterns? When Bushnell refers
to the "formlessness" of truth, he seems to mean a universal
potentiality of form. He postulates a "Logos," or linguistic principle, which inheres both in the outer world and in the mind. In
some way—"how, we cannot discover"—the Logos asserts itself
in human language: "The external grammar of creation answers
to the internal grammar of the soul, and becomes its vehicle."
The patterns of language as we know it have been "insensed"
in things or "imparted" to them by God, so that one may legitimately speak of "the reality of language."

Bushnell's argument is an oblique way of stating an organic
theory. When he approaches the subject more directly, consider-
ing "language as a human product," the God-given forms inhabit
the realm of human experience. They are figurative in the same
way as life itself is a procession of forms, and they partake of

the organic structure of life. Every language, Bushnell maintains, "carries in its bosom some flavor of meaning or import, derived from all the past generations that have lived in it." This over-all pattern or schema conditions every individual act of speech. In every philosophy, similarly, an "atmosphere of meaning" envelops the individual terms:

> There is a form-element in every system of thought or doctrine, which assimilates all the words employed, insinuating into them, or imposing upon them, a character partly from itself; much as food is changed in form, when the *nisus formativus* of a living body imposes its own chemistry and requires it to fill and support its own type of growth and structure.

Every man, finally, has his own universe of discourse, which influences "all the ratios of meaning, or relative forces of words," and every book has an organic unity in which the whole is somehow intended upon the parts:

> Life is organic; and if there be life in his work, it will be found not in some noun or verb that he uses, but in the organic whole of his creations. Hence, it is clear that he must be apprehended, in some sense, as a whole, before his full import can be received in paragraphs and sentences.

Beyond the distinction between the logical doctrine and the poetic figure lies a deeper principle, according to which both, as figures, presuppose the entire configuration into which they enter.

This was only to say, as Bushnell was well aware, that poetry is the norm of language. It was from this standpoint that he leveled his fire against New England rationalism and at the same time caught a glimpse of his own New Jerusalem. For him, logic is a device, an intellectual artifice. Pure logicians "reason, not by or through formulas, but upon them. After the formulas are got ready, they shut their eyes to all interior inspection of their terms, as in algebra." But plainly the value of this method depends upon the initial "power of insight by which premises are seen or ascertained." In so far as the logician, in pursuit of his characteristic method, fails to hold "a constant insight of all terms and constructions," he necessarily departs from truth. In so far as he does keep before him the "latent element of figure" by which his creed is shaped, he approaches the poet. Thus the error of the dogmatist is one of degree. The dogmatist is so unwary as to ignore completely the figurative nature of his terms and to treat them as though they belonged to the "literal department" of language. Semantically naïve, he does not realize that in all discursive thought, as well as in literature, words "have a wholly different relation to their truths—a relation of form or symbol." The result is bitter controversy, which would cease forthwith if doctrines were felt as variant forms of a single stuff, not as mutually exclusive statements of fact: "A very great share of our theological questions, or disputes, originate in the incapacity of the parties . . . to see how the same essential truth may clothe itself under forms that are repugnant."

Bushnell prided himself on his ability to see just that and to act on the perception:

So far from suffering the least consciousness of constraint, or oppression, under any creed, I have been readier to accept as great a number as fell in my way; for when they are subjected to the deepest chemistry of thought, that which descends to the point of relationship between the form of the truth and its interior formless nature, they become, thereupon, so elastic, and run so freely into each other, that one seldom need have any difficulty in accepting as many as are offered him.

In focusing on "the point of relationship between the form of the truth and its interior formless nature," Bushnell comes to the heart of his positive program. His theme is that "religion has a natural and profound alliance with poetry," but more interesting and more important is the ground he finds for this identification. He conceives of religious doctrine as cognate to the paraphrase of a poem. It is necessarily incomplete, since it is cast in logical form, which follows "the atomic relations of inorganic matter"; at the same time, since it is a "formula," and thus ultimately symbolic, it is potentially reconcilable with other versions of the matrix from which it comes:

> It would not be as wild a breach of philosophy itself, to undertake a dogmatic statement of the contents of a tragedy, as to attempt giving in the same manner the equivalents of the life and death of Jesus Christ. The only real equivalent we can give is the representation of the life itself. It is not absurd, however, to say something about the subject, if only we do not assume the adequacy of what we say—we could offer some theoretical views of a tragedy, but our theoretic matter would not be the tragedy.

What, then, is the religious and the poetic fact, of which doctrine and paraphrase are the inadequate translation? We know it immediately as a "living, plastic, organically perfect whole," but we can define it only as a multiple meaning. It is formless, inasmuch as it transcends all its forms; absolute form, inasmuch as it receives every figure proposed. Bushnell in this way arrives at the double principle of poetic realization and poetic paradox. The *end* of the poetic (and the religious) consciousness is a state where all meanings "gravitate inwardly, towards that whole of truth, in which they coalesce." Considered genetically, however, the realization of poetic and religious fact is attained "not by destroying the repugnances, but by allowing them to stand." Poetry is not only Nirvana but also a state of war:

> It will . . . be necessary, on this account, to multiply words or figures, and thus to present the subject on opposite sides or many sides. Thus, as form battles form, and one form neutralizes another, all the insufficiencies of words are filled out, the contrarieties liquidated, and the mind settles into a full and just apprehension of the pure spiritual truth. *Accordingly we never come so near to a truly well rounded view of any truth, as when it is offered paradoxically; that is, under contradictions; that is, under two or more dictions, which, taken as dictions, are contrary to one another. . . .* It will be found, that the poets often express their most inexpressible, or evanescent thoughts, by means of repugnant or somewhat paradoxical epithets; as, for example, Coleridge, when he says—
>
> > "The stilly murmur of the distant sea
> > Tells us of silence."

There is a striking modernity in Bushnell's conception of a literature which frankly relies on "antagonistic figures, paradoxes, and contrarious representations." Though he tends, like Emerson, to jump too quickly to that "pure spiritual truth" where the "contrarieties" of paradox are finally "liquidated," he presents the picture of a language which can attain its goal of symbolic unity only by running the gauntlet of stark opposition. Bushnell brought the Emersonian doctrine to the test of a situation in which "infinite multiplications of opinion, . . . errors and sects and strifes" were the most present of realities. In a sense, he offered a necessary counterweight to the Emersonian stress on the undifferentiated whole of perception and speech. But in another sense one might say—remembering, all the while, that he made no allusion to Emerson and was certainly not a conscious follower—that Bushnell revealed the fertility of the Emersonian vision. He was able to conceive a language of paradox because he lived in the Emersonian universe and set his sights on the mirage of ideal unity. It was only in terms of this goal that the fragmentation of New England religion, as well as his own personal difficulty, took on any meaning at all. Given the ideal of organic knowledge, Bushnell's early dilemma, when "nothing came to give . . . expression," was typical of the daily struggle of the artist, who must *learn* to "embark" on words "as we do when we go to sea." Given the ideal of organic form, logical opposition, constantly renewed, was the occasion and the material of an endless effort toward symbolic unity. Emerson's inadequacies were plain enough, or even more obvious, in Bushnell's redaction. To speak of the "formlessness" of truth was to give away the alarming secret that form, pursued too far, verges into the negation of form. But Emerson came off very well under the circumstances. His rationale, which led him into many a theoretical mist, could also give shape and direction to the literary mind.

For he himself was nothing if not literary. Melville marked in his copy of the *Essays* a passage in which Emerson declared that the poet "disposes very easily of the most disagreeable facts"; and he noted in the margin, "So it would seem. In this sense, Mr. E. is a great poet." Here certainly was the bland inspirationalist, "cracked right across the brow," who was intent on drawing a veil before "the shark-maw of the Devil." Yet, as Melville conceded, Emerson was a "thought-diver." If he generally came to the surface with a premature conclusion that glossed over the battle in the depths, there was another and more important meaning in the very spectacle of his ever-renewed descent. What seemed a sermon was really a kind of object-lesson, a spiritual exercise. Though he was not a great poet, nor even a good poet, he was more a poet than a dogmatist. He was an artist in the medium of theory—in short, a dialectician—and his doctrines are better regarded as themes of his discourse than as elements of a system. He was ultimately faithful to no creed but only to the process of concrete thought which doctrine, as doctrine, always distorts.

"Dialectic" was his own term for his quasi-poetic method:

As there is a science of stars, called astronomy; a science of quantities, called mathematics; a science of qualities, called chemistry; so there is a science of sciences,—I call it Dialectic,—which is the Intellect discriminating the false and the true. It rests on the observation of identity and diversity; for to judge is to unite to an object the notion which belongs to it.

Dialectic claims the autonomous status of a poem, working in a realm constituted by the unification of objects and notions, and "discriminating the false and the true" on the basis of internal coherence rather than correspondence to an external reality. It is not a set of doctrines, but a process—"a long logic"—and "the moment it would appear as propositions and have a separate value, it is worthless." The characteristic form of dialectic is an approximation of symbolic structure:

Each new step we take in thought reconciles twenty seemingly discordant facts, as expressions of one law.... By going one step farther back in thought, discordant opinions are reconciled by being seen to be two extremes of one principle, and we can never go so far back as to preclude a still higher vision.

In the dialectic hierarchy each general law is "only a particular fact of some more general law presently to disclose itself."

Emerson's fifty-year monologue was itself the best example of the genre he described. His ideas, as he pointed out, were like great circles on a sphere: they were "intertranslateable." Conversely, his main subject was the method he professed; he was never far removed from the act of expression as he himself knew it. In his usage a term like "World Spirit," whatever it means as a metaphysical entity, is also "our name for the last generalization to which we can arrive." God is the "algebraic x" in language, standing for a "residuum unknown, unanalyzable," which includes and is implied by the whole of recorded speech. If the writer is a "rhapsodist," and poetic creation is a "surrender of will to the Universal Power," this "attitude of reception" is cognate to the *entertainment* of meaning by which the symbolist and the dialectician extend the boundaries of present reality. In theory and in practice, Emerson cleaved to the concrete awareness which is the basis of literature: the sense of a whole which anticipates its parts; which is implicit in the parts and yet transcends them; which is known, therefore, by continual redefinition; and which is given as an immediate presence. He isolated these principles and thereby made them more available.

Of course, he oversimplified. The facile optimism that Melville censured was more than a matter of personality; it was inherent in the way Emerson put his basic question. "Cannot I conceive the Universe without a contradiction?" He was not fully alive to the complexity of the concrete fact in which he worked and to which his theory referred, for he took it as evidence that "the world of contradictions which the metaphysician finds" is not a real form of nature. Contradiction seemed only to prove that "the universality, being hindered in its primary form, comes in the secondary form of *all sides*. . . . Nature keeps herself whole and her representation complete in the experience of each mind."

He resisted the idea that opposition might be more than a phenomenon, and he was always prepared with comforting reflections on the value of multiplicity:

> The surveyor goeth about taking positions to serve as the points of his angles, and thereby afterwards he finds the place of the mountain. The philosopher in like manner selects points whence he can look on his subject from different sides, and by means of many approximate results he at last obtains an accurate expression of the truth.

Emerson could never feel the potential disunity of thought, word, and object as a tragic dilemma; this was Melville's discovery. At his most skeptical, Emerson is lighthearted:

> It seemed to men that words come nearer to the thing; described the fact; were the fact. They learn later that they only suggest it. It is an operose, circuitous way of putting us in mind of the thing,—of flagellating our attention. But this was slowly discovered. . . . Garrulity is our religion and philosophy.

He calmly foresees the disappearance of all language as "speech becomes less, and finally ceases in a noble silence." By agnosticism, if not by knowledge, the integrity of truth will be preserved.

He is more appealing in those moments of rueful confession when he *cannot* conceive the universe without a contradiction and therefore contradicts himself. As early as his sermon on the Lord's Supper, he was forced to modify his more categorical statements on the unity of thought, word, and object: "We are not accustomed to express our thoughts and emotions by symbolical actions. . . . To eat bread is one thing; to love the precepts of Christ and resolve to obey them is quite another." This disintegration of the symbol was one of the hard realities of a world where it was not always easy to transfigure the material fact. The symbolic ideal was perpetually unattained. "For language itself is young and unformed. In heaven it will be . . . 'one with things.' Now, there are many things that refuse to be recorded,—perhaps the larger half. The unsaid part is the best of every discourse." Emerson was "not so foolish as to declaim against forms," but he was uncomfortably aware that his formalism

walked a narrow path between the recalcitrance of the object
and the vagaries of the imagination. He criticized Margaret Fuller
for erecting a "dazzling mythology" without any "real meaning."
Moreover, form itself was treacherous. The theme of the sermon
on the Lord's Supper is the fossilization to which every form is
subject when it degenerates from a creative force into a static
sign. Even the creative symbol has its "intrinsic defect," for
"language overstates" and exists as self-contradiction. Somehow
"we cannot strongly state one fact without seeming to belie some
other," so that "the only way in which we can be just, is by giving
ourselves the lie." At the same time, language understates, with
the same result: "The thought that I think excludes me from all
other thoughts. . . . The symbols in which I had hoped to convey
a universal sense are rejected as partial." We are sectarians in
spite of ourselves:

> There would be no sect if there were no sect. . . . Something has been
> overstated or omitted by the antecedent sect, and the human mind feels
> itself wronged, and overstates on the other side. . . . Each of our sects
> is an extreme statement and therefore obnoxious to contradiction and
> reproof.

His concessions gave away his case: the world of contradictions, which he regarded as "secondary," became the primary
fact of Melville's experience. Emerson's work has enduring value
because his point of view, partial as it was, implied its opposite.
When he tried to elevate his point of view into doctrine, he
emerged with the jejune concepts for which he is famous. But
in so far as he was faithful to his dialectic method, he himself
was committed to "all sides," and his work pointed like an arrow
at its antithesis. Melville's grudging praise—"Say what they
will, he's a great man"—was the just reward of this "endless
seeker," who transcended his own conclusions and who remained,
as much for good as for ill, a "man without a handle."

V *The Fool of Truth*

> *The calyx of death's bounty*
> *giving back*
> *A scattered chapter, livid*
> *hieroglyph . . .*

HART CRANE, "At Melville's Tomb"

The modernity of Herman Melville is complex. To all appearances it is not distinctively a literary quality. The Melville cult, since its beginning in the 1920's, has been, consciously at least, a response not to an artist but to a man, a personality. Even the fairly sophisticated exegesis of recent years has tended to conceive the author of the novels as an archetypal modern man. He has been heard as the voice of one in trouble, yet full of ironic inflections, and his critics have discovered themselves in him. There is no doubt that Melville invites this sort of interpretation. He would seem a prime example of the demonic writer, carrying all before him by what he *is* rather than what he can *do*. He is often indifferent to the details of structure; his speculations are seldom profound and sometimes juvenile; he offers little variety of fictional character or situation. His greatest gift is a sense of tone and attitude, behind which we cannot help looking for an individual speaker; and this speaker, as it happens, can be taken as a very modern personality.

Yet Melville is no true case of the legendary writer whose life has enveloped his work. On the contrary, his work has been the most important source for his putative quality as a man. "Herman Melville (1819–91)" remains largely unknown, so that all attempts to identify the omnipresent voice of the novels with Melville as he lived and breathed have been self-defeating. What we have is a literary personality, a created figure who inhabits a created world. He is not a portrait of the man who lived in Pittsfield and New York, but a kind of presence—hardly a portrait—of the artist, the author; and his difficulties, whatever else they may include, are aesthetic quandaries. Willard Thorp has given the clearest statement of this fact:

> The conception . . . that Melville was a natural genius who never understood the art he practiced . . . will have to give way to the truer picture of a writer who from the beginning of his career was occupied with the theme of the artist's problems and brooded over the nature of his own creative powers and their relation to the vital center of his spiritual life, until in much of his finest work this theme is deeply involved in the other mysteries with which he wrestled.

From first to last, he presents himself as an artist, and a conscious artist. It is in this character that he seizes our attention.

The intimate connection between his "theme of the artist's problems" and the other themes of his work is in itself a modern quality. And the aesthetic issues that are raised within his books come very close to those that lie behind recent literature. Melville's appeal to the modern reader derives from a community of literary aim—a community of theory and of method and of the relationship between theory and method. At the same time his literary preoccupations help to explain the brevity of his professional career and the long silence that followed, which cannot be accounted for solely on personal grounds. He reached not only a personal, but also a technical, impasse. The logic of his career was the logic of his aesthetic premises; his concept of artistic truth was calculated to lead him into a skepticism of art.

Typee opens with Melville's basic cartography, his division of earth and waters: "Six months at sea! Yes, reader, as I live, six months out of sight of land; . . . the sky above, the sea around, and nothing else!" Land is starting point and conclusion; the sea lies between. But the continents, the limits of the voyage, are beyond the horizon. Nukuheva, where the narrator jumps ship, is not a land mass but an island—neither a beginning nor an end but an episode. Here the waters are the cosmos, and the island is a microcosm. Encompassed by waters, it repeats the circular pattern. Its shore is indented by semicircular bays, from which the land rises to a cluster of mountains in the interior. Valleys and ridges "come down . . . at almost equal distances, all apparently radiating from a common centre." Entering the island at Nukuheva proper, the narrator and his companion follow one of these ridges. They naïvely expect, upon reaching the central plateau, to see the other two principal bays, Typee and Happar, spread out before them. Instead, "the land appeared to retain its general elevation, only broken into a series of ridges and intervales, which as far as the eye could reach stretched away from us." They might as well have been on the ocean. "The whole landscape seemed one unbroken solitude, the interior of the island having apparently been untenanted since the morning of the Creation." After toiling over this no-man's-land, they finally arrive at the head of another group of radiating valleys and ridges, "semicircular" in pattern, down which innumerable streams flow to the ocean. With great difficulty they reach and descend one of the valleys, and at length they find themselves in the territory of the Typees.

The topography of *Typee* is metaphoric. Certainly the book is primarily a travelogue; its scene is the solid earth; and the language does not often *invite* a symbolistic interpretation. Yet here, at the beginning of Melville's literary career, the stuff of his experience seems to hover on the verge of the symbolic expansion it was to undergo in *Mardi* and *Moby-Dick*. *Typee* shadows forth the pattern of Melville's world, which is remarkably like the spherical universe of Emerson. "Line in nature is not found," said Uriel; "unit and universe are round." The sphere (or the circle) was one of Emerson's most frequent images for organic, as opposed to mechanical, structure. Though he used this device in various ways, which may not be wholly consistent, his basic idea was similar to Coleridge's "law of Bicentrality," by which "every whole . . . must be conceived as a possible centre in itself, and at the same time as having a centre out of itself and common to it with all other parts of the same System." It was in this sense that both unit and universe were "round," and it followed, for Emerson, that experience was an infinite series of reformulations. Each unit was a microcosm, in that the universe was organized around it; life was a transition from one sphere to another, each potentially including the former; and the universe was the expanding sphere of spheres, in terms of which every unitary center became a radial element.

Into this world Melville's "Tom" is precipitated, though he does not realize it and one may doubt whether Melville did. The theme of *Typee*, from one point of view, is Tom's education in the complexity of experience and in the vocation of the voyager. This is emphasized by Melville's apparent lack of interest in the *character* of Tom, who is less a man than a capacity for perception. As the narrator moves on through *Omoo* and *Mardi*, he is more and more committed to the voyage as a mode of existence and to a sea where every island, while it constitutes a "centre in itself," points toward some later landfall.

At the beginning of *Omoo* the narrator regains the open sea. At its end still other islands have gone down in the horizon, and the wide Pacific lies ahead. Tom is the prototype of the Melvillian rover, the man destined for an endless voyage. His associate, Toby, is so described: "one of that class . . . you sometimes meet at sea, who never reveal their origin, never allude to home, and go rambling over the world as if pursued by some mysterious fate they cannot possibly elude." And *Omoo,* where Tom's story is continued, gets its title from the Marquesan word for "a rover, or rather, a person wandering from one island to another." As "Taji," he reappears in *Mardi,* again jumps ship, and heads westward in an open boat. After many adventures, he arrives at a new microcosm, vaster than before. The archipelago of Mardi is a planisphere, a world island made up of islands. As on Nukuheva, "towering above all, and midmost, rose a mighty peak." Beyond it "stretched far away, what seemed lands on lands, in infinite perspective," all "grouped within a milk-white zone of reef." This is the setting for the main action of the book, a part-symbolic, part-allegorical, part-fanciful journey "in quest of some object, mysteriously hinted." At the end, once more, the narrator moves on. He is last seen as he strikes out through the "circumvallating reef" and races "over an endless sea."

The subtitle is significant: *And a Voyage Thither.* Melville's development from *Typee* to *Mardi*—from a primarily objective attitude to one that is openly symbolistic—is dramatized within *Mardi* itself. The narrator's journey to the Mardian archipelago is a voyage away from verisimilitude. Even in the first chapter, where he is no more than a restive sailor, he chooses the unlikely expedient of absconding in an open boat in mid-ocean; and the hints of symbolism multiply as the book continues. While he wants to escape from an unjust captain, he is also summoned by visions "leading to worlds beyond." The Kingsmill Islands, which are his goal on a realistic level, are "loosely laid down upon the charts" and a "terra incognita." Beyond them, he often fears, may lie not the Pacific but some "endless sea." When at last he glides through the Mardian reef, he has discovered that his goal and his journey are intellectual. In chapter lii, as a sort of signal that the voyage has become equivalent to mental action and that the scene is "the world of mind," Melville lets down the Mardian backdrop. Thereafter, the voyager inhabits a region where voyaging itself is redefined and where, indeed, life is an object-lesson in the meaning of the term. Seen at close range, of course, Taji's quest is much simpler: the world of mind is no more than the antonym of "fact"—a world of random speculation, loose fantasy, and creaking allegory—and the voyage is merely a device for occasionally changing the subject. But the intellectual odds and ends which constitute the bulk of the book are actually ballast for the main theme, which is intellectual method. Seen from a distance, the voyage takes shape as the symbol of thought. What is thought *about* is a relatively minor matter; Melville's ultimate question is *how*. In the largest view the book is a study of what it entails to regard thinking as a metaphysical journey.

This theme is most explicit in a scattered sequence of chapters where the author merges with the narrator, and both with the Emersonian visionary. The mood is set quite early—even before Taji launches his boat—in an excursus on "sociality," the metaphysical unity of all thought. Taji (and Melville with him) aspires to the condition of his comrade Jarl, in whose language "there was never an idiom." Jarl spoke "a world's language." His "Lingua-Franca of the forecastle" represents organic experience, in terms of which "no custom is strange; no creed is absurd." Thus the circular pattern of the Mardian islands comes as the answer to Taji's prayer: he discovers the organic universe that he predicates. Mardi is not a place but a process, like the boundless West which the voyager apostrophizes—"unattainable forever; but forever leading to great things this side thyself!" It is the universe of the chapter on "Time and Temples," where "the winged soul . . . finds eternities before and behind; and her last limit is her everlasting beginning." Or again, as in "Faith and Knowledge" and the grandiloquent chapter on "Dreams," it is the immediate presence of the whole in every moment of the individual career:

> Beneath me, at the Equator, the earth pulses and beats like a warrior's heart; till I know not, whether it be not myself. . . . And like a frigate, I am full with a thousand souls. . . . In me, many worthies recline, and converse. . . . So, with all the past and present pouring in me, I roll down my billow from afar.

The speaker—Taji or Melville—sails the heaven like the earth itself and, freighted with humanity, sails the sea or *is* the sea of human thought. While he includes past and present, the near and the remote, his goal is a new synthesis. "Sailing On," the last of these regulative chapters, states the credo of the intellectual voyager:

> Oh, reader, list! I've chartless voyaged. With compass and the lead, we had not found these Mardian Isles. . . . Hug the shore, naught new is seen; and "Land ho!" at last was sung, when a new world was sought.

Intellectual adventure in this metaphysical sense is the business of *Mardi*. The whole enterprise is related to what James Murdock, a contemporary writer, described as the rationale of post-Kantian philosophy; and Murdock uses closely related imagery:

> The chief aim of most of these systems was, to penetrate into the *terra incognita* of Kant, that is, into the region of *noumena* and of *supersensible* things. The authors were unwilling to believe we can know so little, as Kant had represented. They therefore attempted to rend the *vail* [*sic*], which conceals the unknowable; or to bridge the *unpassable gulf* of Kant, which separates between phenomena and noumena in the material world, and between ideas and the object of them in the world of thought.

Like Emerson, Melville proposes to bridge the gulf and move through the veil by treating the moment of passage as an end in itself, not a means. His fictive narrator proceeds with no finite goal in view, but claims, for that very reason, the power to encompass any possible goal. The principle that Melville tried to father on Hawthorne (rather ineptly) is the theme of Taji's career: he is "a seeker, not a finder yet," and he glories in the title.

But the Melville whom Hawthorne saw at Liverpool in 1856, hopelessly "wandering to-and-fro," had found inconclusiveness an intolerable state. He yearned for the *noumenon*, the rational object. Latent in *Typee*, explicit in *Mardi*, and violently at odds in *Moby-Dick* and *Pierre*, are two distinct versions of the metaphysical journey. The basic ambiguity of Melville's mind was a double attitude toward the intellectual quest.

In *Typee*, for instance, though the island-hopping hero is a born wanderer, and though the topography of the island suggests an organic world made to his order, the case is not so simple. The majestic mountains at the heart of Nukuheva are badlands, intricate and rough. They afford no easy path from one segment of the circle to another. The concentric valleys of the island are physically isolated from each other by lofty cliffs, and their peoples are eternally at war. Tom's journey is painful and slow. When he moves inland, he imagines the center of the island as a crossroads from which one trail will lead to the "good" Happars and the other to the "bad" Typees. If the mountains teach him, in a sense, that alternatives are not so clear cut, to him this is not, as Emerson would have it, a happy discovery, for he still believes in a real and important difference. And it is more an ironic *contretemps* than evidence of universal harmony that his journey to Happar, like Ahab's and Pierre's after him, ends in Typee. Once arrived, he is again confronted with a multiplicity that defeats as much as it interests him. The Typees are not only difficult to understand; they also belie their conventionally accepted nature, being a compound of good and evil. Tom's situation among the Typees, where he "saw everything, but could comprehend nothing," has little in common with the role of the Emersonian hero, to whom "every thing is in turn intelligible . . . as his on-ward thinking leads him into the truth to which that fact or series belongs."

By "comprehension" Tom means rational knowledge as distinguished from mere realization. It is a distinction that Melville never forgets. He plays the two terms against each other. In *Mardi* the perpetually unattainable West is symbolized by Yillah, who is the formal cause of "the endless journey to no end." But the quest for Yillah becomes, at the same time, an exasperated effort to grasp the *Ding an sich,* which always retreats beyond the horizon. Two ways of thinking fight for control of Taji. On the one hand, as in *Moby-Dick,* "wandering from all mortal reason, man comes at last to that celestial thought, which, to reason, is absurd and frantic." This is only to say that man comes, as Taji does, into a realm where there is no "last," since all rational boundaries have disappeared. Yillah, like the whale, is white, and with the same fundamental meaning: white is the "colorless all-color." She and her polar opposite, Hautia, "in some mysterial way seemed . . . connected." For Emerson, what could be more "celestial"?

> Line in nature is not found;
> Unit and universe are round;
> In vain produced, all rays return;
> Evil will bless, and ice will burn.

For Melville, what could be more infernal? Having followed Uriel to the edge of the vortex down which Yillah disappears, Taji might well echo the elder gods:

> Seemed to the holy festival
> The rash word boded ill to all;
> The balance-beam of Fate was bent;
> The bounds of good and ill were rent;
> Strong Hades could not keep his own,
> But all slid to confusion.

Taji wanders from all mortal reason, but, on the other hand, he is a thorough rationalist. Even at his most expansive, he has reservations. There is bravado in his boast that all the worlds are his kin, and a secret apprehension in his verdict that it is "better to sink in boundless deeps, than float on vulgar shoals." He is unable to regard Yillah simply as the putative end of an infinite process. He seeks her as a finite object and is thereby thrown into a terrible dilemma. For, however much he may come to distrust the whole theory of the voyage, he cannot retreat. He is doomed to apply the endless journey to a purpose for which it was never intended—that is, to attain an end. Ambiguities accumulate; the gulf widens and the veil thickens; despite his mounting horror, he can only drive ahead:

I am the hunter that never rests! the hunter without a home! She I seek still flies before; and I will follow, though she lead me beyond the reef; through sunless seas; and into night and death.

The major question at this point in the book is Melville's attitude toward his hero. The question cannot be answered merely by citing the attitude of Taji's comrades, who plead with him to remain within the Mardian reef. They are appalled by his wilfulness, which is, no doubt, meant to be appalling; but the real issue is whether any other course is open to him. Serenia is no valid alternative. There the philosopher Babbalanja calls a halt, declaring: "My voyage is ended. Not because what we sought is found; but that I now possess all which may be had of what I sought in Mardi." In Serenia, knowledge is love: "The more we love, the more we know; and so reversed. . . . Our wide arms embrace all Mardi like its reef." But for Taji this doctrine would have the ring of his own early enthusiasm. He did not need to reach Serenia in order to learn about "sociality," and the whole bent of his experience has gone to show that the all-embracing is at the same time all-confusing. Serenia would seem to him a spurious haven, an ineffectual attempt to escape the full implications of "the organic law." His only recourse is to accept these implications and to try to get beyond them by aiming at a rational conclusion—even though he strongly suspects that this is equally impossible and that the effort to arrive at an end will merely generate further ambiguity.

Taji's decision to continue the quest may be a "crime," as one of his companions alleges, but if so it is an unavoidable crime, woven into the texture of human existence. Here again, the fact that his quest is inaugurated by an act of violence is no index of Melville's ultimate judgment on him. The death of the priest Aleema is not a clear case of unjustifiable homicide. On the contrary, Taji's sense of guilt is part of his growing sense of the ambiguity of human motives in general and of his own in particular. His self-doubt is the counterpart of the inherent ambiguity of his object, Yillah, for whom he committed the deed. Thus the three vengeful pursuers, who dog him throughout his journey and follow him out to sea at the end, are inseparable from his own pursuit. Their presence does not brand him as a criminal but is the seal of his humanity. This whole phase of the narrative is like an ironic rewriting of Emerson's joyous discovery that "compensation" rules the world: "Every act, every thought, every cause is bi-polar, and in the act is contained the counteraction. If I strike, I am struck; if I chase, I am pursued." In Melville's world the reciprocal becomes the ambiguous, the contradictory, the sinister. But this is not Taji's fault; it is his predicament.

It is Melville's predicament as well—if not Melville the man, of whom we know so little, certainly Melville the author, who plays a leading role in his own works. When Taji departs over an endless sea in the last sentence of *Mardi*, he cannot be regarded simply as a fictive sailor who might return, in accordance with the fictional convention, to tell the tale we have heard. He merges with the author, who is also a voyager, and who has moved and will continue to move with every phase of his own creation. This identification, without which the conclusion of the book is absurd, has frequently occurred earlier: notably in the string of chapters already mentioned, where the intellectual voyage is simultaneously Taji's and Melville's.

The result is a curious and very revealing literary situation, which can be taken in several related ways. Most obviously, the device serves to establish the fact that the intellectual method which is the theme of the book is, at the same time, illustrated by it—that theme and method are one. The two meet in the image of the voyage. Taji's quest implicitly refers to Melville's quest, which the book embodies. Translated into terms of literary theory and practice, Taji's career represents the symbolistic imagination; it is the symbol of symbolism. The opening section of the book, where the hero moves from a realm of fact into a realm of figure, is itself a figure for the characteristic shift of stance by which a symbol is generated. Taji's journey through the Mardian isles dramatizes the imaginative process by which Taji and creatures like him come into being. This is the theme of Babbalanja's account of the composition of Lombardo's "Koztanza," the Mardian epic. Taji listens while his companions, like characters who have found their author, discuss Melville and his book. Babbalanja speaks:

> Of ourselves, and in ourselves, we originate nothing. When Lombardo set about his work, he knew not what it would become. He did not build himself in with plans; he wrote right on; and so doing, got deeper and deeper into himself; and like a resolute traveler, plunging through baffling woods, at last was rewarded for his toils. "In good time," saith he, in his autobiography, "I came out into a serene, sunny, ravishing region; full of sweet scents, singing birds, wild plaints, roguish laughs, prophetic voices. Here we are at last, then," he cried; "I have created the creative."

The whole doctrine of symbolism is in these words, which are presented, nevertheless, as an integral part of the activity they describe. Melville creates the creative, and his subject is creation. "Traveling" is at once the rationale and the chief theme of his work.

Given this intimate connection between theme and method, it cannot be part of Melville's purpose to pass judgment on his hero. For he has deprived himself of any external standpoint from which he might praise or condemn. The kind of literature in which he deals is *problematic*. To use Babbalanja's word (borrowed from Dante), *Mardi* is a "polysensuum"—and in a very radical way, since it even raises the question of its own method. If Taji's voyage corresponds to the symbolistic habit of mind, Taji's impasse is symbolism grown self-critical. *Mardi* would seem to be the thoroughly symbolistic record of a symbolist whose every move forces him to reconsider his working principles. While this situation is paradoxical, it is not necessarily unhealthy. It reflects the real paradox in the situation of the practicing symbolist, as distinguished from the straw man of Emersonian theory. The symbolist is a writer for whom the world, theoretically, is indeterminate, but who spends his life making a place for symbolism in a determinate world. His art treads a thin line between his theoretical premises and certain practical conditions which, if fully admitted, would render his premises null and void. Out of that tension comes his awareness of universal paradox, his sense that "opposite or discordant qualities" are equally as real as the power of reconciliation. And out of the sense of paradox comes his characteristic subject matter, his tendency to seek his theme in the final paradox of his own activity. He saves his chosen method and at the same time does full justice to its practical limitations by making his work a symbolic dramatization of the symbolic process. In *Mardi* Melville fell into a pattern that was to be followed by many modern writers, and he rejected the partiality which is apparent in Emerson and Thoreau. Taji's double loyalty to organic experience and the rational object, to sheer realization and logical conclusion, to the voyage as end and the voyage as means, is tightly bound up with the aesthetic problem of his alter ego, the man who made him and who haunts him throughout his journey.

Yet the problem is put in so radical a way that no creative impulse, however vigorous, could stand the strain. Melville was to become more and more aware of these contradictions and less and less able to distinguish theme and method. Here, of course, one is reduced to pure conjecture, but it would seem that he was destined to lose faith in his technique precisely in the degree that he developed his subject. He was headed toward the view that the symbolistic and the rational attitudes, far from supplementing each other, are mutually destructive—that they entail but damn each other; an interesting theme but a paralyzing methodology. Melville's artistic bankruptcy was postponed by his buoyant spirit, which at first enabled him to regard the whole matter, quite properly, as an ironic game. The somber conclusion of *Mardi* is openly exaggerated for effect; Melville is half-amused both at Taji's histrionics and at his own. This measure of objectivity, however, was not enough. Melville was deeply troubled by an issue which cut at the roots of art and which he could not resolve. When he sets sail with Taji at the end of the book, he is already well on his way toward the predicament described by Hawthorne: "He can neither believe, nor be comfortable in his unbelief; and he is too honest and courageous not to try to do one or the other." By "belief" Hawthorne meant religious faith, but the word can be taken in the larger sense of intellectual confidence and applied to both of the habits of mind involved in *Mardi*. Taji cannot trust absolute experience; he is too much aware of its disintegration into rational opposites, and he is too much drawn to the rational standpoint from which the fusions of experience are mere confusion. On the other hand, the rational object remains entirely hypothetical, and its very nature defeats his desire for immediate knowledge; reason fails him and actually throws him back into the nightmare of his endless journey. He, no less than Pierre, is "the fool of Truth," betrayed by his own honesty. And Melville, no less than Taji, is committed to an intellectual search which holds out no prospect of success but to which there is no alternative.

Melville was not one to be bound by a theory, but he was, so to speak, involved with a principle. He was experimenting with a literary point of view. His stance was neither romantic nor realistic. He postulated a world where "matter and mind . . . unite," where "fact and fancy, half-way meeting, interpenetrate, and form one seamless whole." He was concerned with what he called "significance"—"things infinite in the finite; and dualities in unities." He was drawn to the "deeper meanings" of Hawthorne's tales and to the "deeper and deeper and unspeakable meanings" of Solomon. His letter to Mrs. Hawthorne acknowledging her symbolic interpretation of *Moby-Dick* is remarkable both for what it says and for what it assumes:

> But, then, since you, with your spiritualizing nature, see more things than other people, and by the same process, refine all you see, so that they are not the same things that other people see, but things which while you think you but humbly discover them, you do in fact create them for yourself—therefore, upon the whole, I do not so much marvel at your expressions concern'g Moby Dick. At any rate, your allusion for example to the "Spirit Spout" first showed to me that there was a subtle significance in that thing—but I did not, in that case, *mean* it. I had some vague idea while writing it, that the whole book was susceptible of an allegoric construction, & also that *parts* of it were—but the speciality of many of the particular subordinate allegories, were [*sic*] first revealed to me, after reading Mr. Hawthorne's letter, which, without citing any particular examples, yet intimated the part-&-parcel allegoricalness of the whole.

This is the full-blown doctrine of aesthetic impersonality. Melville regarded the book as a body of potential meaning, and for him there was nothing binding in his own preconceptions. He held, moreover, that the impersonal significance of *Moby-Dick* was thoroughly real. In a companion piece, his eager reply to Hawthorne's letter, selflessness and meaningfulness take on a metaphysical cast:

> I felt pantheistic then—your heart beat in my ribs and mine in yours, and both in God's. A sense of unspeakable security is in me this moment, on account of your having understood the book. . . . Ineffable socialities are in me. . . . I speak now of my profoundest sense of being, not of an incidental feeling. . . . I feel that the Godhead is broken up

like the bread at the Supper, and that we are the pieces. Hence this infinite fraternity of feeling.

Melville's tirade is something more than an author's letter of thanks. It conveys, in a wonderfully immediate way, the faith of the symbolist in that universal "intertranslateability" which for him, as Emerson said, "is not social; . . . is impersonal; is God."

Again, in the "Agatha" letter, offering Hawthorne the materials for a short narrative, "I am," he declared, "but restoring to you your own property—which you would quickly enough have identified for yourself—had you but been on the spot as I happened to be." The materials consist not only of Melville's notes on the scene but also of a diary, which "is instinct with significance." The "tributary items" collected by Melville on his walks find their place in this web of meaning and "seem legitimately to belong to the story, in its rounded & beautified & thoroughly developed state." For "they were visibly suggested to me by scenes beheld while on the very coast where the story of Agatha occurred." But why should he regard these on-the-spot observations as peculiarly appropriate? (He repeats: "These things do, in my mind, seem legitimately to belong to the story.") And why should he suppose that Hawthorne would necessarily have chosen the same elements? He assumes the symbolic reality of the story, which, half-disengaged from the marble, already exists in the words of the diary. "Significance" is the key, and significance is something different from subjective intention and the welter of objective fact. He thinks of the artistic process as governed by an ideal "rightness," which is determined by the inherent meaning and direction of the symbols involved. The entire letter implies the concept of art as a kind of midwifery, active and passive at once: "Then we must introduce the mail-post—no, that phrase won't do, but here is the thing." And in a later letter: "Turn this over in your mind and see if it is right. If not—make it so yourself."

Melville's sketch of the story does not merely assign symbolic meaning. He treats the meaning as substantive, not adjectival. The "poetic reference" of scene to event is focused in the sensibility of the heroine. She is pictured as dimly aware of the metaphoric connections that Melville perceived:

Young Agatha ... comes wandering along the cliff. She marks how the continual assaults of the sea have undermined it; so that the fences fall over, & have need of many shiftings inland. The sea has encroached also upon that part where their dwelling-house stands near the light-house.—Filled with meditations, she reclines along the edge of the cliff & gazes out seaward. She marks a handful of cloud on the horizon, presaging a storm thro' all this quietude.... This again gives her food for thought. Suddenly she catches the long shadow of the cliff cast upon the beach 100 feet beneath her; and now she notes a shadow moving along the shadow. It is cast by a sheep from the pasture. It has advanced to the very edge of the cliff, & is sending a mild innocent glance far out upon the water. There, in strange & beautiful contrast, we have the innocence of the lamb placidly eyeing the malignity of the sea, (All this having poetic reference to Agatha & her sea-lover, who is coming in the storm: the storm carries her lover to her; she catches a dim distant glimpse of his ship ere quitting the cliff)—

The symbols of the Agatha story were to be located in an act of symbolic perception which would establish their *radical* significance.

That is the premise of *Moby-Dick:* "Some certain significance lurks in all things, else all things are little worth, and the round world itself but an empty cipher." As suggested in an earlier chapter, the point of departure of *Moby-Dick* is Ishmael's vision of a symbolic universe:

The great flood-gates of the wonder-world swung open, and in the wild conceits that swayed me to my purpose, two and two there floated into my inmost soul, endless processions of the whale, and, mid most of them all, one grand hooded phantom, like a snow hill in the air.

The white whale of Ishmael's vision is equivalent to the "common centre" of the valleys of Nukuheva and to the "midmost" peak among the islands of Mardi. The whale perspectives represent the total act of symbolic thought, which is not only Ishmael's voyage but also Melville's and that of the reader. Thus *Moby-Dick* defines itself in much the same way as Melville's letter to Mrs. Hawthorne describes the book. It claims the status of a "poly-sensuum," an expanding sphere of meaning. And this kind of self-definition is the business of many other passages, of which the chapter on "The Doubloon" is the best example. Another good instance is the ascent of Father Mapple into his pulpit, when he draws up his rope ladder under Ishmael's inquiring gaze:

> I could not suspect him of courting notoriety by any mere tricks of the stage. No, thought I, there must be some sober reason for this thing; furthermore, it must symbolize something unseen. Can it be, then, that by that act of physical isolation, he signifies his spiritual withdrawal for the time, from all outward worldly ties and connections? Yes, for replenished with the meat and wine of the world, to the faithful man of God, this pulpit, I see, is a self-containing stronghold—a lofty Ehren-breitstein, with a perennial well of water within the walls.

Here, as in the more complex situation of "The Doubloon," emphasis is placed not so much on the particular meanings evolved as on the evolution of meaning. The growth of significance begins with Father Mapple's action, an inherently symbolic piece of language where the physical and spiritual unite. Ishmael both enters into and absorbs this symbolic action. His reading of the symbol is continuous with Father Mapple's action and expands upon it. And the author has much the same relation to Ishmael as Ishmael to Father Mapple. Throughout the book Melville stands half within and half outside the narrator. His is the most inclusive attempt to realize significance—"to read the awful Chaldee of the sperm whale's brow." But it is not a definitive attempt; the entire book, which constitutes his reading, is only "a draught— nay, but the draught of a draught." The reader inherits the job. *Moby-Dick* is a developing meaning. "I but put that brow before you. Read it if you can."

Even the lesser novels, in which symbolic form is kept to a minimum, are colored by a preoccupation with related themes. *Redburn, White Jacket,* and *Israel Potter,* though "beggarly" to their ambitious author, were obviously turned on the same wheel as *Moby-Dick*. In each case (and this is true of all Melville's novels after *Mardi*) the subtitle draws attention to some phase of the metaphysical journey: *Redburn: His First Voyage; White Jacket: The World in a Man-of-War; Israel Potter: His Fifty Years of Exile*. The voyage, the world, and the wanderer—Melville's stock in trade—always tended to gather theoretical overtones.

The subtitle of *Redburn*, which is repeated, usually in italics, throughout the novel, points toward the conception of experience as process; it generalizes the realistic narrative. This theme is most apparent in the Liverpool episode. In effect, what Redburn has been learning is *how* to voyage, and at Liverpool he becomes aware of what he has learned: that the meaning of the voyage lies precisely in change of meaning. He was provided with a guidebook (inherited from his father) which he had studied closely. "For I was determined to make the whole subject my own. . . . I could not but think that I was building myself up in an unerring knowledge of Liverpool." But he discovers that the guidebook and the town are far apart. "This world, my boy, is a moving world," he is forced to tell himself. "Guide-books . . . are the least reliable books in all literature; and nearly all literature, in one sense, is made up of guide-books." The absolute Liverpool is inaccessible; like the ship that Redburn saw in the dock there, "as her timbers must have been frequently renewed in the course of a hundred years, the name alone could have been all that was left of her." The only reality, therefore, lies in the process of becoming; not in the illusory permanence of guidebooks but in the hazards of change. Redburn is the voyaging consciousness, the shifting focus of a transient experience, and his last words look forward to the resurgence of Ishmael at the end of *Moby-Dick:* "But yet, I . . . chance to survive, after having passed through far more perilous scenes than any narrated in this, *My First Voyage*—which here I end."

Similarly, *White Jacket* plays upon "the world in a man-of-war," and *Israel Potter* expands on the theme of "exile." In the former the subtitle has a variety of meanings, which are brought together in the final chapter. It refers to the world as seen from a man-of-war; the world as epitomized in a man-of-war; the world of man, who is warlike; the world in the sense of convention; the world in the sense of the universe. While these variations achieve far less "comprehensiveness of sweep" than the whale of *Moby-Dick*, they show some aspiration toward the all-inclusiveness of that book, where to study cetology is "to have one's hands among the unspeakable foundations, ribs, and very pelvis of the world." The hero of *White Jacket* has less likely material: he is studying the United States Navy. But even so he is more than half an Ishmael, a visionary, and he almost suffers the consequence that Ishmael imagines. He is much given to the "fine feeling . . . that fuses us into the universe of things, and makes us a part of the All." He would follow "the rover's life, . . . not life in a man-of-war, . . . with its martial formalities." America is the symbol of his way of thought—"the advance-guard, sent on through the wilderness of untried things, to break a new path in the New World that is ours." The white jacket that he wears would seem to represent something very like the infinite potentialities of Yillah and the whale.

Yet he tells how this jacket "came near proving his shroud." It caused him to be mistaken for a ghost and led to an attempt on his life; it would have dragged him to the bottom of the ocean, and, as he shook it off, his comrades saw it as a "white shark." Two widely separated chapters—"The Jacket Aloft" and "The Last of the Jacket"—reflect the anxiety, the fear of annihilation, which is the other side of the desire "to nationalize with the universe." Certainly the great passage on falling from the mast, though it is primarily descriptive rather than symbolic, has the same pattern as its counterpart in *Moby-Dick* (the moment when Ishmael, lost in "pantheistic reveries," nearly falls from the mast, and his "identity comes back in horror"). In *White Jacket* the narrator's plunge "toward the infallible center of this terraqueous globe" is an ironic continuation of his quest. But now he recoils into himself: "All I had seen, and read, and heard, and all I had thought and felt in my life, seemed intensified in one fixed idea in my soul . . . as I fell, soul-becalmed, through the eddying whirl and swirl of the maelstrom air." The conclusion of this episode, which is very near the conclusion of the book, anticipates the end of *Moby-Dick* and recalls the end of *Redburn*. Out of a "life-and-death poise" beneath the water, the narrator "at last . . . bounded up like a buoy." He survives as the potentiality of experience, always about to lose himself in the flux and always emerging to face another world.

Though *Israel Potter* is more remote from the voyage theme, he too "began his wanderings very early," and at the end of his adventures "white-haired old Ocean seemed as a brother." His years abroad are linked, through his given name, with various Old Testament exiles: he is Daniel in the lion's den and Samson among the Philistines; he flies to the wilderness; he labors in a brickyard like Israel in Egypt; he is the Wandering Jew. But he is an unwilling exile; unlike the typical Melvillian hero, he is not a seeker, and he lives in a state of passive wonder. Not until he returns home in extreme old age does he become fully aware of what Redburn learned at Liverpool—that "this world . . . is a moving world." *Israel Potter,* written several years after *Moby-Dick* and *Pierre,* is one outcome of the double value with which Melville invested the symbol of voyaging. Here the two aspects that appear in *Mardi* and even in *White Jacket* are not in direct conflict: since Israel aims at no promised land and has little individuality, there is nothing in the book to set against the endlessness of the voyage and the selflessness of the voyager. Yet the journey is depicted solely as man's fate, and it has no vestige of man's hope. The movement of man and the world is inevitable but profitless; real but devoid of human significance. On a foggy November morning, Israel observes the "hereditary crowd—gulf-stream of humanity—which, for continuous centuries, has never ceased pouring, like an endless shoal of herring, over London

Bridge." Individuals are lost in the stream, and the stream has no destination. He himself is lost in the stream, both physically and intellectually, during his forty years in the city. Just as he is physically helpless to escape, he is intellectually lost in the need to "absorb what he saw." His wandering is also a "wondering." In either case he is passive; his life accretes no meaning, and he can only "meditate himself into boundless amazement." Just one "significance" is left him—the evaporation of significance, meaninglessness at the source of meaning. The episode, therefore, is unique; and it is not surprising to find that most of the symbolism in *Israel Potter*, lacking a functional basis, is mechanical and labored.

While these books are a pale reflection of the achievement of *Moby-Dick*, they reveal the extent of Melville's preoccupation with intellectual method, which was the ground not only of his masterpiece but of nearly everything he wrote. A good deal has already been said about *Moby-Dick* as one phase of the American symbolist movement. Consciously departing from naïve irrationalism like that of Whitman, Melville did not fall back on Hawthorne's naïve common sense; nor did he adopt the method of Poe, who cultivated unreason with all the fervor of a man violating his own deeply rational nature. In this literary constellation *Moby-Dick* was a point of balance: Melville seized on the common problem, and there was something of each of the others in his attitude. In his own career the book occupied a similar position. It drew upon and defined a bundle of questions that recurred in various forms throughout his work. It was his most successful attempt to play off the concept of "significance" against all the difficulties that rose in the wake of the symbolistic voyage.

Mardi had suffered from much uncertainty of purpose. The bulk of the book consisted of univocal allegory, which, however it might be justified on other grounds, was obviously the work of a man not yet sure what he meant by "significance." But the Melville of *Moby-Dick* was quite sure. Whereas the quest for Yillah was weakened as a symbol of symbolism by the physical vagueness of the girl—Taji's transmutation of Yillah from object into symbol lost force because Yillah was never sufficiently an object—the whole of *Moby-Dick* demonstrates just that kind of metamorphosis. The whale is simultaneously the most solid of physical things and the most meaningful of symbols. The voyaging intellect of Ishmael interacts with the material world to generate symbolic meaning. Thus the art of *Moby-Dick* depends on the frank acceptance of a methodological paradox, that the realm of "significance" rises from and returns to the dual reality of subject and object, which it would deny. Like *Mardi*, but much more forcibly, *Moby-Dick* exploits the basic paradox of symbolistic method.

At the same time Melville averts the internal clash, which seemed imminent at the end of the earlier book, between method and theme. Not that he removes himself from the arena; the author, as in *Mardi*, is interchangeable with the narrator, so that Ishmael's voyage is equivalent to Melville's creative process. But he establishes a working principle by a division of labor between the two protagonists. Ishmael, by and large, assumes that phase of Taji's quest wherein theme and method are most nearly at one. He does not dwell on the ambiguity of his enterprise. Ishmael is the binder of *Moby-Dick*; he keeps the book from disintegrating in the furnace of Ahab's despair. Ahab, beset by doubt and doomed to failure, inherits the other side of Taji's nature. Ahab's voyage, which realizes the worst fears of Ishmael, is a stinging commentary on the method of *Moby-Dick*. And Melville does not try to disguise this consequence of his own procedure. Though he makes a clear distinction between Ishmael and Ahab, he remains true to his total theme by insisting on their close relationship. Each is endowed with some tincture of the other. Ishmael is capable of rejecting the whole theory of the voyage:

Were this world an endless plain, and by sailing eastward we could forever reach new distances, and discover sights more sweet and strange than any Cyclades or Islands of Solomon, then there were promise in the voyage. But in pursuit of those far mysteries we dream of, or in tormented chase of that demon phantom that, some time or other, swims before all human hearts; while chasing such over this round globe, they either lead us on in barren mazes or midway leave us whelmed.

Ahab, on the other hand, never quite loses the symbolistic faith:

O Nature, and O soul of man! how far beyond all utterance are your linked analogies! not the smallest atom stirs or lives in matter, but has its cunning duplicate in mind.

Just as the method of *Moby-Dick* is a paradox, the theme of the book is an unresolved question—doubly unresolved, since the question is precisely the validity of the method.

The poet Lombardo in *Mardi* "wrote right on; and so doing, got deeper and deeper into himself." As Melville, in the course of writing, got deeper into himself, what he discovered was not so much hidden traits of his own personality, the secret motives of a self-expressive art, but rather the nature of his calling. He saw more and more clearly what he was doing. And he threw it all back into his work. *Pierre* is *Mardi* reconsidered after three years of crowded experience in the artistic process. It is *Moby-Dick* gone sour, off-balance, but the theme and the involuted relationship of theme and method are fundamentally unchanged. Indeed, the bitter tone, the aberrations of style, and the awkwardness of *Pierre* would seem to be closely connected with an artistic insecurity which Melville continued to exploit even as he found it increasingly frustrating. If the Melville of *Mardi* is not yet sure what he means by "significance," though he strongly suspects what it will entail, the Melville of *Pierre* knows all too well.

The culminating symbol of the book carries on from the doubloon of *Moby-Dick*, the image of communication, of meaning, and of value. But in Pierre the coin is counterfeit. The hero's life and work, governed by the noblest aims, are false currency. He so condemns himself: "Now, then, where is this swindler's, this coiner's book? Here, on this vile counter, over which the coiner thought to pass it to the world, here will I nail it fast, for a detected cheat!" He concludes that every supposed truth is a fiction and that every fiction is forgery, imposture, jugglery. Sincerity is impossible:

> For the more and the more that he wrote, and the deeper and the deeper that he dived, Pierre saw the everlasting elusiveness of Truth; the universal lurking insincerity of even the greatest and purest written thoughts. Like knavish cards, the leaves of all great books were covertly packed. He was but packing one set the more; and that a very poor jade set and pack indeed.

Pierre's difficulty is the same as that of his author, of Taji, and of Ishmael-Ahab. His longing for absolute truth discredits the symbolic imagination with which he is endowed. For him the transient "als ob" is a deceptive screen between his mind and permanent reality:

> What, *who* art thou? Oh! wretched vagueness—too familiar to me, yet inexplicable,—unknown, utterly unknown! ... What is that thou hast vailed in thee so imperfectly, that I seem to see its motion, but not its form. It visibly rustles behind the concealing screen. ... I conjure ye to lift the vail; I must see it face to face.

He is determined to "know what *is*."

> Thou Black Knight, that with visor down, thus confrontest me, and mockest at me! Lo! I strike through thy helm, and will see thy face, be it Gorgon!

But each attempt to formulate the fact is exposed as another fiction. His life is a series of fictions, where "one pervading ambiguity [is] the only possible explanation for all the ambiguous details."

Defective as it is, *Pierre,* not *Moby-Dick,* is the best vantage point for a general view of Melville's work. In *Pierre* his fundamental artistic problem is more baldly stated and more fully conceived, even as it becomes more damaging to his artistic self-confidence. And the best clue to the method and meaning of *Pierre* is a novel written seventy-five years later by a distinguished alumnus of the French symbolist school: Gide's *Faux-monnayeurs*.

The structure of *Les Faux-monnayeurs* is an infinite regress. Gide himself appears in the novel as "I," wandering through the pages in assumed perplexity. He is a figure of irony, stripped of the prerogatives of the omniscient author. He is "not sure" of many things; he inquires "with some anxiety where his tale will take him." Thus the largest concept of the book is the making of the book. Its theme is a set of problems raised by its own creation. In form and content the book hinges on the creative process that Gide has recorded in his *Journal des faux-monnayeurs*—his long effort "to objectify the subject" and "subjectify the object." Within this outer circle of Gide's creative experience is the realm of the novelist Edouard. Edouard's unsuccessful attempt to write his own *Faux-monnayeurs* continues the problematic theme. "On one side," as Gide says, "the event, the fact, the external datum; on the other side, the very effort of the novelist to make a book out of it all." But we cannot stop here. The book Edouard conceives will have as its hero a novelist caught "between what reality offers him and what he himself desires to make of it." And the book written by Edouard's hero will presumably repeat the pattern. Gide proposes a world of creative activity, generated by the ceaseless interchange between "the world of appearances" and "our own interpretation."

This activity is "the drama of our lives." The problem is pursued through a vast number of permutations, in each of which there recurs the symbol of the counterfeit coin. The self-deceived and the deceiver, the involuntary and the voluntary pretender, the mystic and the nihilist, the individual and society, fathers and sons—all are counterfeiters. But the artist is the supreme coiner. The artist is the archetypal man, or rather the whole picture of man in the book is a large-scale projection of a portrait of the artist. The false coin is his talisman. It stands for the vision which at any given moment is at once "the real world and the representation of it which we make to ourselves." It is a necessary fiction, forged and reforged in the course of the struggle between the two poles of life. And the artist becomes aware of these poles— the subject and the object—only by means of his counterfeiting. In creating a character, Gide declares, "I forget who I am, if indeed I have ever known"; for "I become the other person." On the other hand, "I stick to Wilde's paradox: nature copies art." The "I" of *Les Faux-monnayeurs* works in a medium "animated with its own life." Similarly, Edouard prides himself on his gift of "depersonalization," and yet is no "slave to resemblance." He writes: "The only existence that anything (including myself) has for me, is poetical—I restore this word its full signification." It follows that the artist has no permanent character. As Edouard says, "I am never anything but what I think myself—and this varies so incessantly, that often, if I were not there to make them acquainted, my morning's self would not recognize my evening's." He is echoing Gide's famous dictum: "I am a creature of dialogue; everything in me is conflicting and contradictory." The "I" of the novel lacks any permanent standpoint; it is lived by the bewildering variety of its own book. The book as a whole is designed to force the reader out of his single-mindedness by giving "the impression of inexhaustibility" and by disappointing his desire for a single "subject." *Les Faux-monnayeurs* presents the fountain of all "subjects," the mint of art, in which men and the world take shape.

Here, in the artistic process, is the reconciliation, as Gide remarks in his autobiography, of those "discordant elements" which would otherwise lead to a state of perpetual warfare. But here also are struggle and inconsistency. The reconciliation is illusory; the coin is counterfeit; art and reality are opposed. The most compelling statement of this point of view is delivered by the old musician La Pérouse. "Have you observed," he asks Edouard, "that the whole effect of modern music is to make bearable, and even agreeable, certain harmonies which we used to consider discords?" For La Pérouse these discords are substantive evil; they cannot be truly resolved into the "perfect and continuous chord" for which he yearns. He is not distracted from his insight by Edouard's feeble rejoinder: "Everything must finally resolve into —be reduced to harmony." According to him, the word of God, which in the beginning was the whole of creation, has been perverted or drowned out by the language of the Devil. "Have you noticed that in this world God always keeps silent? It's only the Devil who speaks." At length, in his final despair, La Pérouse exclaims that "the Devil and God are one." All the mediums of life are radically false. In his old age he has come to feel that he has been "a dupe" all his life. Not merely wife and son, he says, but even "God has fooled me." La Pérouse is an effective critic of Edouard's (and Gide's) aestheticism. Thoroughly the artist, he announces the falsity of art. But Gide is not disposed to argue. His antagonist is his best ally. While he is the advocate and practitioner of art, he calls his own method into question. The fictionality of the artifact, the transience of any resolution of the conflict that goes into its making, and the lawless variety of human creation are thoroughly taken into account by the structure of *Les Faux-monnayeurs*—by that very infinite regress which establishes creativity as the subject.

This, at least in part, is what Gide means when he says that "one character (the Devil)" should "circulate incognito throughout the entire book." The Devil is a principle of thought. He is that factor in experience which mocks aesthetic unity, invalidates the momentary fusion of the ideal and actual, reduces the present vision of reality to a dream. Gide acknowledges that his whole world of counterfeiters is itself a counterfeit by putting himself into the book. As an ironic commentary on the ambiguity of his art—the perilous balance between "the external datum" and his own "effort . . . to make a book out of it all"—he centers his narrative in the creative struggles of Edouard and forces Edouard to resort to the same self-exposure. Fully conscious that the "many beginnings of drama" offered by life "rarely . . . continue and take shape as the novelist is accustomed to spin them out," he mocks the well-made novel—on the one hand, by deliberate artificiality and, on the other, by surrounding Edouard with an embarrassment of riches.

In short, the Devil and God *are* one. But what strikes La Pérouse as the disappearance of all meaning is for Gide the very movement of life. The disintegration of each synthesis is the occasion of the next. Though the "subjects" of art are unsolved problems, of which the greatest is the nature of art, yet it is equally true to say, as Gide does in his Preface to *L'Immoraliste,* that "in art there are no problems—that are not sufficiently solved by the work of art itself." Every phase of *Les Faux-monnayeurs,* while it presupposes the divine harmony, postulates the Devil. To leave him out would be not only to lose all momentum but also to give the father of lies his best opportunity. "The more we deny him, the more reality we give him. The Devil is affirmed in our negation." By the same token, the more we affirm him, the more he is brought to heel. Gide is determined to keep both principles at work. He holds before himself the one certainty in his world of dubieties— the ambiguous process of creation:

A strange liquid substance which, long after you begin, refuses to acquire consistency, but in which solid particles, stirred and shaken every which way, at last clot together and separate from the whey. . . . If he didn't know beforehand from experience that through beating and shaking this creamy chaos he was going to see the miracle repeated—who wouldn't throw up the job?

With extravagant honesty Gide would avoid all the subtle suppressions by means of which fiction ordinarily secures itself from question. He would expose the machinery from which the god descends. But his positive ambition is even more extravagant. Like Edouard, he wants "to put everything" into his novel. When he insists on revealing the seamy side of art—the endless conflict that goes into its making, and the provisional, "counterfeit" quality of the moment when the conflict is resolved—he aspires to a new richness of content, for he has at his command all the variety of subjective intention, objective fact, and mediating fiction.

The preoccupations of *Les Faux-monnayeurs* were Melville's

standing questions, and they led him to attempt in *Pierre* a similar tour de force. As in Gide's novel, every character, including
the author, is a counterfeiter; man's life is a construct; the artist
is the archetypal man. Pierre, the central figure, is "naturally
poetic," first in his relationship with others and ultimately as a
professional writer. The central action of the book is Pierre's
effort to realize the world, and this struggle is epitomized in his
effort to write a novel, which itself has an "author-hero." Melville,
like Gide, broods over his creation. The story unfolds before him,
forcing him to cope with the same methodological problems of
objective event and subjective interpretation as he sets before his
protagonist.

These problems confront Pierre at every turn. His task—"to
reconcile this world with his own soul"—proves to be dangerously
easy and at the same time fearfully difficult. The difficulty is immediate and obvious: the incompatibility between his conceptions
and putative fact. Early in the book, when he is still full of his
romantic love for Lucy, he happens to go into her empty chamber
and there sees "the snow-white bed reflected in the toilet-glass."
While he seems "to see in that one glance the two separate beds—
the real one and the reflected one—" he is filled with a miserable
sense that the two are irreconcilable. Much later, he is confounded
by the face of the philosopher Plinlimmon because it is "a face by
itself," refusing any response to his mind. The face is "something
separate, and apart." Even the triumphant smile that it seems to
show is probably, as "the Kantists might say," merely "a *subjective*
sort of leer in Pierre." Melville keeps this dualism in the fore-
ground by constant allusion to "the two different worlds—that
without, and that within"; to "things, and emotions of things";
to the "vail" that hides the countenance of absolute truth. Like
Gide's Edouard, Pierre works under conditions that are not made
to order for the poet.

He acts as though they were, or, more precisely, as though there
were no conditions. Until he is brought up short by experience, he
is almost totally unaware of any distinction between thought and

fact. He lives in the image. Lucy, his mother, his family history, and his own being are constructs in "the illuminated scroll," the "sweetly-writ manuscript," which for him is present reality. He does not hesitate to doctor the image. Since "a sister had been omitted from the text," he allows himself the "strange license" of addressing his mother as sister. And since this device is too transparently "fictitious," he jumps at the opportunity, afforded by Isabel's letter, to regard her as his "real" sister. To do so, he must readjust his whole picture of the world. He recalls "words and . . . signs" borne in his memory like shrunken seeds; the "cipher" of the past takes on new meaning; "he reads all the obscurest and most obliterate inscriptions . . . and rummages himself all over, for still hidden writings to read." Pierre's materials are symbols, not facts. The "searching argumentative itemizings" of reason have no effect on his conviction that Isabel is his sister and his revered father a sinner. He is "persuaded . . . in spite of them." He lends himself to his vision; he is carried away by "the multitudinous shapes" that the poetic mind "creates out of the incessant dissolvings of its own prior creations."

Similarly with his plan of action—at once to protect the memory of his father and to acknowledge Isabel by pretending that she is his wife. Melville remarks that no man can claim that "his slightest thought or act solely originates in his own defined identity." To understand the origin, especially in the case of Pierre, one must remember that it is impossible always to distinguish between what is "confusedly evolved from out [the mind] itself" and the "vast and varied accessions [which] come to it from abroad." If Pierre, having previously converted his mother into a sister, now proposes to convert his sister into a wife, it is because he has submerged himself in a world where the distinction between external and internal does not exist at all—where the fiction is the thought and the fact. He has habituated himself, as Melville says, "to a certain fictitiousness in . . . the closest domestic relations of life," and he surrenders to the movement of his symbols. His future is determined thereby. The plan "foetally forming in him, ... when it should at last come forth in living deeds, would scorn all personal relationship with Pierre, and hold his heart's dearest interests for naught."

The new picture is constructed by reversals and fusions of image, "awfully symmetrical and reciprocal." Though Pierre's grief in a sense brings him closer to truth, he follows no "covertly inductive reasoning process." His "truth" is a reconstruction of his symbols:

> Not only was the long-cherished image of his father now transfigured before him from a green-foliage tree into a blasted trunk, but every other image in his mind attested the universality of that electral light which had darted into his soul. Not even his lovely, immaculate mother, remained entirely untouched, unaltered by the shock. At her changed aspect, when first revealed to him, Pierre had gazed in a panic; and now, when the electrical storm had gone by, he retained in his mind, that so suddenly revealed image, with an infinite mournfulness.

Pierre's father is represented by two portraits, one showing a middle-aged married man, the other a gay bachelor. The latter, which his mother dislikes, has come into Pierre's possession. Even while he still conceives his father in his mother's terms, he is wont to fall into reverie before the painting in his room, which wears an "ambiguous smile." Leaving "the assured element of consciously bidden and self-propelled thought," he watches "the strangely concealed lights of the meanings" within the portrait. And the smiling figure speaks to him: "Consider in thy mind, Pierre, whether we two paintings may not make only one. Faithful wives are ever over-fond to a certain imaginary image of their husbands; and faithful widows are ever over-reverential to a certain imagined ghost of that same imagined image." The transfiguration of his father is completed when the two portraits merge with a third—the visionary countenance of Isabel, which he cannot drive from his mind. "The face haunted him as some imploring, and beauteous, impassioned, ideal Madonna's haunts the morbidly longing and enthusiastic, but ever-baffled artist." He takes the course of the artist; he effects a metaphoric fusion between the image of his father and the image of his supposed sister:

And now, by irresistible intuitions, all that had been inexplicably mysterious to him in the portrait, and all that had been inexplicably familiar in the face, most magically these now coincided; the merriness of the one not inharmonious with the mournfulness of the other, but by some ineffable correlativeness, they reciprocally identified each other, and, as it were, melted into each other, and thus interpenetratingly uniting, presented lineaments of an added supernaturalness.

On all sides, the physical world of solid objects now slidingly displaced itself from around him, and he floated into an ether of visions; and, starting to his feet with clenched hands and outstaring eyes at the transfixed face in the air, he ejaculated that wonderful verse from Dante, descriptive of the two mutually absorbing shapes in the Inferno:

> "Ah! how dost thou change,
> Agnello! See! thou art not double now,
> Nor only one!"

Pierre is not alone in these habits of mind. The essence of his situation is the incapacity of any of the principals to escape their own imaginations. The conventionality of his mother, like that of the minister Mr. Falsgrave, is a tissue of fictions. It is she who encourages Pierre's little game of calling her his sister. She not only cherishes an "imagined ghost of . . . [an] imagined image" of her husband but also builds up an ambiguous picture of her son as at once "docile" and "heroic." So completely is she dominated by her preconceptions that her only recourse when Pierre violates her dream is to disown him and die. Lucy follows the opposite path for similar reasons. When Pierre abandons her for Isabel, she tries to pretend that nothing has changed. She joins them in the city, where she occupies herself with drawing Pierre's portrait. Different as she is from Mrs. Glendinning, she is equally inflexible. Their imaginations are simplistic.

The full power of symbolic vision is personified in Isabel, who disclaims all rationality:

All my thoughts well up in me; . . . as they are, they are, and I can not alter them, for I had nothing to do with putting them in my mind, and I never affect any thoughts, and I never adulterate any thoughts; but when I speak, think forth from the tongue, speech being sometimes before the thought; so, often, my own tongue teaches me new things.

While the other women strive to see Pierre in their own terms, Isabel is completely malleable. Her personality is no more than a function of her imagination, and she offers herself to the imagination of Pierre:

Thy hand is the caster's ladle, Pierre, which holds me entirely fluid. Into thy forms and slightest moods of thought, thou pourest me; and I there solidify to that form, and take it on, and thenceforth wear it, till once more thou moldest me anew.

Isabel's story of her life is Melville's attempt at a genetic account of a completely impersonal power of vision. She was a child amid an external chaos: "the bewilderingness;—and the stupor, and the torpor, and the blankness, and the dimness, and the vacant whirlingness of the bewilderingness." Only very slowly did she begin "to learn things out of" herself or even to know herself as "something human" in distinction from external things. Now, as an adult, she can only realize, not "comprehend." She yearns for a purely organic life, "as of some plant . . . existing without individual sensation." She is incapable of disengaging the thought from the fact: "Always in me, the solidest things melt into dreams, and dreams into solidities." She moves "amid all sorts of shapes." When she looks at Pierre, his "visible form" gives way to "a second face, and a third face, and a fourth face." As she plays on her guitar, Pierre is overwhelmed by "the utter unintelligibleness, but the infinite significancies of the sounds."

What distinguishes Pierre from his fellow-counterfeiters is his perspective on their common predicament. His suffering, while it leads him to nihilism, at least has the advantage of clarifying his problem. He suffers because he can trust neither reason nor imagination. Reason affords him no certain standpoint outside poetic ambiguity. His pursuit of absolute Virtue and Truth is inconclusive. He is like the Enceladus of his dream, "still turning his unconquerable front toward that majestic mount eternally in vain assailed by him." To accept that condition—the "mixed, uncertain,

heaven-aspiring, but still not wholly earth-emancipated mood"—
would be to acknowledge that reason returns to imagination, that
the quest for the absolute is merely a blind for the continuous re-
constructions of the poet. But Pierre cannot help judging the life of
imagination from the standpoint of reason. He postulates a "solid
land of veritable reality" even as it is "encroached upon by ban-
nered armies of hooded phantoms." He tries repeatedly to condense
the "haze of ambiguities" around Isabel "into some definite and
comprehensible shape." Even while he revels in the fluid world
that has opened before him out of "this common world of every-
days," he rebels against "a mysteriousness wholly hopeless of solution." He wants a solution, not an infinite series of problems. Thus
imagination returns to reason: the poetic fiction is a falsehood. The
result of Pierre's inner conflict is despair and self-contempt. Unlike
the Gide of *Les Faux-monnayeurs,* he cannot regard the paradox of
reason and imagination as the vital center of art. His ultimate
point of view is closer to that of La Pérouse. The Devil and God
are one, not in the sense of a productive duality, but in the sense
that man is "the fool of Truth, the fool of Virtue, the fool of Fate."

These phrases are often interpreted in too narrow a context.
Pierre does not mean simply that, because the noumenon he
sought is unattainable, he was a fool to behave unconventionally.
He means that the principle of man's fate is the ineffectuality of
any principles of knowledge or conduct. "How did he know that
Isabel was his sister?" His conviction, he feels, was "originally
born . . . purely of an intense procreative enthusiasm." He was convinced by the portrait of his father. Yet now, as he reconsiders the
question, he still cannot transcend the realm of portraiture. On
the contrary, he has just come upon a "portrait of a complete
stranger" which bears a striking resemblance to Isabel. "Then, the
original of this second portrait was as much the father of Isabel as
the original of the chair-portrait. But perhaps there was no original
at all to this second portrait; it might have been a pure fancy-
piece." Much earlier, he noted that even his father's picture was
not rationally verifiable: "not Pierre's parent, as any way re-

memberable by him, but the portrait's painted *self* seemed the real father of Isabel."

Noumenon fades into phenomenon; objective truth into fiction. And when everything is fiction, fiction is nothing: "I am a nothing. It is all a dream—we dream that we dreamed we dream." A personality that is no more than the creature of its own projections is nonexistent. Pierre is moving toward this concept from the time of his first impulsive lie to his mother, which seems to make him "a falsifyer" not only *to* his mother but *of* himself. His dim perception that "not always in our actions, are we our own factors" is confirmed by his experience with Isabel. Moreover, even the action is meaningless. Inherently ambiguous, it neutralizes itself. "Look: a nothing is the substance, it casts one shadow one way, and another the other way; and these two shadows cast from one nothing; these, seems to me, are Virtue and Vice." Pierre's "sister" turns out to be his lover, and this fact demonstrates to him "the mere imaginariness of the so supposed solidest principle of human association." Her face, "ever hovering between Tartarean misery and Paradisaic beauty, . . . compounded so of hell and heaven," is really indifferent both to Vice and to Virtue, for, as she herself says, she "knows neither the one nor the other." Her fluidity reduces her to nothingness. And here Isabel, the dark temptress, is on the same ground as Lucy, the "marble-white." If Pierre from the beginning "substituted but a sign—some empty x—" for "the real Lucy," the issue proves to him that no other reality ever existed. Opposite the "Stranger's Head," so that "in secret they seemed pantomimically talking," hangs a portrait of Beatrice Cenci. While Isabel gazes at the former, Lucy stands before the latter. Both are ambiguous. The swarthy "Stranger" is "portentously looking out of a dark, shaded ground, and ambiguously smiling." The Cenci, "seraphically *blonde*," is "double-hooded . . . by the black crape" of crime, so that she almost appears, despite her blondness, to be "vailed by funereally jetty hair." Like Pierre's father and Isabel, Lucy and Isabel in the end are two mutually absorbing shapes. Faced with this consequence of his whole way of thought, Pierre dismisses them both as "two pale ghosts" and adopts a radical nihilism: "Pierre is neuter now."

Gide also takes a neutral stand: "I do not indeed claim that neutrality (I was going to say 'indecision') is the certain mark of a great mind; but I believe that many great minds have been very loath to . . . conclude—and that to state a problem clearly is not to suppose it solved in advance." For Gide, the neutral mind is overflowing with life. For Pierre, it is left void and empty by "mutually neutralizing thoughts." Since nothing can be affirmed, all men, including himself, are "liars" perforce. Theirs is the neutrality of death. Thus his career ends in murder and suicide. Similarly, his book, on which he labors as his nihilism grows, is undermined by his sense of "the universal lurking insincerity of even the greatest and purest written thoughts." Just as every phase of his life leads him back to questions about the validity of any action or concept, so in his literary work his main interest is his own creative process. What occupies him, day after day, is "not the book, but the primitive elementalizing of the strange stuff, which in the act of attempting that book, has upheaved and upgushed in his soul." In each case the result is the same. His experience with "the inventional mysteries" of composition makes him "uncompromisingly skeptical." Earlier, he despised common novels as "false, inverted attempts at systematizing eternally unsystemizable elements." Now he feels that "like knavish cards, the leaves of all great books [are] covertly packed" and that he himself is "but packing one set the more." His former reverence for works that "never unravel their own intricacies, and have no proper endings," takes on new meaning in the bitterness of his final speech, when he sees his life in terms of his book, and both in terms of a self-destructive illogicality, inconclusiveness, and ambiguity:

Here, then, is the untimely, timely end;—Life's last chapter well stitched into the middle! Nor book, nor author of the book, hath any sequel, though each hath its last lettering!—It is ambiguous still.

Both his death and his literary failure confirm the "nothingness" of a world without solid substance and without determinate form.

His book is his link with Melville. The device of the infinite regress is used to good effect in *Pierre*. It comes to a focus when Melville, the "I" of the novel, transcribes several pages in which his hero "seems to have directly plagiarized from his own experiences" to compose a soliloquy for "his apparent author-hero." The experience in question is the experience of authorship. Pierre's "Vivia," like Pierre, is an artist suspicious of his calling. Melville's Pierre, like Melville, like Gide, and like Gide's Edouard, finds his "deep-lying subject" in his own artistic difficulties.

But "difficulty" is too mild a word for Pierre's situation, which comes closer to bankruptcy. His theme is not so much the problem as the impossibility of a valid art. Here two points must be made. On the one hand, the scheme of *Pierre* marks an important change from that of Melville's previous novels. In *Mardi* and *Moby-Dick* the author led a shadowy existence within the voyaging narrator and partook of his triumphs and his doubts. This earlier method was based on an overriding faith in the symbolistic point of view. Melville's presence in the book could only mean, despite all the methodological questions he raised, that in the last analysis he submitted himself to his expanding vision. The "I" of *Pierre* is more skeptical. Though he too inhabits his creation, he is also a free agent, the objective workman and the critical observer. He performs the same function as the "I" of *Les Faux-monnayeurs*— to dramatize the double activity which is the whole artistic process. On the other hand, Melville's skepticism goes farther than Gide's, just as Pierre goes far beyond Edouard. How far does Melville go? He cannot successfully adopt the nihilism of Pierre (whereas Gide *can* associate himself with Edouard). Yet the design of his book requires a parallelism between himself and his hero. Does he manage to overcome this discrepancy?

He does not, and many of the weaknesses of the novel can be traced to the resulting confusion in Melville's attitude. To the extent that he enters into the balanced spirit of Gide, he gives a striking portrait of the artist at work. To the extent that he is carried away by Pierre's negativity—or, what amounts to the same thing, to the extent that Pierre's negativity reflects his own—his outlook becomes uncertain. Both elements are likely to be present in any particular passage. Read in one way, Melville's comments on the progress of the story are very similar to Gide's. He often professes ignorance: "It will be observed, that neither points of the above speculations do we, in set terms, attribute to Pierre.... Possibly both might be applicable; possibly neither." He would "let the ambiguous procession of events reveal their own ambiguousness" and would follow rather than lead: "I shall follow the endless, winding way, ... careless whither I be led, reckless where I land." He represents himself, in short, as the creature of his creation. At the same time he is the conscious creator: "In general terms we have been thus decided in asserting the great genealogical and real-estate dignity of some families in America, because in so doing we poetically establish the richly aristocratic condition of Master Pierre Glendinning." Having likewise established the dignity of Lucy, he asks: "By immemorial usage, am I not bound to celebrate this Lucy Tartan? Who shall stay me? Is she not my hero's own affianced?" Balanced off against one another, Melville's comments reflect the paradoxical workings of the writer's mind.

But he is enough like his hero to regard the paradox as destructive. He mocks his own literary aspirations. The oddly sneering tone that pervades so much of the book is apparent in the two passages just quoted, where he exposes his own "jugglery." William Braswell is surely right when he speaks of the "satirical temper" of *Pierre;* but the root of the satire is self-satire. By way of contrast, Gide is merely ironic at his own expense. He wonders "with some anxiety where his tale will take him." Melville pictures himself as "careless" and "reckless." He blusters when he describes the variability of aesthetic truth:

As a statue, planted on a revolving pedestal, shows now this limb, now that; now front, now back, now side; continually changing, too, its general profile; so does the pivoted, statued soul of man, when turned by the hand of Truth. Lies only never vary; look for no invariableness in Pierre. Nor does any canting showman here stand by to announce his phases as he revolves. Catch his phases as your insight may.

Taken seriously, this passage is a good description of symbolic reality. But the ranting tone discredits the statement. Melville cannot take himself seriously, and he becomes unsure: "There is infinite nonsense in the world on all of these matters; hence blame me not if I contribute my mite. It is impossible to talk or to write without apparently throwing oneself helplessly open; the Invulnerable Knight wears his visor down." After a mock-pompous discussion of the two chief "modes of writing history," he concludes: "I elect neither of these; I am careless of either; both are well enough in their way; I write precisely as I please." *Pierre* is too much like the book one can imagine being produced by its hero. If it fails as a conventional novel, this happens not because Melville is incapable of handling the form but because he is contemptuous of literary form in general. He is not satisfied, like Gide, to disappoint conventional expectations and thus to suggest the "creamy chaos" from which all form emerges; he must devise a preposterous story, so patently absurd that it casts doubt even on the serious use he would make of its symbols. If the style of *Pierre* is grotesque—by turns mawkish, pretentious, and eccentric—it is the style of an author who suspects from the beginning what his hero discovers in the end, that all literature is meretricious. He suspects that the sentimental dithyrambics on nature that he parodies in his opening pages are no more fraudulent than his own "card-packing."

Within five years he would cease to consider himself a professional writer, taking refuge in silence. If *Pierre*, like its hero's book, was "a detected cheat," no other recourse was possible. Silence was the artistic equivalent of Pierre's death. But the theme of *Pierre*, from another point of view, is precisely the ambiguity of silence, which, like the whiteness of the whale, is "at once the most harmless and the most awful thing in all nature." It is the plenum of meaning and the negation of meaning, God and Devil. Though Melville comes close to being strangled by the negativity of his hero, his positive purpose somehow survives: to present his eternally undecided battle "with the angel—Art," which *is* a battle because the angel is also a devil. Melville has a flexibility that Pierre lacks. Both are like the priest who "was in the act of publicly administering the bread at the Holy Sacrament of the Supper, when the Evil One suddenly propounded to him the possibility of the mere moonshine of the Christian Religion." And both differ from the priest in that they cannot defeat the Devil merely by summoning up their faith in supposedly absolute truths. Their job is to find a criterion in the course of their own vital activity, which is itself the "sacrament" that is constantly being called into question. Pierre gives up the battle and grants that all is "moonshine." Melville takes the battle as his absolute. He ranges from one extreme to the other, affirming the Devil so that he may also affirm the divine. "Silence is the only Voice of our God," he writes; and yet, a few pages later, he bitterly asks "how . . . a man [can] get a Voice out of Silence." The stuff of life is "endless significancies," but the exploration of significance ends in nothingness:

Far as any geologist has yet gone down into the world, it is found to consist of nothing but surface stratified on surface. To its axis, the world being nothing but superinduced superficies. By vast pains we mine into the pyramid; by horrible gropings we come to the central room; with joy we espy the sarcophagus; but we lift the lid—and no body is there!—appallingly vacant as vast is the soul of a man!

It is not merely by accident that this, the finest passage in the book, shifts without logical transition from "the world" to "the soul." Significance, which is at once everything and nothing, is both subject and object. Here again we must give the Devil his due. Melville parodies the Emersonian "marriage of mind and nature," wherein "all this Earth is Love's affianced." He doubts the Emersonian doctrine that "from each successive world, the demon Principle is more and more dislodged . . . by every new translation." On the contrary, if there is no "Ultimate of Human Speculative Knowledge," it is because of the "barbarous hordes which Truth ever nourishes in the loins of her frozen, yet teeming North," and which overturn every synthesis. The evolution of thought is a series of revolutions, and it is the Devil who puts his shoulder to the wheel.

Meaning and moonshine, harmony and discord, are logically irreconcilable but supplement each other. The opposition between "heaven" and "earth," which runs through the book and is ostensibly resolved in Plinlimmon's pamphlet, falls into the same pattern. According to Plinlimmon, the beginning of wisdom is the realization that heavenly ("chronometrical") truth is at variance with earthly ("horological") truth; for ours is "an artificial world," more remote from the absolute than China time from Greenwich time. From this standpoint, "a virtuous expediency" is "the highest desirable or attainable earthly excellence for the mass of men," and Pierre's great error is his defiance of convention. Melville often seems to ally himself with Plinlimmon:

> It is not for man to follow the trail of truth too far, since by so doing he entirely loses the directing compass of his mind; for arrived at the Pole, to whose barrenness only it points, there, the needle indifferently respects all points of the horizon alike.

In departing from convention, Pierre achieves nothing positive and yet destroys all human scales of measure. The nearer he moves to the absolute, the more he sees "all objects . . . in a dubious, uncertain, and refracting light." He sees "the most immemorially admitted maxims of men begin to slide and fluctuate, and finally become wholly inverted." But is this the result of Pierre's error or of human fate? The issue as put by Plinlimmon and as Melville sometimes seems to put it—a simple choice between the unattainable absolute and earthly fiction—begs the question, since "there is no China Wall that man can build in his soul" to ward off "sudden onsets of new truth." Man in general and Pierre in particular are "fitted by nature for profound and fearless thought." The issue before them is not how to judge the conflicting claims of the artificial and real but how to survive at all when every step of thought is at once artificial and real, subversive and constructive, barren and fertile.

To this question there can be no answer except in action, which raises the question again and again. Pierre's dream of Enceladus comes close to the root of his troubles. The ever renewed effort of the giant to reach the absolute is symbolized by his ancestry, the repeated match of earth and heaven. At the same time his "organic blended heavenliness and earthliness" is "doubly incestuous." The productivity of thought is also a kind of inbreeding—like Pierre's love for his mother and sister—every stage of which puts the thinker farther from his goal. Even the Plinlimmon pamphlet, which seems to dogmatize, turns out to be one more instance of the problem, not Melville's "solution." Its title is "Ei"—"If"—and it ends abruptly with "Moreover: if—." The rational conclusion, the "then" clause, is conspicuously lacking. From it, Melville says, "I confess, that I myself can derive no conclusion. . . . For to me it seems more the excellently illustrated re-statement of a problem, than the solution of the problem itself." Having postulated an absolute which is wholly incommensurable with human experience, Plinlimmon hastens to add that the two, nevertheless, *are* commensurable: "It follows not . . . that God's truth is one thing and man's truth another; but . . . by their very contradictions they are made to correspond." Plinlimmon plunges back into the unity of contradictions that Melville and Pierre inhabit. Indeed, he himself, as he watches Pierre from his window, is the embodiment of the problematic: silent yet eloquent, homogeneous yet complex, "mystic-mild" yet capable of conveying "to most philosophical observers a notion of something not before included in their scheme of the Universe."

Edouard would like to end his book with the words "Might be continued." Gide virtually does just that. "It must not be neatly rounded off," he tells himself in his journal, "but rather disperse, disintegrate." Pierre's "untimely, timely end" is as inconclusive as the last paragraph of *Les Faux-monnayeurs*. Though his suicide concludes his worldly career, it does not solve his problems. These are "ambiguous still," and the novel, like Plinlimmon's pamphlet, reaches "a most untidy termination." Melville conceives the whole book as an instance of those "profounder emanations of the human mind" which escape from "speculative lies," have "no proper endings," and "hurry to abrupt intermergings with the eternal tides of time and fate." Life and literature, he says, derive from a God whose nature is "inscrutableness"—who is the source of questions, not of final answers. God is a tragic principle. But this conception renders tragedy in a new key. *Pierre* expresses what Melville once called (in a letter to Hawthorne) "the tragicalness of human thought in its own unbiassed, native, and profounder workings." Thought is both hero and villain. Edouard has the same idea:

> There is a kind of tragedy, it seems to me, which has hitherto almost entirely eluded literature. The novel has dealt with the contrariness of fate, good or evil fortune, social relationships, the conflicts of passions and of characters—but not with the very essence of man's being.... There are novels whose purpose is edification; but that has nothing to do with what I mean. Moral tragedy—the tragedy, for instance, which gives such terrific meaning to the Gospel text: "If the salt have lost his flavour, wherewith shall it be salted?"—that is the tragedy with which I am concerned.

Edouard is not concerned with classic tragedy, with the triumph of evil over good and the resurgence of good out of evil, but with what happens when such terms lose their established meaning— when good loses its savor of goodness, or in Melville's language, when it appears that "the uttermost virtue ... [may] prove but a betraying pander to the monstrousest vice." The tragedy of human thought is that the very process of thought is self-betraying. Here indeed "no villain need be"; not because "we are betrayed by what is false within," but because of the inherent falsity of every truth. "As soon as you say *Me*, a *God*, a *Nature*," Melville writes, "so soon you jump off from your stool and hang from the beam." The backbone of *Pierre* is this sense of the tragic convertibility between truth and falsehood, good and evil.

The book's great defect is the inability of Melville and Pierre to preserve that point of view. "Si le grain ne meurt," Gide quotes: life is a series of little deaths, out of which life always returns. The persistence of life and thought disproves the nihilism of Pierre —and of Melville, in so far as he shares his attitude. Pierre twists the valid tragedy into melodrama. He is not strong enough to endure the endless warfare of the spirit. Murder and suicide, though he realizes that they bring no solution, are his attempt to force a conclusion. While he knows that what he calls his "fate" is the intrinsic ambiguity of life, he likes to regard it as externally imposed, and he seeks revenge:

On my strong faith in ye Invisibles, I stake three whole felicities, and three whole lives this day. If ye forsake me now,—farewell to Faith, farewell to Truth, farewell to God; exiled for aye from God and man, I shall declare myself an equal power with both; free to make war on Night and Day, and all thoughts and things of mind and matter, which the upper and the nether firmaments do clasp!

Melville's considerable sympathy with his hero's passionate resentment robs him of aesthetic balance. He tends to see Pierre's tragedy and the parallel problem of his own authorship as though they were contrived by some malevolent external force. Ahab supplants Ishmael within him. For practical purposes, he is about to adopt a less frantic but equally negative approach. This is foreshadowed in the very letter where he speaks of "the tragicalness of human thought." Like Pierre, he pictures man as "a sovereign nature (in himself) amid the powers of heaven, hell, and earth." Man is a diplomat at a parley:

He may perish; but so long as he exists he insists upon treating with all Powers upon an equal basis. If any of those other Powers choose to withhold certain secrets, let them; that does not impair my sovereignty in myself; that does not make me tributary.

What man carries away from the parley is "the visible truth,... the apprehension of the absolute condition of present things as they strike the eye of the man who fears them not." Such truth is frankly subjective, but it has the advantage of escaping the *"Being* of the matter,... the knot with which we choke ourselves." In so doing, it also writes an end to the "tragic phase of humanity" that the letter sets out to define. It substitutes a comfortable skepticism:

For all men who say *yes*, lie; and all men who say *no*,—why, they are in the happy condition of judicious, unincumbered travellers in Europe; they cross the frontiers into Eternity with nothing but a carpet-bag,—that is to say, the Ego. Whereas those *yes*-gentry, they travel with heaps of baggage, and, damn them! they will never get through the Custom House.

After the humorless rantings of *Pierre*, this quizzical self-sufficiency would be welcome. But it would mark the approaching abdication of an author who once wanted to carry the entire universe through the Custom House and boasted that he could assimilate all creeds.

Something of his new attitude is apparent in *The Confidence Man*, his last novel before the thirty years when he wrote nothing but awkward verse. *Pierre* had failed because Melville was not able to maintain Gide's stand: "to rise to the point of accepting and assuming all the contradictions of his too rich nature . . . the point of seeking not to resolve them but to feed them." If *The Confidence Man* is more successful—at once less labored and more controlled —Melville regained his balance not by rising to the complexity of Gide's outlook but by simplification. He is less involved in the action than ever before. Here for the first time the unsolved, insoluble problem of the book is not brought closely to bear on his own artistic processes. To a considerable extent, Melville is the independent ego, the amused observer of a "masquerade"; he watches but does not lose himself in the ceaseless fusion and disintegration which are the world of *The Confidence Man*. For the first time, he does not emphasize the quest for rational objects. He is not trying to "strike through the mask" but is content to take every personage as a *persona:*

"How? Does all the world act? Am *I*, for instance, an actor? Is my reverend friend here, too, a performer?"

"Yes, don't you both perform acts? To do, is to act; so all doers are actors."

Such considerations had led to the artistic uncertainty of *Pierre*. But in *The Confidence Man* Melville is not greatly troubled by questions of fiction and reality. He leaves that for the most part to his characters, the "yes-gentry," who deserve whatever difficulties they encounter:

> The cosmopolitan turned on his heel, leaving his companion at a loss to determine where exactly the fictitious character had been dropped, and the real one, if any, resumed. If any, because, with pointed meaning, there occurred to him, as he gazed after the cosmopolitan, these familiar lines:—
>
>> "All the world's a stage,
>> And all the men and women merely players,
>> Who have their exits and their entrances,
>> And one man in his time plays many parts."

Nevertheless, the theme of the book restates and inherently refers to Melville's old dilemma. Artistic "confidence" is precisely what he was losing through twelve years of writing, and in the last analysis *The Confidence Man* proposes no way to regain it. The book, for all its verve, is essentially valedictory. It is the comic counterpart of *Pierre,* the comedy of human thought, and points just as surely to Melville's retirement.

The major symbols are money and the voyage. The "masquerade" is both the fluid reality of the journey down the Mississippi and the deliberate impostures of the con-men who infest the ship "Fidèle." The life of the great river at the heart of the continent represents the perpetually new world of symbolic experience— endless, expansive, and metamorphic—which had long been identified in Melville's mind with the westward movement of America. "Here reigned the dashing and all-fusing spirit of the West, whose type is the Mississippi itself, which, uniting the streams of the most distant and opposite zones, pours them along, helter-skelter, in one cosmopolitan and confident tide." The action, like the voyage downstream from landing to landing, is episodic yet continuous. Even the hero undergoes a constant change of form and character, a method which Melville defends in terms very like the argument of *Pierre* against rational system:

> That fiction, where every character can, by reason of its consistency, be comprehended at a glance, either exhibits but sections of character,

making them appear for wholes, or else is very untrue to reality; while, on the other hand, that author who draws a character, even though to common view incongruous in its parts, as the flying-squirrel, and, at different periods, as much at variance with itself as the butterfly is with the caterpillar into which it changes, may yet, in so doing, be not false but faithful to facts.

All is inconclusive. The ship never reaches New Orleans. "Might be continued" is the last sentence of the book: "Something further may follow of this Masquerade." And yet Melville claims an organic unity. The con-man is an "original" character in a special sense; he is originative:

The original character, essentially such, is like a revolving Drummond light, raying away from itself all round it—everything is lit by it, everything starts up to it (mark how it is with Hamlet), so that, in certain minds, there follows upon the adequate conception of such a character, an effect, in its way, akin to that which in Genesis attends upon the beginning of things.

This book exemplifies the "history of the genesis" which, Emerson said, "repeats itself in the experience of every child." Though "a work of amusement," it is a creative creation—a kind of fiction where one may "look not only for more entertainment, but, at bottom, even for more reality, than real life itself can show."

On the other hand, this very realm of inconclusive creativity is the habitat of the confidence man. His financial schemes are the manipulation of a token world in which we all necessarily live. In this respect the professional impostor and his victims are alike. All are committed to—one taking advantage of, and the others caught in—a situation where no verification is possible, where confidence and lack of confidence are equally arbitrary. On the river, the "transfer-book" of a stock company is all one can know of the company. It is useless to study the text:

Doubts, maybe, it might suggest, but not knowledge; for how, by examining the book, should I think I knew any more than I now think I do; since, if it be the true book, I think it so already; and since if it be otherwise, then I have never seen the true one, and don't know what that ought to look like.

All the passengers in the "great white bulk" of the "Fidèle," hunters and "still keener hunters after ... these hunters," are "merchants on 'change," dealing in a medium that is subject to infinite revaluations. Their world is like the "Protean easy-chair" invented by the con-man:

> My Protean easy-chair is a chair so all over bejointed, behinged, and bepadded, every way so elastic, springy, and docile to the airiest touch, that in some one of its endlessly changeable accommodations of back, seat, footboard, and arms, the most restless body, the body most racked, nay, I had almost added the most tormented conscience must, somehow and somewhere, find rest.

Anything so responsive is irresponsible. The "confident tide" is the most immediate of experiences, but the insubstantiality and fluidity of experience are such that the very question of confidence becomes absurd.

The basic comedy of the book is the interplay of these two phases of the masquerade: the antics of men who "have confidence, and then again ... have none," who try to choose without any means of choosing, and who fall into all the grotesque postures of their Protean medium. The comedy has its positive side. Their very effort to choose is an act of faith. Paradoxically, they are on firmest ground when they are most troubled. The con-man is the Devil, but as such he has a function. He unsettles; he forces the issue:

> Now, what I would ask is, do you think it sensible standing for a sensible man, one foot on confidence and the other on suspicion? Don't you think ... that you ought to elect? Don't you think consistency requires that you either say, "I have confidence in all men," ... or else say, "I suspect all men" ... ?

Indirectly, the con-man suggests an answer which is neither of the alternatives he offers. There is a *modus vivendi* in the instinctive repudiation of "consistency." True confidence is not the absolute faith he opposes to doubt; nor is the dubious simply "the fiction as opposed to the fact." Life is inconsistent; it is the meeting point of "trust" and "no trust," fiction and reality. Confidence is the process of living these contradictions. In the comedy of human thought, as in the tragedy of *Pierre,* meaning lies precisely in the conflict between the meaningful and the meaningless. The "Fidèle," though honeycombed with falsehood, justifies its name in a roundabout way. An organic unity that thrives on opposition is symbolized by the passage of the sun from the dawn at the beginning of *The Confidence Man* to the gathering darkness of the final pages.

Still, the night does come, and in such a way as to augur no further dawn. As the last chapter opens, the creative "Drummond light" is failing:

In the middle of the gentlemen's cabin burned a solar lamp, swung from the ceiling, and whose shade of ground glass was all round fancifully variegated, in transparency, with the image of a horned altar, from which flames rose, alternate with the figure of a robed man, his head encircled by a halo. The light of this lamp, after dazzlingly striking on marble, snow-white and round—the slab of a centre-table beneath—on all sides went rippling off with ever-diminishing distinctness, till, like circles from a stone dropped in water, the rays died dimly away in the furthest nook of the place.

Here and there, true to their place, but not to their function, swung other lamps, barren planets, which had either gone out from exhaustion, or been extinguished by such occupants of berths as the light annoyed, or who wanted to sleep, not see.

The spherical world expands into nothingness, and the white marble, like the whiteness of the "Fidèle," confuses all clear and distinct ideas. Though the last sentence of the book promises "something further ... of this Masquerade," it is voided by the context: "the waning light expired, and with it the waning flames of the horned altar, and the waning halo round the robed man's brow." What is departing is not merely the image of God but the divine principle of creativity. The genetic power of the imagination is impotent. The last of Melville's voyagers is a helpless old man, "his head snowy as the marble," who sits beneath the fading lamp. When the light goes out, he stumbles off, clutching his "hollow" life-preserver, his money belt, and his useless "Counterfeit Detector." He is guided by the con-man, the "cosmopolitan" of a fraudulent cosmos, who preaches a groundless faith. The comedy of thought is ultimately negative. The theme of *The Confidence Man* leaves Melville, as Starbuck said of Ahab, with "his standpoint . . . stove," a victim of the dilemma which *was* his standpoint throughout his career.

Many have found in *Billy Budd,* thirty years later, a new mood of "acceptance," based on a new, dogmatic standpoint, of which Captain Vere is the spokesman. Like the skeptical concept of "visible truth," Vere's authoritarian dogmatism would seem to be a way to escape the *"Being* of the matter," which is also "the knot with which we choke ourselves." But actually neither *Billy Budd* nor the poetry of Melville's later years can be explained in terms so remote from his characteristic point of view. *Billy Budd* "accepts" in the sense in which everything Melville wrote might be called a *de facto* "testament of acceptance" and at the same time a prophecy of failure. It accepts the problematic, the inconclusive, the contradictory. The dogmatism of Captain Vere, which is set off against his own instincts and the instinct of his plodding officers, is not the conclusion but the problem of the story. The only "solution" lies in the story at large—precisely in the *"Being* of the matter"—where, as Plinlimmon would say, "by their very contradictions they are made to correspond." For Melville, dogmatism and skepticism alike could only be alternatives to art, not possible artistic attitudes. He was committed to the problematic method which had led equally to his moments of triumph and to his capitulation. It was for this reason that he could return, even after *The Confidence Man,* to the occasional practice of his art. The forces that had driven him from the field were the weapons in his own armory. *Billy Budd* marks the indecisive end of a campaign which could neither be wholly lost nor wholly won. And the poems reflect the irrepressible, involuntary withdrawal and return of an artist who "wrestled with the pristine forms / Like the first man," who knew the "hour of such control / As shapes, concretes," as well as the hour of impotence:

> When old forms are annulled, and new
> Rebel, and pangs suspend the birth.

Postscript

The gift of expression, the bewildering, the illuminating, the most exalted and the most contemptible, the pulsating stream of light, or the deceitful flow from the heart of an impenetrable darkness.

CONRAD, *Heart of Darkness*

In brief: the affinity between large areas of American literature and of modern literature brings to light unsuspected aspects of both. In this perspective the classic American writers take on a new unity of direction, a new historical status, and a new subtlety of achievement. Modern literature becomes a less unaccountable phenomenon; it is naturalized in a long, rather covert historical movement, of which American writing is a major phase. And both point toward a rationale of the affinity one finds between them: toward a definition of "symbolism." Together they body forth a large-scale shift of categories through which "the meaning of meaning" becomes the generative question of literature and philosophy.

But the whole process by which idealism and materialism, romanticism and realism, give way to the symbolistic point of view is hedged about with difficulties. The meaning of meaning is a new *question*—not a new answer. The difficulties are at once literary and intellectual, theoretical and practical, specifically aesthetic and broadly humanistic. In general, how can symbolism, having transcended the characteristic oppositions of the last few hundred years, come to grips with all the patent dualisms of life, which are given to reason and epitomized in rational method? In particular, how can a distinctively aesthetic approach, both in theory and in practice, render an adequate account of ethical fact?

These and related problems are brought into focus by critics like T. E. Hulme and Eliot. Against the entire "naturalistic" and "humanistic" bent of philosophy since the Renaissance, Hulme poses what he calls a "religious" Weltanschauung. He holds that these three attitudes are appropriate to three discontinuous areas of reality: the world of mechanistic physics, the "vital" world of organism, and the "world of ethical and religious values." Both the physical and the religious worlds "have . . . an absolute character, and knowledge about them can legitimately be called absolute knowledge," while the middle region is relative. Humanism is able to see the "chasm" between vital and mechanical reality; to this extent it marks an advance on mere naturalism, which confuses the two. But humanism—which leads to romanticism in literature, idealism in metaphysics, liberalism in politics, and relativism in ethics—has fallen into grievous error by failing to preserve the other distinction, between the vital and the religious. Hulme maintains that romanticism, idealism, liberalism, and relativism are "bastard phenomena," the result of seeking absolute values in a realm which is essentially fluid. From the standpoint of the reli-

gious absolute, the prime ethical fact is Original Sin, which sepa-
rates man from the divine perfection; and the prime political fact
is the need for "institutions" and for "discipline." Similarly,
Hulme prescribes and prophesies a "classical" and "abstract" art.
Since the religious outlook limits the nature of man, in contrast to
romanticism, which is "always . . . talking about the infinite," the
great aim of its art will be "accurate, precise and definite description." And since the religious view necessitates a discontinuity between man, the world, and the divine, its art will not reflect "a
happy pantheistic relation between man and the outside world" but
rather "a desire to create a certain abstract geometrical shape,
which, being durable and permanent, shall be a refuge from . . .
flux and impermanence." Abstract art will presuppose an absolute
beyond man and the physical world.

Oddly conjoined with this prophecy of an art founded on a renewed distinction between man and nature, nature and God, is
Hulme's Bergsonian strain. Hulme is deeply drawn to Bergson's vision of a fluid world given to immediate intuition and inaccessible
to the rational intellect. He finds in Bergson an account of the real
"interpenetration" which is the matrix of the work of art. The "distinctively aesthetic emotion," according to Hulme, is a sense that
the rational "veil" has been lifted and that we are in the presence
of the world as it really is. Both the premises and the conclusion of
this theory are far removed from those of Hulme's "religious"
view. When Hulme Bergsonizes, he is setting out from aesthetic
fact and from the problem posed for the artist by the rationalist
metaphysics of modern thought. But when he preaches a new dogmatism, he has in mind primarily the ethical problem raised by a
philosophy that excludes any point of reference beyond the sphere
of human experience. While one problem leads him away from
the method and structure of rational thinking, the other forces him
to return. Though he agrees with Bergson that aesthetic reality is
not geometry, he advocates a geometrical art; though he sees "the
artist . . . placing himself back within the object by a kind of sympathy and breaking down by an effort of intuition the barrier . . .

between him and his model," he contends that the basis of modern
abstractionism is "a feeling of separation in the face of outside
nature." Hulme is caught between a desire to vindicate aesthetic
perception and an even stronger desire, to which the needs of art
are subordinate, to vindicate ethical absolutes.

A similar doubleness complicates the literary theory of Eliot and
has been transmitted to his followers. On the one hand, Eliot's conception of the aesthetic fact is essentially antirational; his conception of "tradition" is avowedly the conception of an "organic
whole." He pictures an impersonal medium "in which impressions
and experiences combine in peculiar and unexpected ways" to form
"a new thing." And the advent of this new thing is part of the becoming which constitutes literature:

> What happens when a new work of art is created is something that
> happens simultaneously to all the works of art which preceded it. The
> existing monuments form an ideal order among themselves, which is
> modified by the introduction of the new (the really new) work of art
> among them. The existing order is complete before the new work
> arrives; for order to persist after the supervention of novelty, the
> *whole* existing order.must be, if ever so slightly, altered; and so the
> relations, proportions, values of each work of art toward the whole
> are readjusted; and this is conformity between the old and the new.

It is apparent that any brand of dogmatism is foreign to this aspect
of Eliot's theory. Pursuing his theme of aesthetic impersonality in
the face of the prevalent romantic-realist system, Eliot is brought
to "doubt whether belief proper enters into the activity of a great
poet, *qua* poet. That is, Dante, *qua* poet, did not believe or dis-
believe the Thomist cosmology or theory of the soul: he merely
made use of it, or a fusion took place between his initial emotional
impulses and a theory, for the purpose of making poetry. The poet
makes poetry, the metaphysician makes metaphysics, the bee makes
honey, the spider secretes a filament; you can hardly say that any
of these agents believes: he merely does." To locate the intellectual
affinities of such a statement, one has only to recall Thoreau's question: "Who shall distinguish between the *law* by which a brook

finds its river, the *instinct* [by which] a bird performs its migrations, and the *knowledge* by which a man steers his ship around the globe?" When Eliot is concerned with literature per se, he falls into line with theories abhorrent to Eliot the dogmatist.

On the other hand, he *is* a would-be dogmatist. In this role he is motivated not by a need to reaffirm the distinctive method of art but by ethical, social, and political considerations. Like Hulme, he requires an absolute beyond experience in order to judge experience; he deprecates relativism, tolerance, and liberty as ideals. To some extent, his two views reinforce one another. In both cases he damns "personality," and in both cases he lauds "tradition." But the same arguments that he directs against romantic individualism would apply to the "peculiar and unexpected" forms of symbolic perception. And Eliot the moralist is more concerned with the way "the present is directed by the past" than with the way the past is "altered by the present"; he is more concerned with the possibility of a rational orthodoxy than with organic tradition. The whole tendency of his discussion of literature when he speaks as the exponent of the new dogmatism is to put a brake on the symbolistic process by means of an external criterion. Having postulated a fluid and inconclusive experience as the province of art, he goes on to contrive a further absolute, in the light of which many possibilities of experience become "heretical."

While Eliot and Hulme avowedly urge their dogmas because they believe them to be true, their usual appeal is to the pragmatics of our current historical situation. Moreover, they argue not so much for a special set of doctrines as for dogmatism in general. And any philosophy which would take the aesthetic fact as its primary datum—any literature which would ground itself in such a philosophy—must make due allowance for the strategic value of their dogmatic absolutism. They allege that ungovernable "individualism" is the inevitable consequence of a failure in orthodoxy; that an ethical relativism is necessarily blind to positive evil; and that "liberalism" is synonymous with a vapid optimism. Such arguments have rightly troubled even the confident humanist, who is "depressed by the obvious fact . . . that liberalism has not been able to produce a literature which can strongly engage our emotions" and by an awareness that there are "certain kinds of behavior which on the whole liberalism has been unable to face or understand." The bases of dogmatism—the impulsion toward objective belief, the necessity of ethical judgment, and the experience of human limitation—are ineluctable. Though dogmas change, the dogmatic principle persists. Dogmatism aside, dogmatizing remains.

But we *can* leave dogmatism aside. If Eliot and Hulme help to locate the besetting problems of modern literature, they are hardly fair to the scope of symbolism (and in this sense one might say that they are hardly fair to themselves). For at his best the symbolist is supremely conscious of the very tensions Eliot and Hulme would reinstate by their emphasis on absolutes. His basic aesthetic problem is the incompatibility between the individual and the impersonal vision; his problem, indeed, is not so much to control as to do justice to his own individuality. The structure of his world is built up by the continuous interplay between real opposition—the compulsion toward moral choice—and real harmony—the compulsion toward moral indifference. And "liberalism" is not, in his hands, a naïve faith in the synthetic power of human reason but a recognition of the diversity that reason contemplates and art resolves. Symbolism, in short, has no need of dogmatism as a corrective; the extravagancies of symbolists like Emerson are corrected in the problematic attitude of symbolists like Melville and Gide. Hulme claims that only the "religious" attitude, by realizing "the *gap* between the regions of vital and human things, and that of the *absolute* values of ethics and religion," can grasp "the *tragic* significance of life." But there is tragedy enough in the gap between the world as given to reason and the world as given to aesthetic apprehension. This it is the mission of the symbolist to render.

Symbolism is humanism, but a critical humanism. The "gift of expression," the specifically human power, is such by virtue of also being the locus of error, confusion, darkness. If Kurtz, who "presented himself as a voice," was all but destroyed by his gift, and if Marlow, himself a voice in the darkness, could not finally disengage the truth from the corrupting lie, both were saved by the articulation of their insecurity. "To the destructive element submit yourself," says Stein in *Lord Jim*, "and with the exertions of your hands and feet in the water make the deep, deep sea keep you up." Something like that is the radical principle—the method and the recurrent theme—of the literature surveyed in this book. It is a viable principle. In that "twilight of the absolute" where painting and sculpture, as Malraux declares, have become their own absolute, literature too is autotelic. But in serving itself alone and thereby furthering "art's eternal victory over the destiny of mankind," it acknowledges the defeat that is always implicit in the victory. Its victory, like that of Marlow, is only "the culminating point of . . . experience," and, like that of Kurtz, is "paid for by innumerable defeats."

Bibliographical Note

A number of works bearing on the theory and practice of symbolism are mentioned in the notes to chapter ii. This bibliographical note will be confined to works on American literature and will be further limited to books and essays, mostly of recent date, which have directly influenced the present study or are closely related in theme. The works listed here represent, as it were, a context for this book as well as an acknowledgment of my major obligations.

Among general surveys of American thought and letters, this study owes most to the following: Norman Foerster, *American Criticism* (Boston, 1928); Joseph Haroutunian, *Piety versus Moralism: The Passing of the New England Theology* (New York,

1932); D. H. Lawrence, *Studies in Classic American Literature* (New York, 1923); F. O. Matthiessen, *American Renaissance* (New York, 1941); Perry Miller, *The New England Mind: The Seventeenth Century* (New York, 1939), together with his Introduction to Jonathan Edwards' *Images or Shadows of Divine Things* (New Haven, 1948), pages 1–41, his biography of Edwards (New York, 1949), and his article, "Jonathan Edwards to Emerson," *New England Quarterly*, XIII (1940), 589–617; the Introduction by Perry Miller and T. H. Johnson to their anthology, *The Puritans* (New York, 1938), pages 1–79; Perry Miller (ed.), *The Transcendentalists: An Anthology* (Cambridge, Mass., 1950); Lewis Mumford, *The Golden Day: A Study in American Experience and Culture* (New York, 1926); K. B. Murdock, *Literature and Theology in Colonial New England* (Cambridge, Mass., 1949); H. B. Parkes, "The Puritan Heresy" and "Emerson," in *The Pragmatic Test: Essays on the History of Ideas* (San Francisco, 1941), pages 10–62; V. L. Parrington, *Main Currents in American Thought* (New York, 1927); R. B. Perry, *Puritanism and Democracy* (New York, 1944); Philip Rahv, "Paleface and Redskin" and "The Cult of Experience in American Writing," in *Image and Idea* (New York, 1949); H. W. Schneider, *The Puritan Mind* (New York, 1930) and *A History of American Philosophy* (New York, 1946); and Yvor Winters, *Maule's Curse* (Norfolk, Conn., 1938).

In the case of Hawthorne the most pertinent biographies have proved to be those by Newton Arvin (Boston, 1929) and Mark Van Doren (New York, 1949), especially the later. On general topics connected with Hawthorne's art the following works should be cited: Walter Blair, "Color, Light, and Shadow in Hawthorne's Fiction," *New England Quarterly*, XV (1942), 74–94; F. I. Carpenter, "Puritans Preferred Blondes: The Heroines of Melville and Hawthorne," *New England Quarterly*, IX (1936), 253–72; Malcolm Cowley, "Hawthorne in the Looking Glass," *Sewanee Review*, LVI (1948), 545–63; Vega Curl, *Pasteboard Masks* (Cambridge, Mass., 1931); Q. D. Leavis, "Hawthorne as Poet,"

Sewanee Review, LIX (1951), 179–205, 426–58; R. H. Pearce, "Hawthorne and the Twilight of Romance," *Yale Review,* XXXVII (1947–48), 487–506; Philip Rahv, "The Dark Lady of Salem," in *Image and Idea* (New York, 1949), pages 22–41; J. W. Schroeder, " 'That Inward Sphere': Notes on Hawthorne's Heart Imagery and Symbolism," *PMLA,* LXV (1950), 106–19; Leland Schubert, *Hawthorne the Artist: Fine-Art Devices in Fiction* (Chapel Hill, 1944).

In recent years many relevant essays have appeared dealing with individual novels and tales of Hawthorne: Darrel Abel, "Hawthorne's Pearl: Symbol and Character," *ELH,* XVIII (1951), 50–66; Edward Davidson, *Hawthorne's Last Phase* (New Haven, 1949); M. E. Dichmann, "Hawthorne's 'Prophetic Pictures,' " *American Literature,* XXIII (1951), 188–202; a series of articles by R. H. Fogle—"Ambiguity and Clarity in Hawthorne's 'Young Goodman Brown,' " *New England Quarterly,* XVIII (1945), 448–65; "An Ambiguity of Sin or Sorrow," *ibid.,* XXI (1948), 342–49; "The Problem of Allegory in Hawthorne's *Ethan Brand,*" *University of Toronto Quarterly,* XVII (1947–48), 190–203; "The World and the Artist: A Study of Hawthorne's 'The Artist of the Beautiful,' " *Tulane Studies in English,* I (1949), 31–52; and "Simplicity and Complexity in *The Marble Faun,*" *ibid.,* II (1950), 103–20; J. C. Gerber, "Form and Content in *The Scarlet Letter,*" *New England Quarterly,* XVII (1944), 25–55; R. B. Heilman, "Hawthorne's 'The Birthmark': Science as Religion," *South Atlantic Quarterly,* XLVIII (1949), 575–83; and Gordon Roper, "The Originality of Hawthorne's *The Scarlet Letter,*" *Dalhousie Review,* XXX (1950–51), 63–79.

Whitman remains largely unexplored except in terms of biography and his democratic "message." In lieu of an adequate general study, G. W. Allen's *Walt Whitman Handbook* (Chicago, 1946) has been of most assistance. Basil de Selincourt's *Walt Whitman: A Critical Study* (London, 1914) is the only large-scale treatment of formal problems. Among shorter studies the chapter on "The Musical Development of Symbols: Whitman" in C. S.

Brown's *Music and Literature* (Athens, Ga., 1948) deserves special mention. Other discussions bearing on the question of Whitman's point of view and method are: J. W. Beach, *The Concept of Nature in Nineteenth-Century English Poetry* (New York, 1936), pages 370–94; F. I. Carpenter, "Walt Whitman's 'Eidólon,'" *College English*, III (1941–42), 534–45; Jean Catel, *Rythme et langage dans la 1ʳᵉ édition des "Leaves of Grass" (1855)* (Paris, 1930); A. H. Marks, "Whitman's Triadic Imagery," *American Literature*, XXIII (1951), 99–126; D. W. Schumann, "Enumerative Style and Its Significance in Whitman, Rilke, Werfel," *Modern Language Quarterly*, III (1942), 171–204; Esther Shephard, *Walt Whitman's Pose* (New York, 1938); G. L. Sixbey, "'Chanting the Square Deific': A Study in Whitman's Religion," *American Literature*, IX (1937–38), 171–95; C. F. Strauch, "The Structure of Walt Whitman's 'Song of Myself,'" *English Journal*, XXVII (1938), 597–607; and Mattie Swayne, "Whitman's Catalogue Rhetoric," *University of Texas Studies in English*, XXI (1941), 162–78. Some illuminating commentary on Whitman's thought has appeared in connection with the alleged influence of Hegel: M. C. Boatright, "Whitman and Hegel," *University of Texas Studies in English*, IX (1929), 134–50; R. P. Falk, "Walt Whitman and German Thought," *Journal of English and Germanic Philology*, XL (1941), 315–30; and O. W. Parsons, "Whitman the Non-Hegelian," *PMLA*, LVIII (1943), 1073–93.

Virtually all current critical interpretation of Melville involves the question of symbolism: see especially Richard Chase, *Herman Melville: A Critical Study* (New York, 1949), and two recent biographies—Geoffrey Stone's *Melville* (New York, 1949) and Newton Arvin's *Herman Melville* (New York, 1950). Symbolistic interpretation has been attacked by E. E. Stoll, "Symbolism in *Moby Dick*," *Journal of the History of Ideas*, XII (1951), 440–65; and advocated by R. W. Short, "Melville as Symbolist," *University of Kansas City Review*, XV (1948–49), 38–46, and Nathalia Wright, "Form as Function in Melville," *PMLA*, LXVII (1952), 330–40.

Relevant studies on general topics—to many of which I am greatly indebted—are the following: R. P. Blackmur, "The Craft of Herman Melville: A Putative Statement," in *The Expense of Greatness* (New York, 1940), pages 139–66; William Braswell, *Melville's Religious Thought* (Durham, N.C., 1943); the essay by F. I. Carpenter listed under Hawthorne; the essay by Vega Curl, also listed under Hawthorne; Stanley Geist, *Herman Melville: The Tragic Vision and the Heroic Ideal* (Cambridge, Mass., 1939); G. C. Homans, "The Dark Angel: The Tragedy of Herman Melville," *New England Quarterly*, V (1932), 699–730; W. E. Sedgwick, *Herman Melville: The Tragedy of Mind* (Cambridge, Mass., 1944); K. H. Sundermann, *Herman Melvilles Gedankengut* (Berlin, 1937); Willard Thorp's Introduction to *Herman Melville: Representative Selections* (New York, 1938), pages xi–cxxix; R. E. Watters, "Melville's Metaphysics of Evil," *University of Toronto Quarterly*, IX (1939–40), 170–82, and "Melville's Sociality," *American Literature*, XVII (1945), 33–49; and Nathalia Wright, *Melville's Use of the Bible* (Durham, N.C., 1949).

On individual works of Melville see especially: H. P. Vincent, " 'White Jacket': An Essay in Interpretation," *New England Quarterly*, XXII (1949), 304–15; H. A. Myers, "Captain Ahab's Discovery: The Tragic Meaning of *Moby Dick*," *New England Quarterly*, XV (1942), 15–34; Charles Olson, *Call Me Ishmael* (New York, 1947); M. O. Percival, *A Reading of Moby-Dick* (Chicago, 1950); H. P. Vincent, *The Trying-Out of Moby Dick* (Cambridge, Mass., 1949); C. C. Walcutt, "The Fire Symbolism in *Moby Dick*," *Modern Language Notes*, LIX (1944), 304–10; R. E. Watters, "The Meanings of the White Whale," *University of Toronto Quarterly*, XX (1950–51), 155–68; William Braswell, "The Satirical Temper of Melville's *Pierre*," *American Literature*, VII (1935–36), 424–38, and "The Early Love Scenes of Melville's *Pierre*," *ibid.*, XXII (1950–51), 283–89; S. F. Damon, "Pierre the Ambiguous," *The Hound and Horn*, II (1928–29), 107–18; E. L. G. Watson, "Melville's *Pierre*," *New England Quarterly*, III (1930), 195–234; H. M. Campbell, "The Hanging Scene in Melville's *Billy Budd*,

Foretopman," Modern Language Notes, LXVI (1951), 378–81; Joseph Schiffman, "Melville's Final Stage, Irony: A Re-examination of *Billy Budd* Criticism," *American Literature,* XXII (1950–51), 128–36; E. L. G. Watson, "Melville's Testament of Acceptance," *New England Quarterly,* VI (1933), 319–27; Charles Weir, Jr., "Malice Reconciled: A Note on Melville's *Billy Budd,*" *University of Toronto Quarterly,* XIII (1943–44), 276–85; Newton Arvin, "Melville's Shorter Poems," *Partisan Review,* XVI (1949), 1034–46; and R. P. Warren, "Melville the Poet," *Kenyon Review,* VIII (1946), 208–23.

Modern appraisal of Poe, like that of Whitman, is inadequate. Among earlier general studies, those by Edward Shanks—*Edgar Allan Poe* (New York, 1937)—and Arthur Ransome—*Edgar Allan Poe: A Critical Study* (New York, 1920)—are most suggestive from our present point of view. Baudelaire's essays on Poe have now been conveniently collected in a translation by L. and F. E. Hyslop, Jr., *Baudelaire on Poe: Critical Papers* (State College, Pa., 1952). Companion pieces are Paul Valéry's essays: "Au Sujet d'Euréka," in *Variété* (Paris, 1924), pages 113–36, and "Situation de Baudelaire," in *Variété II* (Paris, 1930), pages 141–74. Recently two notable attempts to determine Poe's significance have appeared: T. S. Eliot's *From Poe to Valéry* (New York, 1948) and Allen Tate's "Our Cousin, Mr. Poe," *Partisan Review,* XVI (1949), 1207–19. See also Darrel Abel, "Edgar Poe: A Centennial Estimate," *University of Kansas City Review,* XVI (1949–50), 77–96, and "A Key to the House of Usher," *University of Toronto Quarterly,* XVIII (1948–49), 176–85. F. O. Matthiessen contributed a chapter on Poe to *Literary History of the United States,* ed. R. E. Spiller (New York, 1948), I, 321–44.

On Poe's literary theory see the Introduction by Margaret Alterton and Hardin Craig to *Edgar Allen Poe: Representative Selections* (New York, 1935), pages xiii–cxviii; Marvin Laser, "The Growth and Structure of Poe's Concept of Beauty," *ELH,* XV (1948), 69–84; George Snell, "First of the New Critics,"

Quarterly Review of Literature, II (1944–45), 333–40; and Floyd Stovall, "Poe's Debt to Coleridge," *University of Texas Studies in English,* X (1930), 70–127.

Some of the earlier monographs on Emerson's philosophy are still pertinent: K. O. Bertling, *Emerson und die Bildungsideale Neu-Englands* (Breslau, 1911); F. I. Carpenter, *Emerson and Asia* (Cambridge, Mass., 1930); H. D. Gray, *Emerson: A Statement of New England Transcendentalism* (Stanford, 1917); J. S. Harrison, *The Teachers of Emerson* (New York, 1910); Régis Michaud, *L'Esthétique d'Emerson* (Paris, 1927); and E. G. Sutcliffe, *Emerson's Theories of Literary Expression* (Urbana, Ill., 1923). The section on Emerson's philosophy in F. I. Carpenter's Introduction to *Ralph Waldo Emerson: Representative Selections* (New York, 1934), pages xxx–xxxviii, and the chapters on Emerson in J. W. Beach's *The Concept of Nature in Nineteenth-Century English Poetry* (New York, 1936) are especially valuable.

Perceptive recent studies of Emerson's thought are: Darrel Abel, "Strangers in Nature—Arnold and Emerson," *University of Kansas City Review,* XV (1948–49), 205–14; Walter Blair and Clarence Faust, "Emerson's Literary Method," *Modern Philology,* XLII (1944–45), 79–95; S. G. Brown, "Emerson's Platonism," *New England Quarterly,* XVIII (1945), 325–45; Kenneth Burke, "William James, Whitman, and Emerson," in *Attitudes toward History* (New York, 1937), pages 1–41; A. R. Caponigri, "Brownson and Emerson: Nature and History," *New England Quarterly,* XVIII (1945), 368–90; V. C. Hopkins, *Spires of Form: A Study of Emerson's Aesthetic Theory* (Cambridge, Mass., 1951); Sherman Paul, *Emerson's Angle of Vision* (Cambridge, Mass., 1952); and René Wellek, "Emerson and German Philosophy," *New England Quarterly,* XVI (1943), 41–62. A vast collection of materials for the study of Emerson is provided by K. W. Cameron, *Emerson the Essayist* (Raleigh, N.C., 1945).

On Horace Bushnell, who is discussed in relation to Emerson in chapter iv, see Sherman Paul, "Horace Bushnell Reconsidered," *ETC.,* VI (1948–49), 255–59.

The most relevant interpretation of Thoreau is by Sherman Paul: "The Wise Silence: Sound as the Agency of Correspondence in Thoreau," *New England Quarterly*, XXII (1949), 511–27. See also the recent biography by J. W. Krutch, *Henry David Thoreau* (New York, 1948); the critical study by R. L. Cook, *Passage to Walden* (Boston, 1949); and Ethel Seybold's *Thoreau: The Quest and the Classics* (New Haven, 1951).

Notes

[Numerals at the left refer to pages in this book. The initial phrases of each note indicate the beginning and end of the passage in the text to which the note pertains.]

INTRODUCTION

PAGE

1. "As a vast . . . each other."—Emerson, *Journals*, ed. E. W. Emerson and W. E. Forbes (Boston, 1909–14), VI, 59.

2. "All our . . . and skin."—*Ibid.*, p. 191.

   "One morning . . . Milky Way."—Melville, *Moby-Dick*, chap. xcix (*Works* [Standard ed.; London, 1922–24], VIII, 188).

   "rag of . . . my mind."—Hawthorne, "The Custom House" (*Works*, ed. G. P. Lathrop [Standard Library ed.; Boston, 1882], V, 50).

   "l'exception dans l'ordre moral"—Baudelaire, "Edgar Poe, sa vie et ses œuvres," *Œuvres complètes*, ed. Jacques Crépet (Paris, 1922–48), VI, xxviii.

229

2–3. "an atmosphere . . . our depth."—Poe, "The Fall of the House of Usher" (*Complete Works,* ed. J. A. Harrison [Virginia ed.; New York, 1902], III, 276, 273–74).

3. "long panoramas of visions"—Whitman, "When Lilacs Last in the Dooryard Bloom'd," Sec. 15 (*Leaves of Grass,* ed. Emory Holloway [Inclusive ed.; Garden City, N.Y., 1925], p. 282).

"the shows . . . over it."—Whitman, "Democratic Vistas" (*Complete Prose Works* [New York, 1914], p. 244).

Parrington almost . . . "belletristic" considerations.—V. L. Parrington, *Main Currents in American Thought* (New York, 1927), I, iii.

3–4. The first . . . of democracy."—F. O. Matthiessen, *American Renaissance: Art and Expression in the Age of Emerson and Whitman* (New York, 1941), pp. vii, ix, xv.

4. Edmund Wilson . . . modern literature.—Edmund Wilson, *Axel's Castle: A Study in the Imaginative Literature of 1870–1930* (New York, 1931), p. 12.

Winters keeps . . . "American obscurantism."—Yvor Winters, *Maule's Curse: Seven Studies in the History of American Obscurantism* (1938), reprinted in *In Defense of Reason* (New York, 1947), p. 155.

CHAPTER I

6. "I remember . . . particular occasion."—Hawthorne, *The American Notebooks,* ed. Randall Stewart (New Haven, 1932), p. 78.

He admired . . . the earth."—*Ibid.,* p. xcii.

6–7. "none of . . . of society."—Preface to *Twice-Told Tales* (*Works,* I, 16–17).

7. "a neutral . . . the other."—"The Custom House" (*Works,* V, 55).

Whereas the . . . objective world.—Preface to *The House of the Seven Gables* (*Works,* III, 13).

This doctrine . . . *Marble Faun.*—*Works,* III, 13; V, 321–22; VI, 15. Cf. the Introduction to "Rappaccini's Daughter" (*Works,* II, 107–8). Both *Twice-Told Tales* and *Mosses from an Old Manse* are full of references to Hawthorne's mid-world. *Works,* I, 79:

". . . the moment, when waking thoughts start up amid the scattered fantasies of a dream." I, 228: ". . . when fantastic dreams and madmen's reveries were realized among the actual circumstances of life . . ." I, 343: ". . . wide awake in that realm of illusions, whither sleep has been the passport . . ." I, 511–12: "I know these girls to be realities of flesh and blood, yet, glancing at them so briefly, they mingle like kindred creatures with the ideal beings of my mind. . . . Have not my musings melted into . . . rocky walls and sandy floor, and made them a portion of myself?" I, 527: ". . . a train of incidents in which the spirit and mechanism of the fairy legend should be combined with the characters and manners of familiar life." II, 11: ". . . a kind of spiritual medium, seen through which the edifice had not quite the aspect of belonging to the material world." Behind such sketches as "A Select Party" (II, 70–71) and "The Hall of Fantasy" (II, 196–211) lies the question put in "The Old Manse" (II, 32) : "Which, after all, was the most real—the picture, or the original?—the objects palpable to our grosser senses, or their apotheosis in the stream beneath?"

"attempts, and . . . the world."—Preface to *Twice-Told Tales* (*Works*, I, 17).

7–8. He chose . . . and reality."—Preface to *The Blithedale Romance* (*Works*, V, 322).

8. as he complained . . . come by.—Notably in the Preface to *The Marble Faun* (*Works*, VI, 15). Cf. "Legends of the Province House" (*Works*, I, 289–90).

to speak . . . the air."—Preface to *The House of the Seven Gables* (*Works*, III, 15).

"Personify the . . . its prospects."—*The American Notebooks*, p. 108.

9. "It was . . . was mine."—"The Custom House" (*Works*, V, 57).

the vignette . . . scarlet letter.—See above, p. 2.

Hawthorne in . . . quite otherwise.—See the references, dating from long before the Custom House period, in "Endicott and the Red Cross" (*Works*, I, 487) and *The American Notebooks*, p. 107.

As enemy . . . the cartload."—"The Custom House" (*Works*, V, 45, 53–54).

9–10. As his ally . . . seafaring ancestors.—*Ibid.*, pp. 25–27.

10. The discovery . . . persistent meaning.—*Ibid.*, pp. 47–50.

In the opening . . . the Adulteress.—*The Scarlet Letter*, chap. iii (*Works*, V, 91). Cf. the "exaggerated and gigantic proportions" of the letter as reflected in Governor Bellingham's armor in chapter vii (V, 132) and the treatment of the "veil" symbol in "The Minister's Black Veil" (I, 52–69).

10–11. Looking down . . . spectral images."—*The Scarlet Letter*, chap. ii (*Works*, V, 78–80).

11. As the years . . . scarlet letter."—*Ibid.*, chap. xiii (*Works*, V, 197, 199). Cf. chap. xviii (V, 239).

As "the scarlet . . . may take.—*Ibid.*, chap. vii (*Works*, V, 127). Cf. "The Custom House" (V, 50): ". . . I happened to place it on my breast. It seemed to me,—the reader may smile, but must not doubt my word,—it seemed to me, then, that I experienced a sensation not altogether physical, yet almost so, as of burning heat. . . ."

He cannot . . . or otherwise.—*Ibid.*, chap. xvii (*Works*, V, 234, 230). Cf. chap. xi (V, 173–78).

"strange sympathy . . . and body"—*Ibid.*, chap. x (*Works*, V, 168).

yearning for "substance."—*Ibid.*, chap. xvii (*Works*, V, 230).

11–12. his aspect . . . the devil.—*Ibid.*, chap. xiv (*Works*, V, 204–5). Cf. the status of the serpent-symbol in "Egotism; or, The Bosom Serpent" (II, 303–21).

12. Naturally enough . . . our fate."—*Ibid.*, chap. xiv (*Works*, V, 210).

While Hawthorne . . . these ideas.—Cf. "Monsieur du Miroir" (*Works*, II, 192, 195): "Is it too wild a thought that my fate may have assumed this image of myself, and therefore haunts me with such inevitable pertinacity, originating every act which it appears to imitate, while it deludes me by pretending to share the events of which it is merely the emblem and the prophecy? . . . So inimitably does he counterfeit that I could almost doubt which of us is the visionary form, or whether each be not the other's mystery, and both twin brethren of one fate in mutually reflected spheres."

Something like . . . those two."—*The Scarlet Letter*, chap. xii (*Works*, V, 187).

13. Donatello in . . . of art.—*The Marble Faun*, chap. i (*Works*, VI, 21–22). The identification is referred to constantly throughout the book. At various points other characters—Miriam, Hilda, and Miriam's model—are associated with paintings.

"sylvan dance . . . antique vase."—*Ibid.*, chap. x (*Works*, VI, 110). Another device is the carnival in chaps. xlviii and xlix (VI, 493–513).

"The Bronze . . . our glances."—*Ibid.*, chap. xxxv (*Works*, VI, 371).

14. "a knot . . . a drama."—*The Blithedale Romance*, chap. xviii (*Works*, V, 498). Although Coverdale is involved in the action to the extent that he harbors an unexpressed love for Priscilla, he is a prime example of Keats's "negative capability"—the specifically artistic temperament which Hawthorne described in "Sights from a Steeple" (I, 220): "The most desirable mode of existence might be that of a spiritualized Paul Pry, hovering invisible around man and woman, witnessing their deeds, searching into their hearts, borrowing brightness from their felicity and shade from their sorrow, and retaining no emotion peculiar to himself."

Perhaps his . . . and actuality.—This uncertainty lies behind his favorite device of offering several explanations, natural and supernatural, for events that challenge common sense. It is also related to the contrasting themes of those tales which touch on the question of art. Such stories as "Drowne's Wooden Image" and "The Artist of the Beautiful" (*Works*, II, 347–62, 504–36) emphasize the aesthetic reality defined by the storyteller in "The Antique Ring" (XII, 67): "You know that I can never separate the idea from the symbol in which it manifests itself." On the other hand, Owen Warland in "The Artist of the Beautiful" is defeated by gross physical reality, and many of the tales deprecate any mode of thought that removes the thinker from the everyday world of men. Thus the artist becomes a "fiction-monger" (Preface to *The Snow-Image* [III, 387]), and Hawthorne reiterates that "a dreamer may dwell so long among fantasies, that the things without him will seem as unreal as those within" ("Night Sketches" [I, 478]). Cf. "The Village Uncle" and "The Christmas Banquet" (I, 349–63; II, 322–46). In "Peter Goldthwaite's Treasure" (I, 428–54) worthless paper money is used as a symbol of the unreality of imagination, in direct contrast to the imagery of "The Custom House."

Pearl, its . . . broken law."—*The Scarlet Letter,* chap. x (*Works,* V, 164).

"could not . . . be discovered."—*Ibid.,* chap. vi (*Works,* V, 115). Cf. chap. x (V, 164–65): "It was as if she had been made afresh, out of new elements, and must perforce be permitted to live her own life, and be a law unto herself, without her eccentricities being reckoned to her for a crime."

Hawthorne's sense of the combined power and danger in art, and of the corresponding moral problem for the artist, was not simply a survival of Puritanism; nor was it, on the other hand, simply an outcome of his humanitarian reverence for the sanctity of the individual spirit, which the artist coldly investigates. Bound up with these motives was another and better grounded one: an awareness that art claims to be a new and real creation in status and form and, as such, is not subject to any external discipline. In various degrees this theme enters into stories like "The Prophetic Pictures" (I, 192–210), "Edward Randolph's Portrait" (I, 293–305), "The Birthmark" (II, 47–69), "Rappaccini's Daughter" (II, 109–48), "Feathertop" (II, 253–78), "Sylph Etherege" (III, 508–17), and "The Devil in Manuscript" (III, 574–83). Broadly speaking, their problem is the human consequences of the human power of artistic creation. In "Fancy's Show Box" (I, 256) Hawthorne even suggests that "a novel writer or a dramatist, in creating a villain of romance and fitting him with evil deeds, and the villain of actual life, in projecting crimes that will be perpetrated, may almost meet each other half-way between reality and fancy."

15. "the characteristics . . . of humanity"—*The Marble Faun,* chap. i (*Works,* VI, 24).

his crime, from . . . Fall of Man.—*Ibid.,* chap. xix (*Works,* VI, 203–8).

"Was the . . . so perilous."—*Ibid.,* chap. xlvii (*Works,* VI, 491–92). Milton and others before him were not so tender-minded. Cf. A. O. Lovejoy, "Milton and the Paradox of the Fortunate Fall," *ELH,* IV (1937), 161–79. But Hawthorne is especially troubled because he has evoked an opposition not so much between damnation and redemption as between supernatural and natural frames of reference—divine justice and human growth.

He falls . . . of Hilda.—In chapter 1 (*Works*, VI, 519–20) Kenyon espouses Miriam's theory in conversation with Hilda, whose paralyzing answer is "Oh, hush!"

Yet there . . . of regret"—*The Marble Faun*, chap. viii (*Works*, VI, 92–93). The most obvious parallel is "Rappaccini's Daughter" (II, 109–48), where the fascination of Rappaccini's achievement almost outweighs the deprecatory moral. Something of the same attraction toward the eccentric and perverse can be seen in such stories as "The Wedding Knell" (I, 41–51) and "Lady Eleanore's Mantle" (I, 309–26); also, given a comic turn, in "Wakefield" (I, 153–64) and "Mrs. Bullfrog" (II, 149–58).

"Aux objets . . . des appas."—Baudelaire, "Au Lecteur," *Les Fleurs du mal*.

16. "But man . . . elder voyagers."—Emerson, *Journals*, ed. E. W. Emerson and W. E. Forbes (Boston, 1909–14), V, 407.

If man . . . of being.—See above, p. 2.

16–17. "No one . . . or aestheticism."—Whitman, "A Backward Glance o'er Travel'd Roads" (*Leaves of Grass*, ed. Emory Holloway [Inclusive ed., Garden City, N.Y., 1925], p. 535).

17. "the United . . . greatest poem"—Preface to 1855 edition (*Leaves of Grass*, p. 488).

the poet . . . American scene—*Ibid.*, pp. 489–91.

the function . . . heroic citizens.—"Democratic Vistas" (*Complete Prose Works* [New York, 1914], pp. 198–202).

"One main . . . has changed."—"A Backward Glance o'er Travel'd Roads" (*Leaves of Grass*, p. 524). In a footnote to the same essay (*Leaves*, p. 527) Whitman remarks that "point of view" is, "according to Immanuel Kant, the last essential reality, giving shape and significance to all the rest." He had said in the 1855 Preface (*Leaves*, p. 493) that men "expect of the poet to indicate more than the beauty and dignity which always attach to dumb real objects . . . they expect him to indicate the path between reality and their souls."

"to articulate . . . immediate days"—"A Backward Glance o'er Travel'd Roads" (*Leaves of Grass*, pp. 523–24).

"to know . . . traveling souls"—"Song of the Open Road," Sec. 13 (*Leaves of Grass*, p. 131).

"perpetual journey"—"Song of Myself," Sec. 46 (*Leaves of Grass*, p. 70).

18. "child who . . . of him."—"There Was a Child Went Forth" (*Leaves of Grass*, pp. 306–7). Cf. "Song of Myself," Sec. 15 (*Leaves*, p. 37): "And these tend inward to me, and I tend outward to them, / And such as it is to be of these more or less I am, / And of these one and all I weave the song of myself."

"Allons! to . . . superior journeys."—"Song of the Open Road," Sec. 13 (*Leaves of Grass*, p. 130). Cf. "Salut au Monde!" Sec. 1 (*Leaves*, p. 114): "Such gliding wonders! such sights and sounds! / Such join'd unended links, each hook'd to the next. . . ."

"seething principle"—"To Thee Old Cause" (*Leaves of Grass*, p. 4).

"shapes ever . . . other shapes."—"Song of the Broad-Axe," Sec. 12 (*Leaves of Grass*, p. 165).

Whitman's "readjustment . . . into events.—Although his theoretical statements are imprecise and full of irrelevancies, a pattern shines through. He had in mind an "Idealism . . . ever modified even by its opposite" as the basis for "New World metaphysics" ("Democratic Vistas" [*Complete Prose Works*, p. 242]). Hence his starting point and conclusion, as he said in "Beginning My Studies" (*Leaves of Grass*, p. 7), was "the mere fact consciousness, these forms, the power of motion," for here he was not committed to distinct mental and physical substances. In order "to confront the growing excess of arrogance of [physical] realism" ("Democratic Vistas" [*Leaves*, p. 243]), he did not fall back on abstract idealism but on the concept of undifferentiated "Being," which was designed to subsume all rational "creeds" and "conventions" (*Leaves*, p. 223). This "Being" was always Becoming. The soul—"buoyant, indestructible, sailing space forever, visiting every region, as a ship the sea"—was part of "the pulsations in all matter, all spirit," which constituted "the only complete, actual poem," Nature (*Leaves*, p. 245).

"See, steamers . . . my poems"—"Starting from Paumanok," Sec. 18 (*Leaves of Grass*, p. 22).

"It is . . . of you."—"Song of Myself," Sec. 47 (*Leaves of Grass*, p. 72). Cf. Sec. 17 (*Leaves*, p. 38): "These are really the thoughts of all men in all ages and lands . . . / If they are not yours as much as mine they are nothing. . . ." Also "Crossing Brooklyn Ferry," Sec. 8 (*Leaves*, p. 138): "What is more subtle than this which ties me to the woman or man that looks in my face? / Which fuses me into you now, and pours my meaning into you?"

18–19. Most of . . . metaphysical sense.—Perhaps the clearest instance is "In Cabin'd Ships at Sea" (*Leaves of Grass*, p. 2), especially the second stanza: "Here are our thoughts, voyagers' thoughts. / Here not the land, firm land, alone appears, . . . / The sky o'erarches here, we feel the undulating deck beneath our feet, / We feel the long pulsation, ebb and flow of endless motion, / . . . And this is ocean's poem."

19. "new theory . . . imaginative works."—"Democratic Vistas" (*Complete Prose Works*, p. 249).

Even in . . . the writer.—A good instance is the short poem "Whoever You Are Holding Me Now in Hand" (*Leaves of Grass*, pp. 97–98).

"the procreant . . . the world."—"Song of Myself," Sec. 3 (*Leaves of Grass*, p. 25).

"Starting from Paumanok"—*Leaves of Grass*, pp. 12–23.

20. "This subject . . . language experiment."—*An American Primer*, ed. Horace Traubel (Boston, 1914), p. viii.

"*Names* are . . . the soul."—*Ibid.*, p. 18. Italics in text. Cf. "Mannahatta" (*Leaves of Grass*, p. 394): "I was asking for something specific and perfect for my city, / Whereupon lo! upsprang the aboriginal name. / Now I see what there is in a name, a word, liquid, sane, unruly, musical, self-sufficient, / I see that the word of my city is that word from of old, / Because I see that word nested in nests of water-bays. . . ."

"new law-forces . . . told out."—"Democratic Vistas" (*Complete Prose Works*, pp. 248–49).

He is . . . an externality.—*An American Primer*, pp. 5–6.

"Strange and . . . are one."—"A Song for Occupations," Sec. 5 (*Leaves of Grass*, p. 183).

"A perfect . . . uses things"—*An American Primer*, p. 14.

20–21. "Latent, in . . . and authorities."—*Ibid.*, pp. 16–17. Cf. "Song of Myself," Sec. 20 (*Leaves of Grass*, p. 40): "To me the converging objects of the universe perpetually flow, / All are written to me, and I must get what the writing means." Also "I Sing the Body Electric," Sec. 9 (*Leaves*, p. 85): "O my body! . . . / I believe the likes of you are to stand or fall with the likes of the soul, (and that they are the soul,) / I believe the likes of you shall stand or fall with my poems, and that they are my poems. . . ."

21. This kind . . . gymnast's struggle."—"Democratic Vistas" (*Complete Prose Works*, p. 249). Cf. "A Backward Glance o'er Travel'd Roads" (*Leaves of Grass*, p. 531) on "suggestiveness."

The poem . . . and speech.—See above, p. 3.

"Song of the Rolling Earth"—*Leaves of Grass*, pp. 186–91. Cf. "Song of the Answerer" (*Leaves*, pp. 140–43), especially Sec. 2, where he contrasts "the words of the singers" with "the words of true poems" on the ground that "the singers do not beget, only the Poet begets." Also "Eidólons" and "Song of Myself," Sec. 25 (*Leaves*, pp. 4–7, 46–47). The former is a vision of symbolic reality as the essence of the self and the world: "Ever the mutable, / Ever materials, changing, crumbling, re-cohering, / Ever the ateliers, the factories divine, / Issuing eidólons." In the latter, "my voice goes after what my eyes cannot reach, / With the twirl of my tongue I encompass worlds and volumes of worlds."

"new potentialities of speech"—*An American Primer*, pp. viii–ix.

"From the . . . with man."—Preface to 1855 ed. (*Leaves of Grass*, p. 494).

"When Lilacs Last in the Dooryard Bloom'd."—*Leaves of Grass*, pp. 276–83.

24. "Out of the Cradle Endlessly Rocking"—*Ibid.*, pp. 210–15.

25. "a passage . . . itself concluded."—*An American Primer*, p. vii. Cf. Preface to 1855 ed. (*Leaves of Grass*, p. 505): "Has any one fancied he could sit at last under some due authority and rest

satisfied with explanations and realize and be content and full? To no such terminus does the greatest poet bring." Also "Song of Myself," Sec. 3 (*Leaves*, p. 25): "I have heard what the talkers were talking, the talk of the beginning and the end, / But I do not talk of the beginning or the end."

"long varied . . . great organ."—"Song of the Broad-Axe," Sec. 1 (*Leaves of Grass*, p. 156).

26. "Sail forth . . . and all."—"Passage to India," Sec. 9 (*Leaves of Grass*, p. 351).

"limits and . . . materialistic priests."—"Song of the Open Road," Secs. 5 and 10 (*Leaves of Grass*, pp. 126, 129). Cf. "In Paths Untrodden" (*Leaves*, p. 95).

"I know . . . unsettle them."—"As I Lay with My Head in Your Lap Camerado" (*Leaves of Grass*, pp. 271–72). Cf. "Song of the Open Road," Sec. 14 (*Leaves*, p. 132): "My call is the call of battle, I nourish active rebellion. . . ." Also "Adieu to a Soldier," "Reversals," and "Transpositions" (*Leaves*, pp. 274, 299, 362).

"The way . . . perhaps more."—"Whoever You Are Holding Me Now in Hand" (*Leaves of Grass*, p. 97).

26–27. Nowadays we . . . of language.—This necessary distinction plays no part in W. H. Auden's brilliant account of the voyage symbol, *The Enchafèd Flood* (New York, 1950). As his subtitle indicates, he takes his subject to be simply "the *romantic* iconography of the sea." But note that the book comes out of Auden's later phase, when he wants to contend that "we live in a new age in which the artist neither can have . . . a unique heroic importance nor believes in the Art-God enough to desire it, an age, for instance, when the necessity of dogma is once more recognized . . ." (p. 153). Actually, the new age began much earlier than he is prepared to admit, and on a rather different basis. The return to dogma is not a reaction against romanticism but a strategic emphasis *within* symbolism.

27. like Hawthorne . . . with "significance."—Cf. "Song of Myself," Sec. 3 (*Leaves of Grass*, p. 26): "Shall I postpone my acceptation and realization and scream at my eyes, / That they turn from gazing after and down the road, / And forthwith cipher

and show me to a cent, / Exactly the value of one and exactly the value of two, and which is ahead?"

On the other . . . the iconoclast.—Since Whitman's methodology assumed that "all is truth" (see the poem of that title, *Leaves of Grass*, pp. 395–96) and, by the same token, that all is good, he could theoretically "stand indifferent" to established virtue and vice, truth and falsehood (cf. "Song of Myself," Sec. 22 [*Leaves*, p. 42]). These rational distinctions were irrelevant to the aesthetic reality in which he sought to dwell. But in practice he found that rational differences persisted in his own mind and in the world: "I am not the poet of goodness only, I do not decline to be the poet of wickedness also" (*ibid.*) Far from transcending conventional evil and falsehood, he tended to become their partisan in his desire to escape conventional good and rational truth.

"passage to . . . reach'd you."—"Passage to India," Sec. 9 (*Leaves of Grass*, p. 350).

"deep waters . . . is "safe."—*Ibid.*, p. 351.

28. "solid white buttress"—Melville, *Moby-Dick*, chap. cxxxv (*Works* [Standard ed.; London, 1922–24], VIII, 365).

"separate Nature so unnatural"—Whitman, "Passage to India," Sec. 5 (*Leaves of Grass*, p. 346).

"the divine . . . divine sea."—Whitman, "A Song of the Rolling Earth," Sec. 1 (*Leaves of Grass*, p. 188).

28–29. Ishmael opens . . . without meaning."—Melville, *Moby-Dick*, chap. i (*Works*, VII, 1–3).

29. The meaning . . . through it."—*Ibid.*, chap. xxxv (*Works*, VII, 198).

"I become . . . see all"—Emerson, *Works* (Fireside ed.; Boston, 1909), I, 16.

As your . . . in horror."—*Moby-Dick*, chap. xxxv (*Works*, VII, 198). Melville continues: "Over Descartian vortices you hover. . . . Heed it well, ye Pantheists!" There can be no doubt that he is using Descartes's vortices as a symbol for the gap between mind and nature postulated in Cartesian metaphysics, and at the same time as a reference to the vortex—in the sense of a circular flux in which all such distinctions are merged—that was a recurrent image of his fiction. Cf. *Moby-Dick*, Epilogue (VIII, 368), and *Mardi*, chaps. cxiv, cxcv (IV, 395–96, 398). On pantheism cf. *Moby-Dick*, chaps. cxi, cxiv, cxxxii (VIII, 252–53, 263–65, 326–30) and Melville's letter to Hawthorne (June, 1851) in *Representative Selections*, ed. Willard Thorp (New York, 1938), p. 393. In every case, Melville's attitude is ambivalent.

the "still . . . it all."—*Moby-Dick*, chap. i (*Works*, VII, 3–4)

The image . . . into it.—Bulkington and Pip (chaps. xxiii and xciii [*Works*, VII, 132–33; VIII, 169–70]) are variant versions of this principle. The former, dedicated to that "landlessness" where "alone resides the highest truth, shoreless, indefinite as God," gains the glory of immediate knowledge although that entails his "ocean-perishing." The latter, abandoned on the open sea, loses his mind but at the same time apprehends the formative process of the world. He was "carried down alive to wondrous depths, where strange shapes of the unwarped primal world glided to and fro before his passive eyes. . . . Pip saw the multitudinous, God-omnipresent, coral insects, that out of the firmament of waters heaved the colossal orbs. He saw God's foot upon the treadle of the loom, and spoke it; and therefore his shipmates called him mad." Cf. the association between death and "the region of the strange Untried" in chap. cxii (VIII, 256).

30. the alliance . . . and water"—*Moby-Dick*, chap. i (*Works*, VII, 3).

The narrator . . . the air."—*Ibid.*, pp. 6–7. The "Spirit-Spout" in chapter li (VII, 296)—"calm, snow-white, and unvarying; still directing its fountain of feathers to the sky; still beckoning us on from before"—is related to Ishmael's initial vision of the whale. In contrast, see the description of the painting in the entry of the Spouter-Inn in chapter iii (VII, 13–14), which is a kind of alternative vision.

It is significant . . . realize themselves.—Ishmael's character is adapted to his role as narrator; he is susceptible to this kind of apprehension. He can enter completely into Ahab's vision (chap. xli [*Works*, VII, 222]) because he lacks dogmatic principles and, "not ignoring what is good, . . . quick to perceive a horror," can "still be social with it" (chap. i [VII, 7]). He is "neither believer nor infidel" (chap. lxxxv [VIII, 117]), and it is his habit to realize rather than judge. Hence his most persistent trait is a sense of universal relationship: cf. chaps. xxvi, lxxii, xciv (VII, 144; VIII, 48–49, 172). His world is a great web, woven by "the weaver-god," in which chance, free will, and necessity are "working together" (chaps. xlvii, cii [*Works*, VII, 269–70; VIII, 213]).

30–31. In this chapter . . . other approach.—chap. xlii (*Works*, VII, 234, 239). The imaginative "pursuit" is represented not only by Ishmael's entry into the action but also by the introductory matter ("Etymology" and "Extracts") and by the monumental chapters in praise of whaling, with their constant refrain of magnitude, variety, and inclusiveness (e.g., chaps. xxiv, xlv, lv, lxxxii, civ). These passages, especially the "Extracts," are perhaps less important for *what* they say than for the kind of outlook they exemplify and thereby inculcate: the myth-making spirit to which Melville alludes at the end of chapter lxxix (VIII, 83).

31. It is Melville's . . . of Ahab.—Chap. xxxiii (*Works*, VII, 183).

In the sequence . . . "Midnight, Forecastle"—*Works*, VII, 199–221. Cf. chaps. xxix, xxxi, xcix, cviii, cxix–cxxii, cxxvii, cxxix.

32. Father Mapple's . . . of Jonah—Chap. ix (*Works*, VII, 49–59).

Ahab's blasphemous rituals—Chaps. xxxvi, cxiii, cxix, cxxiv (*Works*, VII, 205–8; VIII, 261, 281–84, 296–98).

The pattern . . . they look."—Chap. xcix (*Works*, VIII, 188–95).

"some certain . . . all things."—*Ibid.*, p. 188.

"The drama's . . . step forth?"—Epilogue (*Works*, VIII, 368).

33. "the earth . . . left hand"—Whitman, "Song of the Open Road," Sec. 4 (*Leaves of Grass*, p. 125).

While Melville . . . fluid sea.—Cf. chap. lviii (*Works*, VII, 348–49), where "the subtleness of the sea," its ambiguous mixture of beauty and danger, is associated with "the horrors of the half known life" within the personality, and both are set over against the security of land, the "insular Tahiti, full of peace and joy." But if Melville issues a warning—"Push not off from that isle, thou canst never return!"—he himself has already pushed off, and the whole book is predicated upon doing so. He cannot open "the great flood-gates of the wonder-world" without being forced to accept another phase of imaginative perception, typified in the crew and the pagan harpooners. Such men, entering wholeheartedly into Ahab's evocation of the whale-image, are "unrecking and unworshipping things, that live; and seek, and give no reasons for the torrid life they feel" (chap. xxxvi [*Works*, VII, 204–5]). But their mode of thought differs only in degree from Ishmael's pursuit of the "phantom of life" (chap. i [*Works*, VII, 4]) : in "their unconscious understandings," the whale figures as "the gliding great demon of the seas of life" (chap. xli [*Works*, VII, 233]). Similarly, though Fedallah worships destruction, he is the embodiment of a primitive mentality closely related to Melville's own in its departure from the categories of "civilized, domestic people in the temperate zone." He typifies the "aboriginalness of earth's primal generations, when ... men ... eyed each other as real phantoms ..." (chap. l [*Works*, VII, 291–92]).

The ultimate ... we shrink."—Chap. xlii (*Works*, VII, 243–44). Cf. the description of the giant squid that is momentarily mistaken for Moby Dick (chap. lix [VII, 351]) : "A vast pulpy mass, furlongs in length and breadth, of a glancing cream-colour, lay floating on the water, innumerable long arms radiating from its centre, and curling and twisting like a nest of anacondas, as if blindly to clutch at any hapless object within reach. No perceptible face or front did it have; no conceivable token of either sensation or instinct; but undulated there on the billows, an unearthly, formless, chance-like apparition of life." When Moby Dick at last is sighted in chapter cxxxiii (VIII, 333–35), he embodies the basic ambiguity that runs through all references in this book to the whale and the sea: divinity and destructiveness, beauty and terror. His impressiveness results not from any one of these attributes but from their ambiguous combination, which defies rational categories. More generally, the sea is repellent to the landsman because it remains "an everlasting terra incognita" from the rational standpoint (chap. lviii [VII, 347]) ; and the whale is radically unanalyzable: "Dissect him how I may, ... I but go skin deep; I know him not, and never will. ... How understand his head? much more, how comprehend his face, when face he has none?" (chap. lxxxvi [VIII, 123]; cf. chaps. lv, lxxix [VII, 336; VIII, 81–83]).

Ishmael's presentiment ... own "identity."—Chap. cxxxv and Epilogue (*Works*, VIII, 367–68). What happens to the "Pequod" is strictly parallel to what befell Pip, whose madness, resulting from his immersion in the sea, was at once a loss of selfhood and a revelation. He provided the ship, Melville says, "with a living and ever accompanying prophecy of whatever shattered sequel might prove her own" (chap. xciii [*Works*, VIII, 165]). Melville also points out the parallel between Pip and Ishmael (*ibid.*, p. 170). But Ishmael does not finally go the way of Pip, whose death completes the work of his madness, because Ishmael represents something more inclusive—the problematic point of view which is Melville's closest approach to a positive theme.

33–34. Ahab's motives . . . fraught with meaning.—Chap. xxxvi (*Works*, VII, 203–4). Cf. Melville's account of the sources of Ahab's greatness (chap. xvi [VII, 91–92]): he had "been led to think untraditionally and independently; receiving all nature's sweet or savage impressions fresh from her own virgin voluntary and confiding breast, and thereby chiefly . . . to learn a bold and nervous lofty language. . . ."

34. And in one . . . the whale.—Chaps. xxxvi, cxxxv (*Works*, VII, 204; VIII, 366).

In another . . . at last."—Chaps. cxxxv, cxxv (*Works*, VIII, 365, 300).

In either . . . of defiance.—Chap. xxxvi (*Works*, VII, 204). Ahab's "madness" is only one pole of his nature; the other is a titanic will; both are extreme forms of opposing principles, and each lends a deeper coloration to its opposite. His insanity is simply the final stage of his basic irrationalism. Like Ishmael, whose intellectual voyage is determined by "those stage managers, the Fates" (chap. i [VII, 6]), Ahab feels that his "whole act's immutably decreed," that he is "the Fates' lieutenant" (chap. cxxxiv [VII, 352]). His individuality has become "a vacated thing, . . . a blankness in itself," subservient to his idea, which has assumed "a kind of . . . independent being of its own"; his "thoughts have created a creature" that destroys him as a person (chap. xliv [VII, 252–53]). Cf. chaps. xli, cxxxii (VII, 229–30; VIII, 330). Yet, as he declares in his address to the fire, whose "speechless, placeless power" is the principle of all creativeness, he is supremely the independent ego: "In the midst of the personified impersonal, a personality stands here." And he thinks that he can "dimly see" an absolute reality beyond the creative fire. While he would "fain be welded" with the consuming flame, at the same time he rejects "the sacramental act" in which he has been burned, and he avers that "right worship is defiance" (chap. cxix [VIII, 281–83]). Thus either mode of thought renders to him a hostile, malicious world. When Ahab destroys the quadrant in disgust at the limitations of rational knowledge—falling back on immediate experience—the latter also fails him, for his compass becomes inverted (chaps. cxviii, cxxiv [VIII, 274–75, 295]). The result of this dilemma is, on the one hand, an intensification of his pride and, on the other, a complete surrender to impersonal experience, which has become a "dark Hindu half of nature" (chap. cxvi [VIII, 270]). Ahab's symbolic rituals at once exemplify his yearning for symbolic immediacy and express that defiance which is engendered in him by his disillusionment with immediate knowledge.

One might say that Ahab's final stand in the conflict between rational and symbolic thinking is rational. His two views remain unmediated; as Starbuck says, "his standpoint is stove" (chap. cxix [VIII, 278]). He assumes that there *must* be a conclusion, either death or life, and he reaches a kind of conclusion in death. By way of contrast, Ishmael, who exclaims "God keep me from ever completing anything" (chap. xxxii [VII, 179]), is ultimately indifferent to reason. Both views somehow exist together within him: this is his all-inclusive ambiguity. And for him, not for Ahab, "the coffin is, after all, but an immortality-preserver" (chap. cxxvii [VIII, 310]), because, unlike Ahab, he does not try to solve the apparent contradiction. He entertains it.

35. Melville can . . . of failure.—The sentimental interpretation, which would find the theme of the book in Melville's (and occasionally Ahab's own) horror at Ahab's repudiation of ordinary human ties, is off-center. This matter does come into question, notably in chapter cxxxii (*Works*, VIII, 327–30); but it arises as a problem, and it is subordinate to the deeper—and essentially insoluble—problem raised by the self-defeating nature of the quest itself. It is this unresolved difficulty, rather than any pat solution like a return to the land-life, that constitutes the theme of *Moby-Dick*. The tension between the appeal of land and the appeal of sea, between conventional goods and independent thinking, is merely a special form of the devastating tension *within* the voyage (which after all *is* the book) between rational and antirational principles.

Thus a passage like chapter xcvi (VIII, 180–82), where Ishmael warns "Give not thyself up . . . to fire, lest it invert thee, deaden thee," and where he undergoes this experience, cannot be taken as Melville's recantation; on the contrary, it dramatizes his sense of the parallelism between his own problem and Ahab's.

the "apotheosis" . . . the book—Chaps. xxiii, iii (*Works*, VII, 133, 18).

Ahab's greatest . . . nomine diaboli!"—Chap. cxiii (*Works*, VIII, 261). The letter to Hawthorne (June 29, 1851) is printed by Julian Hawthorne, *Nathaniel Hawthorne and His Wife* (Boston, 1884), I, 400. See Melville's note, in which the phrase first appears, printed by Charles Olson, "Lear and *Moby Dick*," *Twice a Year*, No. 1 (1938), p. 173.

The gentleman . . . rational convention.—Poe, "The Fall of the House of Usher" (*Complete Works*, ed. J. A. Harrison [Virginia ed.; New York, 1902], III, 273–97). Until the very end of the story the narrator is eager to dismiss all his perceptions as "fancies," "superstitions," and "dreams" (pp. 274, 276, 290).

35–36. His "habits . . . nervous restlessness."—"MS. Found in a Bottle" (*Complete Works*, II, 1–2).

36. Meditating his . . . the deck.—*Ibid.*, p. 10.

"A feeling . . . my soul."—*Ibid.*, p. 9.

The new . . . the vortex.—*Ibid.*, pp. 10–15. This symbolic use of the vortex and of whiteness is strikingly similar to the conclusion of *Moby-Dick*. With the vortex image cf. "A Descent into the Maelström" (*Complete Works*, II, 225–47), where the seafarer experiences the same mixture of curiosity and horror. With the image of whiteness cf. the end of "Narrative of A. Gordon Pym" (III, 239–42).

37. "indefiniteness" as a poetic principle—Cf. "Letter to B——" (*Complete Works*, VII, xxxvii–xxxix) and "Marginalia" (XVI, 29, 137–38).

"The Philosophy . . . mathematical problem.—*Complete Works*, XIV, 195: ". . . the work proceeded, step by step, to its completion with the precision and rigid consequence of a mathematical problem." In "Marginalia" (XVI, 170) Poe shows an awareness of the tension between his analytic and his aesthetic tendencies.

PAGE

While he held ... and "suggestive"—For Whitman, the poet works "by curious removes, indirections," and "seldomer tells a thing than suggests ... it." For Poe, he aims at "a suggestive indefinitiveness of meaning." Both are attempting to define the epistemological differentia of poetry, which Emerson described more fully (*Journals*, V, 189; italics in text) : "... these complex forms allow of the utterance of his knowledge of life by *indirections* as well as in the didactic way, and can therefore express the fluxional quantities and values which the thesis or dissertation could never give."

he considered ... a craftsman—Cf. his review of Drake and Halleck (*Complete Works*, VIII, 284–85) and "Marginalia" (XVI, 98–99).

"until we ... indivisible—one."—"Mesmeric Revelation" (*Complete Works*, V, 245–46; italics in text).

His purpose ... of God."—*Ibid.*, pp. 248–49.

37–38. As applied ... continuous activity.—"The Power of Words" (*Complete Works*, VI, 142–44). Although Poe never mentions "transcendentalism" except with contempt, he occasionally speaks in the language of the transcendentalist: cf. "The Island of the Fay" (IV, 193–99) and "A Chapter of Suggestions" (XIV, 186). More important are the occasions when one can see him moving toward a comparable position from an opposite starting point. Thus *Eureka*, the bulk of which assumes a finite universe and a rather deistic God, concludes with a vision of infinite process— "a novel Universe swelling into existence, and then subsiding into nothingness, at every throb of the Heart Divine." And this creative heart, Poe goes on to say, *"is our own"* (XVI, 311; italics in text). Here he is carried beyond his position in "The Power of Words," where God creates "in the beginning, *only.*"

The treatment of "matter" and "spirit" in *Eureka* (esp. pp. 308–13) is complicated by Poe's failure to see that much of what he has to say about "matter" really applies to the more general concept of "substance." The principles of "attraction" and "repulsion," which according to him *"are* Matter," are equally constitutive of any substance, for these laws turn out to be simply the logical principles of inclusion and exclusion. It follows that when Poe envisages the disappearance of matter by reason of the cessation of these principles in absolute Unity, what actually remains is not, as he supposes, pure spirit but a psychophysical totality. This Unity, as Poe says, is "Nothingness . . . to all Finite Perception" and Everything to infinite perception. Compare his picture of "matter without matter" in *Eureka* with the identical matter and spirit of "Mesmeric Revelation."

38. "not a . . . an effect"—"The Philosophy of Composition" (*Complete Works*, XIV, 197).

a poem . . . indeterminate glimpses."—"The Poetic Principle" (*Complete Works*, XIV, 273–74; italics in text).

Both views . . . in trade.—In practice, he tended to reduce his "effect" to a simple, rationally definable emotion, and he identified the beauty attainable *through* the poem with conventionally "beautiful" materials (see the list of "poetic" elements at the end of "The Poetic Principle"). In each case he vulgarized his own theory by substituting a preconceived "effect" or "beauty" for the unpredictable outcome of poetic form. Moreover, his particular predilections were usually in the worst romantic taste. They not only vitiated his verse but tended to obscure the really valuable aspects of his theory under appeals to the "ethereal," the "sublime," and the "heavenly." The important point of "The Poetic Principle" is buried deep in references to "the desire of the moth for the star" and to the "taint of sadness" in "all the higher manifestations of true Beauty" (*Complete Works*, XIV, 273, 279).

"by multiform . . . of Time"—"The Poetic Principle" (*Complete Works*, XIV, 274).

these combinations . . . of "effect."—The effect is constructed through "combinations of event, or tone" ("Philosophy of Composition" [*Complete Works*, XIV, 194]).

In both . . . spiritual reality.—Cf. "The Domain of Arnheim" (*Complete Works*, VI, 180–88), where the central importance of the medium and its dual nature are dramatized by the idea of creating a poem in the physical landscape.

poems are . . . *of new*."—"The Power of Words" (*Complete Works*, VI, 142; italics in text). Cf. "Marginalia" (XVI, 87–90), in which Poe discusses "points of time where the confines of the waking world blend with those of the world of dreams." Such perceptions have *"absoluteness of novelty,"* and Poe argues that they are potentially within "the *power of words*" (italics in text).

Poe was much troubled by the conception of poetic creativity, since his rationalism could not accept it, while his aesthetics demanded it. On the one hand, he went out of his way to attack Coleridge's distinction between imagination and fancy, maintaining that "the fancy as nearly creates as the imagination; and neither creates in any respect" (Review of Moore's *Alciphron* [X, 61–62]). He liked to think of imagination as the mechanical combining of "atomic" elements, which already existed as "previous combinations" ("American Prose Writers. No. 2. N. P. Willis" [XII, 38]). On the other hand, he saw that imaginative collocation of elements, in distinction from the fanciful, possessed what he called a "mystic" or "ideal" force, for "there lies beneath the transparent upper current of meaning [i.e., the completely paraphrasable prose statement] an under or *suggestive* one" (Review of Moore's *Alciphron* [X, 65–66; italics in text]). He saw that "the word ποίησις itself (creation) speaks volumes upon this point" (Review of Longfellow's *Ballads and Other Poems* [XI, 74]). In his review of Drake and Halleck (VIII, 301–2) he shows that "ideality" can hardly be found in a mere "collection of natural objects," though "each individually [be] of great beauty," for it is a function of creative form. "... To view such natural objects as they exist, and to behold them through the medium of words, are different things." In the line "The earth is dark but the heavens are bright," the specifically poetic level of meaning, according to Poe, is created by the word "but."

In general, whenever Poe turned against his rationalistic prejudices, he turned toward the conception of a distinctively imaginative act which is at once creative and cognitive and in which the criterion of truth is a formal consistency. See "A Chapter of Suggestions" (XIV, 187), "Mellonta Tauta" (VI, 201–6), and *Eureka* (XVI, 183, 188–98).

It is this . . . and ethics.—The *loci classici* are the review of Longfellow's *Ballads and Other Poems* (*Complete Works,* XI, 68–70, 84) and "The Poetic Principle" (XIV, 271–72). Cf. also "Marginalia" (XVI, 164). Poe's antididacticism and antirealism are related to his dislike of the simile, which he regarded as merely illustrative, and of allegory, which he considered extra-poetic.

Both were intrusions of rational form into the poetic realm. Cf. the review of Moore's *Alciphron* (X, 68) and the review of Hawthorne's tales (XIII, 148–49).

38–39. Poe takes music . . . rational denotation.—Cf. the review of Longfellow's *Ballads and Other Poems* (*Complete Works*, XI, 74–75) and "The Poetic Principle" (XIV, 274–75). In "Marginalia" (XVI, 29, 137–38) Poe denounces any attempt to give "determinateness of expression" to music, especially any effort at "imitation." Behind his constant references to music is "the Platonic . . . *μουσική*," which, as Poe points out, "included not merely the harmonies of tune and time, but *proportion* generally," and which "referred to the cultivation of the Taste, in contradistinction from that of the Pure Reason" ("Marginalia" [XVI, 163]). Cf. "The Colloquy of Monos and Una" (IV, 203–4 and 204 n.).

39. "this poem . . . poem's sake"—"The Poetic Principle" (*Complete Works*, XIV, 272). Cf. his isolation of the "art-product" as the sole legitimate object of literary criticism ("Exordium" [XI, 7]).

"Donner un . . . la tribu."—Mallarmé, "Le Tombeau d'Edgar Poe."

"l'écrivain des nerfs."—Baudelaire, "Edgar Poe, sa vie et ses œuvres," *Œuvres complètes*, VI, xxviii.

The narrator . . . his senses.—"The Tell-Tale Heart" (*Complete Works*, V, 88).

"perverseness," which . . . be such."—"The Black Cat" (*Complete Works*, V, 146).

"an innate . . . human action."—"The Imp of the Perverse" (*Complete Works*, VI, 146–47). Cf. *ibid.*, p. 149: ". . . because our reason violently deters us from the brink, *therefore* do we the most impetuously approach it" (italics in text). The aberrant state is described in such stories as "The Man of the Crowd" (IV, 139–40), "The Pit and the Pendulum" (V, 68–69), and "A Tale of the Ragged Mountains" (V, 167–68). Most of Poe's attempts at the comic are based on the inversion or destruction of rational order: cf. "Dr. Tarr and Prof. Fether" (VI, 53–77), "The Angel of the Odd" (VI, 103–15), and "The Man That Was Used Up" (III, 259–72).

39–40. The first . . . the sublime."—"The Fall of the House of Usher" (*Complete Works*, III, 273–74). See above, pp. 2–3.

40. "I wondered . . . stirring up."—*Ibid.*, p. 277.

The house itself . . . the tarn.—*Ibid.*, pp. 274, 276–77.

Usher's belief . . . upon them.—*Ibid.*, p. 286. Cf. p. 276.

Their "peculiar . . . family mansion."—*Ibid.*, p. 275. Cf. Usher's poem, "The Haunted Palace" (pp. 284–86) and the narrator's reference to "eye-like windows" (p. 274).

"host of unnatural sensations"—*Ibid.*, p. 280. The narrator cannot connect Roderick's "Arabesque expression" with "any idea of simple humanity," just as he cannot reduce the disquieting effect of the house to any "combinations of very simple natural objects" (pp. 279, 274).

41. He produces . . . knowing not why."—*Ibid.*, pp. 283–84. The Usher family is noted for "a passionate devotion to the intricacies, perhaps even more than to the orthodox and easily recognisable beauties, of musical science" (p. 275). The "morbid acuteness of the senses" brought on by Roderick's disease (p. 280) carries him a step further. As he says in his poem, "Spirits moving musically / To a lute's well-tunèd law" must give way to "Vast forms that move fantastically / To a discordant melody" (p. 285). He loves as much as he hates these eccentric forms.

The dénouement . . . the story.—*Ibid.*, p. 291.

"The City in the Sea"—*Complete Works*, VII, 49.

In "The Masque . . . the masquerade.—*Complete Works*, IV, 250–58.

41–42. In "The Assignation" . . . rapidly departing."—*Complete Works*, II, 116, 123–24.

42. In "The Colloquy . . . and intense."—*Complete Works*, IV, 206. Cf. the end of the world in "The Conversation of Eiros and Charmion" (IV, 6–8), where the approaching destruction is accompanied by "a wild luxuriance of foliage, utterly unknown before," and the actual dissolution is "a species of intense flame, for whose surpassing brilliancy and all-fervid heat even the angels in the high Heaven of pure knowledge have no name."

Yet if . . . personal identity.—The hero of "The Assignation," the original title of which was "The Visionary," lacks any permanent character. Even in life his artistic temperament approaches the impersonality which he seeks in death (*Complete Works*, II, 115) : ". . . his countenance . . . had no peculiar—it had no settled predominant expression to be fastened upon the memory. . . . Not that the spirit of each rapid passion failed, at any time, to throw its own distinct image upon the mirror of that face—but that the mirror, mirror-like, retained no vestige of the passion, when the passion had departed."

"sympathies of . . . always existed."—"The Fall of the House of Usher" (*Complete Works*, III, 289).

what Poe . . . for ever."—"Morella" (*Complete Works*, II, 29; italics in text). In this passage Poe plays on the difference between "the doctrines of *Identity* as urged by Schelling" (i.e., the identity of subject and object) and "that identity which is termed personal" and which "Mr. Locke . . . truly defines to consist in the saneness of a rational being." Poe clearly lines up reason, individuality, and life on one side; irrationalism, impersonality, and death on the other. The same theme, with various emphases, is woven into stories like "Berenice" (II, 16–26), "Ligeia" (II, 248–68), and "Eleonora" (IV, 236–44). In "The Oval Portrait" (IV, 245–49) not the thinker but his object dies in the creation of the aesthetic object.

With them . . . of Usher.—"The Fall of the House of Usher" (*Complete Works*, III, 297). In a sense, by identifying art with death, Poe is saying that art, paradoxically, ceases to exist in the degree that it attains its goal. Similarly, on a more philosophical level, he maintained in *Eureka* (XVI, 310–11) that the conversion of rational structure into absolute unity simultaneously converts the world into absolute nothingness. In "The Colloquy of Monos and Una," while the "wreck and the chaos of the usual senses" are revelatory, the reality to which they lead is nihilistic (IV, 209–12). Its mere "duration" amounts to non-entity: "For *that* which *was not*—for that which had no form—for that which had no thought—for that which had no sentience—for that which was soulless, yet of which matter formed no portion—for all this nothingness, yet for all this immortality, the grave was still a home, and the corrosive hours, co-mates" (italics in text).

CHAPTER II

44. "Je n'ai ... leurs sens."—André Gide, *Journal, 1889–1939* (Paris, 1939), p. 737.

45. "In criticizing ... own life."—T. S. Eliot, "Preface to the 1928 Edition," *The Sacred Wood* (4th ed.; London, 1934), pp. ix–x.

For Pound ... utmost degree."—Ezra Pound, "How To Read," *Polite Essays* (London, 1937), p. 167. Further examples of such dicta might be multiplied indefinitely. Cf. the following: Allen Tate, *Reason in Madness* (New York, 1941), p. 76: "... by his [the poet's] language shall you know him; the quality of his language is the valid limit of what he has to say." J. C. Ransom, "Criticism as Pure Speculation," *The Intent of the Critic*, ed. D. A. Stauffer (Princeton, 1941), p. 109: "... the object of esthetic studies became for me a kind of discourse...." Kenneth Burke, *Counter-Statement* (New York, 1931), p. 54: "Eloquence is ... the end of art, and ... its essence." F. R. Leavis, *Towards Standards of Criticism* (London, 1933), p. 16: "A novel, like a poem, is made of words; there is nothing else one can point to. ... The process of 'creation' is one of putting words together."

This kind of assumption is ubiquitous in recent collections like *Forms of Modern Fiction*, ed. W. V. O'Connor (Minneapolis, 1948), and *Critiques and Essays in Criticism*, ed. R. W. Stallman (New York, 1949). In *The Primary Language of Poetry in the 1940's* (Berkeley, 1951), Josephine Miles shows the extent to which "the word as mediator between object and mind" is the focus of critical discussion in this century. Both J. C. Ransom in *The New Criticism* (Norfolk, Conn., 1941) and S. E. Hyman in *The Armed Vision: A Study in the Methods of Modern Literary Criticism* (New York, 1948) assume the centrality of the concept of language.

For Wordsworth ... powerful feelings"—Wordsworth, Preface to *Lyrical Ballads* (1800) in *Wordsworth's Literary Criticism*, ed. N. C. Smith (London, 1905), p. 15. Similarly, though Shelley has much to say about language as "vitally metaphorical," his point of departure is nonlinguistic; for him, "when composition begins, inspiration is already on the decline" (*A Defense of Poetry*, ed. A. S. Cook [Boston, 1891], pp. 4, 39). Cf. F. W. Bateson, *English Poetry and the English Language* (Oxford, 1934), pp. 90–92, 97, on the romantic bias against "questions of language." In *The Medium of Poetry* (London, 1934), p. 26, James Sutherland has distinguished between Wordsworth and Keats on just this ground. It seems likely that the modern habit of singling out Keats for special favor among the English romantics is immediately connected with the fact that his "poetry is far less *communication,* and far more *making.*" Witness the eagerness with which we have seized on his reference to "negative capability."

45–46. For Eliot ... unexpected ways."—T. S. Eliot, "Tradition and the Individual Talent," in *Selected Essays: 1917–1932* (New York, 1932), p. 9.

46. Zola would ... the form.—Émile Zola, "Le Sens du réel," in *Le Roman expérimental,* ed. Maurice Le Blond (Paris, n.d.), pp. 166–67: "Aujourd'hui, la qualité maîtresse du romancier est le sens du réel. ... Le sens du réel, c'est de sentir la nature et de la rendre telle qu'elle est." As for form, "il arrive que les faits se classent logiquement, celui-ci avant celui-là; une symétrie s'établit. ..."

"Words are ... signalling system."—I. A. Richards, *The Philosophy of Rhetoric* (New York, 1936), p. 131.

"Words, and ... you knew."—R. P. Blackmur, "The Craft of Herman Melville: A Putative Statement," in *The Expense of Greatness* (New York, 1940), p. 157. Cf. Dorothy Walsh, "The Poetic Use of Language," *Journal of Philosophy,* XXXV (1938), 78: "Thus the raw material of his art is not directly the world nor his own private experience but what has been said, what is being said, and what may be said about either. ... Approaching the world not directly, but through a preoccupation with some particular language, the object of his passionate interest is not simply reality and not simply words but the complete identity of the two. ... He wishes to avoid the whole bifurcation between a thing or an event and the words which refer to it."

47. "his writing ... something itself."—Samuel Becket, "Dante ... Bruno. Vico ... Joyce," in *Our Exagmination Round His Factification for Incamination of Work in Progress* (London, 1936), p. 14 (italics in text).

PAGE

In the *Portrait . . . ollam denariorum.*"—Joyce, *A Portrait of the Artist as a Young Man* (London, 1936), pp. 101–2, 203–4.

"It was . . . a stone."—Frank Budgen, *James Joyce and the Making of Ulysses* (New York, 1934), p. 13.

47–48. "Between the . . . of technique."—M. D. Zabel, "The Poetics of Henry James," in *The Question of Henry James*, ed. F. W. Dupee (New York, 1945), p. 214.

48. The Jamesian . . . as construction—Cf. Mark Schorer, "Technique as Discovery," in *Forms of Modern Fiction*, pp. 9–29.

The characters . . . show me."—Henry James, *The Art of the Novel: Critical Prefaces*, ed. R. P. Blackmur (New York, 1946), p. 53 (italics in text).

In his notebooks . . . to it."—Henry James, *Notebooks*, ed. F. O. Matthiessen and K. B. Murdock (New York, 1947), p. 293. James insists that to "cipher out" *is* "to let one's self go": "Well, one does—one *is* letting one's self."

What these . . . will give."—*Ibid.*, p. 346.

James's account . . . expressed it."—James, *The Art of the Novel*, p. 339. He describes "the growth of the immense array of terms, perceptional and expressional, that . . . in sentence, passage and page, simply looked over the heads of the standing terms—or perhaps rather, like alert winged creatures, perched on those diminished summits and aspired to a clearer air."

"The term . . . to be assimilated."—*Ibid.*, p. 342 (italics in text).

48–49. The "it" . . . of rendering.—What for James was largely a tacit principle became the program of the next generation. Cf. Gertrude Stein, *Lectures in America* (New York, 1935), p. 191: "I became more and more excited about how words which were the words that made whatever I looked at look like itself were not the words that had in them any quality of description." Most of the recent accounts by poets of their own creative processes evince a sort of reverence for events in language. See, for example, Brewster Ghiselin, "The Birth of a Poem," *Poetry* (Chicago), LXIX (1946–47); 31–43. On the other hand, the increasingly apparent difference between poets like W. H. Auden and Stephen Spender, who were once lumped together, can be traced to this very factor. Auden is much more distinctively modern because he holds, as he told Spender, that "the subject of a poem is a peg to hang the poetry on." When he said this, as Spender relates in *World within World* (London, 1951), p. 59, "he had indicated ... [a] basic difference between our attitudes. For I could not accept the idea that the poetic experience in reality, which led into a poem, was then, as it were, left behind, while the poem developed according to verbal needs of its own which had no relation to the experience."

49. To consider ... they evince.—My contention is one I can hardly demonstrate here: that the concept of language as autonomous and creative symbol is the reference point for a larger body of modern literary theory, criticism, and practice than can be brought under any other rubric. This is not to say that most, or indeed any, modern writers can be reduced to this concept without remainder. Many recent critical pronouncements are essentially practical counsel, and it is possible that their authors would strenuously object to any such generalization. See, for example, the two articles on "The Intentional Fallacy" and "The Affective Fallacy" by W. K. Wimsatt, Jr., and M. C. Beardsley, *Sewanee Review*, LIV (1946), 468–88, and LVII (1949), 31–55. These are primarily offered as working principles, yet they point by a process of elimination to a symbolistic theory. Again, René Wellek's discussion of the "mode of existence" of literature in "The Analysis of the Literary Work of Art," in *Theory of Literature* (New York, 1949), pp. 139–58, avoids the identification of "the real poem" with language, postulating "a system of norms of ideal concepts which are intersubjective." Yet Wellek remarks that "in this respect ... a literary work of art is in exactly the same position as a system of language." And it is the idea of language that would serve to mediate between his theory and Ransom's "ontology" of poetry (*The New Criticism*, pp. 279–336). On the other hand, much of the opposition to modern symbolistic theory takes place within the same frame of reference as that theory—does not represent a change of venue but a retrial. Yvor Winters, for instance, sets out from the premise that "a poem is first of all a statement in words": *The Anatomy of Nonsense* (1943) in *In Defense of Reason* (New York, 1947), p. 363. While the differentia of Winters' approach is his emphasis on "statement," the determinant of his approach is his awareness of "words."

According to ... our time."—W. M. Urban, *Language and Reality: The Philosophy of Language and the Principles of Symbolism* (London, 1939), pp. 35, 401.

Mrs. Langer ... of philosophy.—S. K. Langer, *Philosophy in a New Key: A Study in the Symbolism of Reason, Rite, and Art* (Cambridge, Mass., 1942), pp. vii–viii, 21–22.

50. As Whitehead ... inside matter."—A. N. Whitehead, *Science and the Modern World* (Cambridge, 1933), p. 70.

51. In *Axel's Castle* ... with Romanticism."—Edmund Wilson, *Axel's Castle: A Study in the Imaginative Literature of 1870–1930* (New York, 1931), pp. 19–20. Although much of what Wilson has to say would tend to qualify this initial definition of symbolism, subjectivism (as his title indicates) represents the essence of the movement for him. Curiously enough, he combines this emphasis with frequent reference to Whitehead, whose philosophy, by dispensing with ultimate dualism, would tend to discourage a subjective leaning.

The aim ... is capable."—*Ibid.*, p. 66. Paul Valéry, "Dernière visite à Mallarmé," in *Variété II* (Paris, 1930), p. 205: "la volonté de mettre en evidence, de conserver à travers les pensées et de développer pour elles-mêmes, les formes du langage." Or, as Mallarmé himself says, "L'œuvre pure implique la disparition élocutoire du poëte, qui cède l'initiative aux mots...." *Œuvres complètes*, ed. Henri Mondor and G. Jean-Aubry (Paris, 1945), p. 366. On the concept of language as the central idea of French symbolism cf. A. G. Lehmann, *The Symbolist Aesthetic in France, 1885–1895* (Oxford, 1950), pp. 306–15, and Elizabeth Sewell, *The Structure of Poetry* (London, 1951).

romanticism, as ... imperfect inspiration."—Allen Tate, "Three Types of Poetry," *Reactionary Essays on Poetry and Ideas* (New York, 1936), p. 94.

Symbolism is ... literary question.—The bankruptcy of Cartesianism and idealism (though not the resulting ascendancy of "language") is treated as the source of modern critical method by W. J. Ong, S.J., "The Meaning of the New Criticism," in *Twentieth-Century English*, ed. W. S. Knickerbocker (New York, 1946), pp. 344–70.

"The truly ... *than either.*"—R. M. Eaton, *Symbolism and Truth: An Introduction to the Theory of Knowledge* (Cambridge, Mass., 1925), p. 287 (my italics).

52. "juggling of abstractions"—Whitehead, *Science and the Modern World*, p. 70.

A literary ... nor subjective.' "—Owen Barfield, *Poetic Diction: A Study in Meaning* (London, 1928), p. 245. An attempt to evade dualism by one device or another (not always by an explicit appeal to "symbolism") is continually turning up in modern literary theory and aesthetics. To take two widely differing instances, cf. Kenneth Burke, *The Philosophy of Literary Form* (Louisiana State University Press, 1941), pp. 8–9, 64, and Edward Bullough's famous article, " 'Psychical Distance' as a Factor in Art and an Aesthetic Principle," *British Journal of Psychology*, V (1912–13), 89–91, 94.

These writers ... relative terms.—Whitehead, *Science and the Modern World*, p. 70; *Adventures of Ideas* (Cambridge, 1933), pp. 244–45.

It undercuts ... significant phrase."—Langer, *Philosophy in a New Key*, p. 12 (italics in text). In addition to Whitehead, both Bergson and Dewey, in their different ways, are notable instances of this kind of strategy in modern thought. Wyndham Lewis, in *Time and Western Man* (London, 1927), was among the first to realize how characteristic of recent thinking this is and how closely it is bound up with the habit of conceiving reality in the temporal category of "process." Cf. esp. pp. 251–57 (on the "fusion of idealism and realism"), 317–66 (on "the extinction of the 'thinking subject' "), and 406–33 (on the extinction of the substantival object).

Whitehead refuses ... to reality.—Cf. Urban, *Language and Reality*, pp. 371, 452–53. Bergson is even more cautious. Whereas Whitehead, in assuming the externality of language, believes that he can redesign this external language to correspond with reality as process, Bergson's notorious distrust of language is founded precisely on the belief that no such method is possible. He associates language with an intellectualization that necessarily misrepresents the fluid reality available to pure intuition. Yet in another sense Bergson, like Whitehead, points toward a redefinition of language as immanent symbol and of knowledge as symbolization.

The case of Dewey is more difficult to fix. For him language is "the cherishing mother of all significance," and significance, if not the "real substance," is the prime characteristic of "experience," which stands beyond the distinction of mind and matter. Cf. *Experience and Nature* (Chicago, 1925), p. 186. But his instrumentalism complicates the issue; the relation of his philosophy to a philosophy of symbolism becomes fully apparent only in the light of his theory of art, which he defines as an activity where instrument and end are united (*ibid.*, p. 361).

"the three ... of the object."—Eaton, *Symbolism and Truth*, p. 34.

the symbols ... of objects"—Langer, *Philosophy in a New Key*, pp. 60–61.

52–53. "Language, which ... first given."—Urban, *Language and Reality*, p. 375.

53. "the mean*ing* ... the meant."—Eaton, *Symbolism and Truth*, p. 157.

In Cassirer's ... with each other."—Ernst Cassirer, *Language and Myth*, trans. S. K. Langer (New York, 1946), pp. 6–10. A number of caveats must be entered here. In the first place, Cassirer's metaphysics and epistemology are generally regarded as very ambiguous. Cf. Iredell Jenkins' review of *The Philosophy of Ernst Cassirer*, ed. P. A. Schilpp (Evanston, 1949), in *Journal of Philosophy*, XLVII (1950), 43–55. As Jenkins points out, this collection of widely diverse critiques evinces great uncertainty "as to what Cassirer's position actually is." In particular, "what reference do symbolic forms make beyond themselves? Are they categories of *what is* or of *what is thought?* ... In sum, do symbolic forms have truth or only meaning?" But I should take this systematic ambiguity as evidence for my own contention that Cassirer's position is consciously *beyond* the categories of "what is" and "what is thought"—that he identifies truth and meaning.

Moreover, none of the writers cited as parallel to Cassirer is precisely parallel. This is notably the case with Urban, who holds —cf. *Beyond Realism and Idealism* (London, 1949)—that there is no possibility of a position beyond *naturalism* and idealism. Metaphysically, he remains an idealist. On the other hand, while

Urban states (*Language and Reality,* p. 392) that "truth, *in the last analysis,* is immanent in discourse and not an external relation of discourse to reality," Eaton ultimately falls back on a correspondence theory of truth (*Symbolism and Truth,* pp. 174–75). And Eaton is solely concerned with the logical structure of language. In Mrs. Langer's book metaphysical implications are largely in abeyance: she explores the practical possibilities of this "philosophy in a new key."

Finally, a distinction should be made between symbolism and Crocean expressionism. Though the latter is cognate to symbolism in its identification of intuition and expression, its concept of language is explicitly opposed to the material medium. Similarly, R. G. Collingwood's theory of "art as language" labors the opposition between the medium and the "work of art" proper, "whose only place is in the artist's mind." But in many respects Collingwood represents a point where expressionism is turning into symbolism. Cf. *The Principles of Art* (Oxford, 1938), esp. pp. 300–308.

53–54. "Certain expressions . . . expressive function."—Rudolf Carnap, "Logic," in *Factors Determining Human Behavior* (Cambridge, Mass., 1937), p. 109.

54. Semantics was . . . it occasions").—I. A. Richards, *Principles of Literary Criticism* (4th ed.; New York, 1930), p. 267. Cf. C. K. Ogden and I. A. Richards, *The Meaning of Meaning* (4th rev. ed.; London, 1936), pp. 11, 149.

"pseudo-statement"—I. A. Richards, *Science and Poetry* (London, 1926), pp. 55–67.

In *Coleridge* . . . is projected."—I. A. Richards, *Coleridge on Imagination* (New York, 1935), p. 109.

In the end . . . the same."—I. A. Richards, "The Interactions of Words," *The Language of Poetry,* ed. Allen Tate (Princeton, 1942), p. 84. The "semiotic" of C. W. Morris attempts to remain faithful to the concept of sign-language while at the same time avoiding the relegation of aesthetic language to "emotion." Cf. "Esthetics and the Theory of Signs," *Journal of Unified Science,* VIII (1939–40), 131–50. But Morris maintains his position by avoiding any discussion of the *process* of meaning—what he calls the "interpretant." He merely assumes a stimulus-response psychology.

54–55. F. W. Bateson . . . use of language.—F. W. Bateson, *English Poetry and the English Language,* p. 25.

55. that "symbols . . . in themselves."—R. P. Blackmur, "Humanism and Symbolic Imagination: Notes on Rereading Irving Babbitt," *Southern Review,* VII (1941–42), 316. To say that modern literature has a new awareness of the medium is to say, with Jacques Maritain, that it has "become aware of itself." See "Poetry's Dark Night," *Kenyon Review,* IV (1942), 149. Maritain adds that while romanticism marks a "deepening of the consciousness of the *art*" [i.e., of art as opposed to science], with Baudelaire we find "a discontinuity, an enormous transformation" of sensibility, "because at the same time it is *of the poetry,* it is *of itself as poetry* that poetry achieves awareness in him" (pp. 150–51; italics in text). H. A. Hatzfeld, in "The Language of the Poet," *Studies in Philology,* XLIII (1946), 94–97, implicitly makes the same point about twentieth-century poetry. This line of thought has been much more generally applied to modern painting and sculpture than to literature. Cf. Lionello Venturi, *Modern Painters* (New York, 1947–50), II, 217–18, and the central thesis of André Malraux's *Psychology of Art,* trans. Stuart Gilbert (New York, 1949–50). A good illustration of the new sensibility they discuss (and themselves exemplify) is Henri Focillon's *Life of Forms in Art,* trans. C. B. Hogan and George Kubler (New Haven, 1942).

"instead of . . . *animal symbolicum.*"—Ernst Cassirer, *An Essay on Man* (New Haven, 1944), p. 26.

Yet Cassirer . . . creative power."—Cassirer, *Language and Myth,* pp. 97–98.

Although Cassirer . . . and fantasy."—*Ibid.,* pp. 98–99.

From this point . . . abstract fiction.—The classic statement is Mallarmé's "Avant-Dire au *Traité du verbe* de René Ghil" (1886) in *Œuvres complètes,* 857–58: "Au contraire d'une fonction de numéraire facile et représentatif, comme le traite d'abord la foule, le Dire, avant tout, rêve et chant, retrouve chez le poëte, par nécessité constitutive d'un art consacré aux fictions, sa virtualité." In poetry, consecrated to fiction, language in effect ceases to be fiction and regains its absolute validity.

56. Given the . . . traditional framework.—This distinction between "romanticism" and "symbolism" has been implicitly challenged by René Wellek. In "Coleridge's Philosophy and Criticism," in *The English Romantic Poets: A Review of Research*, ed. T. M. Raysor (New York, 1950), p. 113, he speaks of "a paradoxical situation" in recent literary theory: "the modern anti-romantic critics appeal constantly to the highly romantic . . . thought of Coleridge, which, in the passages which interest them most, is really the thought of Schelling." In "The Concept of 'Romanticism' in Literary History," *Comparative Literature*, I (1949), 1–23, 147–72, he posits "symbol and myth" as one of the key concepts in "the unity of European Romanticism."

The problem would seem to be one of effective use of terms. We need terminology which will clarify the paradoxical situation that Wellek notes; and to that end romanticism and symbolism should be distinguished. This is not to deny the relevance of the "romantic" symbolism he cites (on the contrary, the purpose of this book is to suggest that the American "romantics" were perhaps even more "symbolistic" than their European counterparts). But it is to say that, in so far as they *were* symbolistic, they were not romantic in the sense to which "the modern anti-romantic critics" are hostile.

Meaning for . . . terms about it."—Langer, *Philosophy in a New Key*, p. 66 (italics in text).

"the fabric . . . the world."—I. A. Richards, *The Philosophy of Rhetoric* (New York, 1936), p. 36.

57. As Cassirer . . . conceptual space."—Cassirer, *Language and Myth*, p. 90.

We usually . . . of meaning.—To attribute "atomism" to logic does not entail the "atomism" of associationist psychology, nor does it involve the "proper meaning superstition" or the "doctrine of usage" castigated by Richards in *The Philosophy of Rhetoric* (pp. 11–12, 51–52). For the discrete structure of logical language does not derive from any of these factors; rather, the discreteness enters into meaning as a structural property of logical language. Moreover, as Eaton says (*Symbolism and Truth*, p. 47), the simple elements of a logical statement "are not affirmed to be absolutely simple, to be irreducible. They are the elementary components of the fact *as it is here expressed* . . ." (my italics).

"two logical . . . been brought"—Cassirer, *Language and Myth*, p. 91.

Two poetic . . . metaphorical meaning.—Cf. Martin Foss, *Symbol and Metaphor in Human Experience* (Princeton, 1949), pp. 61–62: "The metaphorical process . . . is different [from the "symbol"—i.e., the sign]: here the known symbols in their relation to each other are only material; they undergo a complete change in losing their familiar meaning in each other and give birth to an entirely new knowledge beyond their fixed and addible multitude. Creation, judged from the level of fixed symbols, arises out of destruction. . . ."

58. "the logic . . . speaking, propositions."—John Dewey, *Art as Experience* (New York, 1934), p. 85.

In civilized . . . to toe.—In literary usage, then, there still exists virtually the same situation as that imagined by Owen Barfield (*Poetic Diction*, pp. 64–65) to have obtained at "a time when 'spiritus' or πνεῦμα, or older words from which these had descended, meant neither *breath*, nor *wind*, nor *spirit*, nor yet all three of these things, but when they simply had *their own peculiar meaning*, which has since, in the course of the evolution of consciousness, crystallized into the three [logical] meanings specified." What J. M. Murry calls "The Metaphysic of Poetry" —the immanent principle in accordance with which all poets behave—is intrinsically at odds with the implicit metaphysic of rational discourse. See *Countries of the Mind, Second Series* (London, 1931), pp. 45–62.

"Metaphor consists . . . of analogy."—Aristotle, *On the Art of Poetry*, ed. and trans. Ingram Bywater (Oxford, 1909), p. 63.

59. But does . . . at all?—The idea that resemblance is the functional basis of metaphor and simile has been dominant throughout the history of rhetoric. Cf. the group of definitions collected by Gertrude Buck in *The Metaphor* (Ann Arbor, 1899), pp. 75–76. Contrast the German tradition summarized by Max Diez, "Metapher und Märchengestalt," *PMLA*, XLVIII (1933), 74–75.

60. that the relation . . . their likenesses."—Richards, *The Philosophy of Rhetoric*, pp. 96, 127. Cf. his *Interpretation in Teaching* (New York, 1938), p. 132.

On the other ... that relation.—It would be possible, of course, to place the phrase in a *literary* context which would produce an alogical shift of emphasis. We might have our attention directed to the gates in such a way that the park, instead of acting as a whole, would become "adjectival."

A number of recent accounts of poetic structure, though they do not dispense with logical relations, are cast in such a way as to suggest that in poetry these relations become radically different from anything found in truly logical discourse. See, e.g., Philip Wheelwright, "On the Semantics of Poetry," *Kenyon Review*, II (1940), 263–83; W. K. Wimsatt, Jr., "The Structure of the 'Concrete Universal' in Literature," *PMLA*, LXII (1947), 262–80; Allen Tate, "Tension in Poetry," *Reason in Madness* (New York, 1941), pp. 62–81; and the title essay of Kenneth Burke's *Philosophy of Literary Form*, pp. 1–137. Different as these formulations are, they meet in a common attempt to point out the positive structure of literature without reducing it to the distinctive methods of logic. Burke, indeed, might be said to have reduced logic to literature.

61. "It is not ... use either."—Richards, *Interpretation in Teaching*, pp. 284–85.

62–63. The most harmonious ... each other.—Cf. Cleanth Brooks, "The Language of Paradox," in *The Well Wrought Urn* (New York, 1947), pp. 3–20. Brooks, however, makes no clear distinction between the poem *as it exists* and *as it is analyzed*. It is the analysis, generally speaking, that falls into paradoxical form, thus indicating that the poem is not in logical form. Overt paradox is a special case in poetry—a kind of daring of the reader to perform an aesthetic act—and it results from unusual awareness of the problematic relations between poetry and logic.

63. The metaphysical ... of comparison."—Samuel Johnson, "Cowley," *Lives of the Poets*, ed. G. B. Hill (Oxford, 1905), I, 20. Similarly, "mixed metaphor" has been condemned because its terms, having no obvious common denominator of resemblance, "clash" with one another. George Orwell, in "Politics and the English Language," *Modern British Writing*, ed. D. V. Baker (New York, 1947), p. 199, goes so far as to say that the user of a mixed metaphor "is not really thinking." Like many proponents of "resemblance," Orwell is led to this conclusion by his as-

sumption that the purpose of a figure is literally to conjure up a visual image, not to make a meaning. Most evidence from experimental psychology would indicate that the degree of visualization varies greatly in experienced readers and therefore cannot be used as a central factor in the definition of imagery.

"the meaning . . . are aspects."—Michael Roberts, *Critique of Poetry* (London, 1934), p. 26. Cf. Cleanth Brooks, "The Heresy of Paraphrase," in *The Well Wrought Urn*, pp. 176–96. Among modern critics concerned with poetic structure, J. C. Ransom has been the leading dissenter from this conception. In *The New Criticism* he puts forward the picture of a poem as "a *logical structure* having a *local texture*"—a "paraphrasable core" to which "irrelevant" additions are made (pp. 98, 107, 110). While he sets out from the idea of a poem as a kind of discourse, and is even much concerned to establish the "ontological" validity of such discourse (p. 281), he stops short and refuses to give poetic structure any complete autonomy within the universe of discourse. For him, structure is necessarily logical, though why this should be so does not appear. On the other hand, in an effort to demonstrate that Ransom's division of structure and texture is arbitrary, Ruth Herschberger falls off in another direction: structure and texture alike become "fundamentally an expository . . . prose usage." See "The Structure of Metaphor," *Kenyon Review*, V (1943), 433–43.

64. "What precisely . . . blessed spirits."—M. M. Ross, *Milton's Royalism* (Ithaca, 1943), p. 111 (italics in text).

65. This figure . . . the whole."—Cassirer, *Language and Myth*, pp. 91–92.

"Every actual . . . relevant to it."—Whitehead, *Symbolism: Its Meaning and Effect* (New York, 1927), p. 25.

"an occasion . . . is concerned."—Whitehead, *Adventures of Ideas*, p. 226.

Metaphor and . . . they deliver.—Cf. Martin Foss, *Symbol and Metaphor in Human Experience*, esp. chap. iv. In a less metaphysical sense, of course, rational language is distinctively processional (i.e., "discursive"), while poetic form, by transcending the logical sequence, assumes a momentary ("presentational") aspect. This type of alogicality is the theme of Joseph Frank's article on "Spatial Form in Modern Literature" in *Criticism*, ed. Mark Schorer *et al.* (New York, 1948), pp. 379–92.

66. "contains them . . . their 'purity.' "—Kenneth Burke, *The Philosophy of Literary Form*, p. 49.

To take . . . at odds.—This example is presented, in somewhat different terms, by H. F. Dunbar, *Symbolism in Medieval Thought* (New Haven, 1929), pp. 145–47.

67. "The radiance . . . but he."—*Ibid.*, p. 145.

"he [Christ] . . . that Radiance."—*Ibid.*

In any . . . unconsciously presuppose."—Whitehead, *Science and the Modern World*, p. 61. Cf. Langer, *Philosophy in a New Key*, p. 4.

68. The dialectician . . . simply disappears.—I. A. Richards has had much to say of a variety of knowledge that is "a kind of making, i.e., the bringing into being of what is known" (*Coleridge on Imagination*, p. 49), and has often drawn a contrast between this "behaving or thinking with a concept" and objectively thinking "of one" (*The Philosophy of Rhetoric*, p. 31). As he puts it, "if we fix our attention on '*what* is being said,' the utterance becomes doctrine" (*Coleridge on Imagination*, pp. 143–44 [my italics]).

This is the basic insight of Kenneth Burke. Cf. *A Grammar of Motives* (New York, 1945), the whole of which depends on the dialectical method described in the Introduction (p. xix): "Distinctions, we might say, arise out of a great central moltenness, where all is merged. They have been thrown from a liquid center to the surface, where they have congealed. Let one of these crusted distinctions return to its source, and in this alchemic center it may be remade, again becoming molten liquid, and may enter into new combinations, whereat it may be again thrown forth as a new crust, a different distinction."

"opposition can . . . a *whole*."—M. J. Adler, *Dialectic* (London, 1927), p. 165 (italics in text). With this whole discussion of dialectic cf. Adler, *passim*, esp. pp. 14, 73, 100, 104, 157, 217, 249.

68–69. "The universe . . . with confusion."—*Ibid.*, p. 87.

69. "Beatrice is . . . Divine Sun."—Dunbar, *Symbolism in Medieval Thought*, pp. 492–93 (italics in text).

Urban has ... great dilemmas.—Urban, *Language and Reality*, p. 22.

the "semeiotic" of Locke—John Locke, *An Essay concerning Human Understanding*, ed. A. C. Fraser (Oxford, 1894), II, 461–62.

As Mill ... meaning of it?"—J. S. Mill, "Coleridge," in *Dissertations and Discussions* (London, 1859), I, 394.

70. "for," as ... to it."—Locke, *Essay concerning Human Understanding*, II, 461.

71. On the other ... and object.—Cf. Urban's comment on Whitehead's attempt to *describe* reality as process: "We are told that the feeler is the unity emergent from its own feelings. ... [But Whitehead] is constantly being tricked—by the truth, shall we say?—into another kind of language. These very feelings from which the feeler is said to emerge are constantly being given the character of the feeler ..." (W. M. Urban, "Whitehead's Philosophy of Language and Its Relation to His Metaphysics," in *The Philosophy of Alfred North Whitehead*, ed. P. A. Schilpp [Evanston, 1941], pp. 316–17).

And the more ... external world.—Cf. Wyndham Lewis' remark that in philosophies like those of Bergson and Whitehead "you lose not only the clearness of outline ... of the things you commonly apprehend; you lose also the clearness of outline of your own individuality which apprehends them" (*Time and Western Man*, p. 175; cf. p. 181). In place of the "Time-mind," which leads to this predicament, Lewis would reinstate the "spatializing" quality of "the visual intelligence."

Deliberate symbolism ... its subject matter.—The problem here put very abstractly turns up in many particular forms in modern criticism. See, e.g., Louis MacNeice, *Modern Poetry: A Personal Essay* (London, 1938), pp. 21–22; W. K. Wimsatt, Jr., "Verbal Style: Logical and Counterlogical," *PMLA*, LXV (1950), 19–20; R. J. Smith, "Intention in an Organic Theory of Poetry," *Sewanee Review*, LVI (1948), 625–33. J. C. Ransom writes, in "Poetry: the Formal Analysis," *Kenyon Review*, IX (1947), 436, that "we have grown familiar with many exciting turns of poetic language, but we begin to wonder if we are able to define *a poem*" (my italics).

This is the essential argument of R. S. Crane in "Cleanth Brooks; or, The Bankruptcy of Critical Monism," *Modern Philology*, XLV (1947–48), 226–45. What is valid in Crane's attack can be reduced to the necessity of invoking categories denied by monism in order to render monism. But the case is not so desperate as he would have us believe. It is possible to frame a purely structural definition of poetry in such a way as to take account of the extra-poetic. Cf. R. P. Warren, "Pure and Impure Poetry," *Kenyon Review*, V (1943), 251: "...the poet is like the jiujitsu expert; he wins by utilizing the resistance of his opponent—the materials of the poem. In other words, a poem, to be good, must earn itself. It is a motion toward a point of rest, but if it is not a resisted motion, it is motion of no consequence. ...And the good poem must, in some way, involve the resistances; it must carry something of the context of its own creation...."

pathless void... with significance—Cf. Elizabeth Sewell, *The Structure of Poetry* (London, 1951), esp. pp. 102–12, on "Everythingness, Nothingness, and Poetry." As this writer points out, "everything"—every thing—and "nothing"—no thing—ultimately meet. Rimbaud, the exponent of the former, declares "Je ne sais plus parler"; Mallarmé, the exponent of the latter, announces "J'ai presque perdu la raison et le sens des paroles les plus familières." Cf. also A. R. Chisholm, *Towards Hérodiade* (Melbourne, 1934).

72. "The poet... accidental pregnancies."—W. H. Auden, "Squares and Oblongs," in *Poets at Work*, ed. C. D. Abbott (New York, 1948), p. 172.

This equivocation... symbolistic framework.—See, e.g., R. P. Blackmur's attack on E. E. Cummings in *The Double Agent* (New York, 1935), pp. 1–30, on the ground (in effect) that Cummings "makes" when he ought to "find" and "finds" when he ought to "make."

It is plain that neither neoclassicism (e.g., Eliot) nor surrealism (e.g., Herbert Read) is simply a revival. Both are strategic emphases within a frame of reference quite different from that of the older classicism and that of the older romanticism. Eliot's notion of "tradition" (e.g., "Tradition and the Individual Talent") is deeply colored by a kind of Bergsonian becoming. Read's "automatism" is something much more complex than mere unconscious inspiration: cf. "Surrealism and the Romantic Principle" (1936), revised in *Criticism*, ed. Schorer, pp. 95–116.

"How can . . . I say?"—Auden, "Squares and Oblongs," in *Poets at Work*, p. 174.

73. "It was . . . singing, made."—Wallace Stevens, "The Idea of Order at Key West," in *Ideas of Order* (New York, 1936), p. 18.

73–74. These devices . . . of meaning.—For instances of this theme in modern literature (and of the reflexive relationship between theme and method) see George Haines IV, "Forms of Imaginative Prose: 1900–1940," *Southern Review*, VII (1941–42), 755–75. Cf. Henry James on Conrad in "The New Novel," *Notes on Novelists* (New York, 1914), p. 349: "It literally strikes us that his volume sets in motion more than anything else a drama in which his own system and his combined eccentricities of recital represent the protagonist in face of powers leagued against it. . . ." As James was doubtless aware, he was describing himself as well as Conrad.

74. The great . . . nihilistic mood.—Cf. Jacques Maritain, "Poetry's Dark Night," *Kenyon Review*, IV (1942), 149–59; and, as the classic instance, Mallarmé's letter to Henri Cazalis (March, 1866) in *Propos sur la poésie*, ed. Henri Mondor (Monaco, 1946), p. 59: "Malheureusement, en creusant le vers à ce point, j'ai rencontré deux abîmes, qui me désespèrent. L'un est le Néant, . . . et je suis encore trop désolé pour pouvoir croire même à ma poésie et me remettre au travail, que cette pensée écrasante m'a fait abandonner."

Yet even . . . of meaning.—Cf. the comment of Cleanth Brooks in a review of John Peale Bishop's verse, *Kenyon Review*, IV (1942), 244: not only is "Bishop's poetry . . . often poetry about poetry," but also his "basic theme is the loss of form, the loss of myth, the loss of a pattern." A similar method appears in the genre which Sartre has called the "anti-roman." See his Preface to *Portrait d'un inconnu*, by Nathalie Sarraute (1948), pp. 7–8: "Il s'agit de contester le roman par lui-même, de le détruire sous nos yeux dans le temps qu'on semble l'édifier, d'écrire le roman d'un roman qui ne se fait pas, qui ne peut pas se faire. . . ." The most familiar instance is Gide's *Faux-monnayeurs*. Cf. Roger Shattuck, "The Doubting of Fiction," *Yale French Studies*, No.

PAGE

6 (1950), pp. 101–8. Shattuck singles out a group of modern French critics "obsessed by verbal expression and . . . at the same time deeply suspicious of it." Several of these are represented in *Essays on Language and Literature,* ed. J. L. Hevesi (London, 1947).

75. "The most . . . our being."—A summary by G. J. Adler in *Wilhelm von Humboldt's Linguistical Studies* (New York, 1866), p. 16. Cf. Ernst Cassirer, *Philosophie der symbolischen Formen* (Berlin, 1923–29), I, 98–106. For a brief survey of related writers (Vico, Hamann, Herder, Schelling), cf. pp. 89–98.

Seeking to . . . things, too."—S. T. Coleridge, *Unpublished Letters,* ed. E. L. Griggs (London, 1932), I, 156. This phase of Coleridge was first brought into focus by I. A. Richards in *Coleridge on Imagination.* For related aspects, and especially his awareness of the attendant difficulties, cf. Herbert Read, "Coleridge as Critic," *Sewanee Review,* LVI (1948), 597–624, and W. J. Bate, "Coleridge on the Function of Art," *Perspectives of Criticism,* ed. Harry Levin (Cambridge, Mass., 1950), pp. 125–54. Read places Coleridge in a tradition extending from Kant's *Critique of Judgment* to Existentialism. The essay by R. P. Warren, "A Poem of Pure Imagination," appended to *The Rime of the Ancient Mariner* (New York, 1946), indicates that Coleridge, like later symbolists, tended to find his theme in his method.

CHAPTER III

77. "What could . . . the twentieth?"—Henry Adams, *The Education of Henry Adams* (Boston, 1918), p. 4.

78. "This being . . . his head."—John Winthrop, *Journal "History of New England,"* ed. J. K. Hosmer (New York, 1908), II, 347–48.

Cotton Mather . . . should be broken."—Samuel Sewall, *Diary . . . 1674–1729,* in *Collections of the Massachusetts Historical Society,* 5th Series, V–VII (1878–82), V, 402.

As Joshua Moody . . . versed in."—Joshua Moody, *Souldiery Spiritualized* (Cambridge, 1674), in *The Puritans,* ed. Perry Miller and T. H. Johnson (New York, 1938), p. 368.

79. "When they . . . in them."—William Bradford, *History "Of Plimoth Plantation"* (Boston, 1898), p. 97.

"Wee cannot ... the Dragon."—Thomas Shepard, *A Defense of the Answer Made unto the Nine Questions* (London, 1648), quoted in *The Puritans*, p. 119.

When Edward Johnson ... of Aijalon"—Edward Johnson, *The Wonder-working Providence of Sion's Saviour in New England* (London, 1654), ed. J. F. Jameson (New York, 1910), p. 36.

"See, ther's ... his comming."—*Ibid.*, p. 49.

New England ... Common-wealth together."—*Ibid.*, p. 25.

80. "wee are ... upon us."—Peter Bulkeley, *The Gospel-Covenant* (London, 1651), in *American History Told by Contemporaries*, ed. A. B. Hart (New York, 1897–1901), I, 451. This sense of a symbolic role persisted long after the older New England theocracy was dead. As late as 1801 James Dana suggested that God had created the United States in order "to exhibit to the world an instance" of republican government (*Two Discourses ... Delivered in New Haven* [New Haven, 1801], p. 49).

" 'Tis possible ... *to nothing*."—Cotton Mather, *Magnalia Christi Americana, or the Ecclesiastical History of New England* (Hartford, 1855; 1st ed., London, 1702), I, 27 (italics in text).

"For the ... Assyrian army."—Johnson, *The Wonder-working Providence*, p. 30.

80–81. Satan was ... in them.—*Ibid.*, pp. 148, 168.

81. The Wars ... New England"—Mather, *Magnalia*, Book VII (II, 489–681).

In the days ... tragical instances."—*Ibid.*, pp. 447–48. This completely realistic interpretation of the "Wars of the Lord" was felt to be bound up with any realistic conception of the Lord himself. Mather's *Memorable Providences, Relating to Witchcraft and Possessions* (Boston, 1689), in *Narratives of the Witchcraft Cases, 1648–1706*, ed. G. L. Burr (New York, 1914), were designed to prove (p. 96) "That, There is both a God, and a Devil, and Witchcraft; That, There is no out-ward Affliction, but what God may (and sometimes doth) permit Satan to trouble His people withal: That, The malice of Satan and his Instruments, is very great against the Children of God...." Cf. Joseph Glanvill's doctrine in *Saducismus triumphatus* (London, 1681) that the first step toward atheism is the denial of spirits and witches.

As H. W. Schneider points out in *The Puritan Mind* (New York, 1930), p. 17, the New World environment enabled the symbolic consciousness of the Puritans to have full play in daily life: "What was sheer fantasy in England appeared to be a practical and literal reality in New England."

The commissioning ... in these parts"—*Records of the Governor and Company of the Massachusetts Bay in New England,* ed. N. B. Shurtleff (Boston, 1853–54), V, 378.

Memoirs were ... every juncture.—Cf. Roger Clap, *Memoirs* (Boston, 1731), in *American History Told by Contemporaries,* I, 196.

A favorable ... to prayer—Francis Higginson, quoted by Thomas Hutchinson, *A Collection of Original Papers Relative to the History of the Colony of Massachusetts-Bay* (Boston, 1769), in *American History Told by Contemporaries,* I, 191.

the death ... Gods providence"—Bradford, *History "Of Plimoth Plantation,"* p. 90.

the triumph ... indifferent world.—*Ibid.,* pp. 493–96.

Cotton Mather ... by the score—*Magnalia,* Book VI (II, 339–486).

"The things ... sensibly demonstrated."—*Ibid.,* p. 342 (italics in text).

82. In government ... not another."—John Davenport, *A Sermon Preach'd at the Election ... May 19th 1669* (n.p., 1670), in *Publications of the Colonial Society of Massachusetts,* X (1904–6), 6.

"He can ... not devour."—Urian Oakes, *The Sovereign Efficacy of Divine Providence* (Boston, 1682), pp. 18–19.

82–83. "And now ... mans salvation."—Johnson, *The Wonder-working Providence,* p. 121.

83. When she ... by stars—Anne Bradstreet, "Meditations, Divine and Moral," in *Works,* ed. J. H. Ellis (Charlestown, Mass., 1867), p. 67.

In the best ... illustration coalesce.—In the following passage, for example, the conscious intention is to illustrate the "wonderful works" of God. But the writer's eye, at the same time, is on the object, and what emerges is a rather complex symbol of terror and beauty, in which the image and the meaning are indivisible: "... We received instruction and delight in behoulding the wonders of the Lord in the deepe waters, and sometimes seeing the sea round us appearing with a terrible countenance, and as it were full of high hills and deepe vallyes; and sometimes it appeared as a most plain and even meadow. And ever and anon we saw divers kyndes of fishes sporting in the great waters, great grampuses and huge whales going by companies and puffing up water-streames. Those that love their owne chimney corner, and dare not go farre beyond their owne townes end shall neever have the honour to see these wonderfull workes of Almighty God." Francis Higginson, quoted by Thomas Hutchinson, *A Collection of Original Papers Relative to the History of the Colony of Massachusetts-Bay* (Boston, 1769), in *American History Told by Contemporaries*, I, 194. In *The Rise of Puritanism* (New York, 1938), pp. 146–47, William Haller cites a passage from John Downame's *The Christian Warfare* (1609) which provides a revealing contrast. The pilgrim soul goes to sea. If he does not take God's word for his card, "Satan will raise against him such stormie tempests and contrary blasts of temptations" that he "will suffer shipwracke upon the rockes of sinne and bee drowned in a sea of destruction." Downame gives an analytic statement of part of the meaning which Higginson accidentally evokes.

"In the year ... *fire* in him."—Mather, *Magnalia*, II, 495 (italics in text).

84. "While these ... to produce."—*Ibid.*, p. 519 (italics in text). Cf. Mather's "Political Fables," in *The Andros Tracts* ("Publications of the Prince Society" [Boston, 1868–74]), II, 325–32. These are even more consciously "literary" and therefore suffer even more obviously from the prevailing ignorance of aesthetic unity. The terms of each fable hang loosely apart.

Aquinas held ... of reality.—Cf. H. F. Dunbar, *Symbolism in Medieval Thought and Its Consummation in the Divine Comedy* (New Haven, 1929), pp. 498–99.

"It is impossible ... of them."—Samuel Willard, *A Compleat Body of Divinity* (Boston, 1726), p. 44 (my italics).

85. "A Scripture ... manifest consequence."—John Norton, *The Heart of N-England Rent at the Blasphemies of the Present Generation* (Cambridge, 1659), pp. 9–11. Italics in text.

The Puritan ... and commentaries.—Cf. Perry Miller, *The New England Mind: The Seventeenth Century* (New York, 1939), pp. 493–501; and *The Puritans*, p. 30, n. 2.

"This is ... mostly philosophical."—Henry Schorus, *Specimen et forma legitime tradendi sermonis et rationis disciplinas, ex. P. Rami scriptis collecta* (Strassburg, 1572), p. 51, quoted by Perry Miller, *The New England Mind*, p. 316. On the Ramistic rhetoric in general cf. *The New England Mind*, pp. 300–330. The ornamentalism of the doctrine comes out boldly in Omer Talon's *Rhetorica*, the standard text. "Elocution" is defined as "exornatio orationis"; "trope"—the first part of elocution—is that "by which a word is transferred from its primary meaning to another" ("qua verbum a nativa significatione in aliam immutatur"), and "figure" is that "by which the character of discourse is altered from accepted and artless usage" ("qua orationis habitus a recta & simplici consuetudine mutatur"). See Audomarus Talaeus [Omer Talon], *Rhetorica e P. Rami praelectionibus observata* (3d ed.; Frankfort, 1584), pp. 24, 29, 71.

"All Rhetorical ... Grammar of it."—Willard, *A Compleat Body of Divinity*, p. 33 (italics in text).

86. the poetry ... *Bay Psalm Book.*—[Richard Mather], "The Preface," *A Literal Reprint of the Bay Psalm Book* (Cambridge, 1862), sig. **3 verso: "If ... the verses are not alwayes so smooth and elegant as some may desire or expect; let them consider that Gods Altar needs not our pollishings: Ex. 20, for wee have respected rather a plaine translation, then to smooth our verses with the sweetnes of any paraphrase, and soe have attended Conscience rather then Elegance, fidelity rather then poetry...."

Thomas Hooker ... the builder."—Thomas Hooker, "A Preface of the Authour," in *A Survey of the Summe of Church-Discipline* (London, 1648), sig. a4 verso and b.

86–87. Whitehead has shown ... claims to render.—A. N. Whitehead, *Science and the Modern World* (Cambridge, 1933), pp. 49–118, *passim*.

87. The logical ... from Ramus—The best summaries of the Ramistic logic will be found in Miller, *The New England Mind*, pp. 111–53, and *The Puritans*, pp. 28–41.

the Ramistic logicians ... of reality.—Cf. Ramus [Pierre de la Ramée], *Dialecticae institutiones* (1543), in *Antonii Goveani Opera*, ed. Jacob van Vaassen (Rotterdam, 1766), p. 725: "Dialectic is according to nature; that is to say, it is the character, the reason, the mind, the thought of God the father of all things; in short, it is a light, similar to his holy and eternal light, proper to man and born with him." (*"Naturalis* autem *Dialectica,* id est, ingenium, ratio, mens, imago parentis omnium rerum Dei, lux denique beatae illius, & aeternae lucis aemula, hominis propria est, cum eoque nascitur.")

"As a hammer ... many explanations."—Quoted by F. W. Farrar, *History of Interpretation* (New York, 1886), p. 73.

Rules of ... mutually supplementary.—*Ibid.,* pp. 196–97, 294–95; Dunbar, *Symbolism in Medieval Thought,* pp. 21, 275.

88. "multiplex intelligentia"—Farrar, *History of Interpretation,* p. 294.

Aquinas held ... beyond itself.—*Summa theologica,* Part I, Q. I, Art. 10: "Whether in Holy Scripture a Word May Have Several Senses?" Cf. the quotation from Hugh of St. Victor in Dunbar, *Symbolism in Medieval Thought,* p. 491: "It should be known therefore that when Leo is said to signify Christ, not the name of the animal, but the animal itself signifies him."

the meaning ... several meanings."—"Epistle X: To Can Grande della Scala," *Dantis Alagherii epistolae: The Letters of Dante,* ed. and trans. Paget Toynbee (Oxford, 1920), pp. 173, 199: "... sciendum est quod istius operis non est simplex sensus, immo dici potest *polysemos,* hoc est plurium sensuum...."

The meanings ... other meanings."—*Dante's Convivio Translated into English,* trans. W. W. Jackson (Oxford, 1909), p. 75.

The "poetriae" ... for symbolism—C. S. Baldwin, *Medieval Rhetoric and Poetic (to 1400)* (New York, 1928), p. 203.

the medieval ... to fact."—H. O. Taylor, *The Mediaeval Mind: A History of the Development of Thought and Emotion in the Middle Ages* (4th ed.; London, 1930), II, 69. Cf. his comment (II, iii) on the builders whose cathedrals show "with a plastic adequacy ... how completely they thought and felt in the allegorical medium in which they worked." W. M. Urban, *Language and Reality* (London, 1939), p. 25, remarks that "trust in the word is the predominant note of mediaeval culture," so that "nominalism . . . becomes, for this culture, the most fundamental of all heresies."

The Puritans . . . the New.—Samuel Mather, *The Figures or Types of the Old Testament* (2d ed.; London, 1705), p. 52, defines a type as "some outward or sensible thing ordained of God under the Old Testament, to represent and hold forth something of Christ in the New."

These relationships . . . and metaphors.—*Ibid.,* pp. 23, 58–59.

89. "Men must . . . make *Types.*"—*Ibid.,* p. 55 (italics in text).

90. The purpose . . . our *light.*"—Mather, *Magnalia,* I, 33 (italics in text).

"the whole . . . and blood."—Emerson, *Works,* X, 234.

The highly wrought . . . Civil Covenant.—Cf. Schneider, *The Puritan Mind,* pp. 19–24.

they reflect . . . were founded.—Cf. T. C. Hall, *The Religious Background of American Culture* (Boston, 1930), p. 190. H. G. Townsend, *Philosophical Ideas in the United States* (New York, 1934), p. 10, points out a similar relationship between the theocratic conception of government and the New England family.

The earthly . . . been exemplar"—Miller, *The New England Mind,* p. 413.

91. "All the Arts . . . they flow."—Samuel Mather, "To the Reader," in Samuel Stone, *A Congregational Church Is a Catholike Visible Church* (London, 1652), sig. A2 (italics in text).

The Puritan obsession with "method"—Cf. Miller, *The New England Mind,* p. 95: "The great difference between Calvin and the so-called Calvinists of the seventeenth century is symbolized by the vast importance they attached to one word, 'method.' Systematic organization of the creed had indeed been of great concern to Calvin, but never the obsession it was to his followers." Miller observes (p. 111) that the basic doctrines of Puritan belief were often in effect translated into linguistic terms: the fall of man, the loss of God's image, and innate depravity amounted to "a lapse from dialectic . . . the loss of an ability to use the syllogism, and . . . a congenital incapacity for discursive reasoning."

92. "Bernard, upon ... of Christianity."—Mather, *Magnalia*, I, 27.

"Had Ramists ... all at once."—Miller, *The New England Mind*, p. 149. Cf., e.g., George Downame's *Commentarii in P. Rami Dialecticam* (London, 1669; 1st ed., 1610), pp. 24–25, where he answers the question whether arguments are things or words by declaring that they are "things *and* words as far as they are affected to the arguing of other things and words" ("res & voces quatenus ad alias arguendas affectae sunt").

"knowledge is ... faculty knowing"—Willard, *A Compleat Body of Divinity*, p. 41.

93. Arguments were ... them true.—Ramus, *La Dialectique de M. P. de la Ramée* (Paris, 1576), pp. 37–38, quoted by Miller, *The New England Mind*, p. 155. Compare Calvin's answer to the question of how we know the Scriptures to be divine: "This is just as if any one should inquire, How shall we learn to distinguish light from darkness, white from black, sweet from bitter?" (Jean Calvin, *Institutes of the Christian Religion*, trans. John Allen [Philadelphia, 1936], I, 87).

"the light ... is perceived."—Ramus, *Dialecticae institutiones*, pp. 731–32: "... naturae lumen ... seipsum intuentibus ostendit, & huiusmodi dispositionem perspectum naturalis assensio sequitur."

Similarly, a ... and order.—Cf., e.g., Downame's *Commentarii*, p. 473: "For thus this golden chain of method adjusts and connects axioms to each other, so that the prior, as it were, holds out a torch of significance to the following, and whatever follows depends on its antecedent as do the links of a chain." ["Sic enim aurea haec methodi catena axiomata aptat inter se & connectit, ut & prius quasi facem quandam intelligentiae posteriori praeferat, & posterius quodque ex antecedente (ut inter catenae anulos fit) dependeat."] Also Ramus' *Dialecticae institutiones*, p. 734: "The second [part of dialectic] ... deals with *collocation* and the order of many and various arguments cohering among themselves, bound together as a continuous chain, and related with reference to a fixed end." ("Secundus ... *Collocationem* tradit, & ordinem multorum, & variorum argumentorum cohaerentium inter se, & perpetua velut catena vinctorum, ad unumque certum finem relatorum.")

"An argument . . . something else."—Ramus, *Dialecticae libri duo,* ed. George Downame (London, 1669), p. 1: "Argumentum est quod ad aliquid arguendum affectum est."

The axiom . . . and things.—Miller, *The New England Mind,* pp. 133–34: ". . . the stuff of judgment is not the syllogism but the axiom; the aim of an orator or preacher is a succession of sentences, not a display of deductions. When he has laid out the arguments and combined them into several axioms, he then ought to perceive from the axioms themselves what are their interconnections and what is their order. . . ." Cf. Ramus, *Dialectique de Pierre de la Ramée* (1555), quoted by Charles Waddington, *Ramus . . . sa vie, ses écrits et ses opinions* (Paris, 1855), p. 373: ". . . Autant que l'homme surmonte les bestes par le syllogisme, d'autant luy-mesme excelle entre les hommes par la méthode, et la divinité de l'homme ne reluit en nulle partie de la raison si amplement, qu'au soleil de cest universel jugement."

The arguments . . . of things—Alexander Richardson, *The Logician's School-Master* (London, 1657), p. 69, quoted by Miller, *The New England Mind,* p. 131.

"The least . . . extraordinary power."—Nathaniel Ward, *The Simple Cobler of Aggawam in America* (London, 1647), ed. L. C. Wroth (New York, 1937), p. 20. Ramus declares in *Dialecticae institutiones,* p. 729, that "in all modes [of "invention"] . . . the force of proof is double: for now the parts are confirmed by the whole, and now the whole by the parts." ("In omnibus . . . modis gemina probationis vis est: tum enim ex toto partes, tum ex partibus totum confirmatur.")

94. the vogue . . . been explored—Cf. Rosemond Tuve, *Elizabethan and Metaphysical Imagery: Renaissance Poetic and Twentieth-Century Critics* (Chicago, 1947), esp. pp. 331–53. On the relation of "dialectic" to the Renaissance conception of truth cf. Hardin Craig, *The Enchanted Glass: The Elizabethan Mind in Literature* (New York, 1936), pp. 156–57. Craig notes that this concept "suspends truth, not between hypothesis and verification, but between the affirmative and the negative in debate. In such circumstances truth becomes, not a fixed proposition, but a shifting, elusive, debatable thing to be determined by dialectical acumen before it shines forth in rhetorical clarity by its own unassisted

effulgence." Hence, as Craig remarks, the characteristic dramatic form of Elizabethan literature.

"we cannot . . . some other."—Emerson, *Works*, II, 42.

94–95. "it was . . . this case." Winthrop, *Journal "History of New England,"* I, 201.

95. The same . . . a "rule."—Thomas Hutchinson, *History of the Province of Massachusetts-Bay* (London, 1768), in *American History Told by Contemporaries*, I, 384.

John Cotton . . . other sanctification)."—Winthrop, *Journal "History of New England,"* I, 209 (my italics). Miller (*The New England Mind*, pp. 6, 32, 70, 100, 112, 190, 208, 367, 440) and Schneider (*The Puritan Mind*, pp. 64, 70) point out other logically incompatible elements in Puritan thought.

The arbitrary . . . than God.—Cf. Miller, *The New England Mind*, pp. 397, 399, 485, and " 'Preparation for Salvation' in Seventeenth-Century New England," *Journal of the History of Ideas*, IV (1943), 253–86.

"It is his . . . of it."—Thomas Shepard, *Works*, ed. J. A. Albro (Boston, 1853), III, 31, quoted by Miller, *The New England Mind*, p. 198.

95–96. "Revelation had . . . things considered."—Benjamin Franklin, *Autobiography*, in *Complete Works*, ed. John Bigelow (New York, 1887–88), I, 139 (italics in text).

96. "regeneration became . . . an ideology."—Joseph Haroutunian, *Piety versus Moralism: The Passing of the New England Theology* (New York, 1932), pp. 55–56.

"those who . . . *real holiness*"—Nathanael Emmons, *A Dissertation on the Scriptural Qualifications for Admission and Access to the Christian Sacraments* (Worcester, Mass., 1793), p. 51 (italics in text). Cf. Schneider, *The Puritan Mind*, p. 221.

"When it . . . plain nonsense."—Andrews Norton, *A Statement of Reasons for Not Believing the Doctrines of Trinitarians* (2d ed.; Boston, 1856), pp. 169–70. This passage is not in the first edition (Boston, 1819). Contrast Cotton Mather's ability, however limited, to feel the Trinity as a symbolic pattern: "Of Man," *The Christian Philosopher* (London, 1721), pp. 303–4.

PAGE

Norton recognized . . . a passage.—Norton, *A Statement of Reasons* (1st ed.), pp. 38, 42. See his general discussion of language: 1st ed., pp. 36–64; 2d ed., pp. 138–73.

97.   "the Trinitarian . . . "incomprehensible jargon"—Thomas Jefferson, Letter to Timothy Pickering (February 27, 1821), *Writings*, eds. A. A. Lipscomb and A. E. Bergh (Washington, 1903–4), XV, 323.

"the Christian . . . is three"—Thomas Paine, *The Age of Reason*, in *Writings*, ed. M. D. Conway (New York, 1894–96), IV, 58.

They proposed . . . complex symbols.—See chap. iv.

Roger Williams . . . a "seeker."—Williams was horrified by the human consequences of absolute dogma—"soules compelled and forced to *Hypocrisie* in a *spirituall* and *soule rape*" (*The Bloudy Tenent, of Persecution, for Cause of Conscience* [London, 1644], ed. S. L. Caldwell [Providence, 1867], p. 63).

"How all . . . of Heaven."—Ward, *The Simple Cobler of Aggawam*, p. 21 (my italics).

98.   "God's sovereignty . . . *live together*."—W. E. Channing, "Introductory Remarks" (1841), *Works* (Boston, 1883), pp. 2–3 (my italics).

Emerson's defiance of system—Emerson, *Works*, XII, 11.

Horace Bushnell's . . . his way.—Horace Bushnell, *God in Christ* (Hartford, 1849), p. 82.

"language of paradox"—Cleanth Brooks, "The Language of Paradox," in *The Well Wrought Urn* (New York, 1947), pp. 3–20.

Horace Bushnell . . . the tradition.—M. B. Cheney (ed.), *Life and Letters of Horace Bushnell* (New York, 1880), pp. 208–9.

"not art . . . the artisan."—Ramus, *Dialectique* (1555), pp. 137–38, quoted by Waddington, *Ramus*, p. 373: "non pas l'art seullet, mais beaucoup plus l'exercice d'icelluy et la pratique fait l'artisant."

98–99.   Richard Sibbes . . . his trade."—Richard Sibbes, "The Art of Contentment" (1629), in *Complete Works*, ed. A. B. Grosart (Edinburgh, 1862–64), V, 183 (my italics).

PAGE

99. "There is . . . proved it."—Thomas Hooker, *The Application of Redemption . . . The Ninth and Tenth Books* (2d ed.; London, 1659), pp. 53–54.

his "real . . . supernatural light"—Jonathan Edwards, "A Divine and Supernatural Light," in *The Works of President Edwards* (New York, 1856), IV, 440–41. (Unless otherwise stated, quotations from Edwards' *Works* are from this edition.)

Emerson's conviction . . . or logical"—Emerson, *Works*, II, 307.

"There is . . . the latter."—Edwards, "A Divine and Supernatural Light," *Works*, IV, 442.

100. God's power . . . holy gentleness."—Edwards' autobiography (*Works*, I, 16) (italics in text).

"The design . . . and relations."—Edwards, "Dissertation Concerning the End for Which God Created the World" (*Works*, II, 253) (my italics).

Within "those . . . spiritual excellencies."—Edwards, "Excellency of Christ," in *Observations Concerning the Scripture Oeconomy of the Trinity and Covenant of Redemption*, ed. E. C. Smyth (New York, 1880), pp. 93–96.

The "images . . . Newtonian universe.—Edwards, *Images or Shadows of Divine Things*, ed. Perry Miller (New Haven, 1948), pp. 17–23.

101. "As Edwards . . . as thing."—*Ibid.*, pp. 19–20.

"Seeing the . . . have it."—Edwards, MS "Miscellanies," No. 260, quoted in *Images or Shadows of Divine Things*, p. 22.

"doubt whether . . . American disciple."—*Ibid.*

102. "If there . . . in democracies."—Alexis de Tocqueville, *Democracy in America* (1835–40), trans. Henry Reeve *et al.* (New York, 1945), II, 31–32.

On the one . . . of day."—*Ibid.*, p. 25.

Tocqueville reported . . . United States.—*Ibid.*, p. 27.

Yet on . . . expressions."—*Ibid.*, pp. 13–17, 69.

he traced . . . "private judgment."—*Ibid.*, pp. 3–6.

103. Side by . . . of ideas."—*Ibid.*, pp. 66–67.

"They were ... Mr. Locke."—[S. M. F. Ossoli], *The Writings of Margaret Fuller*, ed. Mason Wade (New York, 1941), p. 391.

104. "So speech ... in defining."—A. B. Alcott, *Tablets* (Boston, 1868), p. 175.

"Transcendentalism ... mythi."—Noah Porter, "Transcendentalism," *The American Biblical Repository, Second Series*, VIII (1842), 198.

"the world ... of both"—Alcott, *Tablets*, p. 176. Cf. his *Journals*, ed. Odell Shepard (Boston, 1938), p. 100: "God publishes himself in facts, whether of the corporeal or spiritual world. These are his words."

"Transcendentalism" in ... modern world.—A comprehensive selection from the writings of the New England group, together with biographical and critical comment, has been made by Perry Miller in *The Transcendentalists: An Anthology* (Cambridge, 1950). While Miller's emphasis is on the "religious" character of the movement, he notes and to some extent illustrates the fact that "this revival of religion had to find new forms of expression instead of new formulations of doctrine, and it found them in literature" (p. 9). The point is that aesthetic, and specifically symbolic, expression was so crucial an issue that it may well be regarded as end rather than means. To say that "transcendentalism was fed by deeper springs than mere aesthetics" may be true enough and yet not quite relevant when one must add that "the situation was such that there was almost no other direction in which the waters could flow than into a doctrine and an attempted practice of the beautiful."

104–5. "Certain it is ... entirely new."—Francis Bowen, *Critical Essays on a Few Subjects Connected with the History and Present Condition of Speculative Philosophy* (Boston, 1842), p. 6.

105. "the mode ... British ancestors."—J. W. Alexander and A. B. Dod, "Transcendentalism," *Two Articles from the Princeton Review, Concerning the Transcendental Philosophy of the Germans and of Cousin, and Its Influence on Opinion in This Country* (Cambridge, Mass., 1840), p. 72.

"The very ... for any."—Emerson, *Journals*, V, 293.

"Above his ... manner is."—Emerson, *Works*, II, 329.

105–6. "The movement . . . the cause."—O. A. Brownson, "Two Articles from the *Princeton Review*," *Boston Quarterly Review*, III (1840), 271.

106. In 1715 . . . real motive.—Herbert and Carol Schneider (eds.), *Samuel Johnson . . . His Career and Writings* (New York, 1929), I, 6; II, 186.

He was . . . humane intellect."—*Ibid.*, II, 14, 21, 202.

"One reason . . . general heads."—Jonathan Edwards, *Works*, ed. S. E. Dwight (New York, 1829–30), I, 682–83.

107. Jefferson's "self-evident" . . . without metaphysics."—H. W. Schneider, *History of American Philosophy* (New York, 1946), pp. 36, 41, 48. Similarly, deism never put down deep roots in America as a consciously held doctrine: cf. H. M. Morais, *Deism in Eighteenth Century America* (New York, 1934), esp. p. 28.

By 1800 . . . New Learning—Merle Curti, "The Great Mr. Locke: America's Philosopher, 1783–1861," *Huntington Library Bulletin*, No. 11 (April, 1937), p. 117.

"where the . . . best applied."—Tocqueville, *Democracy in America*, II, 3.

The uniformity . . . "private judgment"—*Ibid.*, p. 10.

"The theology . . . unimportant propositions."—J. W. Alexander and A. B. Dod, "Transcendentalism," *Two Articles from the Princeton Review*, p. 6.

108. The liberalizing . . . eighteenth-century nurture"—V. L. Parrington, *Main Currents in American Thought* (New York, 1927), II, 380.

"They had . . . of evidence."—O. B. Frothingham, *Transcendentalism in New England: a History* (New York, 1876), p. 114.

When the older . . . a Seeker."—W. H. Channing, "Ernest the Seeker," *The Dial*, I (1840–41), 48–58. On the relation between Unitarianism and Transcendentalism cf. H. C. Goddard, *Studies in New England Transcendentalism* (New York, 1908), pp. 21–26. C. H. Faust, in "The Background of the Unitarian Opposition to Transcendentalism," *Modern Philology*, XXXV (1937–38), 297–324, has shown that the bitterness of the Unitarians' attack on the Transcendentalists was caused by the fact that their own Calvinistic opponents had prophesied long before that the principle of freedom of interpretation would lead to intellectual revolution. Perry Miller, "Jonathan Edwards to Emerson," *New England Quarterly*, XIII (1940), 615–16, remarks that "over and over again the rational attack upon Calvinism served only to release energies which then sought for new forms of expression in directions entirely opposed to rationalism." Actually, the crux in every case *was* the "form of expression"—doctrine vs. undogmatic rationalism, and free rational inquiry vs. aesthetic apprehension.

"Protestantism ends in Transcendentalism."—O. A. Brownson, *Works*, ed. H. F. Brownson (Detroit, 1882–87), VI, 113–34.

109. Sampson Reed's . . . to Emerson—Emerson, *Journals*, II, 116.

"rushed into . . . the world"—Edward Everett Hale (who grew up during the period) in his edition of J. F. Clarke's *Autobiography, Diary, and Correspondence* (Boston and New York, 1891), p. 87. For the chronology of "transcendentalism" cf. Goddard, *Studies in New England Transcendentalism*, pp. 33–41.

As Francis Bowen . . . virtually disappeared.—Bowen, *Critical Essays*, p. 35.

But "in . . . whole system."—Whitehead, *Science and the Modern World*, p. 71.

109–10. "Knowledge was . . . for granted."—E. A. Burtt, *The Metaphysical Foundations of Modern Physical Science: A Historical and Critical Essay* (New York, 1932), pp. 1–2.

110. Man, according . . . all things."—Ramus, *Dialectique* (1555), p. 69, as quoted by Waddington, *Ramus*, p. 370: "L'homme a en soy naturellement la puissance de cognoistre toutes choses."

But Descartes . . . of anything.—René Descartes, *Philosophical Works*, trans. E. S. Haldane and G. R. T. Ross (Cambridge, 1911), I, 3, 101, 238.

Similarly, Locke . . . by ourselves."—John Locke, *An Essay Concerning Human Understanding*, ed. A. C. Fraser (Oxford, 1894), I, 9, 122.

"the difficulties . . . his chamber—*Ibid.*, p. 9.

But the "creative . . . and experience."—David Hume, *Enquiries Concerning the Human Understanding and Concerning the Prin-*

ciples of Morals, ed. L. A. Selby-Bigge (2d ed.; Oxford, 1902), p. 19.

111. "It is . . . in reasoning."—*Ibid.,* p. 153.

Kant's new . . . of cognition"—Immanuel Kant, *Critique of Pure Reason,* trans. F. M. Müller (London, 1881), I, 370.

"the primary . . . of experience."—James Gibson, *Locke's Theory of Knowledge and Its Historical Relations* (Cambridge, 1917), p. 326.

He is aware . . . of knowledge."—Kant, *Critique of Pure Reason,* II, 45.

"the Kantian . . . is possible."—Gibson, *Locke's Theory of Knowledge,* p. 332. While Kant proposed to correct Locke and Hume by asserting that objects conform to modes of thought, he did not focus on the inherence of intellectual form *in* objects, "its 'secret' presence in the content of immediate experience" (p. 334).

Kant began . . . unknown to us."—Kant, *Critique of Pure Reason,* I, 398; II, 40.

112. "Now the young . . . for them."—Emerson, *Journals,* IV, 281.

Locke seems . . . or wise."—Emerson, *Works,* V, 231–32.

The founders . . . was based."—F. H. Hedge, quoted by J. E. Cabot, *A Memoir of Ralph Waldo Emerson* (Boston, 1887), I, 244–46.

Their obsession . . . popular joke.—Cf. the anonymous dialogue, "A Plain Discussion with a Transcendentalist," *The New Englander,* I (1843), 503: Mr. B., a critic of the new ideas, makes a preliminary agreement with Mr. A., the transcendentalist, to leave names and systems out of the question. But Mr. A. sets out at once with "Your sensual school of philosophy—." He is interrupted by Mr. B., only to return to his theme after a few moments: "Locke has entirely misled the world in some of the most vital points."

They pictured . . . iron hand."—George Ripley, "Professor Walker's Vindication of Philosophy," *The Dial,* I (1840–41), 259. W. D. Wilson, "The Unitarian Movement in New England," *The Dial,* I (1840–41), p. 422.

"The notion . . . surrounding objects."—Charles Lane, "A. Bronson Alcott's Works," *The Dial*, III (1842–43), 427–28. While Lane was not an American by birth or education, his is perhaps the most eloquent statement of a point of view which is everywhere apparent in *The Dial*. A member of an English group led by one James Pierrepont Greaves, whom Alcott visited in 1843, he came to America under Alcott's auspices.

the absolute . . . United States—James Marsh (ed.), *Aids to Reflection, by Samuel Taylor Coleridge, with a Preliminary Essay* (New York, 1840; 1st American ed., by Marsh, 1829), pp. 47–48.

112–13. In America . . . philosophy, never."—Brownson, *Works*, I, 133–34.

113. The American . . . *ratio cognoscendi*"—F. H. Hedge, review of various works of Coleridge, *Christian Examiner*, XIV (1833), 120–21; J. E. Cabot, "Immanuel Kant," *The Dial*, IV (1843–44), 409.

In 1803 . . . probably inconsistent.—Samuel Miller, *A Brief Retrospect of the Eighteenth Century* (New York, 1803), II, 4, 22–28.

By 1848 . . . it up."—J. B. Stallo, *General Principles of the Philosophy of Nature* (Boston, 1848), p. 189. Between 1801 and 1829 only five articles dealing with Kant appeared in American periodicals, while fifteen appeared between the years 1838 and 1845 alone. See S. H. Goodnight, *German Literature in American Magazines Prior to 1846* (Madison, Wis., 1907), p. 246. The "Scottish School" of realism played a transitional role in this filling-out of the philosophical picture. Cf. E. W. Todd, "Philosophical Ideas at Harvard College, 1817–1837," *New England Quarterly*, XVI (1943), 89. On the influence of Scottish realism in the United States (its chief center being Princeton) see I. W. Riley, *American Thought from Puritanism to Pragmatism* (New York, 1915), pp. 118–39. This school was highly conscious of the historical development of "the Cartesian system." Cf. A. Seth [Pringle-Pattison], *Scottish Philosophy: A Comparison of the Scottish and German Answers to Hume* (Edinburgh, 1885), pp. 5–7.

113–14. The American . . . become disciples—Cf. René Wellek, "Emerson and German Philosophy," *New England Quarterly*, XVI (1943), 41–62; and "The Minor Transcendentalists and German

Philosophy," *New England Quarterly*, XV (1942), 652–80. Not all were as frank as J. A. Saxton, who declares, after giving an account of the origins of "Transcendentalism" in reaction from Locke, that he "knows nothing of the writings of Kant." See "Poetry—Transcendentalism—Progress," *The Dial*, II (1841–42), 90.

114. "the transcendental . . . the intellect"—George Santayana, "The Genteel Tradition in American Philosophy," in *Winds of Doctrine* (London, 1913), p. 195. Santayana notes in *Character and Opinion in the United States* (New York, 1921), pp. 9–10, that the tendency "to imbibe more or less of the spirit of a philosophy" was a peculiarity of nineteenth-century American thinkers. If they burked distinctions in the process, their very looseness enabled them (as Santayana only half grants) to follow paths which were hidden from the more technically expert: "they found new approaches to old beliefs or new expedients in old dilemmas." Emerson speaks of "the American superficialness" (*Works*, X, 323) without apology.

The earliest . . . sound philosophizing."—James Murdock, *Sketches of Modern Philosophy, Especially among the Germans* (Hartford, 1842), p. 47.

Parker "found . . . right road."—John Weiss, *Life and Correspondence of Theodore Parker* (London, 1863), II, 454.

Hedge attributed . . . transcendental method."—Hedge, review of Coleridge, *Christian Examiner*, XIV, 126. Charles Follen, in his *Inaugural Discourse* (Cambridge, Mass., 1831), p. 11, calls German metaphysics "the best gymnastics of the mind," and he adds that the value of gymnastics is "methodically to unfold, invigorate, and refine all the growing powers of man." Follen looked forward to "a new race of thoughts and modes of reasoning." See his letter to James Marsh (1832) in Marsh's *Remains*, ed. J. L. Torrey (2d ed.; Boston, 1845), pp. 151–52.

"not so much . . . premises themselves."—Marsh (ed.), *Aids to Reflection*, p. 10. Cf. John McVickar, in the other early American edition (New York, 1841), p. xvii: Coleridge's aphorisms must be entertained and savored until the reader finds that "he has got embodied some new truth, a new stepping-stone for his foot to rest upon amid the dark waters."

While Coleridge was undoubtedly a major "influence" in America at this time, the wording of Marsh's Preface to his edition of *The Friend* (Burlington, 1831), p. vii, is significant: he hopes that the book will be "instrumental in hastening the change, *which is already taking place,* in our views of logic and metaphysics." The Coleridgean and the American emphasis on method were essentially parallel results of the whole modern philosophic tradition. Each was an attempt to take a stand precisely in the area of vacillation that characterized both empiricism and idealism—the area where thought, the idea, or the subjective comes into immediate contact with sense, the thing, or the objective. When Coleridge declares that true method depends upon "the due mean or balance between our passive impressions and the mind's own re-action on the same"—that it is a means of finding the "ground common to the world and to man"—that "during the act of knowledge itself, the objective and subjective are so instantly united, that . . . there is here no first, and no second; both are coinstantaneous and one"—he is actuated by the very historical forces which, brought to a peculiar concentration in this country, made Americans his most sympathetic readers. See *The Friend,* ed. H. N. Coleridge (London, 1844), III, 116, 196; *Biographia literaria,* ed. J. Shawcross (Oxford, 1907), I, 174. The same is true of Carlyle, whose enormous vogue in America from 1830 to 1860 has been demonstrated by W. S. Vance, "Carlyle and the American Transcendentalists" (unpublished dissertation, University of Chicago, 1941). His view of language as "the Body of Thought," and of the artifact as a symbol with "intrinsic meaning," was the outcome of a similar preoccupation with the clash between empiricism and idealism. See *Works* (Centenary ed.; London, n.d.), I, 57, 177–78. René Wellek, *Immanuel Kant in England, 1793–1838* (Princeton, 1931), pp. 67, 102–3, 108, 187–89, has shown the looseness of Coleridge's and Carlyle's interpretations of Kant, as well as their tendency to lump together all German idealism as one doctrine. Like their American followers, they were working from a standpoint which made it less important to observe technical distinctions than to realize broad directions.

"the state . . . of men."—Emerson, *Works,* II, 289.

"the Idealism . . . *Transcendental* forms."—*Ibid.*, I, 320–21 (italics in text).

115. "left reason ... were irreconcilable."—Stallo, *General Principles of the Philosophy of Nature*, p. 210.

"Spiritualism and ... *equally impossible*."—George Ripley, "Brownson's Writings," *The Dial*, I (1840–41), 27 (my italics). Cf. Hedge's "Questionings," *The Dial*, I (1840–41), 290–91—a poem much admired by Emerson: "Hath this world, without me wrought, / Other substance than my thought? / Lives it by my sense alone, / Or by essence of its own?"

Behind George Ripley's ... of interdependence.—Stallo, *General Principles of the Philosophy of Nature*, pp. 46, 182.

"the subject ... or act."—Brownson, *Works*, V, 128. Cf. I, 65: "... in Life ... the subject and object, me and not me, are one and indissoluble." But Brownson drew a distinction between "Life," which he identified with "thought" or "act," and metaphysical "Being," which he associated with the logical dichotomy of subject and object. In effect, he tried to do justice to both tendencies, and thereby he was able to give a truer account than those, like Alcott, who had no reservations in advocating an "identity-philosophy."

115–16. "All existence ... or spiritual"—Asa Burton, *Essays on Some of the First Principles of Metaphysicks, Ethicks, and Theology* (Portland, 1824), p. 13. Cf. Frederick Beasley, *A Search of Truth in the Science of the Human Mind: Part First* (Philadelphia, 1822), p. 15; Asa Mahan, *Abstract of a Course of Lectures on Mental and Moral Philosophy* (Oberlin, 1840), p. 9.

116. "As thinkers ... cannot tell."—Emerson, *Works*, I, 311.

The transformation ... of the time.—Cf. B. B. Edwards and E. A. Park (eds. and trans.), *Selections from German Literature* (Andover, 1839), pp. 1, 3; I. N. Tarbox, *An Address on the Origin, Progress & Present Condition of Philosophy* (Utica, N.Y., 1843), pp. 18–19. Noah Porter points out the naïveté of this generalization in his article on "Transcendentalism," *American Biblical Repository*, VIII (2d ser., 1842), 203–5.

Here was ... the naturalist's"—Alcott, *Journals*, ed. Odell Shepard (Boston, 1938), p. 171; *Concord Days* (Boston, 1872), pp. 204–5. Cf. Odell Shepard, *Pedlar's Progress: The Life of Bronson Alcott* (Boston, 1937), p. 149, quoting Alcott's *Journal* for 1836: "Spirit and Matter, Man and Nature, are the two members of that original undivided synthesis that is the ground and heart of the Spirit of Man."

"the latest form of infidelity"—Andrews Norton, *A Discourse on the Latest Form of Infidelity* (Cambridge, Mass., 1839). As George Ripley points out in his reply, *"The Latest Form of Infidelity" Examined* (Boston, 1839), Norton shows his lack of understanding by centering his attack on Spinoza and Hume. But Norton, however unwittingly, does manage at one point to hit on a real weakness of his opponents (p. 30): "To the demand for certainty, . . . I answer, that I know of no absolute certainty, beyond the limit of momentary consciousness, *a certainty that vanishes the instant it exists . . .*" (my italics).

By extending . . . the whole.—Alcott, *Concord Days*, p. 73; *Tablets*, p. 175.

The hostile . . . and spirit."—J. W. Alexander and A. B. Dod, "Transcendentalism," *Two Articles from the Princeton Review*, p. 23 n.

that separation . . . of Man."—Emerson, *Works*, III, 76–77.

116–17. To the prelapsarian . . . thing believed."—James Marsh, "Present Literature of Italy—Ancient and Modern Poetry," *North American Review*, XV (1822), 123.

117. "very unhappy . . . be helped"—Emerson, *Works*, III, 76.

"Unless . . . their poetry."—James Marsh, Translator's Preface to Herder's *The Spirit of Hebrew Poetry* (Burlington, Vt., 1833), I, 5.

"We no longer . . . it affords."—Reed, *Observations on the Growth of the Mind*, p. 43. Cf. J. H. Randall, *The Making of the Modern Mind* (rev. ed.; Cambridge, 1940), p. 270, on the shift to biological categories: "If we regard man as a biological creature actively adjusting himself to an environment, and experience not as picture in the mind but such a process of adjustment, and knowledge, not as a copy of a real world, but as a definite relation between an intelligent organism and its environment, then the problem is transformed, and, set in new terms, seems possible of solution." At the same time, of course, another problem arises: organic knowledge is inconclusive. "Growth, expansion," said W. E. Channing (*Works*, p. 15), "is the end"; but growth per se is endless. Brownson pointed out the difficulty toward which the new philosophy was headed when he spoke of its "attempt to identify the subject and object, and to resolve all the categories into one," as its "primal error." For this involves "the denial of substantial forms" ("Transcendentalism," *Works*, VI, 106).

"He tells . . . be identical."—C. Hodge, "The School of Hegel," *Two Articles from the Princeton Review*, p. 98. The conservatives were also puzzled by the neologisms of the "new school," being unable to find the point of view from which the words would be necessary or meaningful. Francis Bowen, in "Transcendentalism," *Christian Examiner*, XXI (1837), 377–78, cited many examples of novel expressions which he found pretentious but which are now well established: adjectives used as abstract nouns ("infinite," "beautiful," "unconscious," "true") ; verbs like "individualize," "materialize," and "externize"; compounds like "adolescent," "symbolism," "unconditioned," "theosophist."

117–18. But to . . . bad sense."—W. D. Wilson, "Channing's Translation of Jouffroy," *The Dial*, I (1840–41), 105.

118. "fact of consciousness"—Brownson, *Works*, I, 68; Reed, *Observations on the Growth of the Mind*, pp. 35–38; Weiss, *Life and Correspondence of Theodore Parker*, II, 454–55; C. A. Bartol, "Transcendentalism," in *Radical Problems* (Boston, 1872), p. 83. Cf. Brownson's reply to Bowen's attack on the language of transcendentalism: "It is impossible to form a tunnel out of common sense phraseology, by means of which, thought may be poured from one mind into another, as we pour wine into a demijohn" (*Works*, I, 13). Similarly, Alcott does not consider himself a "writer" in the ordinary sense (*Journals*, p. 128) : "I am an actor and sayer, rather than a writer. I do not detach my thoughts from my life. I am concrete." This principle of immediate apprehension and speech led to his method of "conversation" (cf. *Journals*, pp. 63–64).

"not mere . . . *formed life*"—C. K. Newcomb, "The Two Dolons," *The Dial*, III (1842–43), 117 (italics in text).

"Syllogistic reasoning . . . with syllogisms."—Reed, *Observations on the Growth of the Mind*, p. 81.

Those who ... the exponent"—F. H. Hedge, review of Sweden-borg's *True Christian Religion,* in *Christian Examiner,* XV (1833), 193.

the true ... *a growth"*—John Wheeler, *A Historical Discourse ... on ... the Semi-Centennial Anniversary of the University of Vermont* (Burlington, 1854), p. 38. This was the avowed prin-ciple of the curriculum at the University of Vermont under James Marsh.

"that through ... Eternal Word."—W. H. Channing, "The Princi-ples of Christian Union" (1843), quoted by O. B. Frothingham, *Memoir of William Henry Channing* (Boston, 1886), p. 187.

Beneath "the discordant ... in nature."—Reed, *Observations on the Growth of the Mind,* pp. 54–55. Margaret Fuller maintained that as long as men continued to use language new forms and cults would continue to arise: "The very people, who say that none is needed, make one at once. They talk with, they write to one another." See R. W. Emerson, J. F. Clarke, and W. H. Channing, *Memoirs of Margaret Fuller Ossoli* (Boston, 1852), II, 81–82. An interesting contrast to the prevalent empirical psychology is F. A. Rauch's *Psychology; or a View of the Human Soul* (New York, 1840). "As the plastic power produces at the same time *sap* and *bark,* *form* and *contents,*" Rauch declares (p. 232), "so reason [i.e., the operation of the human mind] produces *thought* and *language.*" Words also give a new status to nature (p. 242) : "... Language gives a higher and more noble existence to all that it names. As much as *thinking* is superior to mere feeling, to sensations or perceptions, so much is the existence of a thing in language superior to that in mere nature. It is by language, that whatever is in nature is classified, and all confusion is removed from it."

CHAPTER IV

119. "Oh you . . . a handle!"—Quoted by F. O. Matthiessen, *The James Family* (New York, 1947), p. 43.

"transcendentalisms . . . gibberish"—Melville, Letter to Evert Duyckinck (March 3, 1849), in *Representative Selections,* ed. Willard Thorp (New York, 1938), p. 371.

120. the "perception . . . poetic expression"—Emerson, *Works* (Fireside ed.; Boston and New York, 1909), IV, 137.

"the Imagination is Vision"—Emerson, *Journals*, ed. E. W. Emerson and W. E. Forbes (Boston and New York, 1909–14), III, 525–26.

poetic vision . . . of things"—*Works*, VIII, 31.

120–21. "no longer . . . they signify."—*Journals*, VIII, 521.

121. "The sensual . . . own feelings.—*Works*, I, 56–57.

The rationalist . . . creates the rose."—*Ibid.*, IV, 79–80. Emerson's shift from rational observation and judgment to organic activity is reflected in a dream which he records (*Journals*, V, 485): "I dreamed that I floated at will in the great Ether, and I saw this world floating also not far off, but diminished to the size of an apple. Then an angel took it in his hand and brought it to me and said, 'This must thou eat.' And I ate the world." Note the moral implications.

"difficulties of a naïve dualism"—K. O. Bertling, *Emerson und die Bildungsideale Neu Englands* (Breslau, 1911), p. 7.

122. Art was . . . and nature."—*Works*, II, 338.

the "spheral" . . . and essays—*Journals*, VIII, 230.

the awareness . . . manifold meaning"—*Works*, III, 10.

"I affirm . . . these oppositions"—*Journals*, VIII, 86.

123. "A subtle . . . farthest brings."—*Works*, I, 7.

"Brahma" illustrates . . . symbolic order.—*Ibid.*, IX, 170–71.

"A believer . . . behold two."—*Journals*, IV, 248.

The essential . . . his mind—Cf. *Journals*, IV, 435–36: "Write the Natural History of Reason. Recognize the inextinguishable dualism. . . . But also show that to seek the Unity is a necessity of the mind; that we do not *choose* to resist duality, complexity; show that Will is absurd in the matter." Again (VI, 60–61): "The whole game at which the philosopher busies himself every day, year in, year out, is to find the upper and the under side of every block in his way. . . . The head and the tail are called in the language of philosophy Finite and Infinite, Visible and

Spiritual, Relative and Absolute, Apparent and Eternal, and many more fine names."

the "fragmentary . . . his essays.—*Works*, XII, 11.

"the perpetual . . . and mind—*Ibid.*, VI, 46.

123–24. "two boys . . . the pavement."—*Ibid.* Cf. II, 94; IV, 52. In *Journals*, VI, 61, Emerson comments: "It is strange how fast *Experience* and *Idea*, the wonderful twins, the Castor and Pollux of our firmament, change places; one rises and the other instantaneously sets."

124. "The sum . . . his mind."—S. G. Brown, "Emerson's Platonism," *New England Quarterly*, XVIII (1945), 336.

"somewhat better . . . at last"—*Works*, II, 53.

"the discovery . . . we exist"—*Ibid.*, III, 76.

"study of . . . of faculty."—*Ibid.*, XII, 11.

To the Greek . . . signifies sight."—*Journals*, III, 477.

125. "The ancients . . . a smile."—*Ibid.*, p. 558.

"the problems . . . to state"—*Works*, I, 71.

"Philosophically considered . . . name, NATURE."—*Ibid.*, p. 10.

"If, as Hedge . . . pretty dream."—*Journals*, V, 206 (my italics). Although Emerson often called himself an "idealist," he saw that idealism, like empiricism, begins and ends in "the eternal distinction between the soul and the world" (*Works*, I, 67). ". . . This theory," he says, "makes nature foreign to me, and does not account for that consanguinity which we acknowledge to it." In this sense, he was trying to get beyond both idealism and empiricism. Cf. *Journals*, VIII, 255: " 'Tis indifferent whether you say, all is matter, or, all is spirit; and 'tis plain there is a tendency in the times to an identity-philosophy." From this point of view, it became "a small and mean thing to attempt too hardly to disprove the existence of matter" (*ibid.*, IV, 32; cf. VI, 141): it was more important to accept and go beyond matter. Cf. also *ibid.*, VIII, 78, where he portrays the "Modern" tendency as the resultant of "Greek" naturalism and "Christian" idealism.

126. "the relation . . . and thoughts"—*Works*, I, 71.

"poetry had . . . and false"—*Ibid.*, p. 67.

"the marriage . . . and things."—*Journals*, III, 519. Cf. *Works*, VIII, 67; *Journals*, VIII, 78. This is the basic image of Coleridge's "Dejection" Ode and of the "Prospectus" to Wordsworth's *Excursion*, ll. 62–71.

"the act . . . are one"—*Works*, II, 253.

each reprise . . . reconcile themselves."—*Ibid.*, I, 333. Cf. III, 78: "Marriage (in what is called the spiritual world) is impossible, because of the inequality between every subject and every object."

127. The paradoxical . . . undisciplined abstraction—A. N. Whitehead, *Adventures of Ideas* (Cambridge, 1933), pp. 226–27.

"oneness and otherness"—*Works*, IV, 49: "But every mental act, —this very perception of identity or oneness, recognizes the difference of things. Oneness and otherness. It is impossible to speak or to think without embracing both."

Emerson's "hide-and-seek . . . of Thoughts"—*Journals*, IX, 176.

"intellectual perception . . . he converses"—*Works*, XII, 41.

"affection"—*Ibid.* The whole passage is worth quoting: "The intellect that sees the interval ["between the mind and the object"] partakes of it, and the fact of intellectual perception severs once for all the man from the things with which he converses. Affection blends, intellect disjoins subject and object. For weal or woe we clear ourselves from the thing we contemplate. We grieve but are not the grief; we love but are not love."

"every fact . . . to morals"—*Works*, IV, 143. He continues: "The game of thought is, on the appearance of one of these two sides, to find the other. . . ."

"the soul . . . into nature"—*Journals*, IV, 473.

"unsolved, unsolvable wonder"—*Works*, XII, 15: "To Be is the unsolved, unsolvable wonder. To Be, in its two connections of inward and outward, the mind and nature. . . . Who are we and what is Nature have one answer in the life that rushes into us."

"a continual . . . the thought"—*Journals*, III, 519.

"the knowing . . . put it."—R. M. Eaton, *Symbolism and Truth* (Cambridge, Mass., 1925), p. 288.

128. "the study . . . eyes see"—*Works*, XII, 11.

To become . . . see all—*Ibid.*, I, 16. Cf. II, 304: "Its [the mind's] vision is not like the vision of the eye, but is union with the things known."

"this manner . . . the consciousness"—*Ibid.*, I, 312.

"the habitual . . . mind—beholding"—*Journals*, IV, 249.

"a pernicious . . . term *subjective*"—*Works*, XII, 181 (italics in text). The crucial point, Emerson says (p. 182), is "the tendency of . . . [the] composition; namely, whether it leads us to nature, or to the person of the writer." Cf. *Journals*, V, 287: "Nature mixes facts and thought to evoke a poem from the poet, but our philosophy [i.e., current philosophy] would be androgynous, and itself generate poems without aid of experience."

"he does not . . . concerns him"—*Works*, I, 312.

"*subjectiveness* itself . . . the answer"—*Journals*, X, 469 (italics in text).

the precepts. . . . single maxim.—*Works*, I, 88. Cf. the very early passage (1826) in *Young Emerson Speaks: Unpublished Discourses on Many Subjects*, ed. A. C. McGiffert, Jr. (Boston, 1938), p. 5: "For it is the very root and rudiment of the relation of man to this world, that we are in a condition of wants which have their appropriate gratifications within our reach; . . . that we are full of capacities that are near neighbors to their objects. . . ."

129. "There is . . . a row."—*Works*, XII, 18. Cf. III, 220 ("In the famous dispute with the Nominalists, the Realists had a good deal of reason"); I, 39 ("The relation between the mind and matter is not fancied by some poet, but stands in the will of God, and so is free to be known by all men. It appears to men, or it does not appear"); *Journals*, III, 383 ("Let a man work after a pattern he really sees, and every man shall be able to find a correspondence between these works and his own . . .").

"Nature works . . . human Imagination"—*Journals*, VIII, 9.

"what is . . . human mind?"—*Works*, I, 87. Cf. I, 60: ". . . the solid seeming block of matter has been pervaded and dissolved by a thought: . . . this feeble human being has penetrated the vast masses of nature with an informing soul, and *recognized itself* in their harmony, that is, *seized their law*" (my italics).

"the analogy . . . and Mind"—*Works*, I, 42.

the common . . . "emblem in nature."—*Journals*, III, 163, 226. Cf. *Unpublished Discourses*, p. 44.

129–30. "The constructive . . . the universe."—*Works*, II, 312. Cf. II, 27: "Every thing the individual sees without him corresponds to his states of mind, and every thing is in turn intelligible to him, as his onward thinking leads him into the truth to which that fact or series belongs."

Hence the ambiguity of "creation" and "discovery" (I, 91): "The soul active *sees* absolute truth, or *creates*." Again (I, 79): "Nature is not fixed but fluid. Spirit *alters, moulds, makes* it" (my italics). The ambiguity results from Emerson's concentration on the advent of form per se. Thus he writes (I, 20): "Such is the constitution of all things, or such the plastic power of the human eye, that the primary forms, as the sky, the mountain, the tree, the animal, give us a delight *in and for themselves . . .*" (italics in text).

The dynamic quality of form is an important aspect of Emerson's conception. Cf. *Journals*, V, 349–50: "I will never quarrel with a man because he makes little of the forms, laws, and usages of the world. He cannot do so, if he be thoughtful and earnest, but by the force of his perception. He sees that the soul is a creator, and instantly makes light of all your present works, since he knows it can very easily make more when these are gone. . . ." Similarly (*Works*, II, 78), "every new mind is a new classification," and (III, 37) "the quality of the imagination is to flow, . . . not to freeze. The poet did not stop at the color or the form, but read their meaning; neither may he rest in this meaning, but he makes the same objects exponents of his new thought."

130. "idealistic minimum"—W. M. Urban, *Language and Reality* (London, 1939), p. 375.

He is concerned . . . "animal rationale"—Ernst Cassirer, *An Essay on Man* (New Haven, 1944), p. 26. This emphasis is fully apparent only when one tries to take all Emerson's statements into account—the purpose of this whole discussion. But see his summary of principles drawn up in preparation for a course of lectures in 1836 (*Journals*, IV, 118–19) and another summary in the same year (IV, 33).

"So must . . . an influence."—*Works,* I, 196. Cf. I, 89: "The scholar of the first age received into him the world around; brooded thereon; gave it the new arrangement of his own mind, and uttered it again. It came into him life; it went out from him truth." Again (*Journals,* III, 395): "He who makes a good sentence or a good verse . . . launches out into the infinite and builds a road into Chaos and old Night, and is followed by those who hear him with something of wild, creative delight." Historically, the mere "Aye and No" of the primitive mind "have become nouns and verbs and adverbs" (*Works,* XII, 34).

"endeavor to . . . a name."—*Journals,* IV, 459.

"remoteness from . . . of words"—*Ibid.,* III, 491.

"intertranslateable language"—*Ibid.,* VII, 313.

"Words," Emerson . . . of words."—*Works,* III, 14.

"the figure . . . subtile language."—*Ibid.,* VI, 163.

"not *what,* but *how*"—*Ibid.*

131. the chestnut . . . the dance.—W. B. Yeats, "Among School Children."

"there lie . . . momentary thought."—*Works,* II, 311. Cf. I, 36: "This imagery is spontaneous. It is the blending of experience with the present action of the mind. It is proper creation." It is characteristic of Emerson that he makes no distinction between the word and the visual image (he himself was apparently a visualizer) just as he tries to eliminate the distinctions between word and thought, word and thing.

Language, the . . . their fathers."—*Journals,* VIII, 100. Cf. remarks on "the wisdom of words" in *Journals,* VIII, 17, and X, 466, and the following passage (*Works,* VIII, 25): "This power is in the image because this power is in nature. It so affects, because it so is. . . . The selection of the image is no more arbitrary than the power and significance of the image. The selection must follow fate."

"The great . . . been aroused."—*Journals,* IV, 358–59. For remarks on the interpretive function of the symbolic word or image see *Works,* II, 22, 136–37; III, 229; *Journals,* III, 408; IV, 276; IX, 272–73.

PAGE

132. "the seer is a sayer"—*Works*, I, 133.

"that which . . . not thought."—*Ibid.*, XII, 38.

the word . . . it back."—*Ibid.*, VI, 216. Cf. *Journals*, VI, 132.

"nature is . . . new word"—*Journals*, III, 227. Cf. IV, 133, and X, 236.

that speech . . . be said."—*Ibid.*, IV, 33. Cf. *Works*, III, 231: "All persons, all things which we have known, are here present, and many more than we see; the world is full."

The section . . . as symbol.—*Works*, I, 31. Cf. the eulogy of language, dating from early in his career (1829), in *Unpublished Discourses*, pp. 60–61; and the following passage from the *Journals* (VI, 84–85), where "expression" is treated as at once impersonal and nonrepresentational: "The man is only half himself. Let me see the other half, namely, his expression. Strange, strange, we value this half the most. We worship expressors; we forgive every crime to them. Full expression is very rare. Music, sculpture, painting, poetry, speech, action, war, trade, manufacture is expression. A portrait is this translation of the thing into a new language." Shakespeare is discussed from this point of view in *Works*, IV, 203–4 (cf. IV, 20).

the "Namer . . . the poet.—*Works*, III, 26.

poetic speech . . . when liberated."—*Ibid.*, p. 28. Cf. I, 14: "There is a property *in* the horizon which no man has but he *whose eye can integrate* all the parts, that is, the poet." My italics. More generally (I, 34): "Because of . . . [the] radical correspondence between visible things and human thoughts, savages, who have only what is necessary, converse in figures. As we go back in history, language becomes more picturesque, until its infancy, when it is all poetry, or all spiritual facts are represented by natural symbols." Again (VIII, 69): "In proportion as a man's life comes into union with truth, his thoughts approach to a parallelism with the currents of natural laws, so that he easily expresses his meaning by natural symbols, or uses the ecstatic or poetic speech."

133. "The poet . . . a tree"—*Ibid.*, III, 26.

The "progress . . . be written."—*Journals*, I, 348–49.

"poetry preceded . . . sustained thought"—*Ibid.*, III, 492.

All language ... poetic origin."—*Works*, III, 26.

The basic ... the fact"—*Ibid.*, II, 269 (italics in text).

"speak about ... things themselves"—*Journals*, VIII, 126 (1850). Cf. *Journals*, II, 422 (1831), and IV, 277 (1837). The phrases were derived from Schelling. This, said Emerson, "remains by far the most important intellectual distinction." A passage (1830) in *Unpublished Discourses*, pp. 92–93, puts this difference in language that shows its close relationship to the distinction made by Hooker and Edwards between rational judgment and immediate perception.

Emerson saw the unity of word and thing as perpetually lost and re-established (*Journals*, IV, 146): "Only words that are new fit exactly the thing. ... But in new objects and new names one is delighted with the plastic nature of man as much as in picture or sculpture."

133–34. to turn about ... and ob-jective."—*Works*, X, 13. Cf. VIII, 47: "In dreams we are true poets." The autonomy of dreams illustrated the autonomy of all images: "We call the phantoms that rise, the creation of our fancy, but they act like mutineers, and fire on their commander ..." (X, 13). Again, "they speak after their own characters, not ours;—they speak to us, and we listen with surprise to what they say" (VIII, 47).

134. "all becomes poetry"—*Ibid.*, VIII, 44. Cf. *Journals*, VIII, 321.

he lost ... also *made*.—By the same token, he eliminated the idea of tragedy. He was aware of this, pointing out (*Works*, XII, 262 ff.) that "the only ground ... of tragedy in literature" is "the belief in a brute Fate or Destiny; the belief that the order of nature and events is controlled by a law not adapted to man, nor man to that. ..." To the extent that he took a purely aesthetic approach, he verged toward his well-known view (*ibid.*, I, 123; cf. III, 80) that "evil is merely privative, not absolute"; and he was forced to minimize the moral struggle imposed by a discordant world.

"a mixture ... of choice"—*Ibid.*, II, 313.

his theory ... for decision.—He distinguished between rational "choice" and the "whole act of the man" (*ibid.*, p. 133). But the latter was a process by which the poet "put himself in the way to receive aid" (VII, 50) from "the universal nature, too strong for the petty nature of the bard," which wrote "through his hand" (II, 37).

"perception makes"—*Journals*, VIII, 321.

135. Emerson made ... am pursued."—*Works*, X, 13–14.

"the artist ... efforming matter"—*Journals*, VIII, 563.

"the marriage ... with Nature"—Thoreau, *Writings* (Walden ed.; Boston, 1906), VIII, 413: "The intellect of most men is barren. They neither fertilize nor are fertilized. It is the marriage of the soul with Nature that makes the intellect fruitful, that gives birth to imagination."

135–36. "I think ... the objects)."—*Ibid.*, XVI, 164–65 (italics in text).

136. Thoreau's antidote ... his speech."—*Ibid.*, IX, 236.

"Essentially your ... lamb's bleat."—*Ibid.*, XVII, 386. Cf. his advocacy of "untamed, free, and wild thinking" (VIII, 97).

"a continual ... a sentence."—Emerson, *Journals*, VI, 515.

"I only ... is you."—*Writings*, X, 291. Cf. XVIII, 155, where he illustrates how "double, if not treble, even, are we."

"A poem ... same time."—Emerson, *Journals*, IV, 180.

137. For him ... own ground.—*Writings*, V, 205–6.

Having been ... ridicule only!"—*Ibid.*, XI, 4.

"Once I . . . of her."—*Ibid.*, IX, 378.

137–38. objective method . . . to stone."—*Ibid.*, XI, 45.

138. "Sometimes I . . . reflecting surface."—*Ibid.*, XVI, 164.

Emerson had . . . which imports."—Emerson, *Journals*, V, 461. Cf. *Works*, XII, 9: "What is life but the angle of vision?"

Thoreau tried . . . his eye."—*Writings*, XI, 45.

"intellectual ray"—*Ibid.*, XV, 466.

"intention of . . . and eye."—*Ibid.*, XVII, 285. Cf. XVII, 153.

But the realm . . . unrelated thing.—By emphasizing the angle of vision, Thoreau avoids a lapse into subjectivism. When he declares (*Writings*, XV, 466) that "in the largest sense, we find only the world we look for," or even (XVIII, 367–68) that "there is no beauty in the sky, but in the eye that sees it," he is defining the moving point by which the relational reality is perpetually renewed. This reality is multiplex, and it is no more "subjective," though Thoreau uses the word to describe his method, than it is objective. Cf. XI, 203: "Ever and anon something will occur which my philosophy has not dreamed of. The limits of the actual are set some thoughts further off. That which had seemed a rigid wall of vast thickness unexpectedly proves a thin and undulating drapery. The boundaries of the actual are no more fixed and rigid than the elasticity of our imaginations."

the reflection . . . and hill.—*Ibid.*, XVI, 96–97. Cf. XVI, 156–57: "It is only a reflecting mind that sees reflections."

"more or . . . the substance."—*Ibid.*, XV, 172.

138–39. "In a sense . . . to possess."—*Ibid.*, XX, 118. Cf. the whole passage, pp. 117–20.

139. The "most poetic . . . and best."—*Ibid.*, XIII, 56.

Conversely, "with . . . poetic even."—*Ibid.*, XVII, 137.

his "affirmations . . . not forethought"—*Ibid.*, XIX, 238: "The fruit a thinker bears is *sentences*,—statements or opinions. He seeks to affirm something as true" (italics in text).

"Much verse . . . at all."—*Ibid.*, I, 350.

"the sense . . . the words"—*Ibid.*, XV, 58.

"it is not . . . thoughts shall be."—*Ibid.*, IV, 320.

"the lecturer . . . best heard."—*Ibid.*, XVIII, 9.

the "tyrannous, inexorable meaning"—*Ibid.*, IV, 327. Thoreau is impressed by the union of manner and matter in Carlyle, and he wonders "how so much, after all, was expressed in the old ways" (p. 326). Noting that older people find Carlyle unintelligible, whereas to many boys these writings are quite clear, he judges that "merely reading, even with the best intentions, is not enough: you must almost have written these books yourself" (p. 322). In his own case, he was aware of two main stylistic problems. Form must be revolutionary (XII, 100): "I fear only lest my expression may not be extravagant enough,—may not wander far enough beyond the narrow limits of our ordinary insight and faith, so as to be adequate to the truth of which I have been convinced." And form must disappear in content (IX, 86): "As all things are significant, so all words should be significant. . . . A style in which the matter is all in all, and the manner [qua manner] nothing at all."

140. "My thought . . . my thought."—*Ibid.*, X, 410. Cf. XII, 131–32: "Each and all such disguises and other resources remind us that not some poor worm's instinct merely, as we call it, but the mind of the universe rather, which we share, has been intended upon each particular object."

"in all . . . evening teem"—*Ibid.*, VII, 386–87.

"the present . . . be forgotten"—*Ibid.*

"types almost . . . the magnet."—*Ibid.*, XII, 133.

the object . . . is *musketaquidding.*"—*Ibid.*, XVIII, 390. Cf. p. 389: "Talk about learning our *letters* and being *literate!* Why, the roots of *letters* are *things.* Natural objects and phenomena are the original symbols or types which express our thoughts and feelings. . . ." Italics in text. Again (XVI, 190–91): "Here I have been these forty years learning the *language of these fields* that I may the better *express myself*" (my italics).

Thoreau has little to say on symbolic structure, but in one passage he seems to see that metaphor is the structural aspect of the relational status of language. The trope is a renewal of the tropical essence of speech (XIX, 145): "As in the expression of moral truths we admire any closeness to the physical fact which in all language is the symbol of the spiritual, so, finally, when natural objects are described, it is an advantage if words derived originally from nature, it is true, but which have been turned (*tropes*) from their primary signification to a moral sense, are used, *i.e.*, if the object is personified" (italics in text).

"the perfect . . . to man"—*Ibid.*, XVI, 127. Cf. X, 126: "With our senses applied to the surrounding world we are reading our own physical and corresponding moral revolutions."

"something more than association"—*Ibid.*, VIII, 155.

141. objects affect . . . is absolute.—*Ibid.*, XI, 359: "Is it not as language that all natural objects affect the poet? He sees a flower or other object, and it is beautiful or affecting to him because it is a symbol of his thought, and what he indistinctly feels or per-

ceives is matured in some other organization. The objects I behold correspond to my mood."

"we have . . . within us"—*Ibid.*, VIII, 155. Cf. VIII, 300.

"get rid . . . total apprehension."—*Ibid.*, XVIII, 371 (italics in text).

"Who shall . . . the globe?"—*Ibid.*, XII, 278 (italics in text).

"a man . . . is going."—*Ibid.*, IX, 123 (italics in text). Cf. his letter to Helen Thoreau (VI, 25–26) in which he attacks the empirical theory of knowledge as static and divisive, "making Imagination and Memory to lie still in their respective apartments like ink-stand and wafers in a lady's escritoire. . . ." His own theory arose in a very personal exasperation with all mediate apprehension. Cf. VII, 61: "We may believe it, but never do we live a quiet, free life, such as Adam's, but are enveloped in an invisible network of speculations. Our progress is only from one such speculation to another, and only at rare intervals do we perceive that it is no progress. Could we for a moment drop this by-play, and simply wonder, without reference or inference!"

"to be . . . be significant."—*Ibid.*, XII, 236–37. Cf. XVIII, 372, where he compares the distinction between rational knowledge and total apprehension to that between analysis of a sentence in terms of type, ink, paper, etc., and the perception of meaning.

"The poet's . . . say it."—*Ibid.*, XIX, 69–70.

He can . . . poetic speech.—Cf. *ibid.*, X, 174: "Nature is reported not by him who goes forth consciously as an observer, but in the fullness of life. To such a one she rushes to make her report. To the full heart she is all but a figure of speech."

"Whatever things . . . are significant."—*Ibid.*, VIII, 442. Cf. XI, 135.

141–42. "I would . . . I deal."—*Ibid.*, IX, 99. Cf. VIII, 152: "I do not know where to find in any literature, whether ancient or modern, any adequate account of that Nature with which I am acquainted. Mythology comes nearest to it of any."

142. "A fact . . . is impotent."—*Ibid.*, IX, 85–86.

"My life . . . utter it."—*Ibid.*, I, 365. Thoreau did not mean simply that the business of living left him no time for writing.

He meant that "utterance" in his sense of the word precluded utterance in the ordinary sense. He had so thoroughly submitted the individual to the symbolic activity that the former became enslaved by the latter: "The true poem is not that which the public read. There is always a poem not printed on paper, coincident with the production of this, stereotyped in the poet's life. It is *what he has become through his work*. Not how is the idea expressed in stone, or on canvas or paper, is the question, but how far it has obtained form and expression in the life of the artist" (italics in text).

an "allegorical . . . a myth"—*Ibid.*, XI, 203. Cf. IX, 438: "I am serene and satisfied . . . when the events of the day have a mythological character, and the most trivial is symbolical."

"See how . . . it alone."—*Young Emerson Speaks*, p. 207. Cf. *Works*, VI, 40: ". . . Observe how far the roots of every creature run, or find if you can a point where there is no thread of connection. Our life is consentaneous and far-related."

143. *"so to . . . to know."*—*Works*, II, 298 (italics in text). Cf. the converse statement (XII, 9): "By how much we know, so much we are."

But human . . . a part.—Here, as in so many other aspects of his thought, Emerson was determined to have his cake and eat it too. He sometimes shifted the meaning of "being" from organic development (the antonym of rational knowledge) to an unchanging substance. Cf. *Works*, II, 116: "Under all this running sea of circumstance . . . lies the original abyss of real Being. Essence, or God, is not a relation or a part, but the whole." Again (II, 297): "Whilst the eternal generation of circles proceeds, the eternal generator abides." Yet elsewhere, and more characteristically, he treated ultimate Being as one with Becoming, and the whole as a system of changing relationships, so that there was no interval between man and God. In the famous passage (II, 251–52) beginning "Man is a stream whose source is hidden," the question of source is quickly pushed aside in the vision of "that flowing river." In order for man to become "part or parcel of God," both man and God must be translated into process: "the currents of the Universal Being circulate through me" (I, 16). Thus God as substance or person would seem to be a projection of human thinking, which is identical with God as process. Cf. *Journals,* III, 537 ("The human mind seems a lens formed to concentrate the rays of the Divine laws to a focus, which shall be the personality of God") and IV, 55 ("Theism must be, and the name of God must be, because it is a necessity of the human mind to apprehend the relative as flowing from the absolute, and we shall always give the absolute a name").

"He is . . . without man."—*Works,* I, 33.

He is . . . the world."—*Ibid.,* II, 39. Cf. *Journals,* IV, 78 ("God is within you. The self or self creates the world through you, and organizations like you") ; *Works,* I, 67 (". . . the Supreme Being does not build up nature around us but puts it forth through us . . .") ; XII, 15 (". . . the genius of man is a continuation of the power that made him and that has not done making him").

he is . . . and marry."—*Journals,* IV, 78. Cf. *Works,* VI, 27: "Man is . . . a stupendous antagonism, a dragging together of the poles of the Universe. . . . Here they are, side by side, . . . riding peacefully together in the eye and brain of very man."

144. "A man . . . unmarriageable facts."—*Works,* I, 197–98. This is the basic meaning of the word "representative" in *Representative Men.* Cf. *Works,* IV, 14: "Men are . . . representative; first, of things, and secondly, of ideas."

a single . . . birth, growth."—*Ibid.,* III, 25.

"The intelligent . . . it returns."—*Journals,* IV, 107. Cf. *Works,* VI, 42–43 ("Person makes event, and event person. . . . The event is the print of your form. It fits you like your skin") and II, 266 (". . . accepting the tide of being which floats us into the secret of nature, [we must] work and live, work and live, and all unawares the advancing soul has built and forged for itself a new condition, and the question and the answer are one").

"to think is to act."—*Works,* II, 154. Cf. *Journals,* IX, 88: "I see the selfsame energy and action in a boy at football, that I admire in the intellectual play of Burke or Pindar." Cf. also *Works,* I, 10: "Every man's condition is a solution in hieroglyphic to those inquiries he would put. He acts it as life, before he apprehends it as truth."

Mind is . . . becomes other."—Works, II, 303. Cf. I, 77 ("Is not prayer also a study of truth,—a sally of the soul into the unfound infinite? No man ever prayed heartily without learning something") ; II, 254 (". . . the soul in man is not an organ, but animates and exercises all the organs . . .") ; II, 264 (". . . the power to see is not separated from the will to do, but the insight proceeds from obedience, and the obedience proceeds from a joyful perception") ; III, 12 (". . . the Knower, the Doer, and the Sayer . . . each of those three has the power of the others latent in him, and his own, patent").

"it is . . . to both."—*Journals,* VII, 81–82. In *Journals,* III, 416–17, speaking of a man's "genius, or his nature, or his turn of mind," Emerson says: "This determination of his character is to something in his nature; something real. This object is called his Idea. . . . It can only be indicated by any action, not defined by anything less than the aggregate of all his genuine actions; perhaps then only approximated."

Man whether . . . being reported."—*Works,* IV, 251. Cf. IV, 250: "In nature, this self-registration [self-recording in the environment] is incessant, and the narrative is the print of the seal. It neither exceeds nor comes short of the fact. But nature strives upward; and, in man, the report is something more than print of the seal. It is a new and finer form of the original. The record is alive, as that which it recorded is alive."

145. We ourselves . . . inhabit symbols."—*Ibid.,* III, 24.

"The value . . . are tropes."—*Ibid.,* VIII, 20. Cf. I, 38: "The world is emblematic. Parts of speech are metaphors because the whole of nature is a metaphor of the human mind. The laws of moral nature answer those of matter as face to face in a glass."

"a man . . . selecting principle."—*Ibid.,* II, 136–37.

To symbolize . . . melted wax."—*Ibid.,* I, 316. The "I" is not a static subject, but a "thought which is called I." Cf. II, 21: "A painter told me that nobody could draw a tree without in some sort becoming a tree. . . ."

"this refers . . . everything refers."—*Ibid.,* I, 191.

"the delight . . . his Destiny."—*Journals,* IV, 33.

"I notice . . . solitary observations."—*Ibid.,* VIII, 504. Cf. *Works,* XII, 36: "Insight assimilates the thing seen. Is it only another way of affirming and illustrating this to say that it sees nothing alone, but sees each particular object in just connections,—sees all in God?"

146. "The metamorphosis . . . capricious classification."—*Journals*, VI, 18. Conversely (III, 291): ". . . there is no need to fear that the immense accumulation of scientific facts should ever encumber us, since as fast as they multiply they resolve themselves into a formula which carries the world in a phial. . . . And every man's mind at this moment is a formula condensing the result of all his conclusions." Again (*Works*, III, 23): "Every new relation is a new word."

"A work . . . the world."—*Works*, I, 29.

"the identity . . . the observed."—*Ibid*., IV, 16–17: "The possibility of interpretation lies in the identity of the observer with the observed." Cf. II, 154: "The rich mind lies in the sun and sleeps, and *is* Nature" (my italics).

147. "suffers the intellect to see"—*Ibid*., II, 306. Cf. the whole passage: "We do not determine what we will think. We only open our senses, clear away as we can all obstruction from the fact, and suffer the intellect to see. We have little control over our thoughts. We are the prisoners of ideas."

"not instruction, but provocation."—*Ibid*., I, 126.

"A man . . . new aspects."—*Ibid*., p. 204. Cf. *Journals*, III, 201: "Every act puts the agent in a new condition."

"cannot help . . . to himself"—*Journals*, IV, 33.

"there is . . . of nature"—*Works*, III, 22.

"the entire . . . every particle"—*Ibid*., II, 95.

"experience identifies"—*Ibid*., VIII, 261.

"*one thing* . . . same moment"—*Ibid*., III, 225 (italics in text). Cf. VIII, 29, where he refers to "metonymy, or seeing the same sense in things . . . diverse."

"Rhetoric or . . . of Discourse."—*Journals*, IV, 336. Cf. X, 361: "All conversation and writing is rhetoric." Emerson had defined the status of rhetoric for himself as early as 1824 (*Journals*, I, 313): "Considered with relation to our whole existence, that habits of thought are better than [objective] knowledge—was the original position of my rhetoric." In an even earlier passage (I, 105), dating from 1822, he noted that "poetical expression . . . seems to resemble algebra" to the extent that both are distinctively exercises in language: "both make language an instrument and depend solely upon it without having any abstracted use."

"gives ... the stones"—*Ibid.*, X, 219.

148. "shall thrill . . . to him"—*Ibid.*, III, 478–79. This passage is Emerson's attempt to give a structural description of that "atmospheric influence . . . , not accounted for in an arithmetical addition," which "we are practically skilful in detecting," but "for which we have no place in our theory, and no name" (*Works*, III, 219). Cf. Thoreau, *Writings*, I, 350: "The expressions of the poet cannot be analyzed; his sentence is one word, whose syllables are words." And Mallarmé, "Avant-Dire au *Traité du verbe de René Ghil*" (1886) in *Œuvres complètes* (Paris, 1945), p. 858: "Le vers . . . de plusieurs vocables refait un mot total, neuf. . . ."

"bounded fact"—*Journals*, VIII, 501.

a "point ... a focus."—*Ibid.*, III, 373.

each "noun ... and meaning."—*Works*, VI, 288. Cf. III, 10.

"A man ... new sense."—*Journals*, IV, 337. Cf. II, 402.

symbols, each ... one side"—*Works*, I, 50. Cf. *Journals*, III, 408–9: ". . . every thought is one side of Nature, and really has the whole world under it."

"It is . . . the world."—*Works*, II, 330–31. Cf. III, 26: "Each word was at first a stroke of genius, and obtained currency because for the moment it symbolized the world to the first speaker and to the hearer." Again (II, 328) : "What is that abridgement and selection we observe in all spiritual activity, but *itself the creative impulse?* for it is the inlet of that higher illumination which teaches to convey a larger sense by simpler symbols" (my italics).

149. "poetry seems ... of name"—*Journals*, VIII, 296. Emerson continues: "Poetry calls a snake a *worm*" (presumably a reference to *Antony and Cleopatra*, V, ii).

"Why should . . . and think?"—*Journals*, V, 233–34.

"every word ... is million-faced"—*Ibid.*, VI, 139.

Emerson was ... literary speech.—"Man is architectural" (*ibid.*, X, 192) and beauty is compositional (II, 401; III, 298). Emerson was anxious to believe that a "mere enumeration of ... objects would be found to be more than a catalogue,—would be a symmetrical picture, ... as when we first perceive the meaning of a sentence which we have carried in the memory for years" (III, 484). More particularly, he saw that American art was "formless" (VII, 286–87). By urging his radical formalism, he was trying to obviate the external formalism by which "poetry is degraded and made ornamental" (*Works*, V, 242). Thus he demanded a poetry which would be "the gift to men of new images and symbols, each the ensign and oracle of an age; that shall assimilate men to it, mould itself into religions and mythologies, and impart its quality to centuries;—poetry which tastes the world and reports of it, upbuilding the world again in the thought. . ." (*Works*, VIII, 65).

"if we go ... merely tautology."—*Journals*, V, 84. Cf. his criticism of Swedenborg's system (*Works*, IV, 128): "There is no individual in it. . . . There is an immense chain of intermediation, extending from centre to extremes, which bereaves every agency of all freedom and character. . . . All his types mean the same few things. All his figures speak one speech."

149–50. "our tuition ... the phantasms."—*Works*, VI, 301.

150. his poet ... of Hosts"—*Journals*, VI, 18. The notion that "everything is significant" (II, 478) had come to mean that anything can signify anything else (*Works*, II, 35): "I can symbolize my thought by using the name of any creature, of any fact, because every creature is man agent or patient." Even more pointedly (*Works*, IV, 117): "In nature, each individual symbol plays innumerable parts, as each particle of matter circulates in turn through every system. The central identity enables any one symbol to express successively all the qualities and shades of real being." Cf. *Works*, I, 49; *Journals*, IV, 21.

In *Works*, III, 175, Emerson makes his own reply to his contention that some "fixed scale" is still possible under these circumstances: "That identity makes us all one, and reduces to nothing great intervals on our customary scale." Similarly (III, 22), he remarks that "the distinctions which we make in events and in affairs, of low and high, honest and base, disappear when nature is used as a symbol."

He goes . . . particular impressions."—*Journals,* V, 326–27. Cf. V, 385, 392–93. Emerson's ethical difficulties are parallel. He saw very early in his career that he must "beware of Antinomianism" (*Journals,* IV, 449; cf. *Works,* I, 317). He tried, on the one hand, to appeal to a "law of consciousness" (*Works,* II, 73) and, on the other hand, failing that, to bluster it out (*Works,* II, 2): " 'But these impulses may be from below, not from above.' I replied, 'They do not seem to me to be such; but if I am the Devil's child, I will live then from the Devil.' "

"he is . . . the symbol"—Matthew Arnold, "Emerson," *Discourses in America* (London, 1896), p. 179.

151. "Preliminary Dissertation . . . and Spirit"—Horace Bushnell, *God in Christ: Three Discourses, . . . with a Preliminary Dissertation on Language* (Hartford, 1849), pp. 9–117.

three sermons . . . great stir.—On the controversies surrounding Bushnell's views, see *Life and Letters of Horace Bushnell,* ed. M. B. Cheney (New York, 1880), pp. 211–61, esp. pp. 214–16.

"Language and Doctrine."—Horace Bushnell, *Christ in Theology: Being the Answer of the Author . . . for the Doctrines of the Book Entitled "God in Christ"* (Hartford, 1851), pp. 15–89. A later statement is "Our Gospel a Gift to the Imagination," *Hours at Home,* X (1869–70), 159–72.

"I had . . . and where."—*Life and Letters,* p. 208.

What was . . . poetic method.—Bushnell had some difficulty in defining the exact scope of his inquiry. He said (*God in Christ,* p. 12) that his chief object was "to speak of language as regards its significancy, or the power and capacity of its words, taken as vehicles of thought and of spiritual truth." Thus he was actually a student of semantics rather than the philosophy of language. Though he found himself compelled to take up philosophical questions in order to justify his semantic theory, the focus of his investigation was "the real applicability of words" (*ibid.,* p. 45). He saw all intellectual history as "a gradual culture in the meaning of words and symbols" (*Christ in Theology,* p. 63), and he tried to give a functional description of that meaning.

"Without being . . . settle them."—*God in Christ,* pp. 92–93.

151–52. This failing . . . universes all."—*Christ in Theology,* pp. 70–72.

152. "I discovered . . . *we glide.*"—*Life and Letters*, p. 209. Italics in text.

153. even animals . . . of things."—*God in Christ*, p. 24.

"names of . . . of thought"—*Ibid.*

"vehicles of . . . spiritual truth"—*Ibid.*, pp. 12–13.

In language . . . of form.—*Ibid.*, p. 43: "On the one hand, is form; on the other, is the formless. The former represents, and is somehow fellow to, the other. . . ."

"The universal . . . form-element"—*Christ in Theology*, p. 40. Cf. *God in Christ*, p. 50.

"The particle . . . little particle."—*Christ in Theology*, p. 50.

"Thinking, in . . . their forms."—*God in Christ*, p. 52. Cf. *Christ in Theology*, p. 51: "There is no such thing . . . as getting clear of form in human language." Bushnell admits (*ibid.*, p. 15) that "the soul may have truth present immediately to it, or may directly intuit truth, without symbols or representations of language." But he seems to regard such a case as marginal.

He postulates . . . the mind.—*God in Christ*, pp. 21–22: "It is only as there is a Logos in the outward world, answering to the logos or internal reason of the parties, that they can come into a mutual understanding in regard to any thought or spiritual state whatever. To use a more familiar expression, there is a vast analogy in things, which prepares them, as forms, to be signs or figures of thoughts, and thus, bases or types of words. Our bodily mechanism, and the sensible world we live in, are, in fact, made up of words, to represent our thoughts and internal states. . . ."

In some way . . . its vehicle."—*Ibid.*, pp. 43, 28.

The patterns . . . of language."—*Ibid.*, p. 102. Bushnell's account of the metaphysical status of language is not wholly consistent. While he was anxious to treat form as realistic, he was also under the influence of theological prejudices which made him unwilling to draw mind, nature, and truth too close together. His theory of the Logos was unitive; his other term, "analogy," was divisive. Faced with F. A. Rauch's *Psychology*, he objects (*God in Christ*, pp. 37–38) that Rauch conceives of an "identity" of reason and nature in the word.

"language as a human product"—*God in Christ*, p. 18. Cf. p. 17: ". . . all these different languages are so many free developments of the race; though all from God, in the sense that he has created in all human beings a certain free power of self-representation or expression, which is itself a distinct capacity for language, and, in one view, language itself."

154. "carries in . . . in it."—*Ibid.*, p. 84.

"There is . . . and structure."—*Christ in Theology*, p. 46.

Every man . . . of words"—*Ibid.*, pp. 46–47.

"Life is . . . and sentences."—*God in Christ*, p. 85. Cf. p. 64: "We look at the whole body as a vital nature, and finding every function alive, every fibre active, we perceive that all the parts, even the minutest, exist and act as mutual conditions one of another. And so it is in the spiritual life." Bushnell goes so far as to say that "no religious truth . . . is really true, that is not organific" (*Christ in Theology*, p. 69).

Pure logicians . . . in algebra."—*God in Christ*, p. 59. Bushnell contrasts "simple presentation, as a soul is expressed or presented in a face," with "the formula of a merely logical calculus" (*Christ in Theology*, pp. 15–16) ; "the impressions . . . [a word] is to produce in us" with "the theories of scientific versions we . . . produce of it" (*God in Christ*, p. 91) ; "the simple decision of consciousness" with "argument, whether good or bad" (*ibid.*, p. 63) ; being "busied *about* and *upon* truth, as a dead body offered to the scalpels of logic," with "giving ourselves *to* truth as set before us in living expression" (*Christ in Theology*, p. 32) (italics in text).

initial "power . . . or ascertained"—*God in Christ*, p. 58. For "their premise contains their conclusion, and somewhat more...."

155. "a constant . . . and constructions"—*Ibid.*, pp. 60–61.

"latent element of figure"—*Ibid.*, p. 80.

The dogmatist . . . of language.—Cf. *Christ in Theology*, p. 81: ". . . we are in constant peril of setting one symbol, or class of symbols, above the others, and reducing these to system under the former, taken as being the literal truth...." In such a case (*God in Christ*, p. 80), "that which was true, at the beginning, has . . . become untrue—and that, however paradoxical it may seem, by being assented to." The symbol has become a sign.

words "have ... or symbol."—*Christ in Theology*, p. 16: "We must hold them in a way of inspection...." Similarly, words "do not literally convey, or pass over a thought out of one mind into another, as we commonly speak of doing. They are only hints, or images, held up before the mind of another, to set *him* on generating or reproducing the same thought ..." (*God in Christ*, pp. 45–46). Bushnell speaks of "the impossibility of definitions as determinate measures of thought" (*ibid.*, p. 57) ; for the word, though it has "a dictionary meaning that is settled," is "to every man what his own life-experience, and his theories, and mental struggles have made it ..." (*ibid.*, pp. 47–48).

"A very ... are repugnant."—*Ibid.*, p. 49. Cf. *Christ in Theology*, p. 85: "Hence the eternal changes noted in the history of philosophy; which, though it is ever dealing with the real truths of consciousness, has never yet been able to fix immovably any one doctrine, and never will be; for the manifest reason, that no one form is so related to any one truth, that another may not be conceived for it which has not *some* advantages, and will not better accommodate some other speculative system."

"So far ... offered him."—*God in Christ*, p. 82.

"religion has . . . with poetry"—*Ibid.*, pp. 74–75. Cf. *Christ in Theology*, p. 87: "... there is a livelier and more competent medium of truth than any that classes in the modes of speculation; I mean the medium of simple expression. The poetic forms of utterance are closer to the fires of religion within us, more adequate revelations of consciousness, ... better and more adequate revelations of truth than theology, in its best form, can be."

logical form ... inorganic matter"—*God in Christ*, p. 62.

156. "It would not ... the tragedy."—"A Discourse on the Atonement" (*God in Christ*, p. 204). Cf. *Christ in Theology*, p. 33: "It is a great trouble with us that we can not put a whole scheme of redemption, which God could execute only by the volume of expression contained in the life and death of his incarnate Son, into a theologic formula or article of ten words. It is as if, being unable to compress the whole tragic force of Lear into some one sentence of Edgar's gibberish, we lose our patience, and cry out upon the poverty of language and conception in the poem."

It should be noted that Bushnell's statements on the relations between reason, poetry, and truth are somewhat ambiguous.

PAGE

When he is contrasting logical with aesthetic apprehension, he takes the position (in effect) that logic is external, and poetry internal, to truth. On the other hand, he frequently invokes his theory of "analogy," according to which *all* words are external to truth; e.g., *God in Christ*, p. 48: "They impute *form* to that which really is out of form." But this seems inconsistent with the whole tendency of his organicism. Cf. his vacillation between the concepts of "Logos" and "analogy."

"living, plastic, . . . perfect whole"—*God in Christ*, p. 73. Cf. the whole passage, in which Bushnell maintains that "in mental science, the investigators are . . . only trying to see if they can make up a true man out of some ten or twenty or forty words in the dictionary," whereas "the only way to make up a real man is to put the whole dictionary into him. . . . Poets, then, are the true metaphysicians, and if there be any complete science of man to come, they must bring it."

"gravitate inwardly . . . they coalesce."—*Ibid.*, p. 71.

"not by . . . to stand"—*Ibid.*

"It will . . . of silence.' "—*Ibid.*, pp. 55–56 (my italics).

157. "antagonistic figures . . . contrarious representations."—*Ibid.*, p. 62. Bushnell pointedly remarks that an organic, as opposed to a mechanical, whole will act "a little mysteriously sometimes, . . . diseasedly and contrarily, as if life had let in death, and a quarrel for possession were going on within" (*ibid.*, p. 73). He would look for truth in a writer only "if we find him multiplying antagonisms, offering cross views, and bringing us round the field to show us how it looks from different points" (*ibid.*, p. 67).

"infinite multiplications . . . and strifes—*Ibid.*, p. 40.

157–58. Melville marked . . . great poet."—Emerson, *Works*, III, 23. William Braswell, "Melville as a Critic of Emerson," *American Literature*, IX (1937–38), 324.

158. Here certainly . . . thought-diver."—Melville, Letter to Evert Duyckinck (March 3, 1849), in *Representative Selections*, p. 372.

"As there . . . to it."—Emerson, *Works*, IV, 62.

Dialectic claims . . . external reality.—Cf. Emerson's definitions of "culture" (*Works*, IV, 271; VI, 132) and his description of the method of Christ, "of whose instructions it is one of the most remarkable features that he does not reason at all. He proves nothing by argument." Emerson goes on (*Unpublished Discourses,* p. 91): "He simply asserts.... Every one of his declarations is a naked appeal to every man's consciousness whether the fact be so or not." Out of this kind of method emerge "natural classifications containing their own reason in themselves, and making known facts continually" (*Journals,* III, 294; cf. II, 95). Cousin's eclecticism, though superficially similar to Emerson's, is "mechanical" (*Works,* I, 166). Dialectic is an organic "process in the mind" (*Journals,* II, 446): "Domesticate ... [facts] in your mind, do not force them into arrangement too hastily, and presently you shall find they will take their own order. And the order they assume is divine. It is God's architecture."

It is not ... is worthless."—*Works,* II, 307. Emerson often returned to this contrast between logic as process and logic as proposition. The former is a "silent method" (II, 307), an "unspoken logic" (*Journals,* VI, 79); it is "humanized" (*Works,* XII, 12). The contrast lies between the thinker who "invites me to be present with him at his invocation of truth, and to enjoy with him its proceeding into his mind," and the thinker who simply "gives me results" (*Works,* I, 269; cf. I, 136, and *Journals,* V, 92).

158–59. "Each new ... higher vision."—*Works,* II, 287.

159. each general ... disclose itself."—*Ibid.,* p. 284. Emerson continues: "... the eye soon gets wonted to it, for the eye and it are effects of one cause...." Cf. VI, 303: "... each thought which yesterday was a finality, today is yielding to a larger generalization."

His ideas ... were "intertranslateable."—*Ibid.,* XII, 11. *Journals,* II, 478; VIII, 230. Cf. *Journals,* III, 489.

"our name ... can arrive"—*Journals,* V, 5. Emerson continues: "... and, of course, its sense differs today and tomorrow." Cf. *Works,* III, 75: "... we give to this generalization the name of Being, and thereby confess that we have arrived as far as we can go." Again (*Journals,* III, 235): "The best we can say of God, we mean of the mind as it is known to us."

God is the "algebraic x"—*Journals,* VIII, 4.

a "residuum unknown, unanalyzable"—*Works*, II, 286. Cf. II, 131 ("The last analysis can no wise be made") and X, 32 ("... behind all your explanations is a vast and potent and living Nature, inexhaustible and sublime, which you cannot explain").

the writer ... Universal Power"—*Works*, I, 203.

"attitude of reception"—*Ibid.*, II, 252.

"Cannot I ... a contradiction?"—*Journals*, IV, 249.

"the world ... of nature.—*Ibid.*, VI, 122–23. Cf. *Works*, II, 126.

"the universality ... each mind."—*Works*, III, 231 (italics in text). Cf. *Journals*, VIII, 536: "... the thoughts are few, the forms many; the large vocabulary, or many-coloured coat of the indigent Unity." Hence (II, 478; cf. V, 99–100), "to be at perfect agreement with a man of most opposite conclusions you have only to translate your language into his." While he saw "the power to detach" as "the essence of rhetoric" (*Works*, II, 330), he was more impressed by "the principle of iteration" (*Journals*, IX, 447; cf. IX, 285). Similarly (*Journals*, VIII, 251–52), he saw history as "a vanishing allegory," which "repeats itself to tediousness, a thousand and a million times."

160. "The surveyor ... the truth."—*Journals*, II, 523.

"It seemed ... and philosophy."—*Ibid.*, VI, 274–75.

"speech becomes ... noble silence."—*Ibid.*, VI, 275. Cf. *Works*, II, 319.

"We are ... quite another."—*Works*, XI, 23–24.

"For language ... every discourse."—*Journals*, III, 492. Elsewhere (IV, 495) Emerson adds: "O poet! thou wert ten times a poet, if thou couldst articulate that unsaid part." Cf. IV, 266. What Emerson meant by his reference to "heaven" (borrowed from Sampson Reed) is indicated by the following passage (III, 236): "The Understanding, listening to Reason [i.e., intuition], on the one side, which says *It is*, and to the senses on the other side, which say *It is not*, takes middle ground and declares *It will be*. Heaven is the projection of the Ideas of Reason on the plane of the understanding." Heaven was a concession to his own skepticism. Cf. III, 488.

"not so ... against forms"—*Works*, XI, 25.

161. He criticized ... "real meaning."—R. W. Emerson *et al.*, *Memoirs of Margaret Fuller Ossoli* (Boston, 1852), I, 268, 279–80.

The theme ... static sign.—Emerson sees the whole development of Christianity as an effort "to redeem us from a formal religion, and teach us to seek our well-being in the formation of the soul" (*Works*, XI, 26–27). Cf. similar remarks in *Works*, II, 15, 56, 78–79. Normally, "all symbols are fluxional; all language is vehicular and transitive"; but the symbol tends to become "too stark and solid" (III, 37–38), so that "the truth itself becomes distorted, and, as it were, false" (*Journals*, IV, 380).

Swedenborg was Emerson's favorite whipping boy on this point, for Swedenborg's doctrine of "correspondence," unlike Emerson's theory of symbolism, postulated static meanings. Cf. *Journals*, VIII, 63–64: "What I want to know is, the meaning of what I do. ... This is one kind of symbolism. A more limited one is Swedenborg's fancy that certain books of Scripture were exact allegories. ..."

Even the ... self-contradiction.—*Works*, I, 190.

"we cannot ... some other"—*Ibid.*, II, 42.

"the only ... the lie."—*Ibid.*, III, 233.

"The thought ... as partial."—*Journals*, VI, 56–57.

"There would ... and reproof."—*Ibid.*, IV, 135–36.

Emerson's work ... its antithesis.—As a final instance, take the following passage, where puzzlement gives way to reaffirmation, and yet the affirmation is precisely what has led him to see the difficulty (*ibid.*, V, 135–36): "Gladly would I solve, if I could, this problem of a vocabulary which, like some treacherous, wide shoal, waylays the tall bark, the goodly soul, and there it founders and suffers shipwreck. In common life, every man is led by the nose by a verb. ... [But] it must be from everlasting and from the infinitude of God, that when God speaketh, he should then and there exist; should fill the world with his voice, should scatter forth light, nature, time, souls, from the centre of the present thought; and new date and new create the whole."

"Say what ... great man"—Melville, Letter to Evert Duyckinck (February 24, 1849), in *Representative Selections*, p. 371.

"endless seeker"—Emerson, *Works*, II, 296–97: "...Let me remind the reader that I am only an experimenter....I unsettle all things....I simply experiment, an endless seeker with no Past at my back."

CHAPTER V

162. "The calyx ... livid hieroglyph."—Hart Crane, "At Melville's Tomb," *Collected Poems* (New York, 1946), p. 100.

The Melville ... a personality.—One of the earliest critics, J. W. N. Sullivan, in *Aspects of Science: Second Series* (New York, 1926), pp. 190–91, summarizes a view which was to preoccupy much more pretentious exegetes: "We are not in the presence of what is usually called a work of art, something that can be separated off from its author in the same way, although not to the same degree, as a scientific theory...." *Moby-Dick* is "an account of the mighty, mysterious, and troubled soul of Herman Melville."

163. "Herman Melville ... largely unknown—Jay Leyda's exhaustive compilation of biographical data in *The Melville Log* (New York, 1951)—like Leon Howard's attempt in *Herman Melville: A Biography* (Berkeley, 1951) to frame a "life" chiefly on the basis of such data—is largely negative in its total effect: one is less aware of the presence of Melville than of the distance between the man, as we now can know him, and the complicated being who moves through the language of his writings.

"The conception ... he wrestled."—Willard Thorp (ed.), *Herman Melville: Representative Selections* (New York, 1938), p. xl.

164. "Six months ... nothing else!"—*Typee: A Peep at Polynesian Life* (1846), chap. i (*Works* [Standard ed.; London, 1922–24], I, 1).

Encompassed by ... common centre."—*Ibid.*, chap iv (*Works*, I, 28–29). As C. R. Anderson points out in *Melville in the South Seas* (New York, 1939), pp. 70–72, this description is almost certainly based on a passage in C. S. Stewart's *Visit to the South Seas, in the U.S. Ship Vincennes*. But Melville imposes a greater symmetry on the scene: the sentence quoted has no counterpart in Stewart's description.

Instead, "the ... from us."—*Typee*, chap. vii (*Works*, I, 53).

"The whole ... the creation."—*Ibid.*, chap. vii (*Works*, I, 57).

164–65. After toiling ... the ocean.—*Ibid.*, chap. vii (*Works*, I, 64).

165. "Line in ... are round."—Emerson, "Uriel" (*Works*, IX, 22).

The sphere ... same System."—Coleridge, Unpublished MS C, p. 108, quoted by J. H. Muirhead, *Coleridge as Philosopher* (New York, 1930), p. 122. Cf. Emerson's essay on "Circles," which begins (*Works*, II, 281): "The eye is the first circle; the horizon which it forms is the second; and throughout nature this primary figure is repeated without end. It is the highest emblem in the cipher of the world. ... Our life is an apprenticeship to the truth that around every circle another can be drawn; that there is no end in nature, but every end is a beginning; that there is always another dawn risen on mid-noon, and under every deep a lower deep opens."

166. At the beginning ... lies ahead.—*Omoo: A Narrative of Adventures in the South Seas* (1847), Introduction and chap. lxxxii (*Works*, II, 1, 375).

"one of ... possibly elude."—*Typee*, chap. v (*Works*, I, 40).

And *Omoo* ... to another."—*Omoo*, Preface (*Works*, II, ix).

The archipelago ... of reef."—*Mardi: And a Voyage Thither* (1849), chap. lii (*Works*, III, 186).

"in quest ... mysteriously hinted."—*Ibid.*, chap. lxv (*Works*, III, 230).

He is last ... endless sea."—*Ibid.*, chap. cxcv (*Works*, IV, 399–400).

Melville's development ... *Mardi* itself.—This involuted relationship between theme and method, which is apparent in the book itself, is substantiated by Melville's letter to John Murray (March 25, 1848) in *The Melville Log*, I, 274–75: "Well: proceeding in my narrative of *facts* I began to feel an incurable distaste for the same. ... So suddenly abandoning the thing alltogether, I went to work heart & soul at a romance. ... It opens like a true narrative—like Omoo for example, on ship board—the romance & poetry of the thing thence grow continuly, till it becomes a story wild enough I assure you & with a meaning too."

While he ... worlds beyond."—*Mardi*, chap. i (*Works*, III, 7–8).

166–67. "loosely laid ... the charts"—*Ibid.* (*Works*, III, 7).

167. "terra incognita"—*Ibid.*, chap. xvii (*Works*, III, 59).

Beyond them . . . "endless sea."—*Ibid.*, chap. xii (*Works*, III, 44). Cf. the description of a calm in chapter xvi (III, 55): "Everything was fused into the calm ... The silence was that of a vacuum. No vitality lurked in the air. And this inert blending and brooding of all things seemed gray chaos in conception." The endless voyage (i.e., the possession of everything) tends toward its opposite—static nothingness.

"the world of mind"—*Ibid.*, chap. clxix (*Works*, IV, 277).

The mood ... is absurd."—*Ibid.*, chap. iii (*Works*, III, 14–15).

the boundless ... side thyself!"—*Ibid.*, chap. clxviii (*Works*, IV, 270).

167–68. "the winged ... everlasting beginning."—*Ibid.*, chap. lxxv (*Works*, III, 269).

168. "Beneath me ... from afar."—*Ibid.*, chap. cxix (*Works*, IV, 53–54). Cf. chap. xcvii (*Works*, III, 344–45).

"Oh, reader ... was sought."—*Ibid.*, chap. clxix (*Works*, IV, 276).

"The chief ... of thought."—James Murdock, *Sketches of Modern Philosophy, Especially among the Germans* (Hartford, 1842), pp. 93–94 (italics in text).

169. "a seeker ... finder yet"—"Hawthorne and His Mosses" (1850), *Representative Selections*, p. 340.

But the Melville ... to-and-fro"—Nathaniel Hawthorne, *The English Notebooks*, ed. Randall Stewart (New York, 1941), pp. 432–33.

The concentric ... at war.—*Typee*, chap. iv (*Works*, I, 30, 34–35).

When he ... "bad" Typees.—*Ibid.*, chap. vii (*Works*, I, 53).

If the ... important difference.—*Ibid.*, chap. viii (*Works*, I, 66–67).

Tom's situation ... comprehend nothing"—*Ibid.*, chap. xxiv (*Works*, I, 239). Cf. Preface (I, ix) and chap. xxx (I, 297).

Not only is Tom unable to fix on the ultimate "good" and "evil" of the Typees; he also cannot decide the meaning of "civilization" and "savagery." Throughout the book there runs the unanswered question posed much later in *Israel Potter* (chap. xix [*Works*, XI, 173]): "Is civilization a thing distinct, or is it an advanced stage of barbarism?"

The issue was especially important because of Melville's association of primitive modes of thought with the extra-rational dimension that both attracted and repelled him. This association becomes fully apparent in *Moby-Dick*. In *Typee* it is suggested by his reference to the incomprehensible religious ceremonies of the islanders as "much like seeing a parcel of 'Freemasons' making secret signs to each other." Cf. the allusion in *Moby-Dick* (chap. lxxxvi [*Works*, VIII, 123]) to the "Free-Mason signs and symbols" with which the whale "intelligently conversed with the world," and a similar expression applied to "the Problem of the Universe" in a letter to Hawthorne (March, 1851), *Representative Selections*, p. 388.

170. "every thing is . . . series belongs."—Emerson, *Works*, II, 27.

"the endless . . . no end."—T. S. Eliot, "Ash Wednesday," II.

"wandering from . . . and frantic."—*Moby-Dick*, chap. xciii (*Works*, VIII, 170).

Yillah, like . . . "colorless all-color."—Cf. *Moby-Dick*, chap. xlii (*Works*, VII, 243). The motif of "whiteness" first appears in *Mardi* in chapter xiii (*Works*, III, 48), where the White Shark raises certain doubts in the mind of the optimistic voyager. Cf. chap. xxxviii (III, 140–41). After the encounter with Yillah, not only her whiteness but that of the narrator is emphasized, until at one point the three avengers hurl "white curses" on the "white heart" of the "white . . . murderer" (chap. c [*Works*, III, 356–57]). Mardi is first sighted "within a milk-white zone of reef" (chap. lii [*Works*, III, 186]), which is frequently mentioned, notably at the conclusion: ". . . on the circumvallating reef, the breakers dashed ghost-white" (chap. cxcv [*Works*, IV, 399]). Similarly, Flozella, Hautia's island, is introduced by a reference to its "white marge" (chap. cxcii [*Works*, IV, 387]).

She and . . . connected."—*Mardi*, chap. cxci (*Works*, IV, 386).

"Line in . . . will burn."—Emerson, "Uriel" (*Works*, IX, 22).

"Seemed to ... to confusion."—*Ibid.* Cf. *Mardi*, chap. cxcv (*Works*, IV, 398): "Conflicting currents met, and wrestled; and one dark arch led to channels, seaward tending. Round and round, a gleaming form slow circled in the deepest eddies:— white, and vaguely Yillah."

171. his boast ... his kin—*Mardi*, chap. cxix (*Works*, IV, 53).

"better to ... vulgar shoals."—*Ibid.*, chap. clxix (*Works*, IV, 277).

"I am ... and death."—*Ibid.*, chap. clxxxix (*Works*, IV, 382).

They are ... his wilfulness—*Ibid.*, chap. cxcv (*Works*, IV, 399– 400).

"My voyage ... in Mardi."—*Ibid.*, chap. clxxxix (*Works*, IV, 380).

"The more ... its reef."—*Ibid.*, chap. clxxxvii (*Works*, IV, 370).

"the organic law"—*Ibid.*, chap. clxxxviii (*Works*, IV, 376).

172. The death ... the deed.—*Ibid.*, chaps. xli–xlii. (*Works*, III, 152– 57). Cf. chap. xlvi (III, 168): "As we glided along, strange Yillah gazed down in the sea, and would fain have had me plunge into it with her, to rove through its depths. But I started dismayed; in fancy, I saw the stark body of the priest drifting by. Again that phantom obtruded; again guilt laid his red hand on my soul." Also chap. clxxxix (IV, 382): "Then sweet Yillah called me from the sea;—still must I on! but gazing whence that music seemed to come, I thought I saw the green corse drifting by: and striking 'gainst our prow, as if to hinder."

Thus the three ... own pursuit.—Cf. the first appearance of the pursuers in chapter c, entitled "The Pursuer Himself Is Pursued" (*Works*, III, 354). Also the last sentence of the book (chap. cxcv [*Works*, IV, 400]): "And thus, pursuers and pursued fled on, over an endless sea."

"Every act ... am pursued."—Emerson, *Works*, X, 13–14. This theme, omnipresent in *Mardi* (e.g., chap. cxci [*Works*, IV, 386]: "Yillah I sought, Hautia sought me"), recurs in *Moby-Dick* (e.g., chap. cxxxv [*Works*, VIII, 355]: "Aye, he's chasing *me* now; not I, *him*").

173. Taji's journey ... into being.—Cf. *Mardi*, chap. cxci (*Works*, IV, 385): "As if Mardi were a poem, and every island a canto,

the shore now in sight [Hautia's island] was called Flozella-a-Nina, or the Last-Verse-of-the-Song."

"Of ourselves . . . the creative.' "—*Ibid.*, chap. clxxx (*Works,* IV, 326). Melville's family referred to *Mardi* as the "Koztanza." See letter from Augusta Melville to Elizabeth Melville (January 27, 1849) in *The Melville Log,* I, 286–87.

Babbalanja, of all Taji's comrades, comes closest to Taji's (and Melville's) preoccupations. His problems, like those of Taji, grow out of his initial belief in organism: "that there is no place but the universe; no limit but the limitless; no bottom but the bottomless" (chap. cxliii [*Works,* IV, 161]). He is very much aware of "something going on in me that is independent of me . . . so present . . . that I seem not so much to live of myself, as to be a mere apprehension of the unaccountable being that is in me. Yet all the time this being is I, myself" (*ibid.*, pp. 155–57).

174. To use . . . a "polysensuum"—*Mardi,* chap. cxv (*Works,* IV, 42). Cf. *Dantis Alagherii epistolae: The Letters of Dante,* ed. and trans. Paget Toynbee (Oxford, 1920), p. 173.

Babbalanja uses the word "polysensuum" to describe a story he tells about nine blind men who once fell to quarreling, each claiming to have found the "original and true" trunk of an ancient banyan tree. If the story is polysensuous, it is at the same time, like the whole of *Mardi,* concerned with multiple meaning and the concept of organism. It is, in fact, Babbalanja's comment on the multiple gods of Mardi—the *idola mentis,* but taken in a thoroughly realistic sense—which had already led Taji to think of "the Jew that rejected the Talmud, and his all-permeating principle, to which Goethe and others have subscribed" (chap. lvii [*Works,* III, 204]).

Mardi would . . . working principles.—Although Lombardo is represented as, in one sense, originating nothing "of himself, and in himself," he is "critic" as well as "creator." "It is *I,*" he emphatically declares, that "scrutinize . . . , remorseless as a surgeon" (chap. clxxx [*Works,* IV, 331]).

"opposite or discordant qualities"—S. T. Coleridge, *Biographia Literaria,* ed. J. Shawcross (Oxford, 1907), II, 12.

Taji's double . . . his journey.—The same might be said of Babbalanja, who, when asked, "What is truth?" replies that the "question is more final than my answer" (chap. xciii [*Works*, III, 329]). Though he maintains that "much of the wisdom here below lives in a state of transition" (chap. cxliii [*Works*, IV, 160]), he is alive to the objection put by Media (*ibid.*, p. 158)— that this way of thinking "would seem to relieve all Mardi from moral accountability." He sees man as "soul and body glued together, . . . seamless as the vestment without joint, . . . yet divided as by a river, spirit from flesh" (chap. cxxxvi [*Works*, IV, 131]). While he persists in his speculations, he laments that "the more we learn, the more we unlearn; we accumulate not, but substitute; and take away more than we add" (chap. cxxiv [*Works*, IV, 80]). Cf. other relevant passages, chaps. cix and cxxxv (*Works*, IV, 21, 123–25).

175. The somber . . . his own.—*Mardi*, chap. cxcv (*Works*, IV, 400): "He's seized the helm! eternity is in his eye!"

"He can . . . the other.—Hawthorne, *The English Notebooks*, p. 433. Yet note that Melville was capable of aesthetic perspective even on this predicament. His own comment on the conversation reported by Hawthorne was simply "Good talk." See *Journal Up the Straits*, ed. Raymond Weaver (New York, 1935), p. 5.

"the fool of Truth"—*Pierre: Or, the Ambiguities* (1952), ed. R. S. Forsythe (New York, 1941), p. 398.

And Melville . . . no alternative.—An important sidelight in this connection is Melville's letter to Hawthorne of June, 1851 (*Representative Selections*, p. 393). Written toward the end of the composition of *Moby-Dick*, this letter shows Melville's characteristic attraction, repulsion, and anticipation of bankruptcy when he faces up to the assumptions of his art. He refers to one of Goethe's sayings—"Live in the all"—and comments that "this 'all' feeling," with its transcendence of "separate identity," has "some truth" but yet a good deal of "nonsense" in it. Just before he brings up this subject, he has spoken of his own career, using a metaphor of organic development but foreseeing, in terms of the same metaphor, that mere process can only result in dissolution: "Until I was twenty-five, I had no development at all. From my twenty-fifth year I date my life. Three weeks have scarcely passed, at any time between then and now, that I have not unfolded within myself. But I feel that I am now come to the inmost leaf of the bulb, and that shortly the flower must fall to the mould."

176. He postulated . . . seamless whole."—*Mardi*, chap. clxxx (*Works*, IV, 328) ; *Moby-Dick*, chap. cxiv (*Works*, VIII, 264).

"things infinite . . . in unities."—*Mardi*, chap. clxxx (*Works*, IV, 328).

"deeper meanings"—Letter to Evert Duyckinck (February 12, 1851), in *Representative Selections*, p. 386. Cf. "Hawthorne and His Mosses," *ibid.*, p. 332.

"deeper and . . . unspeakable meanings"—Letter to Hawthorne (June, 1851), in *Representative Selections*, p. 392.

"But then . . . the whole."—"An Unpublished Letter from Herman Melville to Mrs. Hawthorne in Explanation of 'Moby Dick,'" *American Art Association—Anderson Galleries Catalogue of Sale*, No. 3911 (New York, 1931), p. 9. Also printed in *The Portable Melville*, ed. Jay Leyda (New York, 1952), pp. 455–56.

This is . . . own preconceptions.—Cf. "Hawthorne and His Mosses," *Representative Selections*, p. 328: "Would that all excellent books were foundlings, without father or mother, that so it might be we could glorify them, without including their ostensible authors!" Again (*ibid.*, p. 337): "The trillionth part has not yet been said; and all that has been said, but multiplies the avenues to what remains to be said." Much later, Melville marked as "admirable" the passage in Emerson's "The Poet" in which language is described as "fossil poetry," constantly revived by the artist (*The Melville Log*, II, 649). Just as Lombardo in *Mardi* gives birth to a work which is "part of Mardi: claiming kin with mountains" (chap. clxxx [*Works*, IV, 332]), Melville equates his work with reality as meaning: "Why, ever since Adam, who has got to the meaning of his great allegory—the world? Then we pygmies must be content to have our paper allegories but ill comprehended." See letter to Hawthorne (November, 1851), in *Representative Selections*, p. 394.

There is no indication anywhere in Melville's writings of a distinction between "allegory" and "symbolism." Like Emerson, he used these words interchangeably, and they meant for him what we ordinarily mean by the latter.

176–77. "I felt . . . of feeling."—Letter to Hawthorne (November, 1851), in *Representative Selections*, pp. 394–95. Running through the same lines is another theme—that community of meaning is somehow related to ethical indifference: "I have written a wicked book, and feel spotless as the lamb. . . . It is a strange feeling— no hopefulness is in it, no despair. Content—that is it; and irre- sponsibility; but without licentious inclination." This corollary to the concept of meaning had already begun to trouble Mel- ville in *Mardi* (cf. the mysterious connection between Yillah and Hautia) and would become a major issue in *Pierre*. We have seen (chap iv above) that Melville was contemptuous of Emer- son's poet, "who reattaches things to nature and the whole" and thereby "disposes very easily of the most disagreeable facts."

177. universal "intertranslateability" . . . is God."—Emerson, *Journals*, V, 326; *Works*, II, 260. In his copy of Emerson's *Essays*, Mel- ville commented "Bully for Emerson!—Good" next to a passage from "Spiritual Laws" which declares that "a man cannot bury his meanings so deep in his book, but time and like-minded man will find them. . . . Therefore Aristotle said of his works, 'They are published and not published.' " See William Braswell, "Mel- ville as a Critic of Emerson," *American Literature*, IX (1937– 38), 320.

the "Agatha" letter—"Melville's 'Agatha' Letter to Hawthorne," ed. S. E. Morison, *New England Quarterly*, II (1929), 296–307.

"Turn this . . . so yourself."—Letter of October 25, 1852, tran- scribed by Harrison Hayford in "The Significance of Melville's 'Agatha' Letters," *ELH*, XIII (1946), 301.

177–78. Melville's sketch . . . the cliff)—"—"Melville's 'Agatha' Let- ter to Hawthorne," p. 299. This kind of focusing was Mel- ville's usual method in working up documentary materials. A notable instance is "Benito Cereno," in which the most important change from Delano's *Narrative of Voyages* is not the addition of particular incidents but rather the whole process of *trying to understand* which is imputed to Delano. The source of the story is reprinted by H. H. Scudder, "Melville's *Benito Cereno* and Captain Delano's Voyages," *PMLA*, XLIII (1928), 503–29.

178. "Some certain . . . empty cipher."—*Moby-Dick*, chap. xcix (*Works*, VIII, 188).

"The great . . . the air."—*Ibid.*, chap. i (*Works*, VII, 7).

179. the chapter on "The Doubloon"—*Ibid.*, chap. xcix (*Works*, VIII, 188–95).

"I could . . . the walls."—*Moby-Dick*, chap. viii (*Works*, VII, 47–48). Cf. Ahab on the coffin life-buoy (chap. cxxvii [*Works*, VIII, 310]).

to read . . . whale's brow."—*Ibid.*, chap. lxxix (*Works*, VIII, 83).

"a draught . . . a draught."—*Ibid.*, chap. xxxii (*Works*, VII, 179).

"I but . . . you can."—*Ibid.*, chap. lxxix (*Works*, VIII, 83).

"beggarly"—Letter to Evert Duyckinck (December 14, 1849), in *Representative Selections*, p. 376.

180. The subtitle . . . realistic narrative.—*Redburn: His First Voyage* (1849), chaps. i, xiii, xxx, lxi, lxii (*Works*, V, 9, 80, 191, 398, 401, 403).

"For I . . . of Liverpool."—*Ibid.*, chap. xxxi (*Works*, V, 192–93).

"This world . . . guide-books."—*Ibid.*, chap. xxxi (*Works*, V, 200–201).

The absolute . . . of her."—*Ibid.*, chap. xxxii (*Works*, V, 209). Cf. the next chapter (V, 211–17), where the Liverpool docks, the crossing point of "past voyages and future prospects," become "an epitome of the world"; and where, finally, America, whose "ancestry is lost in the universal paternity," is celebrated as the New World. When Redburn approaches the end of his first voyage, he notes "the long devious wakes from Europe, Africa, India, and Peru converged to a line, which braided them all in one" (chap. lx [V, 384]).

"But yet . . . I end."—*Ibid.*, chap. lxii (*Works*, V, 403). Wellingborough Redburn, the comic hobbledehoy, is also the prototypical voyager. Note his comment as his ship begins to move (chap. xiii [V, 84]): "Then was I first conscious of a wonderful thing in me, that responded to all the wild commotion of the outer world; and went reeling on and on with the planets in their orbits, and was lost in one delirious throb at the center of the All." In order to live out this intuition, he must come to terms (and to some extent does) with more than the menial tasks which recall him to empirical reality: he must come to terms with the phenomenon of another voyager, the infamous Jackson (chap. xii [V, 71–79]).

181. It refers . . . the universe.—*White Jacket: The World in a Man-of-War* (1850), chaps. xix, xxx, xxxix, xlii, xlix, l, liv, lxxxiii, xcl, xciii (*Works*, VI, 96–97, 154, 199, 204, 212, 217, 259–60, 262–63, 282, 433, 493, 502–4).

"comprehensiveness of . . . the world."—*Moby-Dick*, chaps. civ, xxxii (*Works*, VIII, 220; VII, 166). Cf., in *White Jacket*, the expansive passage on Rio Bay (chap. l [VI, 261–63]).

He is . . . martial formalities."—*White Jacket*, chap. xix (*Works*, VI, 96–97). The social criticism in *White Jacket*, growing out of the rigid code and formal hierarchy of the warship, is often generalized into a philosophic criticism of all rational order. Cf. the comment on a Polynesian aboard ship: "Our creed he rejected: his we. . . . Had the case been reversed . . . , our mutual opinion of each other would still have remained the same. A fact proving that neither was wrong, but both right" (chap. xxviii [VI, 148]). One aspect of the theme of the book is that a man-of-war (i.e., a ship or a man dedicated to fixed laws) is anomalous. The true voyage is incompatible with mechanical rules. Cf. the view of science symbolized by the contrast between the "inorganic" Surgeon Cuticle and the man on whom he is operating (chap. lxiii [VI, 324]).

America is . . . is ours."—*Ibid.*, chap. xxxvi (*Works*, VI, 189).

The white . . . the whale.—The narrator identifies the jacket with his "castle" and hence, implicitly, with himself (chap. ix [*Works*, VI, 44]); so much so, that eventually "certain involuntary superstitious considerations" make him afraid to part with it (chap. xlvii [VI, 253]). He feels that if he throws it away, he himself will die. Elsewhere, anticipating Ishmael's image in "The Whiteness of the Whale," he perceives "how that evil was but good disguised, and a knave a saint in his way; how that in other planets, perhaps, what we deem wrong may . . . be deemed right; *even as some substances, without undergoing any mutations in themselves, utterly change their colour, according to the light thrown upon them*" (chap. xliv [VI, 230]; my italics).

Yet he . . . the universe."—*Ibid.*, chaps. xix, xcii (*Works*, VI, 96–99, 494–98). Carrying on the image of whiteness, the narrator wants to give the jacket a distinct color in order to escape from the consuming "colorless all-color": "Jacket, ... you must change your complexion! you must hie to the dyers and be dyed, that I may live. I have but one poor life, ... and that life I cannot spare. I cannot consent to die for *you*, but be dyed you must for me. You can dye many times without injury; but I cannot die without irreparable loss, and running the eternal risk" (chap. xix [VI, 98]). To the same effect, he becomes aware through study of Bland that there *is* such a thing as "an organic and irreclaimable scoundrel" (chap. xliv [VI, 234]); and he perceives that the sea, the symbol of "the All," is at the same time "the home of many moral monsters" (chap. xc [VI, 475]).

(the moment ... in horror").—*Moby-Dick*, chap. xxxv (*Works*, VII, 198).

181–82. In White Jacket ... a buoy."—*White Jacket*, chap. xcii (*Works*, VI, 495–97).

182. He survives ... another world.—Something like this, rather than the pat moral stated in the final chapter ("Life is a voyage that's homeward bound"), is the theme that emerges from the book as a whole. Cf. chap. lxxv (*Works*, VI, 404): "But all events are mixed in a fusion indistinguishable. ... Yet though all this be so, nevertheless, in our own hearts, we mould the whole world's hereafters. ..."

he too ... a brother."—*Israel Potter: His Fifty Years of Exile* (1855), chaps. ii, xxvi (*Works*, XI, 7, 221).

His years ... Wandering Jew.—*Ibid.*, chaps. i, v, xxi, xxii, xxiii, xxiv, xxvi (*Works*, XI, 5, 36, 189, 198, 204, 209, 214, 220).

182–83. On a foggy ... boundless amazement."—*Ibid.*, chap. xxv (*Works*, XI, 210–13).

183. The episode ... and labored.—An exception might be made in favor of the symbolism surrounding Paul Jones, who embodies "the primeval savageness which ever slumbers in human kind" (chap. xi [*Works*, XI, 82]). At the same time, Jones is the "sailor of the universe" (chap. x [XI, 73]). Melville, by associating these two qualities, seems again to be calling the voyage theory into question. America, which figured for White Jacket as the symbol of process, is here "the Paul Jones of nations" (chap. xix [XI, 158]). Note that Jones's savagery is typified by his tattooed

arm, covered with "large, intertwisted ciphers ... elaborate, laby-rinthine, cabalistic" (chap. xi [XI, 81]). Savagery is not merely ferocity but a mysterious way of thinking, at odds with the vested interests of civilization.

184. The whale ... symbolic meaning.—It is in this light that Mel-ville's "affidavit" as to "the natural verity" of his story must be viewed (chap. xlv [*Works*, VII, 254–64]). In order to bring about the symbolistic effect he desires, he must establish that Moby Dick cannot be dismissed as *merely* "a monstrous fable, or still worse and more detestable, a hideous and intolerable allegory."

Not that ... creative process.—See chap. i above. Something simi-lar to what happened in the course of writing *Mardi*—the shift from fact to symbol which is recorded in Melville's letter to John Murray (January 17, 1848)—may also have occurred, on a higher level, during the composition of *Moby-Dick*. The book was supposedly "half way" done in May, 1850, and "mostly done" in August, but it was not actually completed until nearly a year later (see *The Melville Log*, I, 274–75, 374, 385). That year very possibly saw the development of the deeper sense of "the meaning of meaning" which marks the advance of *Moby-Dick* beyond *Mardi*. Here Melville *began* with the concept of symbol and the method of symbolism; his development lay in a new ex-perience of the difficulties of his method, which he introduced into his subject.

184–85. "Were this ... us whelmed."—*Moby-Dick*, chap. lii (*Works*, VII, 300).

185. "O Nature ... in mind."—*Ibid.*, chap. lxx (*Works*, VIII, 38).

"Now, then ... detected cheat!"—*Pierre: Or, The Ambiguities* (1852), ed. R. S. Forsythe (New York, 1941), p. 397. In the case of *Pierre*, references will be made to this edition, which provides a carefully corrected text, rather than to the *Works*.

186. "For the more ... pack indeed."—*Ibid.*, p. 377. See Charles Olson, "Lear and *Moby Dick*," *Twice a Year*, No. 1 (1938), p. 173, for a note written by Melville on the flyleaf of his Shake-speare, apparently with *Moby-Dick* in mind. "... Madness is un-definable," Melville says, and yet "it & right reasons [are] ex-tremes of one," this "one" being "not the (black art) Goetic

but Theurgic magic." It is worth remarking, though it may be no more than a coincidence, that "goetic" in the Greek has the primary connotation of trickery and cheating. The word appears near the end of Book III of *The Republic*, when Plato seeks to demonstrate that, in contrast to "lying poets," the gods "are not magicians who transform themselves, neither do they deceive mankind in any way." In effect, between *Moby-Dick* and *Pierre* Melville became ready to believe that art was goetic, not theurgic, magic. Pierre is a more thoroughgoing Plato.

"What, *who* ... to face."—*Pierre*, p. 46.

He is determined ... it Gorgon!"—*Ibid.*, p. 73.

"one pervading ... ambiguous details."—*Ibid.*, p. 249.

187. Gide's *Faux-monnayeurs.*—André Gide, *Les Faux-monnayeurs* (Paris, 1925). Quotations in this discussion follow the translation by Dorothy Bussy—*The Counterfeiters* (New York, 1951)—and the appended translation by Justin O'Brien (*ibid.*, pp. 367–432) of Gide's *Journal des faux-monnayeurs* (Paris, 1927). Reference will also be made in the notes to the text of *Les Faux-monnayeurs* and *Journal des faux-monnayeurs* in Gide's *Œuvres complètes* (Paris, 1932–39), Vols. XII and XIII.

The affinity between *Pierre* and *Les Faux-monnayeurs* is briefly noted by Willard Thorp in his Introduction to *Representative Selections*, p. lxxvii.

He is "not sure" ... take him."—See, e.g., *The Counterfeiters*, pp. 22, 32, 202 (*Œuvres*, XII, 48, 64, 317).

his long ... the object."—*Journal*, p. 381 (*Œuvres*, XIII, 15–16).

"On one ... it all." *Journal*, p. 392 (*Œuvres*, XIII, 31): "D'une part, l'événement, le fait, la donnée extérieure; d'autre part, l'effort même du romancier pour faire un livre avec cela."

The book ... of it."—*The Counterfeiters*, p. 173 (*Œuvres*, XII, 271): "entre ce que lui offre la réalité et ce que, lui, prétend en faire."

"the world ... own interpretation."—*The Counterfeiters*, p. 189 (*Œuvres*, XII, 297).

"the drama of our lives"—*Ibid.*

"the real ... to ourselves."—*Ibid.*

188. In creating ... other person."—*Journal*, p. 405 (*Œuvres*, XIII, 48).

"I stick ... copies art."—*Ibid.*, p. 384 (*Œuvres*, XIII, 18).

"animated with ... own life."—*Ibid.*, p. 406 (*Œuvres*, XIII, 50).

Edouard prides ... to resemblance."—*The Counterfeiters*, pp. 149, 171 (*Œuvres*, XII, 239, 269).

"The only ... full signification."—*The Counterfeiters*, pp. 64–65 (*Œuvres*, XII, 110): "Rien n'a pour moi d'existence, que *poétique* (et je rends à ce mot son plein sens)—à commencer par moi-même." Cf. p. 144 (XII, 231): "I cannot feel that anything that happens to me has any real existence until I see it reflected here" [in his journal].

"I am ... my evening's."—*Ibid.*, p. 64 (*Œuvres*, XII, 109).

"I am ... and contradictory."—*If It Die ... An Autobiography*, trans. Dorothy Bussy (New York, 1935), p. 250. *Si le grain ne meurt* ... (nouv. éd.; Paris, 1924), III, 44: "Je suis un être de dialogue; tout en moi combat et se contredit."

"the impression of inexhaustibility"—*Journal*, p. 415 (*Œuvres*, XIII, 60).

disappointing his ... single "subject."—*Ibid.*, p. 409 (*Œuvres*, XIII, 53); *The Counterfeiters*, p. 172 (*Œuvres*, XII, 270–71).

Here, in ... perpetual warfare.—*If It Die*, p. 14. *Si le grain ne meurt*, I, 26: "Souvent je me suis persuadé que j'avais été contraint à l'œuvre d'art, parce que je ne pouvais réaliser que par elle l'accord de ces éléments trop divers, qui sinon fussent restés à se combattre, ou tout au moins à dialoguer en moi."

188–89. "Have you observed ... to harmony."—*The Counterfeiters*, p. 151 (*Œuvres*, XII, 241–42).

189. According to him ... are one."—*Ibid.*, pp. 364–65 (*Œuvres*, XII, 548–49).

In his ... fooled me."—*Ibid.*, p. 108 (*Œuvres*, XII, 176).

La Pérouse is ... into question.—The same effect is achieved through a totally different character, the cynic Strouvilhou, who delivers a shocking parody of Gide's theories. If Gide would say that men are in some sense the creatures of their constructs, Strouvilhou likes "to imagine . . . a servile humanity working towards the production of some cruel master-piece." If Edouard decries realism, Strouvilhou envisages a literature in which the nonrepresentational method will be extended until "all sense, all meaning will be considered antipoetical." Like Gide and Edouard, he invokes the symbol of the counterfeit coin, but his instincts are wholly destructive: his aim is simply "to demonetize fine feelings, and those promissory notes which go by the name of *words*" (*The Counterfeiters,* pp. 305–8 [*Œuvres,* XII, 464–68]).

"one character . . . entire book."—*Journal,* p. 385 (*Œuvres,* XIII, 21).

Fully conscious . . . well-made novel—*Ibid.,* pp. 412–13, 382 (*Œuvres,* XIII, 57–58, 16).

190. "in art . . . art itself."—*The Immoralist,* trans. Dorothy Bussy (New York, 1930), p. viii. André Gide, *L'Immoraliste* (7th ed.; Paris, 1914), p. 9: "A vrai dire, en art, il n'y a pas de problèmes —dont l'œuvre d'art ne soit la suffisante solution."

"The more . . . our negation."—*Journal,* p. 384 (*Œuvres,* XIII, 19): "Plus on le nie, plus on lui donne de réalité. Le diable s'affirme dans notre négation."

"A strange . . . the job?"—*Ibid.,* pp. 390–91 (*Œuvres,* XIII, 27): "Étrange matière liquide qui, d'abord et longtemps, refuse de prendre consistance, mais où les particules solides, à force d'être remuées, agitées en tous sens, s'agglomèrent enfin et se séparent du petit-lait. . . . S'il ne savait d'avance, par expérience, qu'à force de battre et d'agiter le chaos crémeux, il verra se renouveler le miracle—qui ne lâcherait la partie?"

"to put . . . his novel.—*The Counterfeiters,* p. 172 (*Œuvres,* XII, 271).

190–91. The preoccupations . . . standing questions—Melville seems also to have regarded them in a more general way, as properly questions for the time. Poetry is no longer "a consecration and obsequy to all hapless modes of human life" (*Pierre,* p. 152)— least of all, those modes that pertain to the question of poetry itself. The "Church of the Apostles" has passed from its congregation into the hands of lawyers, and finally, deserted even by most of these, is inhabited by impoverished "poets, painters . . .

and philosophers" (pp. 296–300). It is here, where poetry is reduced to its last extremity "in a bantering, barren, and prosaic, heartless age" (p. 152), that Pierre puts the ultimate validity of the imagination to a more strenuous test than ever before.

191. "naturally poetic"—*Pierre,* p. 156. Cf. p. 272: "... Pierre himself possessed the poetic nature...."

His task ... own soul"—*Ibid.,* p. 231.

Early in ... are irreconcilable.—*Ibid.,* p. 43.

much later ... in Pierre."—*Ibid.,* p. 326.

"the two ... absolute truth.—*Ibid.,* pp. 152, 227, 46, 73. Cf. the title of Book III: "The Presentiment and the Verification."

192. Lucy, his ... present reality.—*Ibid.,* p. 7.

Since "a ... as sister.—*Ibid.,* pp. 7, 5.

He recalls ... to read."—*Ibid.,* p. 78.

The "searching ... of them."—*Ibid.,* pp. 155–56.

"the multitudinous ... prior creations."—*Ibid.,* p. 92.

Melville remarks ... his symbols.—*Ibid.,* p. 197.

193. The plan ... for naught."—*Ibid.,* p. 119.

The new ... and reciprocal."—*Ibid.,* p. 118.

Though Pierre's ... infinite mournfulness."—*Ibid.,* pp. 99–100.

Even while ... imagined image."—*Ibid.,* pp. 93–95.

"The face ... ever-baffled artist."—*Ibid.,* p. 54.

194. "And now ... only one!' "—*Ibid.,* pp. 95–96.

builds up ... and "heroic."—*Ibid.,* p. 22.

she occupies ... Pierre's portrait.—*Ibid.,* p. 398.

194–95. "All my thoughts ... new things."—*Ibid.,* p. 137.

195. "Thy hand ... me anew."—*Ibid.,* p. 360.

She was ... external things.—*Ibid.,* pp. 136–37.

Now, as ... not "comprehend."—*Ibid.,* p. 348.

She yearns ... individual sensation."—*Ibid.,* p. 133.

"Always in ... fourth face."—*Ibid.,* p. 131.

As she ... the sounds."—*Ibid.*, p. 141. Cf. Isabel's reaction to the sea (pp. 394–95). She is the true descendant of Taji and Ishmael: " 'The motion! the motion! ... Don't let us stop here. ... Look, let us go through there! ... out there where the two blues meet, and are nothing. ...' "

He is ... by him."—*Ibid.*, p. 383.

195–96. the "mixed ... earth-emancipated mood"—*Ibid.*, pp. 385–86.

196. He postulates ... hooded phantoms."—*Ibid.*, p. 54.

He tries ... comprehensible shape."—*Ibid.*, pp. 169, 152.

Even while ... of solution."—*Ibid.*, pp. 155, 143.

"the fool ... of Fate."—*Ibid.*, p. 398.

"How did ... pure fancy-piece."—*Ibid.*, pp. 392–93.

196–97. Much earlier ... of Isabel."—*Ibid.*, p. 220 (italics in text).

197. "I am ... we dream."—*Ibid.*, p. 305.

his first impulsive ... own factors"—*Ibid.*, p. 56.

"Look: a ... and Vice."—*Ibid.*, p. 305.

Pierre's "sister" ... human association."—*Ibid.*, p. 159.

Her face ... and heaven"—*Ibid.*, p. 48.

she "knows ... the other."—*Ibid.*, p. 305.

"marble-white."—*Ibid.*, p. 366.

"substituted but ... real Lucy"—*Ibid.*, p. 202.

Opposite the ... jetty hair."—*Ibid.*, pp. 390–91.

two mutually absorbing shapes.—*Ibid.*, p. 96. The parallel to Yillah and Hautia at the end of *Mardi* is obvious. Note that very early in *Pierre* (p. 70) it is the *"bad angel"* who tells Pierre to destroy Isabel's note, and the "good angel" who tells him to read it.

197–98. Pierre dismisses ... neuter now."—*Ibid.*, p. 401.

198. "I do not ... in advance."—Gide, *The Immoralist*, p. viii; *L'Immoraliste*, p. 8.

"mutually neutralizing thoughts"—*Pierre*, p. 395.

all men ... "liars" perforce.—*Ibid.*, pp. 396–97, 399.

"the universal . . . written thoughts."—*Ibid.*, p. 377.

What occupies . . . his soul."—*Ibid.*, p. 338.

His experience . . . "uncompromisingly skeptical."—*Ibid.*, p. 393.

Earlier, he . . . unsystemizable elements."—*Ibid.*, pp. 157–58.

Now he . . . the more."—*Ibid.*, p. 377.

His former . . . proper endings"—*Ibid.*, p. 158.

"Here, then . . . ambiguous still."—*Ibid.*, p. 400.

199. It comes . . . author-hero."—*Ibid.*, p. 336.

"deep-lying subject"—*The Counterfeiters*, p. 189 (*Œuvres*, XII, 297): "le 'sujet profond.' "

200. "It will be . . . possibly neither."—*Pierre*, p. 233.

He would . . . own ambiguousness"—*Ibid.*, p. 202.

"I shall . . . I land."—*Ibid.*, p. 121.

"In general . . . Pierre Glendinning."—*Ibid.*, p. 12.

"By immemorial . . . own affianced?"—*Ibid.*, p. 27.

"As a statue . . . insight may."—*Ibid.*, p. 375.

201. "There is . . . visor down."—*Ibid.*, pp. 288–89. Melville clearly points at himself as parallel to Pierre by his reference to the Knight: cf. Pierre's speech, p. 73. Similarly, if Pierre comes to regard all constructs as false yet unavoidable, Melville anticipates him (p. 78, apropos of Isabel's letter): "Such a note . . . can be easily enough written, Pierre; impostors are not unknown in this curious world; or the brisk novelist, Pierre, will write thee fifty such notes. . . ."

After a . . . I please."—*Ibid.*, p. 272.

the sentimental . . . opening pages—*Ibid.*, pp. 35–38.

Silence was . . . Pierre's death.—Melville's frequent references in his letters to his yearning for "frankness" and to the impossibility of attaining it (see *Representative Selections*, pp. 372, 376, 390, 393) are generally put on the rather superficial ground of a conflict between social conventions and "truth." Yet it is plain that his problem lay deeper. When he remarks to Hawthorne that "Solomon was the truest man who ever spoke, and yet . . . he a little *managed* the truth with a view to popular conservatism" (p. 393), he points at the whole question of "management" —what Pierre calls "jugglery"—which is inherent in the situation of the artist. Thus he declares to Evert Duyckinck (p. 376) that he will "write such things as the Great Publisher of Mankind ordained ages before he published 'The World' "; and then he immediately exclaims: "What a madness & anguish it is, that an author can never—*under no conceivable circumstances*—be at all frank with his readers" (my italics). Melville could not accept the paradox that Emerson easily swallowed (*Journals*, V, 521): "There is no deeper dissembler than the sincerest man." What he valued in Shakespeare was the moment when, as it seemed to him, a character "tears off the mask"; the "Art of Telling the Truth" by indirections remained for him a *pis aller* ("Hawthorne and His Mosses," *Representative Selections*, p. 334).

"at once . . . in nature."—*Pierre*, p. 227.

battle "with the angel—Art"—Melville, "Art," *Poems* (*Works*, XVI, 270).

202. Both are . . . into question.—*Pierre*, p. 228.

"Silence is . . . our God"—*Ibid.*, p. 227.

and yet . . . of Silence."—*Ibid.*, p. 232.

The stuff . . . a man!"—*Ibid.*, p. 317.

Melville parodies . . . new translation."—*Ibid.*, pp. 36–37.

On the contrary . . . every synthesis.—*Ibid.*, p. 186.

The evolution . . . the wheel.—It was the Emersonian Nature itself —which "intended a rare and original development in Pierre"— that "proved ambiguous to him in the end" (pp. 14–15). As Melville notes, a relevant motto is "Nemo contra Deum nisi Deus ipse," which turns out to mean all of its possible constructions: that man is divine and not divine; that the divinity of man is incompatible with the divinity of a transcendent God; and, finally, that God is and is not divided against himself.

203. According to . . . of convention.—*Ibid.*, pp. 234–40.

"It is not . . . horizon alike."—*Ibid.*, p. 184.

The nearer . . . wholly inverted."—*Ibid.*

"there is . . . new truth."—*Ibid.*, p. 186.

"fitted by . . . fearless thought."—*Ibid.*, p. 184.

203–4. Pierre's dream . . . his goal.—*Ibid.*, pp. 385–86. The whole episode is shot through with this double meaning and with references to intellectual method. It is introduced by the passage on "the Mount of the Titans," which changes its aspect as its name is changed from "the Delectable Mountain" (p. 380). This "chameleon . . . height," the scene of Enceladus' attempt to scale heaven, is steadily overgrown by the white amaranth, the token of "sterileness" (p. 381). But the amaranth also expresses, more truly than "the Bunyanish old title," man's "ever-encroaching appetite for God" (pp. 381, 383). Note that the Enceladus story, like the mountain itself, is treated as an instance of the mode of thought on which it is a commentary. It is a "vision which . . . strangely . . . supplied a tongue to muteness" (p. 385).

In connection with the incest motif as a symbol of the inbreeding which is inseparable from its opposite (the productivity of thought), cf. the imagery in Melville's definition of productivity (p. 288): "For though the naked soul of man doth assuredly contain one latent element of intellectual productiveness; yet never was there a child born solely from one parent; the visible world of experience being that procreative thing which impregnates the muses; self-reciprocally efficient hermaphrodites being but a fable."

204. Its title . . . problem itself."—*Ibid.*, p. 234. Cf. *Moby-Dick*, chap. cxiv (*Works*, VIII, 264): ". . . manhood's pondering repose of If."

"it follows . . . to correspond."—*Pierre*, p. 236.

Indeed, he . . . the Universe."—*Ibid.*, pp. 324–26.

Edouard would . . . be continued."—*The Counterfeiters*, p. 310 (*Œuvres*, XII, 472).

"It must . . . disperse, disintegrate."—*Journal of "The Counterfeiters*," p. 415 (*Œuvres*, XIII, 60): "Il ne doit pas se boucler, mais s'éparpiller, se défaire. . . ."

"a most untidy termination."—*Pierre*, p. 240.

204–5. those "profounder . . . final answers.—*Ibid.*, p. 158.

205. "the tragicalness...profounder workings."—Letter to Hawthorne (March, 1851), in *Representative Selections*, p. 388. Cf. the transcript of this letter in *The Portable Melville*, p. 427.

"There is...am concerned."—*The Counterfeiters*, pp. 112–13. (*Œuvres*, XII, 183): "Une sorte de tragique a jusqu'à présent, me semble-t-il, échappé presque à la littérature. Le roman s'est occupé des traverses du sort, de la fortune bonne ou mauvaise, des rapports sociaux, du conflit des passions, des caractères, mais point de l'essence même de l'être....Il y a ceux qui se proposent des fins d'édification; mais cela n'a rien à voir avec ce que je veux dire. Le tragique moral—qui, par exemple, fait si formidable la parole évangélique: 'Si le sel perd sa saveur, avec quoi la lui rendra-t-on?' C'est ce tragique-là qui m'importe."

"the uttermost...monstrousest vice"—*Pierre*, p. 304.

"no villain...false within"—George Meredith, "Modern Love," XLIII.

"As soon...the beam."—Letter to Hawthorne (March, 1851), in *Representative Selections*, p. 388.

"Si le...his attitude.—Cf. *Pierre*, p. 9: "...the most mighty of nature's laws is this, that out of Death she brings Life."

205–6. Pierre twists . . . a conclusion.—Note Melville's remark that Pierre found his vision of Enceladus "repulsively fateful and foreboding" because he failed to "flog this stubborn rock as Moses his, and force even aridity itself to quench his painful thirst (*Pierre*, p. 385).

206. "On my...do clasp!"—*Pierre*, p. 120. Cf. Pierre's behavior at "the Memnon stone" (p. 150). This stone is a symbol of subjectivity in contact with external things. It is balanced on a single small boulder, and "beside that one obscure and minute point of contact, the whole enormous and most ponderous mass touched not another object in the wide terraqueous world" (p. 147). In placing himself in "the horrible interspace" between the stone and the earth, Pierre is acting out the situation in which he really finds himself, but in a spirit of bravado.

206–7. Like Pierre . . . Custom House."—Letter to Hawthorne (March, 1851), in *Representative Selections*, p. 388. Cf. the transcript of this letter in *The Portable Melville*, p. 427.

207. "to rise ... feed them."—*Journal of "The Counterfeiters,"* p. 414 (*Œuvres*, XIII, 58–59).

"'How? Does ... are actors.'"—*The Confidence Man: His Masquerade* (1857), chap. vi (*Works*, XII, 41).

208. "The cosmopolitan ... many parts.'"—*Ibid.*, chap. xli (*Works*, XII, 297–98).

"Here reigned ... confident tide."—*Ibid.*, chap. ii (*Works*, XII, 9).

208–9. "That fiction ... to facts."—*Ibid.*, chap. xiv (*Works*, XII, 90).

209. "Something further ... this Masquerade."—*Ibid.*, chap. xlv (*Works*, XII, 336).

"The original ... of things."—*Ibid.*, chap. xliv (*Works*, XII, 318).

"history of ... every child."—Emerson, *Works*, I, 196.

Though "a ... can show."—*The Confidence Man*, chap. xxxiii (*Works*, XII, 243–44).

On the river ... look like."—*Ibid.*, chap x (*Works*, XII, 73).

210. All the passengers ... on 'change"—*Ibid.*, chap. ii (*Works*, XII, 7–8). "Auctioneer or coiner," Melville continues, "with equal ease, might somewhere here drive his trade."

"My Protean ... find rest."—*Ibid.*, chap. vii (*Works*, XII, 50).

Anything so ... is irresponsible.—The point is also made in the ironic dialogues which argue that disease is as "natural" as health, in opposition to the aesthetic vision of a Nature which "cannot work ill" or "work error" (chaps. xvi and xxi [*Works*, XII, 106, 140–41]). Similarly, the "backwoodsman," Ishmael in a new guise, is committed to a "metaphysics of Indian-hating," which "grows in ... [him] with the sense of good and bad, right and wrong" (chap. xxvi [*Works*, XII, 192–95]). Cf. the character of "Goneril"—"one of those natures, anomalously vicious" (chap. xii [*Works*, XII, 76]).

"have confidence ... have none"—*Ibid.*, chap. xlii (*Works*, XII, 305).

"Now, what ... all men'?"—*Ibid.*, chap. xlii (*Works*, XII, 305). This function of the con-man is most fully developed in the "cosmopolitan," who enters almost precisely in the middle of the book (chap. xxiv [XII, 175]) and increasingly dominates the action. While he preaches the gospel of confidence, his advocacy is calculated to raise questions. In his assumed naïveté, he exposes both the uncritical confidence and the uncritical distrust of those he converses with. The most notable case is that of "Mark Winsome," Melville's version of Emerson, and Winsome's practical disciple Egbert (chaps. xxxvi–xli [XII, 250–98]). On the one hand, the cosmopolitan draws out Winsome on such Emersonian doctrines as aesthetic impersonality and irresponsibility (chap. xxxvi [XII, 251–53]) or inconsistency (*ibid.*, pp. 255–56). Winsome is put in the position of outdoing the very incarnation of confidence. Note that Melville here is criticizing not only Emerson but himself. For he himself is on record (chap. xiv [XII, 90]) in favor of inconsistency; and Winsome's description of "advance into knowledge" as "like advance upon the grand Erie canal, where...change of level is inevitable" (chap. xxxvi [XII, 255–56]), is a good description of *The Confidence Man.* On the other hand, in conversing with Egbert, the cosmopolitan exposes an essentially skeptical aspect of Emerson's approach: Winsome's philosophy is congenial to this "practical poet in the West India trade" because it deals in tokens and does not require any sense of immediate personal relationships (chaps xxxvii–xxxix [XII, 262–75]).

"the fiction...the fact"—*Ibid.*, chap. xxxv (*Works*, XII, 248).

Life is...these contradictions.—As one of the con-man's victims almost comes to see, the human situation requires him "to doubt, to suspect, to prove" as part and parcel of the act of belief (chap. xvi [*Works*, XII, 109]). But he falls into the trap of supposing that "to have all this wearing work to be doing continually ...is evil." Small wonder that the con-man, who teaches him good doctrine, is able at the same time to sell him a worthless bottle of medicine.

211. the passage...final pages.—*Ibid.*, chaps. i, xlv (*Works*, XII, 1, 336). Cf. other references to the sun: chaps. xvi (p. 100), xx (p. 133), xxiii (p. 172).

"In the middle...not see."—*Ibid.*, chap. xlv (*Works*, XII, 320).

"the waning...man's brow."—*Ibid.*, chap. xlv (*Works*, XII, 336).

The last ... groundless faith.—*Ibid.*, chap. xlv (*Works*, XII, 321, 331–32, 335–36). Here, as throughout his role in the book, the "cosmopolitan" is at once the prophet of false confidence and, by virtue of that very fact, a spur to the critical consciousness. Compare Gide's conception of a Devil who would "circulate incognito" through *Les Faux-monnayeurs* and whose "introductory motif" would be: "Why should you be afraid of me? You know very well I don't exist" (*Journal of "The Counterfeiters,"* p. 386 [*Œuvres*, XIII, 21]). But in *The Confidence Man* humanity is ultimately unable to manage both the existence and nonexistence of the Devil. The old man simply vacillates, and his world dissolves. His dealings with the cosmopolitan, instead of sharpening his sense of provisional truth against the latter's demand for absolute faith, deliver him into the Devil's hands.

212. The theme . . . his career.—Cf. *Moby-Dick*, chap. cxix (*Works*, VIII, 278). *The Confidence Man* completed, Melville went abroad. In Egypt he saw the pyramids: "It has been said in panegyric of some extraordinary works of man, that they affect the imagination like the works of Nature. But the pyramid affects one in neither way exactly. Man seems to have had as little to do with it as Nature. It was that supernatural creature, the priest. ... And one seems to see that as out of the crude forms of the natural earth they could evoke by art the transcendent mass & symmetry & voids of the pyramid, so out of the rude elements of the insignificant thoughts that are in all men, they could rear the transcendent conception of a God." The pyramid was not merely the symbol of God; it was most impressive as the token of a creative power, resident in man, which had made what Emerson called "a second nature, grown out of the first," and had in this way actually constructed the image of God. As such, it embodied both "the Intelligence, Power, the Angel," which Melville had invoked years before in notes for *Moby-Dick* (Olson, "Lear and *Moby Dick*," p. 173) and "a terrible mixture of the cunning and awful." The latter aspect is the one Melville dwells upon: "... for no holy purpose was the pyramid founded." In this monument "there is no stay or stage. It is all or nothing. ... It refuses to be studied or adequately comprehended." Here was the antithesis of the "Loomings" of *Moby-Dick*: "Pyramids still loom before me—something vast, indefinite, incomprehensible, and awful. ... Desert more fearful to look at than ocean." See

Journal Up the Straits, ed. Raymond Weaver (New York, 1935), pp. 58–59, 63–64. Also printed in *The Portable Melville,* pp. 566–68.

"testament of acceptance"—A phrase applied to *Billy Budd* by E. L. G. Watson, "Melville's Testament of Acceptance," *New England Quarterly,* VI (1933), 319–27.

The dogmatism . . . to correspond."—A more valid version of the interpretation which emphasizes "acceptance" is based on Billy's lack of resistance, his blessing of Captain Vere, and his ascension amid "the full rose of the dawn." See *Billy Budd,* ed. F. B. Freeman (Cambridge, Mass., 1948), pp. 242, 264, 266. But if this phase of the story asserts the reality of absolute good, it is simply the counterweight to the unequivocal assertion of absolute evil in Claggart (pp. 185–87). The story comes into focus not in either of these characters but in the spiritual drama of Vere, who must decide how to deal with a world where good and evil, as Auden says in his poem on *Billy Budd,* inevitably attract each other, so that "both are openly destroyed before our eyes."

This drama remains logically unresolved. Vere's solution by a reliance on "forms, measured forms" (p. 272), simply raises the whole question of form, as was Melville's consistent habit. Note that Billy's human frailty is pointedly symbolized by a defect of speech (p. 149); that the blow he strikes is his inadequate attempt at expression (pp. 225–26, 239); that Claggart is marked by "a bit of accent in his speech" (p. 168); that his death is described as a "lasting tongue-tie" (p. 241); and, finally, that the dissidence of the crew is expressed in an articulate murmur (pp. 254, 269–70). In this context, what is distinctive in Vere is his power of statement, by which he stands out "against primitive instincts strong as the wind and the sea" (p. 243). But Melville does not regard Vere's rationalism as definitive. Almost immediately following Vere's dictum on "measured forms" comes the opening paragraph of chapter xxix: "The symmetry of form attainable in pure fiction cannot so readily be achieved in a narration essentially having less to do with fable than with fact. Truth uncompromisingly told will always have its ragged edges; hence the conclusion of such a narration is apt to be less finished than an architectural finial" (p. 274). After the burial of Billy, "the circumambient air in the clearness of its serenity was *like smooth white marble in the polished block not yet removed from the marble-dealer's yard"* (p. 273) (my italics). Cf. p. 233.

"wrestled with ... the birth."—*Clarel,* Part I, xvii; Part III, xxi (*Works,* XIV, 74; XV, 100). Cf. the dialectic relationship between a poem like "Timoleon," with its obvious, even verbal reminiscence (Sec. VII) of *Pierre,* and the paradoxical quatrain in "Pebbles" (VII): "Healed of my hurt, I laud the inhuman Sea— / Yea, bless the Angels Four that there convene / For healed I am even by their pitiless breath / Distilled in wholesome dew named rosmarine." Art still grew out of and dissolved into struggle, as in the poem "Art"; it was still the problematic imposition and discovery of form, as in "The Great Pyramid": "Craftsmen, in dateless quarries dim, / Stones formless into form did trim, / Usurped on Nature's self with Art, / And bade this dumb I AM to start, / Imposing him." See *Poems* (*Works,* XVI, 247–53, 244, 270, 294).

Similarly, in *Clarel* "the intersympathy of creeds" leads into "thy hollow, Manysidedness" ("The apprehension tempest tossed — / The spirit in gulf of dizzying fable lost"); and yet it also can issue in the faith of the Syrian monk: "Content thee: in conclusion caught / Thou'lt find how thought's extremes agree— / The forethought clinched by afterthought, / The firstling by finality." See *Clarel,* Part I, v; Part III, xvi; Part II, xviii (*Works,* XIV, 28; XV, 85; XIV, 244).

POSTSCRIPT

213. "The gift ... impenetrable darkness."—Joseph Conrad, "Heart of Darkness," *Youth* (Garden City, N.Y., 1931), pp. 113–14.

214–15. Against the ... for "discipline."—T. E. Hulme, "Humanism and the Religious Attitude," *Speculations,* ed. Herbert Read (New York, 1924), pp. 3–71, esp. pp. 3–11.

215. Similarly, Hulme ... physical world.—"Modern Art and Its Philosophy," *Speculations,* pp. 75–109. "Romanticism and Classicism," *ibid.,* pp. 113–40.

Oddly conjoined ... really is.—"Bergson's Theory of Art," *Speculations,* pp. 143–69.

216. "the artist . . . his model"—*Speculations*, p. 144.

"a feeling . . . outside nature."—*Speculations*, p. 85.

his conception . . . "organic whole."—T. S. Eliot, "The Function of Criticism," *Selected Essays, 1917–1932* (New York, 1932), p. 12.

He pictures . . . unexpected ways"—"Tradition and the Individual Talent," *Selected Essays*, p. 9.

"a new thing."—*Ibid.*, p. 10.

"What happens . . . the new."—*Ibid.*, p. 5.

216–17. "doubt whether . . . merely does."—"Shakespeare and the Stoicism of Seneca," *Selected Essays*, p. 118.

217. "Who shall . . . the globe?"—See above, p. 141.

On the other . . . as ideals.—Notably in *After Strange Gods: A Primer of Modern Heresy* (New York, 1934).

But the same . . . symbolic perception.—"What is disastrous," Eliot declares, "is that the writer should deliberately give rein to his 'individuality'. . ." (*After Strange Gods*, p. 35). But he is actually opposed to *any* emphasis on "novelty or originality" (*ibid.*, p. 24).

And Eliot . . . the present"—In contrast to his earlier view, in which he does not "find it preposterous that the past should be altered by the present as much as the present is directed by the past" ("Tradition and the Individual Talent," *Selected Essays*, p. 5).

While Eliot . . . be true—Cf. Hulme's statement (*Speculations*, pp. 70–71), approvingly cited by Eliot in "Second Thoughts on Humanism," *Selected Essays*, p. 402.

their usual . . . in general.—This is quite obvious in the case of Hulme. In the case of Eliot, see especially "Religion and Literature," *Essays Ancient & Modern* (London, 1936), pp. 93–112.

218. Such arguments . . . or understand."—Lionel Trilling, "A Rejoinder to Mr. Barrett," *Partisan Review*, XVI (1949), 655; Richard Chase, "Liberalism and Literature," *Partisan Review*, XVI (1949), 651.

PAGE

Hulme claims ... of life."—Hulme, *Speculations*, pp. 32, 34.

219. Kurtz, who ... a voice"—Conrad, "Heart of Darkness," *Youth*, p. 113.

Marlow, himself . . . corrupting lie—*Ibid.*, pp. 114, 156–62.

"To the destructive ... you up."—Conrad, *Lord Jim* (Garden City, N.Y., 1931), p. 214.

In that ... own absolute—André Malraux, *The Twilight of the Absolute* [*The Psychology of Art*, Vol. III], trans. Stuart Gilbert (New York, 1950), pp. 117–34.

"art's eternal ... of mankind"—*Ibid.*, p. 154.

Its victory ... innumerable defeats."—Conrad, "Heart of Darkness," *Youth*, pp. 51, 151.

Index

Alcott, A. B., 104, 106, 116, 282, 289–90, 291

Allegory, 8, 14–15, 32, 326

Ambiguity: of American language, 103; concept of, 62–64, in Bushnell, 155, 156, in Emerson, 121, in medieval theory of language, 87–88, in Melville, 30–31, 172, 186, 195–96, 324, in Puritan theory of language, 88–89, 96

American literature: affinity to modern literature, 4, 5, 43, 75–76, 89–90, 105, 120, 123, 162–64, 174, 186–87, 213–14; symbolistic strain in, 1–5, 42–43, 75–76, 89–90, 119–20, 183

Antirationalism; see Rationalism

Aquinas, Thomas, 84, 88

Aristotle, 58–59

Arnold, Matthew, 62, 150

Auden, W. H., 72–73, 255–56, 344

Bacon, Francis, 102, 112

Barfield, Owen, 52, 263

Bateson, F. W., 54–55

Baudelaire, Charles, 15, 39, 261

Beardsley, M. C., 256

Bergson, Henri, 215–16, 258, 267

Blackmur, R. P., 46, 268

Blake, William, 74

Bowen, Francis, 104–5, 109, 291

Bradford, William, 79

Bradstreet, Anne, 83

Brooks, Cleanth, 264, 269

Brownson, O. A., 105–6, 108, 113, 115, 289, 291

Bullough, Edward, 258

Burke, Kenneth, 253, 258, 264, 266

PHOENIX BOOKS
Literature and Language

PHOENIX BOOKS
in Art, Music, Poetry, and Drama

PHOENIX POETS